CHILDREN AND TELEVISION

Children and Television

edited by
Ray Brown

Collier Macmillan
London

A Collier Macmillan book published by
Cassell & Collier Macmillan Publishers Ltd
35 Red Lion Square, London WC1R 4SG
Sydney, Auckland, Toronto, Johannesburg

An affiliate of Macmillan Publishing Co. Inc.
New York

First published 1976

ISBN 02 977290 7

Photoset by Red Lion Setters, Holborn, London
Printed in Great Britain by Fletcher & Son Ltd, Norwich
Bound by Richard Clay Ltd.

To George Westby, Jim M'Comisky,
and the reduction of certainty

Preface

We devote more man hours per year to television than any other single artifact. It's not surprising that books about television are now quite numerous. But it is surprising, to me at least, that so few books have been published which deal with children and television. Although a few new texts have emerged recently they are, in the main, focused on children's exposure to televised violence and the consequences of such exposure. In part this is because a considerable proportion of the total research budget has been directed to this area. Nevertheless, since Hilde Himmelweit's classic British study of the effect upon children of the onset of television there has steadily accumulated a 'literature' on children and television. Since no specialist journals exist for the area, and since researchers themselves are likely to come from different disciplines, their published output is often difficult to locate.

In this book I have attempted to bring together enough diverse material to give a newcomer to the field an idea of what has been going on over the last twenty years. The contributions were selected in order to give a more balanced picture of research into children and television than is presently available. They are a mixture of original research papers and review articles, many of which appear in print for the first time. Authors were not asked to toe any particular party line in preparing their chapters, but they were asked to bear in mind that the book as a whole should present research and its findings in a manner which is useful to both laymen and practitioners of communications research, those who are involved in the production of children's television and those who are close to its audience as parents or teachers. However, where complex thoughts or arguments could not be expressed in a simple manner, authors were encouraged to include them in their complexity rather than exclude them or present them in a fashion which would be injurious to their purpose. If the reader finds a particular sequence incomprehensible, then he or she might well move to other contributions. The article which proves too difficult at first attempt will be much more manageable after the reader has assimilated some of the less complicated pieces.

The book taken as a whole presents my own notion of a balanced picture of the field. However, this does not necessarily mean that I agree with all of the perspectives and arguments put forward by my colleagues. Whilst I have selected topics, authors have been free to present their own analyses and overviews of these topics. Although described as aiming at a 'balanced picture' I have deliberately avoided being representative in the sense that a random or quota sample is representative. Had I desired such a representative picture then perhaps half of the book would have been devoted to the question of television's possibly causal role in childhood aggression. Imitation studies would have been more prominent and those chapters emphasizing the importance of family and the child's functional orientation to television would have been drastically reduced in length.

After a brief introduction, which is a backdrop rather than an overview, the book follows a simple three-part structure. Chapters in the first section, 'Children as an audience', deal with the prerequisites of any effects. The intention here is to give the most accurate assessment presently available of the extent to which children do watch television, and to indicate that their watching is neither the global addiction suggested by such common expressions as 'glued to the set', nor random, patternless behaviour. Clearly there are several simple questions pertinent to this section which remain unanswered: What types of programmes do children find most satisfactory? How do favoured characteristics of television content change as the child grows older? And so on.

Part II is yet more 'patchy'. I have concentrated on two influences on the child's viewing behaviour: the family (an external consraint), and the child's 'functional orientation', what he expects to 'get out of' viewing (an internal constraint). Unfortunately other relevant studies have yet to be conducted. For example, we require considerable research into the influence of the child's peers and school on his viewing (external constraints), and we know little at all of other internal constraints: his or her ability to understand the conventions of television, his or her ability to judge the reality and realism of television content, and the effects upon the viewing experience of the child's emotional state. These and other 'internal constraints' are likely to play an important part in determining the effects that television has on children.

Part III deals with television's effects. This area has received more research attention than any other, and consequently the emphasis is on articles which review the results from several studies.

The structure is by no means an ideal; each part combines quite dissimilar aspects of the overall effects process. However, a more conceptually sophisticated structure would be redundant at this stage since it would necessarily contain a number of empty sections, for example, those relating to content analysis, the production process, reality assessment and long-term effects. If the present division of articles into three groups imposes an order, then it has served its secondary purpose. Its primary purpose is to emphasize that we can only begin to understand the role and influences of television in children's lives by taking into account the complexity of the relationship which exists between children and television.

Silly questions beget silly answers. I have brought together some of today's silly answers in the hope that this will help all of us, public and researchers alike, to ensure that tomorrow's questions are a little more sensible.

RAY BROWN
Leeds University

Autumn 1974

Acknowledgements

Sue, James, Sally and Dem — my family — also Jay Blumler and Michael Gurevitch are among those who felt the repercussions of my involvement with this book and reacted with sympathy, tolerance and good advice. I am particularly grateful to Michael Charters, Cecilia von Feilitzen, Dennis Howitt, Olga Linné, Denis McQuail and Jane Steedman for their many helpful suggestions. From 1971 to 1974 I worked with Joyce Cramond and Bob Wilde; much of my present thinking stems from that period of collaboration with its countless conversations, conflicts, cock-ups and comedy.

My greatest debt is to May Kitching, whose constant good humour, secretarial skills and detailed criticisms were invaluable. May was responsible for many improvements and none of the faults; she also maintained the fiction that researchers can spell.

For permission to reproduce items in this volume acknowledgement is made to the following:

for Bradley S. Greenberg, 'Viewing and Listening Parameters among British Youngsters', from *Journal of Broadcasting*, Spring 1973, to the Broadcast Educations Association;

for Jack Lyle and Heidi R. Hoffman, 'Explorations in Patterns of Television Viewing by Pre-school-age Children', and Scott Ward, 'Effects of Television Advertising on Children and Adolescents', from Rubinstein, Comstock and Murray (eds), *Television and Social Behaviour*, IV, *Television in Day-to-day Life: Patterns of Use,* US Government Printing Office, Washington DC, 1971, to the National Institute of Mental Health, Alcohol, Drug Abuse and Mental Health Administration, United States Department of Health, Education, and Welfare;

for Grant Noble, 'Concepts of Order and Balance in a Children's TV Programme', from *Journalism Quarterly,* XLVII:i, Spring

1970, to the Association for Education in Journalism;

for Bradley S. Greenberg, 'Television for Children: Dimensions of Communicator and Audience Perceptions', from *AV Communication Review*, XIII:4, Winter 1965, to the Association for Educational Communications and Technology;

for Dennis Howitt and Guy Cumberbatch, 'The Parameters of Attraction to Mass Media Figures, from *Journal of Moral Education*, XII:3, 1973, to Pemberton Publishing Company Ltd;

for John D. Murray, 'Television and Violence: Implications of the Surgeon General's Research Programme', from *American Psychologist*, June 1973, to John D. Murray.

Contents

About the Contributors

Jane Delano Brown is a Ph D student in the School of Journalism and Mass Communication at the University of Wisconsin (Madison). She earned her BA from the University of Kentucky in 1972 and her MA from the University of Wisconsin in 1974. She is interested in examining the media's role in the socialization process, especially in terms of sex role development.

Ray Brown, a social psychologist, is Research Fellow in the Centre for Television Research, University of Leeds. He has conducted research into the gratifications sought by committed viewers of selected broadcast programmes, the functions of local radio, and the role of television as an agent of child socialization.

Joyce Cramond, a psychologist, served as Research Assistant in the Centre for Television Research, University of Leeds, from 1972 until 1974. She has conducted research into children's attitudes to alcohol and drinking habits, and is presently working as a Clinical Psychologist.

Guy Cumberbatch graduated in psychology from University College, Cardiff, in 1966, and did research on short-term memory for his Ph D at Leicester University. From 1969 to 1972 he did post-doctoral research at Leicester's Centre for Mass Communication Research. He is now Lecturer in Applied Psychology at Birmingham's Aston University. Current research activities include curriculum development in psychology, short-term memory and the social psychology of crowds.

Richard Dembo received his BA from New York University, his MA in Sociology from Columbia University in 1965 and his Ph D in Sociology from New York University in 1970. He has been employed as a New York State Parole Officer (1966-1969), worked as a Research Scientist for the New York State Narcotic Addiction Control Commission from 1969-1970 and as a Research Officer at the University of Leicester Centre for Mass Communication Research from 1970-1973. He is currently an Associate Research Scientist in the New York State Drug Abuse Control Commission.

Bradley S Greenberg is Professor of Communication at Michegan State University. His research has centred on the impact of the mass media, particularly television, on children and minority groups. He has been a visiting professor at the London School of Economics, The University of Leeds and the University of Lund.

Heidi Hoffman has done her graduate work in education at The University of California, Los Angeles (UCLA). She has specialized in problems of education of young children and has extensive personal experience in this field.

Dennis Howitt completed a first class honours degree in psychology at Brunel University in 1967 and his D.Phil. at the University of Sussex. Since 1970 he has been Research Officer at Leicester University. His research interests cover complex human cognition, child development and socialization, and criminal behaviour.

Bromley Kniveton gained his Ph D in 1969 at the University of Nottingham. Following this he was a Research Fellow for the Mental Health Trust and Research Fund, and then Research Officer in the Adult Education Department at Nottingham. He moved to his present post as Lecturer in Social Psychology at Loughborough University in 1973. His main research interest concerns children's imitation of filmed models.

Olga Linné received her Ph D in sociology from the University of Stockholm, Sweden, in 1971. From 1964 to 1968 she worked as a Mass Communication Researcher in the Audience and Programme Research Department of the Swedish Broadcasting Corporation, and from 1969 to 1970 as a Sociologist in Kenya, East Africa, for the University of Uppsala and Sida, Sweden. She is at present Research Director for Mass Communication Research at the Danish Broadcasting Corporation. Her main interests are the concepts of violence on television, mass communication theories, and the relationships between communicator and audience members.

Jack Lyle received his doctorate in mass communication research from Stanford University in 1959. He has worked extensively in the field of media and society, particularly children and television and educational utilization of media. Among the books he has written or co-authored is *Television in the Lives of our Children*. He presently is Director, Communication Institute, The East-West Center in Honolulu, Hawaii.

Robin McCron was born in Ayrshire in 1948. He took a psychology degree at Glasgow University, followed by postgraduate research at the University of Leicester Centre for Mass Communication Research, where he is currently a Research Assistant. His main research interest is in studying the role of the mass media in socialization.

Jack M McLeod is a Professor of Journalism and Mass Communication, and Chairman of the Mass Communications Research Center at the University of Wisconsin (Madison). He received his Ph D in social psychology at the University of Michegan. His research focus over the last decade has been on co-orientation and interpersonal communication processes, socialization, and professionalization in the mass media.

Denis McQuail, born in 1935 and educated at St Anselm's College, Birkenhead, and Corpus Christi College, Oxford, worked at the newly founded Granada Television Research Unit at Leeds University from 1959 to 1965, on problems concerned with the political, educational and cultural implications of the mass media. Since 1965 he has taught sociology at the University of Southampton, spending a year at the Annenberg School of Communication, University of Pennsylvania.

John P Murray gained his Ph D from the Catholic University of America in 1970. For three years he was Research Co-ordinator at the United States Surgeon General's Scientific Advisory Committee on Television and Social Behavior. He has also done research, lecturing and practice in pediatric/child psychology at the

University of North Carolina Medical School, and is currently Senior Lecturer in Psychology, School of Behavioural Sciences, Macquarie University, Sydney, Australia. His ongoing research includes a longitudinal study of the impact of the introduction and diffusion of television in three rural communities.

Grant Noble is Research Psychologist with the Public Service Board of Papua New Guinea. He gained his Ph D at Birkbeck College, London, and after working as a Research Officer at the Centre for Mass Communication Research, Leicester, became Lecturer in Psychology at Trinity College, Dublin. He has published extensively in the field of children and mass media, his particular interests being the processes of children's involvement in television and theoretical interpretations of television's place in urban society.

Cecilia von Feilitzen is Head of the Children's Studies Research Group at the Audience and Programme Research Department, Swedish Broadcasting Corporation. She has been a Researcher with the Swedish Broadcasting Corporation since 1964 and was awarded her Ph D from the University of Stockholm in 1971. Her main research interests are sociology of mass communications, mass communications theory, and children and mass media.

Scott Ward is Associate Professor of Business Administration at Harvard University, and a Research Associate at the Marketing Science Institute in Cambridge, Mass. His research has focused on the effects of television advertising on children, and his current interests are in the area of consumer socialization.

Introduction

Consider the multi-million population of humans who live in industrialized societies. Pick one at random. What can we say of it? We would have a fifty-fifty chance of guessing its sex, but political or religious affiliations, income and language couldn't be predicted with any degree of accuracy. However, some few things could be said about him or her: in each block of twenty-four hours he or she is highly likely to sleep, eat, drink, defecate and watch television.

Like the wheel and the cooking vessel, television 'catches on' wherever it becomes available, but unlike many other artifacts it is difficult to explain why we apparently need television. And it is also difficult to tease out the social and individual consequences of daily exposure on television. The two questions 'Why do we watch?' and 'What are the consequences of watching?' may not always appear immediately relevant to the work of some researchers in this area, but they are basic to the field.

In terms of scientific research 'Why?' questions are usually unanswerable, therefore researchers often modify the question into a 'What?' form: What types of personality or psychological predispositions are related to television exposure? And so on. The second question 'What are the consequences of watching television?' is a generalized question that can only be answered by summarizing the results of many studies, and after the question itself has been clarified (Consequences for whom? Watching television for how long? etc). Obviously, then, we need to explore these two basic questions by framing a multitude of specific, answerable questions. Unfortunately such a strategy often leads to the evolution of distinct, non-related research traditions. Some kind of schema or conceptual framework is required which not only brings together the various investigations, but also indicates new and important research questions. One such integrative framework can be generated by considering children's use of television in the context of child socialization.

Socialization is the process by which a new-born child is gradually trained to 'fit into' a particular part of society. It entails learning verbal and non-verbal languages, and quantities of attitudes, values, opinions, skills and 'knowledge'. All of this information, which has to be processed by every child, comes from somewhere 'outside' and most of it is directed towards the child by the so-called 'agencies' of socialization, the more important being family, school, peers and media of mass communication. The relative influence of these agencies varies from society to society, sub-group to sub-group, time to time, and child to child. For example, in Britain the influence of organized religion has waned over the last few decades, but there are still large groups of people within Britain for whom 'the church' can rightly be considered as an important source of influence upon their children's training. Whilst some aspects of this shaping of individuals are, of course, non-conscious, others are quite formal and deliberate. Church and school are agencies where formal training with formalized ·objectives obtain. The influences of peers are much less likely to be thought through and formalized into rigorous training periods. And the family will typically maximize both consciously directed behaviour modification ('Don't speak with your mouth full.' 'Do learn to say "Please" and "Thank you".') and the more subtle shaping which occurs when people interact: the parent usually doesn't take a conscious decision to 'turn on' anger or pleasure in order to shape his or her child, it just happens that way.

Communications media are potential agencies of socialization because they too, like family, school and peers, direct information towards the child and present him with examples of behaviour. And it is reasonable to assume that because television has easily interpreted, naturalistic, verbal and visual images which command so much of the child's attention, it is likely to be the most influential of mass media. The perspective of socialization not only helps us to ask a lot of sensible and related questions about children's use of television (and other media), it also constantly reminds us that answering these questions is a relatively important task which may have implications for the futures of our industrialized societies. The disparaging remarks directed towards television, 'chewing gum for the mind', 'idiot box', 'one-eyed monster', 'moving wallpaper', encourage us to underemphasize its potency. Those members of the establishment and public who suggest that children's viewing is of little consequence are as wide off the mark as the more vociferous group who condemn it as a source of anti-social behaviour and moral decline. The socialization perspective encourages us to reject such superficial judgements; it moves away from asking whether television is 'good' or 'bad' towards a more general assessment of its role in children's lives. The emphasis is no longer on a particular type of programme and its potential effects; rather we become concerned to interpret the whole of television's output. And the child is no longer a neutral entity to be pushed this way and that by television's image; he is a conscious, creative element existing in a number of interacting social and psychological contexts. In short, television becomes an integrated part of a matrix of influence *within* which the child exists and *upon* which the child himself can be influential. The implications are numerous.

The remainder of this 'backdrop' to the body of the text describes three general foci which together might form a socialization based approach to the study of children and television, these foci are termed the matrix of influence, the contexts of exposure, the contexts of effect.

The word matrix suggests enclosure, womb, a moulding or shaping; it is probably derived from the Latin *mater*. So the notion of a 'matrix of influence' should carry the same overtones of meaning. The child is as embedded in a particular matrix of influence as he was in the mother's womb. For many years the child is incapable of breaking out of this social womb, and the majority of us never do. We are defined during our childhood and carry the same set of constraints or directives throughout life. But that is not to say that we are fully shaped by the matrix. During childhood we can react differently to elements of the matrix. This is especially true of those countries where the matrix is inconsistent, for here it will often direct to the child opposing messages. Sometimes there is conflict between agencies, school versus family, or, more likely, peer group versus school and family. Because of this conflict the child is able to behave as if he were choosing between different values or behaviours; indeed the child often does quite consciously choose between alternative examples or messages. The child will often attempt to evaluate 'messages' by presenting them to representatives of different agencies. He seeks his friends' evaluations of statements made by parent or teacher, the parents' evaluation of statements made by friends.

As an element in the matrix of influence, television has certain unique advantages and limitations: it transcends certain social, geographical and temporal barriers which are more or less common to the other agencies; on the other hand it cannot *react* to the child's progress in the manner of other agencies. And it has one other characteristic which sets it apart: typically it is itself embedded in another agency — the family. Perhaps this last characteristic partly explains why there is a noticeable tendency to denigrate television, overemphasizing its harmful effects, or arguing that it encourages passive states of mind. As an agency within an agency it can cause embarrassment or discomfort to the family. Its messages and images will often be inconsistent with those generated by parents. The parent loses degrees of control over the information available to the child. Unlike books or verbally presented material, television usually offers Hobson's choice. The parent reacts to this in one or more of several ways: rigorous control of viewing, the blacklisting of certain programmes, attempts to structure and shape the child's interpretation and assessment of broadcast material, or by passing over to television companies the responsibility to produce programmes 'suitable for children'. Similarly the child's peers will influence his use of television, by discussing and recommending particular programmes, explaining story lines and informing him of their own parents' reactions. And school teachers often have their two pennyworth, ranging from special lessons on television through to sarcastic quips directed at sleepy children.

These ripples of interaction which run through the child's social environment and originate in television programmes allow him access to different evaluations of television content. He will gradually build his own unique relationship to television programmes by, as it were, 'working on' the primary experience of viewing and the assessments and reaction of others. In this way the child creates the internal or psychological elements of the context of exposure, a complex processing plant which he brings with him and which shapes his viewing experience. But there is also an external aspect to the context of exposure, and this usually is formed by elements of the matrix of influence: parents, siblings or friends. Viewing is likely to be an accompanied activity, and a truly social activity. Viewers comment on programmes, praise or denigrate the actions of real or fictitious people represented on the screen. Each programme viewed adds to the child's experience of

Introduction

23

television content, his experience of his own reactions to such content, and his experience of other people's reactions to the content. A final point on the context of viewing is that it has certain physical features which are influential. (Grant Noble, in his forthcoming book, *Children in Front of the Small Screen*, convincingly argues that the different content and physical contexts of cinema and television encourage totally opposing notions of identification. In the cinema we are urged to *lose* our identity in favour of the hero; in TV we are asked to *retain* our identity in order to *interact* with the represented people.) For example, a young child will commonly be involved in some play activity whilst viewing; the older children might well be scanning a comic. Time of viewing is probably important, especially proximity to bedtime (because of increased interaction between parent and child, and also because viewing immediately before bed perhaps intensifies the consequences of the child's emotional response since there is less chance of dissipation through physical or verbal activity). Other elements of the environment intrude, including noise, light reflections on the screen and the instrument's 'tuning'. Physical environment, along with the intra- and interpersonal elements of the context, ensure that no two children ever see *exactly* the same programme.

So far, then, we have seen that TV can be treated as one element in an interlocking system, the matrix of influence, which has a primary function of shaping the child's behaviour and experience in order to produce of 'socialized' unit, that is one which can exist in, and help to maintain, a particular society. Furthermore we have seen that through its presence during viewing, and also because the child brings to the viewing situation his past experience, the matrix of influence is a dominant element of the context of children's everyday viewing. Now we can consider the effects of television, but first it should be clear that 'television' has now become one element in the matrix; it does not exist in a vacuum and its effects are dependent upon its position in the matrix. Furthermore its effects are mediated and modified by the interpersonal and intrapersonal contexts of viewing. We are dealing with a conceptually complex system which cannot be expressed in terms of a simple stimulus-response model.

Naturally television has many effects and exhaustive lists are out of the question. In this brief introduction we can do no more than mention some of the categories of effect in order to emphasize that

o, the child is still contained by the matrix of influence.
mes we forget the most obvious influence of television, that
xtent to which children and adults are prepared to watch it.
We think of exposure as something separate, but viewing itself is a
rather staggering effect; it is a very clear example of television
shaping our behaviour. The viewing situation is also one of the
contexts of influence. Whilst the child views responses are elicited
from him; he cries or laughs; he makes mental associations with the
screened images; he feels fear or excitement. These are fairly
immediate phenomenological consequences of exposure. Another
category of effect has been labelled *displacement effects*, and refers
to those activities which we give up in order to view. Here again
context is important since the extent and direction of displacement
is apparently related to such broader dimensions of context as the
child's socio-economic position, the size of his family, the
characteristics of his built environment and the range of activities
and amenities open to him.

However, in general, 'effects' refer to changes in behaviour
after viewing, and they can be crudely categorized according to
duration of effect and its location in time. Firstly there is the short
term effect, probably produced shortly after viewing and likely to
be explained in terms of arousal dissipation, exploration of the
viewing experience (in play, fantasy or questioning) and imitation.
Secondly there are more sustained changes: the introduction of
significant information, a new interpretation, a habit of speech or
behaviour imitated and maintained. Such consequences might take
some time to develop but can be traced back to a particular
televised sequence. And thirdly we might expect the daily ingestion
of televised material to have general amorphous consequences for
the child's overall orientation to society and, of course, society's
overall orientation to the child. Is context essential to the study of
'effects'? The child has expectations of how others will react to
screened behaviours if he attempts to reproduce them; he knows
that in one situation a certain activity is highly valued whilst being
proscribed in another. Social context is particularly influential
since its elements can evaluate the child's behaviour and instruct
him or her by reacting to it.

History, experience and the psychological laboratory have all
amply demonstrated that the individual who stands against the
group is rare (and sometimes punished for it). Rather we are
prepared to ignore the evidence of our senses and the outcome of

our own thoughts and beliefs in favour of conforming to the group. It would be meaningless to ask in which of the three phases of influence context assumes the greatest authority, but certainly the argument for studying context is clearest when we consider the context of effects.

We have seen that the mainly social contexts in which television as a purveyor of socializing messages is embedded, in which viewing takes place and in which effects occur, can all act to modify the effects which television might have on children. One implication of such an analysis might be that controlled laboratory studies of the effects of viewing ten minutes' violence are infinitely distant from that useful fiction of layman and scientist alike, 'the real world'. But this is not so. The laboratory study of, for example, imitation can be located in the overall framework, and thus becomes related to other research foci rather than divorced from them. It is true that the methods of social science are, in the main, badly retailored hand-me-downs from the natural sciences, which are incapable of matching man's first-hand experience of social reality but, taken together, they can and do reveal some of the complexities of social behaviour. And, for the time being, they are all we have. Whether they have been used to good effect, so that the studies in this book can be integrated into a picture, albeit a bitty and lopsided picture, of the role of television in children's lives, is an open question which the reader is encouraged to consider.

Part I
Children as an Audience

Broadcasting organizations are similar to manufacturing industries; they manufacture a product for the public, but they also 'manufacture' a public as their product. A large proportion of television programming is financed by selling an audience to advertisers. Audience research, sometimes termed 'head counting', enables the calculation of 'cost per thousand': the price an advertiser must pay in order to direct his message to 1,000 viewers. Organizations financed by government levy or licence fees are also concerned to discover how many people watch their programmes. Audience measurement is an aid to programme planning; it is a form of feedback from an otherwise largely silent audience which affords producers and programme planners some indication of success or failure; it facilitates 'audience building'. For these reasons most broadcasting organizations regularly assess the size of their audiences. Audience measurement is equally important to the student of mass communications; it provides an overall outline of the phenomenon to be investigated, and 'head counting' alone can indicate some of the complexities of the area. However, the first two chapters in this book represent more than simple head counting. Greenberg's analysis of the younger audience for British television (and radio) clearly reveals the seasonal nature of viewing and the way in which exposure to television is related to age, social class and sex. Lyle and Hoffman report an intensive study of pre-school-age children's viewing in America. In this paper other complexities of 'audience behaviour' begin to emerge: Who selects the programmes? Which types of programme do the youngest viewers find most satisfactory? Which television characters are most memorable? The third and fourth chapters delve more deeply into the 'audience', particularly the audience for children's television (as opposed to the television programmes watched by children).

Noble and Greenberg, in independent studies, compare the producers' assumptions about certain characteristics of their programmes with the audience members' reactions. The chapters illuminate both the child's involvement with particular programmes and features of the production process which influence the content and structure of the same programmes. Both aspects of the investigations are of value, but of particular importance is the attempt to span the process of communication by involving television producers *and* their audience in the same study. Research of this type can allow the audience some say in what is given to them. Perhaps of more consequence, they can be an educative experience for the producer, who is often in the invidious position of attempting to assess objectively the satisfactoriness of his programme by reference to audience figures which group together old and young and which may reflect little more than the time at which his programme was broadcast; little wonder that the producer often comes to rely on intuition, tradition and the reactions of his peers. Taken together, the four chapters are a foundation for the studies which follow of viewing and its consequences. Emerging from them is the realization that whilst an audience can be sold on the basis of cost per thousand, the audience member is rather more thoughtful, active and selective than a quick-frozen pea.

1

Viewing and Listening Parameters among British Youngsters

Bradley S Greenberg

That children watch a good deal of television is known by broadcasters, parents and teachers alike. However, precise information is lacking on the extent of TV viewing by children of different ages or children from different social backgrounds. The classic English study of children and television is now over a dozen years old (*Himmelweit et al*, 1958). Neither that study nor both dated and recent efforts in the United States and Japan were based on national data, but on data from particular regions or cities (*Schramm et al*, 1961; *Furu*, 1971). Radio listening is also recognized as widespread among children, but clear statements as to how much radio listening is done by whom are conspicuously lacking.

The present study describes the current status of television and radio exposure among five- to nineteen-year-old British children. It places this behaviour against the background of similar data from the last half decade. In addition, the sex, age and social class of the children are examined to determine just who are the greatest fans and 'non-fans' of each medium in England. The hope is that comparable data can be obtained in other countries for an eventual cross-national examination of children's television and radio behaviour.

Certain propositions are readily available. These serve primarily to revalidate findings demonstrated by the earlier, non-national studies. It would be expected that boys would do more TV watching than girls, and working-class children more than their middle-class counterparts. Television exposure should increase in relatively large doses among children until their early teens, when it will peak and drop back. For radio, girls are traditionally expected to be the more avid listeners, especially among working-class families. But the age variable should operate differently from the way it operates in television. Radio listening should increase with age among youngsters, and indeed not peak until the oldest of the teen-age groups.

Beyond these simplistic hypotheses, it is possible to test the relative import of these variables. Do certain of these factors play a more prominent role in media behaviour than others? Indeed, are some spurious when information about other characteristics is available? Rather than guess in advance as to the combinatorial nature of these factors, the present study attempts to answer such questions through an intensive sub-group analysis of the children's media behaviour.

This study is limited to the nature of the data that were available for secondary analysis. It does not lend itself to such issues as the effects of media exposure, nor the gratifications associated with media exposure. It does not burrow into the social and psychological attributes of the children. However, it presents a base of information against which such additional issues may be more meaningfully probed — at least in the British context.

METHOD

Each day of each week, the Audience Research Department of the BBC collects viewing and listening data for each programme on the two BBC television channels, the four BBC national radio outlets, the independent television channel (ITA), and Radio Luxembourg (an English-language station readily heard throughout Britain, with commercials clearly aimed at an English audience). The method of data collection is the field survey. The daily national sample goal is 2,500 interviews. Some 200 part-time interviewers use an aided-recall system for audience assessment. The sample itself is constructed by a quota method; in different geographic regions, interviewers are assigned quotas of people to interview, within specified sex, age, and social-class categories. Interviews with children from five to fourteen are done with parental permission. The resultant data are placed on magnetic tape and retained for a specified but restricted period of time.

The taped data for the first ten months of 1971 provided the bulk of the information used in this report. The present analysis began in November 1971. Data for seven two-week periods were used, beginning with the first two weeks of the calendar year 1971, and proceeding with weeks 7-8, 13-14, 19-20, 25-26, 30-31, and 37-38.

Exposure levels for television and radio were averaged over each fourteen-day period.[1] This was done in order to ensure adequate numbers of respondents for sub-group analyses. For the age range five to nineteen, each two-week period yielded an average of 1,600 to 2,000 interviews. For certain analyses, e.g., boys' versus girls' viewing levels, this meant a minimum of 800 of each sex for major comparisons. With more complex breakdowns, e.g., twelve-to-fourteen-year-old middle-class boys, the cell size would be approximately 150. In most cells reported in the most complex cross-classifications, the number of respondents was 200 to 300. No sub-group contained fewer than 100 respondents.

TELEVISION VIEWING

Recent Trends
In order to place the 1971 data in an appropriate context, some data from prior years were examined to provide baselines. For the years 1967 through 1971, we obtained viewing data averaged over two weeks in midwinter and two weeks in midsummer for each of four child age groups. Between 1967 and 1971, viewing in midsummer increased some :37/day (37 minutes per day) for five- to seven-year-olds, :38 for children seven to eleven, :27 for those twelve to fourteen, :04 for those fifteen to nineteen, and :13 for the adult population. The midwinter increases for the same sequence of age groups were :06, :25, :30, :17, and :20/day.

In terms of total viewing, the net effect of these increases was to diminish the 1967 midwinter-midsummer difference for the two youngest age groups. Whereas in 1967, the five- to seven-year-olds were watching 2:00/day (2 hours per day) in winter and 1:30/day in summer, their 1971 levels were 2:12 and 2:08/day for winter and summer. For the eight- to twelve-year-olds, a :28/day seasonal difference in 1967 was reduced by one-half, or 3:14/day in the winter and 2:59 in the summer. For twelve- to fourteen-year-olds there remained approximately :20/day greater viewing in the winter, with average viewing of 3:35/day in the winter and 3:12 in the summer. Viewing for fifteen- to nineteen-year-olds varied from 2 to 2:15/day, which was equivalent to most adult levels.

Current Levels
Across all the youngsters and the various seasons, television was watched 2:25/day. Seasonal variations maximized TV watching

during January-February when it was just short of 3:00/day and minimized it during May-June, when it was 2:10/day. Midsummer and March levels were intermediate, averaging 2:30/day.

Subgroup Viewing
Here the mode of analysis was to examine the relation between each of three social indicators — sex, age and social class — and overall television viewing. Then we looked at these social indicators separately for BBC-TV and ITV. Finally, the combined effect of these variables, controlling for two of them while looking at the third and the simultaneous relation of all three, were analysed.

Table 1.1A presents the basic *sex* differences in television viewing, by season and by channel.[2] On the average, boys watch television :09/day more, and seasonal fluctuations are minor, ranging from :04 to :13 for the seven time periods. All the difference is attributable to greater watching of BBC by boys with no sex difference found for ITV. Therefore, sex is a minor correlate of TV viewing for children aged five to nineteen.

Table 1.1B presents parallel information for two *social groupings* — working-class and middle-class children. Working-class children are consistently higher viewers, averaging some :15/day more than their middle-class peers. Greater seasonal fluctuation is found here than for sex, with maximum :25 differences in the winter season, the differences of half to a third that size in the other time periods. Channel differences are even more marked: Middle-class children watch :10/day more of BBC-TV than do working-class children, who, in turn watch :24/day more of ITV. Indeed, middle-class watching of BBC is equivalent to the working-class child's watching of ITV. The overall class difference in total watching can be fully accounted for by the working-class child's greater watching of BBC-TV, in comparison to the middle-class youngsters' level of ITV viewing. Class and channel choice interact in a significant way for the British child.

Data for viewing patterns for the various *age* groups are in Table 1.1C. Viewing for all age groups is maximum during January-February and shows sharp drops in other seasons. These decreases are less so for the fifteen to nineteen age group. Variations for the three youngest groups extend to a full hour in different months, but fluctuate only within a half hour for those fifteen to nineteen.

The largest viewing jump is between the five-to-seven and

TABLE 1.1
Sex, class and age differences in duration of TV viewing
(hours: minutes/day)*

Seasonal

	All TV average for two weeks in:							Daily average across seasons		
	Jan	Feb	Mar	May	June	Aug	Sept	all TV	BBC-TV	ITV
A SEX										
Boys	3:01	2:52	2:33	2:17	2:11	2:33	2:06	2:30	1:18	1:12
Girls	2:48	2:47	2:29	2:04	2:04	2:18	1:58	2:21	1:08	1:13
B CLASS										
Working	3:03	2:56	2:33	2:16	2:11	2:30	2:04	2:31	1:10	1:21
Middle	2:38	2:32	2:26	2:00	2:00	2:19	1:56	2:16	1:19	:57
C AGE										
5–7	2:35	2:23	2:00	1:33	1:32	2:01	1:25	1:56	:59	:57
8–11	3:15	3:17	2:52	2:31	2:18	2:50	2:19	2:46	1:21	1:25
12–14	3:40	3:32	3:12	2:52	2:48	3:13	2:44	3:09	1:32	1:37
15–19	2:28	2:20	2:13	1:55	2:01	1:58	1:54	2:07	1:06	1:01

*The age range represented is 5–19. All data are from 1971.

TABLE 1.2
All television viewing by sex, age and social class*

		Age and Class Groups							
		5–7 MC	5–7 WC	8–11 MC	8–11 WC	12–14 MC	12–14 WC	15–19 MC	15–19 WC
A BASIC DATA	Boys	1:50	2:09	2:41	3:02	3:01	3:22	2:01	2:06
	Girls	1:34	1:57	2:25	2:46	2:48	3:12	1:56	2:13
B SEX DIFFERENCES		:16	:12	:16	:16	:13	:10	:05	:07
C WC-MC DIFFERENCES	Boys	:19		:21		:21		:05	
	Girls	:23		:21		:24		:17	
D AGE DIFFERENCES			(8–11) – (5–7)		(12–14) – (8–11)		(15–19) – (12–14)		
	Boys		:51	:53	:20	:21	– 1:00	– 1:16	
	Girls	:51	:49	:23	:26	– :52	– :59		

Minus signs mean more viewing by girls, or middle-class or younger children.

TABLE 1.3
Viewing differences for BBC-TV and ITV by sex, age and class*

| | Age Groups | | | | | | | |
| | 5–7 | | 8–11 | | 12–14 | | 15–19 | |
	MC	WC	MC	WC	MC	WC	MC	WC
A SEX								
BBC-TV	:11	:08	:11	:11	:14	:13	:07	:05
ITV	:05	:04	:05	:05	-:01	-:03	-:02	-:12
B WORKING AND MIDDLE CLASS	B	G	B	G	B	G	B	G
	WC				MC			
BBC-TV	-:05	-:02	-:09	-:09	-:08	-:07	-:13	-:11
ITV	:24	:25	:30	:30	:32	:31	:18	:28
C AGE DIFFERENCES	B	G	B	G	G			
					MC			
(8–11) – (5–7)								
BBC-TV	:22	:19	:26	:26	:26	:25		
ITV	:31	:30	:25	:25				
(12–14) – (8–11)								
BBC-TV	:13	:11	:12	:08	:09	:14		
ITV	:08	:15						
(15–19) – (12–14)								
BBC-TV	-:30	-:22	-:25	-:35	-:18	-:34		
ITV	-:46	-:37						

*The tabled figure is the difference between the two sub-groups. For example, in the 5–7, middle-class group, boys watch: 11 more of BBC-TV per day than girls. Minus signs mean more viewing by girls, or middle-class or younger children.

TABLE 1.4
Ordered viewing/listening groups

All-TV Order	Sex	Age	Class	Daily Viewing	Daily Listening	BBC-TV Order	ITV Order	Listening Order
1	B	12–14	WC	3:22	:53	2	2	7
2	G	12–14	WC	3:12	1:14	5.5	1	5
3	B	8–11	WC	3:02	:33	5.5	3	11
4	B	12–14	MC	3:01	:50	1	6	8
5	G	12–14	MC	2:48	1:05	4	5	6
6	G	8–11	WC	2:46	:40	9.5	4	9
7	B	8–11	MC	2:41	:19	3	8	14
8	G	8–11	MC	2:25	:34	7	10.5	10
9	G	15–19	WC	2:13	2:11	13.5	7	1
10	B	5–7	WC	2:09	:31	13.5	9	12
11	B	15–19	WC	2:06	1:56	11.5	12	3
12	B	15–19	MC	2:01	1:45	8	15	4
13	G	5–7	WC	1:57	:30	16	10.5	13
14	G	15–19	MC	1:56	1:58	9.5	13.5	2
15	B	5–7	MC	1:50	:18	11.5	13.5	16
16	G	5–7	MC	1:34	:27	15	16	15

TABLE 1.5
Radio listening by sex, age and social class*

| | | Age and Class Groups | | | | | | | |
| | | 5–7 | | 8–11 | | 12–14 | | 15–19 | |
		WC	MC	WC	MC	WC	MC	WC	MC
A BASIC DATA	Boys	:31	:18	:33	:29	:53	:50	1:56	1:45
	Girls	:30	:27	:40	:34	1:14	1:05	2:11	1:58
B SEX DIFFERENCES		:01	–:09	–:13	–:05	–:21	–:15	–:15	–:13
C WC-MC DIFFERENCES	Boys	:13		:04		:03		:11	
	Girls	:03		:06		:09		:13	
		WC	MC						
D AGE DIFFERENCES (8–11) – (5–7)	Boys	:02	:11						
	Girls	:10	:07						
(12–14) – (8–11)	Boys	:20	:21						
	Girls	:34	:31						
(15–19) – (12–14)	Boys	1:03	:55						
	Girls	:57	:53						

*Minus signs mean more viewing by girls, or middle-class or younger children.

eight-to-eleven age groups — fully :50/day more. A second rise occurs with the twelve- to fourteen-year-olds who view an additional :35/day. Viewing then drops steeply, by an hour a day in the fifteen to nineteen age-group. This is so for both BBC-TV and ITV to virtually identical levels. So, viewing explodes between eight and eleven, is at its maximum from twelve to fourteen and then drops and stabilizes in the fifteen to nineteen age-group. Age is easily the best of the three demographic measures used here for probing exposure behaviours.

The next analysis examines the multiple relation among these social indicators and overall television viewing. The relevant data are in Table 1.2.

The observed sex difference in television exposure across all British children (:09) is relatively consistent. Certainly the younger age groups exceed that average, which is largely affected by the smaller sex differences among the fifteen- to nineteen-year-olds. In a similar fashion, the overall social-class difference of :15/day is exceeded in the age groups from five to fourteen, and also among fifteen- to nineteen-year-old girls, when both age and sex are controlled. Thus, sex and social class persist as somewhat weak correlates of TV viewing. Although it may be tempting to consider as minor the absolute level of differences, :10 and :15/day, the reader may quickly calculate that boys watch some 55 hours more per year than girls, and working-class children approximately 80 hours more.

Controlling for the effects of both sex and social class does not at all affect the impact of age on this choice of leisure time behaviour. Within each age sub-group, there is a climb of :50/day of TV watching among eight- to eleven-year-olds, and another increment of :23/day among the twelve- to fourteen-year-olds. Age is the most critical correlate of television watching identified here.

Given the relations of these social indicators with overall television viewing, the analysis turned to possible channel differences. Table 1.1 suggested that BBC and ITV cater somewhat differently to segments of the child audience (and/or their parents). Table 1.3 presents parallel data for BBC and ITV.

Table 1.3A demonstrates that boy-girl differences, when age and social class are controlled, are confined to BBC through the age of fourteen. Boys watch :11/day more of BBC-TV than girls. For ITV, sex differences are negligible, save for fifteen- to nineteen-year-old working-class children, where it is the girls who watch a dozen minutes more per day than the boys.

Table 1.3B shows that the social-class difference in television watching is persistently in terms of a half hour more of watching of ITV each day among working-class children in each age-sex sub-group. Although middle-class children consistently favour BBC-TV, size of the daily difference is small.

The age variable, as in Table 1.3C, is not affected by channel, except among the fifteen- to nineteen-year-olds. There is minimal variance associated with a :25/day increase per channel between the ages of five to seven and eight to eleven, and a further :10/day rise for the twelve- to fourteen-year-olds. Viewing of course drops for all fifteen- to nineteen-year-olds, but it is ITV viewing which drops a fairly consistent quarter hour more than BBC.

We also identified the maximum and minimum viewing groups for each of the seven sample periods. The TV fan is the twelve- to fourteen-year-old working-class boy in six of seven comparisons, and in the seventh that segment of boys was exceeded only by their female peers. Across seasons, the fan averaged 3:22/day. Least viewing is done by five- to seven-year-old middle-class girls, in six of seven comparisons. Their TV level was 1:32/day. Subsequent data for January 1972 show that twelve- to fourteen-year-old working-class boys were still watching the most and five- to seven-year-old middle-class girls watched 2:10/day, again the minimal viewing level found.

Table 1.4 is an elaboration of the viewing sub-groups, ordering them across seasons from highest to lowest viewing levels. The initial order (the left-hand column) is that of total television exposure. Although the table collapses across the seven seasons, the correlation among seasons in sub-group ordering is .916.[3] Thus the order shown does not mask internal deviations of any magnitude. The table also indicates how the sub-groups order for BBC-TV and ITV. Again, seasonal differences were minor; for BBC-TV, the consistency from season to season correlated .798 while for ITV, it was .911.

One remaining question is the extent to which sub-group ordering for all TV correlates with viewing group order of individual channels. The ITV order correlates .940 with the all-TV order, reflecting the greater watching of ITV by the working-class children and their greater proportion in the sample. The BBC order correlates .779 with the overall order. The BBC and ITV orders correlate .584 with each other, reflecting the kinds of audience differences noted previously.

RADIO LISTENING

Recent Trends

As with television, we obtained background data on radio-listening
levels by re-examing data from 1967 through 1971. For each of five
years, we averaged listening for two weeks in midwinter and two
weeks in midsummer, for each of the major age groups of children.
Among five- to seven- and eight- to eleven-year-olds, no perceptible
change occurred over time in either season. For the former,
listening amounts to :15/day in midwinter and :24 in midsummer
and has been within a few minutes of those levels for the five-year
period. For the eight- to eleven-year-olds one half hour is given
each day to radio, and that has undergone little change in five
years.

Among twelve- to fourteen-year-olds, listening has increased
:20/day in each season, from :30 to :50, in February, and from :57
to 1:20 in August. Radio listening has also increased substantially
for the fifteen- to nineteen-year-olds. In 1967, the level was
1:00/day in midwinter and had grown to 2:00 by 1971; a similar
increase from the same base levels was found for midsummer. Thus
the recent trend in radio listening has been no change before the age
of twelve, an increase of :20/day for twelve- to fourteen-year-olds,
and nearly a full hour per day for those between fifteen and
nineteen. During the same five years, adult listening has grown from
1:15 to 1:30/day.

Current Levels

Over all children, radio listening averaged a few minutes more than
an hour a day. Seasonal variability was not great, ranging from a
low of :55/day in January to 1:19 in August. Some 70 to 80 per cent
of all listening by British youngsters is confined to Radio 1 (popular
music) and most of the remainder goes to Radio 2. Our analysis did
not differentiate among radio channels.

The daily listening average is consistently greater for girls (1:10)
than boys (:57), for working-class children (1:10) than middle-class
ones (:51), and for each successive age group. Across the seven
periods, girls listened :13/day more than boys, and working-class
children :19/day more than their middle-class counterparts. But the
most significant differentiator is age. Radio listening time is
composed of :30/day among the younger groups, 1:00/day among
twelve- to fourteen-year-olds, and hits its maximum among

fifteen- to nineteen-year-olds, at 2:00/day; it remains close to that level among twenty- to twenty-nine-year-olds, but drops significantly for all older adult groups.

Sub-group Listening

Table 1.5 divides radio listening by the sex, social class and age of the children simultaneously. This permits us to determine whether some of the differences noted in the last section remain or disappear when other demographic characteristics are controlled. Thus, for the overall boy-girl difference of :13/day, this table isolates the locus of that difference in the age categories of twelve to fourteen and fifteen to nineteen. Sex is not a strong differentiator of radio listening among British children until they are twelve or older; or, boys and girls from five to eleven listen to nearly the same extent.

Even more strikingly, when we control for age and sex, the social-class difference of :19/day is virtually wiped out in half the sub-groups. It is diminished by a minimum of :06/day in the remainder. Thus social class becomes an even weaker correlate of radio listening, when only two other factors — sex and age — are controlled.

In contrast, the original age differences are retained to fully the same extent. Listening rises slightly among eight- to eleven-year-olds, sharply among those twelve to fourteen, and even more steeply for fifteen- to nineteen-year-olds. Within-sub-group variance is not great. Therefore, the best predictor here of overall attention to radio is simply the age of the youngster.

For the seven seasons, the most avid radio listener would be a fifteen- to nineteen-year-old girls, listening 2:15/day. The least-developed listener would be a five- to seven-year-old, middle-class boy, listening :15/day.

Table 1.4 includes the sub-group listening levels, and their rank order. The order reflects the persistence of age as the critical demographic factor in amount of listening, and the lesser consistency of sex and social class as viable predictors. Although the table represents data collapsed across seven seasonal periods, we did look at the ordering for each season. The degree of agreement across seasons was .904, which reflects near-unanimity for the different time periods analysed.

Finally, we examined the extent to which the radio sub-groups correspond to the television sub-groups in terms of exposure time.

This was done separately for BBC-TV, ITV and total television exposure. In essence, the group ordering for radio (from highest to lowest listening) is uncorrelated with the group ordering for any of the television exposure components. The correlations ranged from Rhos of .160 (BBC-TV) to .220 (total TV). These may be interpreted as trivial relationships. As examples, the maximum radio-listening sub-group is ninth in terms of total television watching; the maximum television-viewing sub-group is seventh in total radio exposure.

SUMMARY

Television Viewing

Young British viewers, aged five to seven, watch 2:00/day in 1971, up :25 from 1967. The remainder of the pre-teen set were watching 2:45/day, up :30 and the youngest teen-age group was watching more than 3:00/day, another thirty minute jump. The fifteen to nineteen group watched about 2:15/day, up :10.

Sex is not a strong correlate of television watching, and what difference is found occurs only in BBC-TV viewing. Working-class children spend nearly a half hour more per day with ITV, but a quarter hour less with BBC. Thus social class and channel interact in the viewing choices of British children.

Age is the strongest correlate of TV watching. Projected over a thirty-day month, a child who is five to seven watched 60:00/month in 1971; an eight- to eleven-year-old watched 83:00, a twelve- to fourteen-year-old watched 95:00, and the lesser viewing among fifteen- to nineteen-year-olds still accounted for some 63:00/month. Controlling for both sex and social class does not diminish the age relations, and age does not interact with channel choice.

Working-class boys and girls, aged twelve to fourteen, are the most avid fans of television; five- to seven-year-old middle-class children are the least ardent.

Radio Listening

British teens have enlarged greatly their radio exposure in the last five years. Those twelve to fourteen listen :20/day more than they did in 1967, yielding :50/day averages in the winter and 1:20/day in the summer. The older teen group has added an hour per day of radio to their 1967 seasonal averages of one hour. The younger children, aged five to eleven, seldom average a half hour a day.

As to correlates of radio usage, girls listen :15/day more than boys, and working-class children some :20 more than middle-class children. As age increases in the five- to nineteen-year-old span, there are successive leaps in daily radio listening. When one controls for other demographic characteristics, the relations between sex and social class with radio usage are weaker or disappear entirely. Age, however, retains its strong relations to usage.

The biggest radio fans are fifteen- to nineteen-year-old working-class girls, listening about 2:15/day. The other sex-social class groupings in that age bracket do not lag far behind in their enthusiasm for radio.

DISCUSSION

Most useful of course would be comparative data for these British children. Two kinds of comparisons would be enlightening. One would be with earlier data, from perhaps 1957 to 1961 or 1961 to 1965. However, individual data are not retained in the BBC data archives for such time periods. So one hope would be to repeat such an analysis from parallel British sources in a future decade. The second form of comparison is perhaps more feasible sooner. Similar data are generated by the Swedish Broadcasting Corporation, Japan's NHK, and perhaps by some United States networks. To what extent would equivalent viewing levels and patterns emerge? The Furu, Himmelweit, and Schramm studies have all shown that the maximum viewing group is the early adolescent one. But in what doses is there maximum or penultimate viewing, given countries in which the broadcast day ranges from six hours per day to twenty-four? For instance, the 3 to 3:30-hour level in Britain for twelve- to fourteen-year-old children is not very different from what has been obtained in the United States studies. This is so although the English broadcast day is eight hours, and that of United States more like eighteen hours. Is there 'optimal' viewing, in terms of so much possible — despite the amount available? How does this optimum differ across various groups? What are the cut-off criteria used by children and their peers — or their parents?

Further, we are minimally aware of the whys for the viewing levels described. Why does it maximize between the ages of twelve and fifteen, and then why does it drop off drastically in the next age cycle? Such whys cannot be accounted for by the present set of demographic attributes. After all, demographic indicators seldom explain. They are largely a means of more precise description of behavioural patterns. More sensitive and subtle social indicators are needed, e.g. interpersonal characteristics, alternative leisure time possibilities, social groupings information, and introversion tendencies.

These life-cycle clusters of child fans of television and radio require elaboration. Intensive studies of the functions and gratifications of the media (see, Blumler and Katz, 1974) should lead to more adequate understanding of the children's needs. Then, one can examine the children's attempts to satisfy those needs through the mass media. Subsequently, the extent to which the media do provide needs-satisfaction must be independently assessed. Future work may turn in such directions for greater theoretical development.

Notes

1 The raw data were weighted by appropriate sampling fractions in accord with population figures. We processed one time period by both weighted and unweighted data, and no significant differences were found.
2 BBC-1 and BBC-2 viewing are combined. BBC-2 viewing by five- to seven-year-olds is less than :30/week, is :40/week among eight to elevens and 1:15/week among twelve to fourteens and fifteen to nineteens. Between 1967 and 1971, viewing of BBC-2 had increased among five- to seven-year-olds, :20/week; among eight- to eleven-year-olds, :35/week; among those twelve to fourteen and fifteen to nineteen, 1:00/week. All increases have been gradual and linear.
3 See Siegel (1956) pp. 229-38.

References

Blumler, J G and *Katz, E* (eds) (1974), *The Use of Mass Communications: Current Perspectives on Gratifications Research,* Sage, Beverly Hills.
Furu, T (1971), *The Function of Television for Children and Adolescents,* Sophia University Press, Tokyo.
Himmelweit, H, Oppenheim A and *Vince P* (1958), *Television and the Child: An Empirical Study of the Effect of Television on the Child,* Oxford University Press, London.
Schramm, W, Lyle J and *Parker E B* (1961), *Television in the Lives of our Children,* Stanford University Press, Stanford.
Siegel, S (1956), *Nonparametric Statistics,* McGraw-Hill, New York, 229-38.

2

Explorations in Patterns of Television Viewing by Pre-school-age Children

Jack Lyle and Heidi R Hoffman

It is generally accepted that the pre-school years are among the most important in a child's development. With television present in almost every American home, this medium undoubtedly is a factor contributing to the developmental experiences of young children. Yet very little is known about the norms of viewing behaviour among this age group. Most of what has been reported is based on interviews with mothers about the behaviour of their young children.

This study was an attempt to gather information directly from pre-school-age children themselves. It focused on use of television and other media together; some questions also probed children's cognitive reactions to television.

In effect, it was an exploratory study. The sample is not a random one; rather, selection was purposeful to guarantee inclusion of a variety of types of children. The children were recruited through the co-operation of day-care centres and nursery schools. These ranged from centres operated with public funds to private and church programmes. Follow-up interviews were obtained with mothers of approximately half the children. (See Appendix A on p.59 for a fuller discussion of methodology.)

THE SAMPLE

Basic demographic characteristics of the 158 children interviewed are detailed in Table 2.1. There was a roughly even division between boys and girls and between students in half-day and full-day programmes. Four-year-olds constituted about half the sample; the remainder was divided about equally between three-

and five-year-olds. Over half the children were Caucasian, but sufficient numbers of blacks and Mexican-Americans were included to make comparisons possible. The Mexican-Americans tended to be older than the other groups. The age profiles for boys and girls were relatively even.

TABLE 2.1
Characteristics of the sample

	N=158		N=158
Girls	48.7%	Negro	23.4%
Boys	51.3	Mexican-American	17.7
		Other	3.1
Age 3	24.7%		
Age 4	52.5	Poverty level	41.7
Age 5	22.2	Middle-class	58.3
Age 6	.6		
		Full-day students	48.7%
Caucasian	55.7%	Part-day students	51.3

Four of every ten children came from poor or welfare families. These were primarily the minority children, and review of the cross-tabulations suggested that the two were basically redundant. Therefore, in the analysis which follows, the emphasis has been on ethnic rather than on socio-economic comparisons.

RESULTS

Before beginning a discussion of the responses provided by these children and their mothers, let us caution the reader against extrapolation of the data. Certainly it cannot be said that the sample is a representative one. However, we do feel that the results are suggestive of the patterns of media use and development. Differences between some of the groups within the sample are particularly intriguing.

Despite the fact that there were many quite poor children in the sample, only two youngsters reported that there was no television in their home. Colour was present in 52 per cent of the homes and actually was more prevalent in the poor homes than in the middle-class homes. Two-thirds of the Negro children said they had colour, compared with 55 percent of the Caucasian and 36 per cent of the Mexican-American youngsters.

The living room was the most common location of the television set, with 65 per cent of the children citing that location and 22 per cent citing the family room. But 45 per cent of the children reported that their parents had a set in their bedrooms and 12 per cent said they had a set in their own bedrooms. The percentages add to more than 100 per cent reflecting the presence of multiple sets in many homes.

Television is immensely popular: 98 per cent of the children said they do like to watch television.

Since children of this age generally have not developed the ability to tell time, it was impractical to ask them for reports on viewing time. Instead, they were asked if they were allowed to watch at various periods of the day. The results are shown in Table 2.2. The afternoon figures as the predominant viewing time; nine out of ten say they are allowed to watch then. But over 80 per cent said they also can watch in the evening after supper and in the mornings. Six out of ten say they are allowed to watch while eating.

TABLE 2.2
Periods of television viewing

| | *Are you allowed to watch television* | | | | |
	In the afternoon	After supper	While eating supper	In the morning	Saturday morning
All children	91.1%	82.8%	62.0%	82.3%	84.8%
Full-time students	93.7%	80.5%	61.0%	76.6%	88.3%
Part-time students	88.8	85.0	63.0	87.7	81.5
Mother works	90.6%	90.6%	56.3%	71.9%	84.4%
Mother doesn't work	90.5	78.6	52.4	95.2	83.3

There was a marked difference between ethnic groups in these reponses. For instance, 78 per cent of the Negro youngsters said they could watch while eating, compared to 64 per cent of the Mexican-American and only 53 per cent of the Caucasian children.

Children whose mothers work were more likely than their peers to watch after supper, but the other children were more likely to say they could watch in the morning. This latter difference reflected the fact that they were more likely to be part-time students and hence at home where television was available in the morning period.

To provide a rough index of total viewing time, responses to these five items were summed. This provided possible scores of 0-5. Table 2.3 presents the distribution of index scores. Over three-quarters of the youngsters responded that they were allowed to watch in at least four of the five time periods. Mexican-American children had the highest scores, followed by blacks; Caucasians had the lowest scores. However, the basic difference between the groups was whether they said they could watch in four or five of the time periods. Similar patterns of differences were found between full-time and part-time students and between those whose mothers worked and those whose mothers did not.

TABLE 2.3
Number of time periods child can view

	0–3	4	5
All children	23.5%	32.5%	43.9%
Girls	29.0%	25.0%	46.1%
Boys	18.0	39.5	42.0
Caucasian	24.1%	37.9%	37.9%
Negro	24.3	27.0	48.6
Mexican-American	21.1	21.4	57.1
Full-time student	25.9%	37.7%	36.4%
Part-time student	21.2	27.5	51.3
Mother works	24.9%	43.8%	31.3%
Mother doesn't work	23.8	35.7	40.5

Solitary watching was definitely a rarity: only 11 per cent of all the children said they did so. The major difference here was that such viewing was higher among the younger children: 17 per cent of the three-year-olds said they viewed alone, compared with 11 per cent of the four-year-olds and 6 per cent of the five-year-olds.

An age difference was also apparent in responses to the question of who selects programmes for viewing. The pattern of responses is shown in Table 2.4. The majority of five-year-olds say they make their own selections, compared with only about one-third of the three- and four-year-olds. Selection by mother falls sharply after age three. Children whose mothers work are more likely to say they make their own programme selection or that they acquiesce to older siblings, while the influence of non-working mothers is stronger.

TABLE 2.4
Who selects programmes

	I do	Mother	Older sibling
All children	39.2%	16.3%	15.0%
Girls	33.3%	19.4%	18.1%
Boys	44.4	13.6	15.0
Mother works	43.8%	12.5%	21.9%
Mother doesn't work	38.1	26.2	7.2
Age 3	33.3%	27.8%	13.9%
Age 4	35.4	13.4	18.3
Age 5	52.9	11.8	8.8

Other responses account for missing percentages.

Children were asked to name their favourite programme, and the responses were categorized according to programme type. The results are shown in Table 2.5. Cartoon shows of various types accounted for almost two-thirds of the choices.

The cartoon show *The Flintstones* led in popularity with over one quarter of the children naming it. *Sesame Street*, named by 16 per cent, was the only other individual programme achieving a sizable frequency.

It is interesting to note that *Sesame Street* was the most popular among the youngest children, the three-year-olds. It also was much more frequently named by Caucasian youngsters than by minority youngsters.

The Flintstones' popularity increased with age and it also scored much higher among girls than among boys, among minority groups than among Caucasians.

The violent action character cartoons were mentioned by 11 per cent, pulling higher response among boys than among girls, among older children than among the three-year-olds.

Almost one-fifth, 19 per cent, of the youngest group did not comprehend the concept of a favourite programme.

Children were shown a series of photographs of persons featured in various television series and asked if they could name them. The characters were selected to provide a cross-section of both cartoon and regular programmes, of both adult and child characters.

The responses are detailed in Table 2.6.

Given the popularity of *The Flintstones*, it should be no surprise that Fred Flintstone was the most frequently identified character. His wife, Wilma, scored considerably below Fred but still was one of the three most frequently identified characters. The second best-known character was Big Bird from *Sesame Street*.

Although the other *Sesame Street* characters presented to the children obtained good recognition levels, they were far less well known than Big Bird. It is impossible to say whether this is due to the character's inherent attraction or to the fact that Big Bird has been more widely featured than his colleagues in guest appearances on major network programmes.

There were marked differences in the level of recognition of *Sesame Street* characters among ethnic groups. In all instances Caucasian children had the highest levels of recognition and, with the exception of Big Bird, black children the lowest. There also was a consistently higher recognition level of these characters among boys than girls. The fact that the human character and the two hand-puppet characters were all males may have contaminated this difference.

A similar sex difference was apparent for Fred Rogers. However, far more marked was the ethnic difference. Only 6 per cent of the Negro children recognized him, compared with 27 per cent of the Mexican-American and 53 per cent of the Caucasian youngsters.

Generally there was relatively low recognition of child characters from family situation comedies. This was particularly true among the younger children. Several characters — Buffy of *Family Affair,* Eddie and *Julia's* Cory — showed a sharp increased recognition among the five-year-olds.

But several adult characters from situation comedy programmes scored much higher than any child character. Lucy, Gilligan and his foil Skipper, together with Samantha of *Bewitched* were particularly well known. It should be noted that these are characters in programmes which are broadcast as repeats during daytime hours. The other adult characters — and, indeed, all the child characters — are on programmes shown only in the evening.

TABLE 2.5
Favourite programme categories

	All Children	Girls	Boys	Age 3	Age 4	Age 5	Caucasian	Negro	Mexican-American
Flintstones	26.1%	39.3%	19.0%	10.8%	28.9%	36.4%	17.2%	34.3%	40.7%
Mickey Mouse type cartoon	5.2	6.7	3.8	2.7	3.6	12.1	4.6	2.9	7.4
General cartoon	11.8	9.3	13.9	8.1	15.7	6.1	10.3	14.3	7.4
Violent cartoon	11.1	5.3	16.5	2.7	14.5	12.1	12.6	5.7	14.8
Bozo, etc.	3.3	4.0	2.5	8.1	2.4	–	3.4	5.7	–
Sesame Street	16.3	17.3	15.2	29.7	13.3	12.0	25.3	8.6	–
Misterogers	2.0	–	3.8	2.7	2.4	–	3.4	–	–
Situation comedy	4.6	5.3	3.8	–	3.6	12.1	5.7	2.9	3.7
Family situation comedy	3.9	4.0	3.8	5.4	2.4	6.1	4.6	5.7	–
No favourite	4.6	4.0	5.1	5.4	4.8	3.0	3.4	2.9	11.1
Don't understand	7.2	8.0	6.3	18.9	3.6	3.0	4.6	11.4	11.1

(Miscellaneous programme choices account for the missing residual percentages.)

The fact that adult characters like Malloy, Julia and Tom Corbett were most widely recognized by five-year-olds may be a reflection of this situation, since they are apt to be allowed to view later into the evening.

There was no age difference in recognition of Gilligan, a daytime-only character. Lucy's recognition did increase markedly with age, but she was seen both in daytime repeats as well as in her current evening series.

Perhaps most interesting of all the differences is the recognition of black characters. Bill Crosby was identified by only one-quarter of the total sample, but over half the Negro children named him. Similar differences are seen for Julia and for her son, Cory. By contrast, however, Gordon, a black adult from *Sesame Street*, was identified by over 60 per cent of the Caucasian youngsters, but only 19 per cent of the black children knew him. He even did better among Mexican-American children, 38 per cent of whom knew him.

Since the children who were in the centres and nursery schools all day generally had less time for television viewing than their peers who were there only part of the day, it was thought that they might have lower levels of recognition. However, there were no consistent patterns of differences when these two groups were compared — not even for daytime programmes.

It is interesting to compare the recognition of characters by these pre-school youngsters with the first graders studied by Lyle and Hoffman (1971). The pattern of best-known characters is quite similar, particularly among the five-year-olds: Lucy, Gilligan, Samantha and, above all, Fred Flintstone. Two differences do stand out: the higher recognition of *Sesame Street* characters and of Fred Rogers by these young children, and their lower level of recognition of child characters. The first graders tended to have higher recognition of child characters than of adult ones; this was not true of these pre-school-age youngsters.

The children were asked whether or not they 'played things they saw on television' in their activities with friends. Over half — 55 per cent — of the children said that they did not. However, there was a marked tendency for such play to increase with age. Whereas 64 per cent of the three-year-olds said they *didn't* engage in such play, 61.5 per cent of the five-year-olds said that they did. The types of things used as models for play were too varied to present any meaningful pattern.

Another question put to the children was, 'What kinds of scary things are there on television?' Two-thirds of the children named 'scary' things, and the responses overwhelmingly dealt with 'monsters'. Only 26.7 per cent said that there weren't any scary things; another 8.7 per cent did not understand the question. As noted in the report on first graders, care must be taken in equating this with an unpleasant experience. Many children responded with obvious relish at the thought of these 'scary monsters' of television.

Several questions were included to try to ascertain whether or not the child had any concept of people on television as 'real'. The children were asked, 'How do kids get to be on your TV?' 16 per cent did not understand the question, and another 40 per cent stated that they did not know. Only 22 per cent showed signs of real comprehension about the nature of television. A parallel question asked 'Where do the people and kids and things on your TV go when your TV is turned off?' On this item 24 per cent couldn't understand the question and another 29 per cent didn't know; only 20 per cent showed understanding. The major increase in comprehension came between ages three and four, but even among the older children the vast majority still did not grasp the nature of television pictures.

The youngsters were also asked whether or not they thought the children they saw on television were like themselves and their friends. 55 per cent replied yes. Minority children were somewhat more likely to think this way than were Caucasian children; 71 per cent of the Mexican-American youngsters replied yes, compared with 59 per cent of the Negroes and 51 per cent of the Caucasians.

Follow-up interviews were obtained from 76 mothers of children interviewed. Because of difficulties encountered in contacting minority group mothers, these tended to be mostly Caucasian mothers. Of those interviewed, 58 per cent were employed and 42 per cent did not work.

Since the educational stations in the Los Angeles area are UHF channels, it was necessary to ascertain the availability of reliable UHF reception in the homes. Only 13 per cent of the mothers said they did not have UHF receivers. 22 per cent said they had receivers but could not get good reception. 64 per cent indicated they had adequate UHF reception in their home.

The mothers were asked to estimate the amount of time their children spent watching television in different periods of the day. The results are detailed in Table 2.7. Generally, viewing appeared

TABLE 2.6
Levels of identification for characters
(Percent able to identify characters from pictures)

	All children	Girls	Boys	Age 3	Age 4	Age 5	Caucasian	Negro	Mexican-American
Fred Flintstone	92.3%	89.3%	95.1%	87.2%	92.6%	97.1%	89.8%	100.0%	92.6%
Wilma Flintstone	71.6	71.6	71.6	61.2	72.5	82.9	64.4	77.8	85.2
Scooby Do	48.4	45.2	51.3	25.6	52.6	65.7	40.2	55.6	65.4
Lucy	64.1	68.0	60.5	53.8	66.7	71.4	59.1	83.3	59.3
Malloy (Adam-12)	17.6	18.1	17.1	8.1	16.9	27.3	5.9	32.4	41.7
Bill Cosby	24.7	21.9	27.2	17.9	26.3	29.4	17.2	52.8	11.5
Samantha (Bewitched)	49.7	54.1	45.6	28.2	54.4	62.9	38.6	63.9	70.8
Gilligan	57.5	54.8	60.0	48.7	54.4	71.4	53.4	63.9	70.8
Skipper (Gilligan)	54.6	50.7	58.2	46.2	52.6	65.7	52.9	55.6	66.7
Tom Corbett (Eddie's Father)	24.0	18.9	28.8	23.1	20.3	34.3	18.4	40.0	25.9
Julia	11.8	13.3	10.3	5.4	8.8	25.7	3.4	31.4	15.4

Table 2.6 continued

	All children	Girls	Boys	Age 3	Age 4	Age 5	Caucasian	Negro	Mexican-American
Danny Partridge	21.3%	20.3%	22.2%	17.9%	23.5%	20.6%	11.4%	38.9%	34.6%
Buffy (Family Affair)	25.2	27.0	23.5	23.1	21.0	38.2	15.9	44.4	26.9
Marcia Brady	13.0	15.1	11.1	20.5	7.4	18.2	8.0	30.6	7.7
Eddie (Eddie's Father)	23.4	17.6	28.8	20.5	20.3	34.3	18.4	40.0	22.2
Cory (Julia)	11.3	12.0	10.5	8.1	8.9	20.6	1.2	35.3	15.4
Sesame Street									
Big Bird	77.6	73.3	81.5	74.4	76.5	82.9	85.2	75.0	51.9
Ernie	50.4	41.3	56.8	48.7	54.3	40.0	62.5	22.2	44.4
Bert	50.3	43.2	56.8	58.7	55.0	42.9	64.4	22.2	44.4
Gordon	46.1	37.0	54.3	41.0	49.4	45.7	60.9	19.4	38.5
Fred Rogers (Misterogers)	36.8	31.1	42.0	33.3	36.3	42.9	53.4	5.6	26.9

to be heaviest on weekday afternoons and Saturday mornings. With the exception of weekday mornings, there was no marked difference in the responses of working and non-working mothers. However, 61 per cent of the non-working mothers said their children were not allowed to watch on weekday mornings, compared with only 21 per cent of the working mothers.

TABLE 2.7
Children's viewing time, reported by mother

	Weekday morning	Weekday afternoon	Weekday evening	Saturday morning	Sunday morning
None	37.9%	20.3%	10.5%	8.0%	16.4%
1 hour or less	34.9	9.5	36.9	25.3	38.4
1.5–2 hours	24.2	47.3	21.1	30.7	28.7
2.5 hours or more	3.0	36.5	19.7	34.7	16.4

Most of the children were up by 7 a.m., and most were put to bed by 8 p.m. Non-working mothers said their children got up earlier, although they were not put to bed any earlier than those of working mothers. However, 94 per cent of the non-working mothers said their children went to sleep immediately, compared with 80 per cent of the working mothers. On the other hand, only 34 per cent of the children of non-working mothers were said to take naps, compared with 51 per cent of those of working mothers.

There was little difference between the responses of working and non-working mothers to questions about use of television deprivation as a punishment or extended viewing as a reward. Less than one-quarter of the mothers said they used these techniques. There was a difference in their reports of selecting programmes for their children: 70 per cent of the working mothers said they did select programmes, but only 41 per cent of the non-working mothers said they did so.

Almost three-quarters, 74 per cent, of the mothers said their young children sang commercial jingles learned from television, 62 per cent saying that this had begun the time the child was age two, another 31 per cent saying by age three.

The impact of advertising was further emphasized by the fact that 87 per cent of the mothers said their pre-school-age children asked for food items they saw on television; 91 per cent, said their children asked for toys they saw on television. Only 22 per cent of the mothers said they usually denied the request outright, but working mothers were twice as likely as non-working mothers to do so. The most typical action was to sidetrack the child's request.

Most of the mothers felt that their children were learning both good and bad things from television. Nine out of ten felt that beneficial learning did occur, 17 per cent citing learning 'about life'. 28 per cent felt there was 'school-readiness' learning, and another 22 per cent mentioned learning from *Sesame Street* and *Misterogers*. A variety of other responses accounted for the remainder.

As to bad learning, only 9 per cent were certain that no bad learning occurred; another 28 per cent were not sure. The only type of bad learning specified with any marked frequency had to do with violence. 24 per cent of these mothers felt that their young children were learning violent or aggressive behaviour from the things they viewed on television.

Slightly more than half the mothers, 53 per cent, thought their children were sometimes frightened by television. Monsters were specified by 2.1 per cent of the mothers as the cause; this was the only specific type of stimulus mentioned by a sizable number. As we have pointed out, the children themselves also most frequently said they were frightened by television monsters.

Only 12 per cent said their children's sleep was interrupted by bad dreams; another 66 per cent said this occurred only infrequently, and 22 per cent said it didn't happen at all. Only 4 per cent of the mothers could recall dreams they could trace to television.

USE OF OTHER MEDIA

The children were asked about the availability of radios and phonographs in their homes. These were equally present: 84 per cent of the children said they had a radio, and 86 per cent said they had a phonograph or record player. 19 per cent said they had records of their own. Interestingly, the children seemed to have more access to record players than to radios. When asked if they were allowed to play them when they wanted to 64 per cent said they had free access to the record player; only 51 per cent said they had access to the radio. As might be expected, there was a general age progression on these responses; the five-year-olds reported more accessibility to both radio and phonograph than did the younger children.

Books appeared to be generally available to the children; 87 per cent said they had books of their own. When asked what were their favourites, the three most frequent categories named were classic story books (29 per cent), books like the *Sesame Street* series (27 per cent), and the Dr. Seuss books (13 per cent).

When asked if their mother ever read to them, only 15 per cent said no; 48 per cent said she did so at bedtime. The remainder named different times but indicated that she did read for them. There was clear evidence of decreased reading by mothers as children grow. Only 3 per cent of the three-year-olds said their mothers did not read to them, compared with 27 per cent of the four-year-olds and 41 per cent of the five-year-olds.

Particularly marked were differences in parental reading among the ethnic sub-groups. Whereas 87 per cent of the Caucasian youngsters said their mothers read to them, only 61 per cent of the Negro and 52 per cent of the Mexican-American children reported reading.

As can be seen from Table 2.8 these children did spend considerable time in play activities, particularly with siblings and friends.

TABLE 2.8
Children's play time, reported by mother

Play with	Alone	Siblings	Friends	Mother	Father
1 hour or less	57.3%	29.3%	9.6%	77.6%	69.3%
2 hours	22.7	17.3	11.0	10.5	13.3
3 hours or more	20.0	53.3	79.4	11.8	17.4

SUMMARY

The responses of these three-, four- and five-year-olds drawn from disparate backgrounds provide strong testimony to the fact that mass media — and particularly television — do play an important part in their lives, do claim large shares of the children's time. Even the youngest children indicated that they do watch television regularly on a daily basis. Viewing was particularly heavy during afternoons and on Saturday mornings, but the majority also indicated that they watched on weekday mornings and in the evenings.

Even the youngest children generally had favourite programmes and showed high ability to identify at least some television characters; almost nine out of ten of the three-year-olds could identify Fred Flintstone; seven out of ten could identify Big Bird from *Sesame Street*; over half of them knew Lucy.

Almost nine out of ten of the mothers said their children had learned commercial jingles from television, and that the children were stimulated by commercials to ask for food and toy items featured in television commercials.

Sex and ethnic differences were already apparent in the programme choices of these pre-school-age youngsters.

Generally, then, the responses of these children and their mothers strongly support the thesis that much of the framework of a child's patterns of television use and reactions to the television stimulus has already begun taking shape before the child begins his formal education in the first grade.

APPENDIX A

A Note on Methodology
As noted at the outset, this study was an exploratory one. Not only did it attempt to gather data on a segment of the population about whose media use knowledge is sketchy, but it attempted to gather this data by direct interview with the young children themselves rather than by using reports from mothers. Interviewing with very young children is still a relatively rare and undeveloped area of field survey research.

For the present study, the techniques employed were developed primarily as adaptations of those used in the interviews with the first graders in the major portion of this study (Lyle and Hoffman, 1971). The junior author was primarily responsible for developing the techniques and in doing so was able to draw upon considerable personal experience in working with young children in day-care centres and nursery schools. In addition, helpful ideas and suggestions came from the authors of several other studies in this series who drew upon their experiences with young children, particularly Aimee Leifer, Donald Roberts and Aletha Stein and her associates. Conversations with Dr Fred Gottleib of UCLA's Neuropsychiatric Institute and Dr Alberta Siegel of Stanford's Psychiatry Department provided other valuable inputs.

In the early stages of development, it was anticipated that it might be necessary to rely heavily on projective devices. However, pretesting soon showed that even three-year-olds were knowledge-able about television and, for the most part, could respond directly to verbal questioning. As a result, the technique used in the field relied upon direct questioning together with a series of photographs of television characters which the children were asked to identify.

Great care was taken in recruiting interviewers who could relate to children of this age group and could make them feel at ease while still keeping their attention directed. The interviewers were young adults who had experience working with young children.Negro children were interviewed by Caucasians after consultation with Negro teachers or directors of the centres and nurseries. Mexican-American children were interviewed in Spanish where it appeared that this was necessary to put them at ease.

Most interviewing was done within the nursery-school or day-care-centre environment. This procedure allowed the inter-viewer to appear on the scene before beginning to interview and to be accepted as part of the group before dealing with a child individually.

All interviews were conducted on an individual basis; the interviewer provided reinforcement and reassurance as needed to keep the child's attention and confidence. The interview consisted of twenty-four questions, after which the child was allowed to rest or stretch before being presented with the twenty-one photographs for identification.

The photographs were purposely kept until last to serve as something of a reward, since identifying them was found to be a generally pleasurable game-type activity for the children.

An interesting informal observation was that although the word 'test' was never used by the interviewers, a number of the children themselves applied this term in inquiring when their turn would come. Even in the pre-school ages, these youngsters had already become 'test conscious'.

Some difficulty was encountered both with the question about favourite programmes and with the picture identifications. The responses were something of a puzzle. With regard to favourite programmes, this was primarily due to the apparent tendency for some children to fail to distinguish among programmes and between programmes and commercials. In some instances, the children had definite answers which were not immediately meaningful to the interviewers. A wide knowledge of programmes and characters was of prime necessity for the interviewers so that they could understand the response. Similarly, in response to the picture identification, children sometimes answered, not with the actual 'name' of the character, but with a mimicking of the character's behaviour or pet phrases.

The most serious difficulty encountered was the difficulty some children had in verbalization. At all three age levels considerable diversity of verbal skills was encountered. For instance, some children showed physical evidence — facial expression, body motion — that they recognized characters, but they couldn't respond with a verbal identification. Generally the difficulties in verbalization were more likely to be related to minority group membership and disadvantaged background than to age.

REFERENCES

Lyle, J and *Hoffman H* (1971), 'Children's use of television and other media', *Television and social behaviour, IV*, US Government Printing Office, Washington DC.

3

Concepts of Order and Balance in a Children's TV Programme

Grant Noble

How do producers and viewers differ in the way they would organize items in a magazine-format television programme? This question, especially as it applies to children as viewers, was of such interest to the European Broadcasting Union that it commissioned the study reported here.

The programme chosen to test hypotheses concerning programme format was *Blue Peter*, a twice-weekly television programme for children between the ages of five and twelve which attracts audiences of between eight and twelve million viewers for the BBC. Because this age range includes children who might have difficulty in conceptualizing television programme content, the investigation included viewer age as a variable.

M D Vernon has reported it is the first half of a television programme that is best recalled (1953). Perhaps this can be explained by what television producers and directors call 'button apathy': the need to 'hook' an audience very early in the programme. The purpose of hooking an audience is to prevent the viewer changing stations and this is achieved by presenting the most interesting material at the beginning. Thus it was expected that television producers would choose to start a magazine-type programme with the most interesting item. On the other hand, it was thought that children would order items in a magazine programme so that interest would be maintained throughout.

Noble (1969) has found that children below the age of seven are unable to comprehend the story of a film and that such abilities are not apparent until after the 'cognitive revolution' has taken place (which Piaget (1954) places at six to seven years). It was therefore hypothesized that children of seven years and below would not be able to discriminate between items transmitted live from the studio and items filmed on location.

'Items' are presented in the studio with background props which have been used throughout the series, and it was felt that children would feel secure because studio items were familiar to them. It was expected that five- and six-year-old children would most like items they thought were made in the studio.

METHOD

The 'intentions' (aims) of the three producers of the children's magazine programme *Blue Peter* were studied by both participant and non-participant observation. Scripts were examined at various stages of completion and special attention directed at the way items were ordered in the programme. The author observed several rehearsal sessions and the changes made during these sessions. It was found that the structure of the programme was given very careful consideration.

Questionnaires were designed to assess both children's and producers' reactions to the concepts used by producers when structuring the *Blue Peter* programme. 300 children were asked to watch BBC television from 4.30 to 5.50 p.m. on Monday 29 January 1968. Eighty-five children were selected at random from these 300 and were interviewed the day after transmission. The children were unaware that it was *Blue Peter* which was to be investigated; it could have been any one of three programmes transmitted in that time. The method used to assess the ordering of items was to present each child with seven still photographs representing the items presented in that programme and ask him to select his own running order as if he had been in charge of the programme. An identical procedure was adopted for television producers except that only five photographs were used. Two photographs (A and C in Figure 3.1) were not included because these were replicate photographs of the same items. These duplicate photographs were given to the children to find out whether they first wished to see the compères or the objects used in that item.

Both children and producers were asked why they would have placed each photograph in the order they had selected. Children then evaluated each photograph for the speed of the item (fast to slow), the length of the item (short or long) and the excitement of the item (exciting to dull). These three dimensions were those which the *Blue Peter* producers had been found to use when maintaining a balance between items.

Figure 3.1 Running order identity of photos used

Running order	Photograph	Item
1	A	Shot of Traction Engines.
2	B	John and Peter play with Traction Engines.
3		John and Peter plough with the two Traction Engines.
4		Val joins John and Peter with old print and *Blue Peter* Tractor.
5	C (close-up)	John as a clown (film).
	D (long-shot)	
6	E	Valerie shows how to make clown coat-hanger.
7	F	John and Peter with 'I'm backing Britain' tee shirts.
8		Film about Ospreys.
9	G	Val and John Murray with Osprey in the studio.
10		All three close programme.

To find out if the items were perceived as similar, Osgood D scores and McQuitty's cluster analysis techniques were applied by plotting preference order against transmitted order in a matrix. The children were individually interviewed by trained interviewers while producers were asked to complete their own questionnaires. Both producers and children made evaluations for each of the three compères on a semantic differential grid.

Although the selected date was known to the producers, no attempt was made to produce a 'special' programme. A brief description of the programme arranged in terms of the items as they were presented is given in Figure 3.1. The running order is abridged from the original script. The letters refer to the photographs used in the exercise.

The programme was introduced by a team of three compères (two men and one woman) who were regularly responsible for the presentation of all the items and the continuity between items. The script was edited by a team of two producers and a senior editor who were responsible for the content of the programme and the direction of the actors.

The children were selected at random from two schools. Twenty-four children aged five and six years were selected from a modern primary school in a middle-class residential suburb, sixty children aged between seven to eleven years from a typical urban school in a city and twelve children, six boys and six girls, at random from each of the seven- to eleven-year age groups.

The sample of television producers was not randomly selected. It consisted of the forty producers of children's television programmes who were gathered in London for a workshop organized by the European Broadcasting Union. The producers were asked to complete a questionnaire immediately after seeing a videotape of the selected programme.

RESULTS

Producers' Intentions
The *Blue Peter* producers considered it very important that a balance be maintained between items in the programme. The main criteria used when ordering items were, firstly, that equal use be made of the three compères; secondly, that no one compère should present several consecutive items; and thirdly, that consecutive items should vary in terms of length, pace and excitement.

Two types of items are always presented in *Blue Peter*, those which are transmitted live from the studio and those which are previously filmed on location using one, two or three of the compères. Filmed material (usually considered the high spot of the programme) was never used to open or close the programme but was sandwiched between items presented in the studio. The reason the programme both begins and ends with items transmitted live from the studio is that studio items are thought to establish a sense of security in the viewing child while a need for adventure (contained in outside film items) could later be satisfied.

Children's Concept of Order and Balance
Only four of the eighty-six children interviewed chose the running order used in the programme. To discover how children would have ordered the items, a matrix was constructed (Table 3.1). Photographs A to G were listed across the top of the matrix (columns), and the running order, expressed in terms of the items

TABLE 3.1
Frequencies, children's preference order, contrasted with programme running order

Running order selected	Photographs						
	A	B	C	D	E	F	G
1	22	14	15	2	9	15	9
2	12	26	15	10	11	5	7
3	9	6	17	16	13	14	11
4	9	7	17	22	9	9	13
5	12	6	10	16	20	12	10
6	9	15	11	11	20	13	7
7	12	12	1	10	3	18	28

First selected running order: A, B, C, D, E, F, G.

Second selected running order: B, A, G, C, D, E, F,

which would be presented first, second, third ... seventh, was placed down the side of the matrix (rows). All the choices for all the children were summed within the matrix format. The modal score was found for each column and this was taken to be the average running order position selected by the children. Two modes were often found in a single column, suggesting that there were two positions available in the running order for that item; e.g. (Table 3.1) photograph C could be placed either third or fourth in the running order. When such a condition was found, the row was inspected to see if any of the other running orders had already been allocated, and if so, whether the modal score for that column was higher than the modal score for the column in doubt. For example the fourth position in the running order in Table 3.1 had already been allocated, so item C was placed in the third position.

The running order selected by the children was found by this method to be the same as that transmitted in the programme, namely, A, B, C, D, E, F, G. These modal scores were eliminated from the matrix and the procedure repeated. A second running order was found to be B, A, G, C, D, E, F (Table 3.1).

The differences between the second running order selected by the children and that used in the programme were of interest, since children did not give the same reasons for their choices as did the *Blue Peter* producers. Firstly, the Traction Engine photographs were reversed. Photograph A, chosen first, was a long shot of the traction engines upon which captions were super-imposed and was therefore chosen as the first shot of the programme. The children, however, evidently preferred first to see the compères rather than the traction engines and to follow the traction engine item with the item about Ospreys. The Osprey item was therefore shifted from the last position in the programme to follow the traction engine item. The children did not choose to end the programme with the Osprey item but rather with the tee shirt item. The tee shirt item had been transmitted live from the studio and had been presented by all three compères, and they might have preferred to end with this safe and humorous studio item.

The reasons given by the children for placing the photographs in their chosen order were examined, and it was found that 17 per cent placed an item at the beginning of the programme because it was the most important item; 12 to 13 per cent placed an item first because the item was good or funny, while 4 per cent placed the least interesting item in first place. The reasons for placing an item second in the running order were that it should be good or interesting (21 per cent) or should logically follow from the first item (20 per cent). The reasons given for placing an item third showed that only 4 per cent of the children wanted the best item in the middle of the programme while the same percentage placed an item in third place because it was dull. The most important reasons given for placing an item third in the running order were that the item followed logically from the previous item (20 per cent) or that it was good (10 per cent) or funny (8 per cent). The reasons given for placing an item fourth, fifth and sixth in the running order were the same as for third. 16 per cent of the children placed an item last because it was the least interesting, 13 per cent because it was the most interesting, 4 per cent because of logical continuation of the previous item. The rest of these answers could not be categorized.

Osgood D scores were then calculated (Osgood *et al* 1957) preference order (rows) against transmitted order (columns), to ascertain the similarities of items in the running orders selected by the children (Table 3.2). McQuitty's elementary linkage analysis (1957) was applied to the D score matrix to find out if several items (rather than pairs of items) were similarly perceived. The strongest

TABLE 3.2
D matrix between items

	B	C	D	E	F	G
A	18.57	17.75	25.42	21.26	13.23	21.86
B		21.35	29.07	24.60	24.21	27.98
C			18.36	17.80	21.67	29.95
D				19.34	21.24	23.24
E					20.27	30.50
F						14.32

association was between items A (the two traction engines), F (the tee shirt item) and G (the Osprey item). This cluster most probably consisted of informational items. A second cluster was one of clown items consisting of items C (close-up of John as a clown), D (long-shot of John as a clown) and E (Valerie making a clown-coat hanger). The children perceived very strong similarities between items A (the traction engines) and B (John and Peter with the traction engines). Children thus perceived similarities between items in terms of content.

Finally, each child was asked to rate each item as he had ordered them for speed, length and excitement. There were no significant differences between such ratings for the *items* they had placed first, second ... seventh in the running order. The modal ratings were found for the first ... seventh positions. The children would have started with the shortest and fastest item, which was also exciting. The second item would have been slow, long and the most exciting, while the third item would have been slowest, longest, but also exciting. The fourth item would have been a fast, short item which was less exciting. The fifth item would have been slow, less exciting and long, while the sixth would have been slow, less exciting and short. The final item would then be slow, short and the least exciting.

Children would, therefore, have commenced with an item which would demand their attention for a short period of time, followed by an item which was longer, slower but more exciting. The third item was then the slowest and longest, but was still exciting. After

TABLE 3.3
Frequencies, children's correct estimation of where items were made, by age

	5-6 years	7-11 years		5-6 years	7-11 years
Correct photographs chosen	7	58	Incorrect photographs chosen or don't know	13	9

X^2 = 21.68 (significant beyond 0.1% level)

this point both the pace and length varied and the programme ended with two short, slow and less exciting items. The three dimensions used by the producers would, therefore, seem to be relevant to the children. The children wanted to be 'hooked' by a short item and their interest then held by the most exciting item. Children were less concerned than the producers about the ending.

Age Difference in Children's Reactions

Having found in a previous study that children of five and six years were unable to comprehend the story line of a puppet film, (*Noble*, 1969) it was expected that, prior to the 'cognitive revolution', children would not be able to discriminate between items transmitted live from the studio and items previously filmed on location. Five- and six-year-olds were significantly less able than children aged seven and older to correctly choose photographs representing items transmitted live from the studio, as opposed to photographs representing items previously recorded on film (Table 3.3). Since children aged seven did not confuse the two types of item, the ability to discriminate evidently develops abruptly.

35 per cent of the five- and six-year-old children thought the traction engine item must have been filmed outside the studio and a further 15 per cent aged five and six thought the Osprey item was not transmitted live from the studio. At these ages the children thought the traction engine might 'blow up' and that the Osprey 'might peck you' or 'be frightened off its nest'. Items considered dangerous were thus seen as items which were filmed outside the studio. One five-year-old thought *Blue Peter* was made 'at home'. These answers suggest that the studio provides a sense of security for young children. Indeed 80 per cent of the children who preferred studio to outside items did so because it was familiar; one ten-year-old girl, when asked why she liked something familiar,

replied 'because it is safe'.

While five- and six-year-old children preferred items transmitted live from the studio because they were familiar, older children preferred items previously recorded on film because they were unusual (significant $X^2 = 2.87$, p < .05 one tail). Children would, therefore, appear to outgrow a need for security expressed in a preference for items transmitted live from the studio.

Children aged seven and older were significantly different from younger children in that the older children more frequently mentioned that items should have followed one another in the running order because of logical continuity ($X^2 = 13.8$, p < .01). Five- and six-year-old children would not have placed photographs A and B (both of traction engines) after one another in the running order. Similarly, they would not have placed photographs C, D and E (the clown and clown coat-hanger item) together in the running order. Older children placed these photographs together.

Differences were also apparent between children of different ages as regards both the speed and length of items as placed in their selected running orders. Five- and six-year-olds reserved running order positions, three and seven for 'fast' items. All other positions would have been occupied by slow items. The seven- and eight-year-olds placed the only fast item in the middle of the running order. Nine to eleven-year-olds placed the faster items first and fifth. The pattern selected by five- and six-year-olds seemed illogical, as was expected.

Five- and six-year-olds placed a long item first and then finished the programme with three long items. Seven- and eight-year-old children ordered items so that the third and sixth items were longer. Nine- to eleven-year-old children placed longer items in the second and third positions. Seven and eight-year-olds would have had long items both after two short ones and again just before the closing item. While children aged seven and above concentrated long items at the beginning, younger children concentrated them at the end.

Television Producers' Concept of Order and Balance

The same method used with children's data was used to find out how producers of children's television programmes would have ordered the same items. It was found that producers emphatically chose the same running order as was used in the programme (much more so than the children). (Table 3.4.)

Producers and children were also asked which items in the programme they liked best. It was found that producers most liked

TABLE 3.4
Frequencies, producers' preference order, contrasted with programme running order

Running order	Photographs						D score matrix between items			
	B	D	E	F	G		D	E	F	G
1	13	11	1	4	2	B	10.29	16.31	12.77	14.46
2	5	13	5	1	7	D		18.28	19.67	14.53
3	4	3	15	4	6	E			15.78	12.61
4	7	1	6	14	3	F				13.64
5	4	3	4	3	12					

First running order: B, D, E, F, G.

Second running order: D, G, F, B, E.

the clown item (39 per cent), followed in turn by the Osprey item (30 per cent), the tee shirt item (11 per cent), thus making the clown coat-hanger item (8 per cent) and the traction engine item (7 per cent) the least liked. The running order selected by the producers was, therefore, to place the item they most liked first in the running order, the item they liked second best second in the running order and so on. Examination of the reasons items were ordered in this way showed that 52 per cent of the produces would have started with the most important or definite items, 15 per cent would have started with funny items, while 11 per cent would have had a quiet, easy starter. An item was placed second in the running order because it was funny (16 per cent), interesting (13 per cent) or a logical follow-on from a previous item (13 per cent). An item was placed third in the running order because it was interesting (14 per cent), activated practical work (10 per cent) or achieved a balance between male and female presenters (10 per cent). The fourth position in the running order was where the least interesting item was placed (15 per cent), or because an item was funny (15 per cent) or continued logically from the previous item (15 per cent). The final position in the running order was reserved for funny items (27 per cent) or for the dullest items (14 per cent). Producers therefore put the most interesting material at the beginning of the programme and the least interesting material at the end. It would appear that producers ordered material so as to capture the audience's

TABLE 3.5
Frequencies, selected running orders of children and producers by liking of items

| | Running order | | | | | |
	1	2	3	4	5	Total
Producers liking item best	39	30	11	7	8	95
Children liking item best	20	17	36	17	1	91
Totals	59	47	47	24	9	186

$x^2 = 32.55$ df = 4 (p < .01)

*Spearman's rank order correlation, order of items with order of liking,
for producers r = 0.95 (p < .05); for children r = 0.23 (n.s.)*

attention at the beginning of the programme.

D scores were calculated and cluster analysis was applied to the producers' preference order matrix (Table 3.4). The strongest association was between items B (traction engine) and D (John in the circus). Both these items were presented by John and this cluster would seem to be a 'John' cluster. The second cluster was one of Items E (clown coat-hanger) and G (Osprey). These two items relied heavily on Valerie for presentation and would seem to be a Valerie cluster. The tee shirt item (F), seemed to be independent. This item was presented by all three compères. Producers thus appeared to have seen similarities between items in terms of the compères who presented those items.

Comparison of Producers and Children

Producers were far less varied than were the children in their selection of items. Given the choice, they overwhelmingly chose the running order used in the programme. Very few children chose that order. Producers placed the item they most liked first in the running order, the next most liked item second, and the item they least liked at the end. Children were significantly different from producers in that they did not order items in terms of liking (Table 3.5).

Producers clearly ordered items so as to present the most interesting and striking item first. Children would have both started and ended with the most interesting items (Table 3.6). Producers would have started with an item previously recorded on film.

TABLE 3.6
Frequencies, producers' and children's placing of most important
items first and last

| | Most important items | |
	First	Last
Producers	52	9
Children	17	13
$X^2 = 7.47$ (p .01)		

Children reserved such items for the middle of the programme and
chose to both start and end with items transmitted live from the
studio. These findings could be regarded as indicating that children
wished to start and finish in safe, familiar surroundings and to have
a high point in the middle. Producers' intentions were to capture
the largest audience possible with the first item.

TABLE 3.7
Analysis of variance contrasting producers' evaluation of the activity of Peter,
John and Valerie (low score = inactive).

Source of variation	Variance	Degrees of Freedom	Mean Square	Variance Ratio	Compere	Producers' Mean	Children's Mean
between comperes	113.31	2	56.65	79.79	Peter	8.32	5.66
between producers'	57.50	81	0.71		Valerie	9.21	5.67
Total	170.81	83			John	11.11	5.83

Children F = 0.97, df = 2/258 (n.s.)

*Tukey's Gap = 0.44 (Therefore John evaluated significantly more actively than
either Peter or Valerie, and Valerie evaluated significantly more active than
Peter by producers.)*

Producers saw similarities between items in terms of the
presenter of the item, whereas the children had far more varied
criteria of association; for example, they saw all the clown items as
being related. There were no significant differences in the ratings

made by the children as regards activity, potency and evaluation of the three compères, who were all seen in similar terms by the children. Producers, however, evaluated John significantly more favourably than Valerie or Peter (Table 3.7). Producers also thought John was significantly more active than Valerie, who in turn, was seen as being significantly more active than Peter. Whereas the children saw the compères as homogeneous, the producers clearly saw John as the most dominant compère. These findings may help explain why the children saw similarities between items in terms of content and the producers in terms of the compère who presented it. Thus producers may not be fully aware of what may be termed the child's apparent liking for a concrete material link between items.

NOTE

The work reported here was supported by the European Broadcasting Union. The idea of building a piece of research into the European Broadcasting Union Workshop was originally conceived at a meeting between J D Halloran and Miss Doreen Stevens.

REFERENCES

McQuitty, L L (1957), 'Elementary Linkage Analysis', *Educational and Psychological Measurement, XVII,* 207-29.

Noble, G (1969), 'Young Children's Comprehension of a Televised Film', in Dunn W. (ed), *Aspects of Education Technology,* II, Methuen, London.

Osgood, C E, Suci G J A and *Tannenbaum P H* (1957), *The Measurement of Meaning,* University of Illinois Press, Urbana.

Piaget, J (1954), *The Construction of Reality in the Child,* Basic Books, New York.

Vernon, M D (1953), 'Perception and Understanding of Instructional Television Programmes', *British Journal of Psychology, XLIV,* 116-26.

4

Television for Children: Dimensions of Communicator and Audience Perceptions

Bradley S Greenberg

How does a child organize his perceptions of commercial television programmes designed to enlighten and entertain him? How does the creator of such programmes structure his perceptions of his own programming? What criteria does that professional communicator think his child audiences use in judging his programmes?

Numerous theoretical issues are involved in these much-discussed questions; little research has been developed to answer them. Most models of the communication process focus on the empathy and rapport that should be established between communicator and receiver as a critical concern. (*Gerbner,* 1956). Communication is presumed to be impeded to the extent that frames of reference differ, that common criteria are not used, that language has different meanings. As adult communicator differs with child receiver in perception of message content, message acceptance is likely to be deterred.

In this vein, Westley and Jacobson explored the relative perceptions of teachers and students regarding the introduction of instructional television in the college classroom (*Westley* and *Jacobson,* 1962). They identified the dimensions of judgement of instructional television applied by teachers; they compared the attitudes of teachers using instructional television with teachers not using that medium; they examined the reactions of students taught by television with students taught conventionally. In essence, the investigators sought to probe the differential meanings of this use of television for two relevant kinds of audiences.

Here we shall focus on two audiences also, but the present stratification will be by level of expertness and age rather than implied status or authority. We wish to compare the perceptions of programmes directed at both younger and older pre-teen-agers. Then, for reasons of theoretical and practical significance, we wish to use the communicators' programme perceptions as a reference point for such judgements. Recently, for example, we found among readers and editors marked discrepancies between judgements of weekly newspapers and the ideal newspaper (*Greenberg,* 1964a). To the extent that the communicator (the editor) perceives and makes use of some attribute not perceived or having a different meaning for the receiver (reader), there is increased opportunity for 'noise' in the communication system.

In essence, the present study is more one of description than of hypothesis testing. It is necessary to establish the parameters of judgement used by communicators and receivers of children's television programmes prior to manipulation or experimentation. However, the general hypothesis which has guided this study is that the professional television communicator has developed a response set which bears little similarity to that used by his audience. Further, it is anticipated that his professional estrangement inhibits his empathy with the audience — decreases his ability to 'play the role' of child viewer.

METHOD AND PROCEDURE

For this study, it was necessary to gain access to a group of professional communicators responsible for creating and producing children's television programmes. Then it was necessary to obtain similar access to (*a*) groups of children who might already be in the viewing audience for the programmes produced by that professional staff or (*b*) groups of children who could be exposed to representative programmes from that staff's output. Perceptions of specific children's television programmes would be obtained from both the communicators and the viewers, and comparisons made among their relative perceptions.

The Respondents
For professional communicators, the writer worked with the staff of one network television programme, the *Discovery* series produced for the ABC television network by Jules Power Productions, Inc.[1]. This was a half-hour programme for youngsters from seven to twelve years old, presented five days a week in the late afternoon. Today, it is a once-a-week programme,

generally broadcast early on Sunday. The programme staff, all of whom served as respondents in half-hour personal interview sessions, consisted of the three script writers, the producer, associate producer, director and associate director. These individuals had crucial differentiated responsibilities in the conception, writing, filming, and presentation of each programme; e.g., the associate producer was responsible for technical production aspects, the director planned the staging and the visual-verbal integration.

For appropriate viewers, third and seventh graders were used. They spanned the intended age range for the series. Different age groups enabled comparisons among their perceptions, as well as the audience-communicator comparison. The students were from the Denver, Colorado, and the Los Angeles, California, public schools. In Denver, six classes of third graders (n = 157) and six classes of seventh graders (n = 169) participated; in Los Angeles, three classes of third graders (n = 96) and three classes of seventh graders (n = 84) participated. All classes were selected from 'middle-class' schools. The sex distribution in each class approached 50-50.

The Programmes
The concept of children's television programming as used in this study is confined to the single series whose programme staff was tested. This series attempts to combine information with entertainment. Television industry peers have acknowledged the general quality of the series.

A complete set of scripts for three months was obtained (n = 62). A sample of seven programmes was randomly selected from this collection. Content of the sample dealt variously with animals, general semantics, boating, rocketry, and agriculture.

The Data
Each member of the programme staff received a complete set of the seven sample scripts in separate interviews. Anonymity was promised. The general instructions given the programme staff members were to read each script thoroughly as a refresher for the specific programme content. After reading each script, the respondent was asked for his impressions of certain aspects of the programme.

The semantic differential was used to obtain judgements or

perceptions of the programmes (*Osgood et al.,* 1957). With this instrument, each communicator assessed each programme with a set of sixteen seven-step bipolar adjective scales. The scales used were: interesting-dull; good-bad; new-old; soft-hard; fast-slow; sad-funny; cool-warm; big-small; wise-foolish; useless-useful; light-heavy; serious-silly; loud-quiet; important-unimportant; easy-hard; and pretty-ugly. Responses could range, for example, from 'very interesting' to 'very dull'. Scales were presented in a random fashion with the scale ends rotated. Each communicator judged the programme he had just reviewed against the entire set of scales, then moved to the next programme, etc.

These particular adjective scales were chosen on the basis of consultation with public-school teachers who thought that the younger child viewers (the third graders) would have adequate facility with the words listed. Eventually, it would be necessary to compare the viewer judgements with the communicator judgements and, to this end, judgements on identical instruments were mandatory. Thus, the scales isolated the specific meaning of each programme for each member of the programme staff.

In practice, each communicator was asked to make two sets of judgements about each programme. First, he was asked to rate the programme as he perceived a typical child viewer would react to it. Then, he rated the programme in terms of his own perceptions of it. In this manner, we obtained both an anticipation of the audience reactions as well as a personal assessment from the programme staff members.

The communicator data consist of the ratings of seven programmes by seven individuals on each of sixteen scales.

Viewer perceptions were obtained in a different fashion. Rather than relying on recall of programme viewing among any segment of the students used, we deliberately exposed all student classes to some portion of the sample of television programmes. For this purpose, two of the seven programmes were transferred from videotape to film by kinescope recording. The method of selection of the two programmes shown is reported in detail elsewhere (*Greenberg,* 1964b). It is sufficient here to indicate that for one programme the professional staff had maximum interpersonal agreement in their ratings of that programme from among the entire sample judged; for the other, they were in maximum disagreement as to its attributes.

All commercial content was deleted from the programmes. The

students saw the filmed programmes in their regular classrooms. The experimenter introduced the film as a copy of an actual television programme. Many students had watched the series at some time, but only a handful had seen the actual programmes used in the study. In Denver, half the classes saw one film, the other half saw the other; in Los Angeles, each class saw both programmes, with the order of presentation alternated between classes. Viewers were told they would not be tested on the programme's content, but they would be asked to indicate what they thought of the programme. After seeing a programme, each viewer completed the same instrument used with the programme staff.

The viewer data consist of the ratings of two programmes by two groups of seventh graders (n = 169 + 84) and two groups of third graders (n = 157 + 96) on each of sixteen scales. Because two programmes were rated by each child in Los Angeles, and one by each child in the Denver sample, we made separate analyses of the data.

RESULTS

The method of analysis consisted of a principal axis factor analysis of the interscale correlations. Separate factor analyses were obtained from the scale judgements of the communicators (across all seven programmes) and the third and seventh graders in each city (across the two programmes viewed). Then, each factor analysis was submitted to a varimax rotation, and this section will present the results of those rotated solutions.

In general, the purpose of the factor analysis of the separate scale judgements is to determine how each of these sub-groups organizes its perceptions of children's television programming, taking this particular series as an example of such programming.

The Communicators' Perceptions
Originally, two sets of programme judgements were obtained from all members of the programme staff — their own perceptions of the programmes and their predictions as to how their child viewers would react to the programmes. There were virtually no differences in these two sets of ratings. The average discrepancy across all programmes they rated and across all sixteen scales was approximately eight scale units, or half a scale difference per scale.

This difference is trivial; it is the similarity that is strikingly significant — the correlation between the two sets of ratings approaches .90. The communicators failed to make any major distinctions between their own perceptions of the programmes and how they anticipated children would react to the same programmes. The factor analysis was made on the communicators' personal programme judgements; a similar analysis based on the alternate set of ratings would have yielded almost identical results.

The factors emerging from the communicators' judgements are shown in Table 4.1. Two major factors are identifiable; the remaining two factors account for proportionately less of the cognitive structure.

TABLE 4.1
Dimensions of children's television programmes as perceived by programme staffs*

Scales	Factors and Factor loading (Varimax solution)			
	I	II	III	IV
big-small	.76			
fast-slow	.71			
hard-easy	.68			
heavy-light	.66			
hard-soft	.70	.54		
funny-sad	.76	.40		
warm-cool	.86	.86		
new-old		.79		
interesting-dull		.65		
important-unimportant	.65	.42		
wise-foolish			.83	
pretty-ugly			.72	
serious-silly	.63		.45	
useful-useless		.53	.49	
good-bad				.78
loud-quiet				.63
% Common variance	(38%)	(28%)	(18%)	(15%)

*In this table, only loadings of .40 or higher are shown

The first principal cluster of attributes represents a *stylistic* dimension of judgement used by the professional television staff. Such components of style as pacing (fast-slow), complexity (hard-easy, hard-soft), and scope (big-small, heavy-light) are reflected on this factor. These appear to be the kinds of attributes professional communicators use in assessing programme style — rather than a straightforward consideration of content, for example. Together, this particular clustering of attributes (the first factor in Table 4.1) accounts for 38 per cent of the variation in total judgements among these television professionals. It is an orientation to programme style which best characterizes the considered judgements of children's television programmes among those responsible for preparing such programmes.

The second major dimension of judgement found in the communicators' ratings may be interpreted as one of programme *interest*. The TV fare is considered in terms of its novelty (new-old), its general interest (interesting-dull), its receptivity (warm-cool), and, to some minor degree, the importance of its message (important-unimportant). The factor of programme interest is another principal frame of reference used by professional communicators in assessing their output.

Not until the third and subsequent factors do we find any concerted emphasis on programme *evaluation*. Clustering of such scales as wise-foolish, serious-silly, and useful-useless appears as the third factor extracted — with the single scale 'good-bad' appearing as still another reference point for the communicators. Those scales which generally account for outright evaluation of programme content tend, in several instances, to be spread across several factors rather than comprising any single factor in their own right. In contrast, most previous analyses of individual judgements of the mass media generally produce a strong evaluative factor — noticeably absent from these data (*Tannenbaum* and *McLeod*, 1963). This cannot be explained by any assumption that unanimous agreement among these respondents as to the general value of their programmes left them free to consider other dimensions of programme judgement. If they completely agreed as to the importance, wisdom, goodness, etc., of the programmes, such scales would have emerged as a dominant factor. Instead, their appearance is fragmentary, scattered, and substantially less important in describing the structure of these judgements than the components of style and interest. It appears that the professional communicator confounds his general programme evaluation or subsumes it under the other predominant judgemental factors. It is programme style and programme interest which claim the major portions of the communicators' professional assessment. General evaluation is tertiary.

The Seventh Graders' Perceptions

The dimensions of judgement used by the older children are shown in Table 4.2. Two trends are apparent; (*a*) Very similar factor structures are found among these students in the two cities,

TABLE 4.2
Dimensions of children's television programmes among seventh graders in two communities*

Cities:**	Factors and factor loadings (Varimax solution)									
	I		II		III		IV		V	
'Scales	D	LA	D	LA	D	LA	D	LA	D	LA
important-										
unimportant	.81	.86								
useful-useless	.69	.83								
good-bad	.81	.66								
serious-silly	.65	.71								
interesting-										
dull	.76	.72								
wise-foolish	.73	.57								
heavy-light			.70	.78						
hard-soft			.47	.74	.42					
cool-warm			.55	.59		.56				
loud-quiet				.51		.41	.56			
big-small						.75	.77			
hard-easy				.48	.69					
funny-sad							.69	.78	.41	
fast-flow								.49	.79	.48
new-old	.44						.49			.78
pretty-ugly						.50		.50		
% Common										
Variance	(41%)	(36%)	(15%)	(22%)	(15%)	(14%)	(14%)	(13%)	(15%)	(15%)

* In this table, only loadings of .40 or higher are shown.
** D = Denver (n = 169); LA = Los Angeles (n = 84).

regardless of whether they were making judgements of one or two programmes; (*b*) the obtained judgemental structure is quite different from that observed among the programme staff.

The perspective which the twelve- and thirteen-year-old viewers used in rating this particular kind of television fare is couched largely in *general evaluative* terms. The programmes are good or bad, important or unimportant, interesting or dull, etc. The six scales which form this dimension have high loadings (> .40) only on this dimension in both communities, except for one scale; the other ten scales fail to be represented on this factor for either community, again with one exception. Both exceptions have substantially lower factor loadings than the average scale loadings on this factor.

For the seventh graders, the second component of judgement — and the third as well, it seems — is one of programme *difficulty*. The content is heavy, hard, and cool, or warm, soft, and light. There is, for the two cities, sufficient overlap with the third factor to suggest that programme scope (the bigness and loudness of the programme) is also part of this general frame of reference. We cannot satisfactorily interpret the differences between the second and third factors extracted, but suggest that both may be accommodated under the general notion of how easy or how difficult the fare is.

The remaining scales do not cluster. Judgements of how funny or sad a programme is, how fast or slow, how new or old, and how pretty or ugly remain independent distinctions in the judgements of these viewers.

There is almost no similarity between the factor structures in Tables 4.1 and 4.2. The point of view of the professional television communicator — at least among those whose views were studied here — markedly contrasts with that of the child viewer. Earlier, we indicated that the professional's personal judgements do not differ from his anticipations of the child's judgements. Thus, he fails to empathize with the child's point of view. Whereas the communicator perceives that the child is concerned primarily with the programme's style, its interest, and, only minimally, with its general quality, these children emphatically focused on general evaluation and then on programme difficulty. If not in conflict with each other, these varying reference points certainly would suggest quite different working assumptions in the preparation or encoding of this kind of television content.

The Third Graders' Perceptions

Data collected from the third graders in the two cities may be described only in tentative terms. The younger respondents could not handle the rating instrument as well as had been hoped; a split-half scale reliability check indicated unsatisfactory ability to use the seven-point scale. Preliminary analysis of the structure of their judgements, however, resulted in a rather dominant evaluative frame of reference. Their ratings clustered only in terms of the scales contained in the first factor for the seventh graders. The other scales showed no general clustering pattern, no ability to make distinctions other than how good or bad they thought the programmes were. To what extent this was a function of instrument difficulty or actual lack of judgemental differentiation is unanswered in these data.

DISCUSSION

These findings are limited to the extent that we dealt with a single television series, sample programmes from the series, that series' programme staff, and the indicated groups of child viewers. Such generalizations as may be attempted from the present data remain speculative.

In summary, the view of the world — the world of children's television programmes — is essentially a view of two different worlds. For the child, the world is one that is good or bad, and hard or easy. One is tempted to suggest that it is a simple world, if not a simple-minded one. For the professional programmer, the child's view of television is conceived of as no different from his own. And his own revolves around programme style, the building of programme interest, and thence with the general quality of the programming.

If pressed at this age to stipulate reasons for his particular affective response, the child may well have difficulty in doing so. Further, his reasons would likely not be in terms expected by the programme creators. The latter's reactions to their own programmes appear to be framed in the more denotative qualities of value to their profession. Their experience, training, and professionalization focus their concern on stylistic features; presumably they believe that a certain set of style characteristics can lead to greater interest or to more positive reactions. This suggests a promising area for subsequent research — obtaining definitions from programmers of the styles that should be employed for various contents and then determining if such style variations do result in different evaluations, interest levels, and/or comprehension.

Professional values are not the same as viewer values, nor perhaps should they be. If they were, even more pap would likely be available. Yet it seems reasonable that if the professional fails to understand or misinterprets viewer values, the process of communication may well be hindered — certainly such circumstances could not facilitate communication. This would appear to be the case particularly where the goal of the communication effort is to transmit information — as in a direct educational effort or, as in commercial programming, where the information is embedded in a more popular or entertaining format.

One final aspect of this study warrants discussion. Of more than passing interest would have been comparative judgements of these same programmes from groups of parents and groups of teachers. What would have been the similarities and differences between these additional groups? How would their viewing framework have corresponded with their children or students and with the professional communicators? As the child matures, adds to his education, or just gains more exposure to television programming, do his sensitivity and discrimination increase? There is some evidence that this does occur. The third graders in this study were unanimous in their praise of both programmes — both were rated extremely good and useful. Significantly more variance existed in the programme evaluations by the seventh graders: they were less lavish in their ratings.[2] Further, as the child grows up with television, it is possible that new dimensions of judgement develop beyond that of general evaluation. This might explain the emergence of the 'difficulty' factors among the seventh graders. We might also anticipate more or different dimensions of judgement invoked by parents or teachers. An expanded list of programme attributes might better tap this possible phenomenon.

What we are suggesting is that a child's early exposure to television, regardless of the content, contains much that portends of a halo. It is all good. It amuses, entertains and watches over the child. The child, left to his own devices, makes indiscriminate use of the medium. When he is good, he is rewarded with more exposure; when bad, he is often punished by denied use. From these kinds of contacts, standards, tastes and discriminations find no formative roots.

When the child grows up, even to the status of sixth or seventh grader, school and other activities not only interfere with earlier pastimes but also presumably provide some new or changing standards. It may no longer be normative to watch quite so extensively or loosely. Some things will be considered 'better' than others, whether by self-selection or peer and parental pressure. The process of socialization to use of television (among other objects) will have taken hold and be manifested in differential judgements of programme content. Further research among these kinds of concerns appears promising.

NOTES

1 This project was supported by a grant from the American Broadcasting Company. Dr John Hayman, Jr, director of research services for the Denver public schools, arranged for use of the students in Denver. Mrs Marilyn Maron arranged for the classes in Los Angeles.

2 For example, variance on the scale 'good-bad' for the third graders was .73 and 1.62 respectively. On the scale 'wise-foolish', variance for the third graders was .51 and .67; for the seventh graders, it was 1.42 and 2.07.

REFERENCES

Gerbner, G (1956), 'Toward a General Model of Communication', *AV Communication Review,* IV, 171-99.

Greenberg, B S (1964), 'Community Press as Perceived by its Editors and Readers', *Journalism Quarterly,* XLI, 437-40.

Greenberg, B S (1964), 'The effects of Communicator Incompatibility on Children's Judgements of Television Programmes', *Journal of Broadcasting,* VIII, 157-71.

Osgood C, Suci, G and *Tannenbaum, P* (1957), *The Measurement of Meaning,* University of Illinois Press, Urbana.

Tannenbaum, P and *McLeod, J* (1963), 'Public Images of Mass Media Institutions,' in Danielson (ed), *Paul J. Deutschmann Memorial Papers in Mass Communications Research,* Scripps-Howard Research, Cincinnati, 51-9.

Westley, B H and *Jacobson, H K* (1962), 'Dimensions of Teachers' Attitudes toward Instructional Television', *AV Communication Review,* X, 179-85.

Westley, B H and *Jacobson, H K* (1962), 'Teacher Participation and Attitudes toward Instructional Television', *AV Communication Review,* X, 328-33.

Westley, B H and *Jacobson, H K* (1963), 'Instructional Television and Student Attitudes toward Teacher, Course, and Medium', *AV Communication Review,* XI, 47-60.

Part II
Individual and Social Factors which Shape the Viewing Experience

It is a truism to say that no two people ever experience the same thing in exactly the same way. Not surprisingly, then, the assumption that an individual television programme will have the same effect on all its viewers no longer has any place in mass communications research. In order to study the effects of television it becomes necessary to define groups of viewers who may be influenced in distinctive ways. One way of doing this is to use traditional demographic variables such as age, sex, socio-economic class, place of domicile and so on, but another approach is to define groups in terms of 'communication variables'. In this second approach the researcher focuses his or her attention on those characteristics of the audience member which are clearly relevant to the act of viewing. How is the medium and its content 'used' by the viewer? How does the viewer feel about programmes and characters? How important are family and peer group in influencing the child's choice and interpretation of programmes? What satisfactions does the viewer seek and are they achieved? The list is potentially lengthy since it includes social contexts of viewing and the intrapersonal factors which influence the viewer's experience of television. However, it is important that research into 'communication variables' should proceed if we are to clarify the role that television plays in the lives of children and adults. The investigations described in this selection do not feature 'effects' as such, but an effects perspective is present in as much as they are concerned with factors that are probably active in modifying television's influence. Although the desire to study the dynamics of viewing in detail is in part a reaction against the simplistic 'stimulus-response' model of television's effects, the resulting investigations stand in their own right as contributions to a developing discipline of mass communications research. Indeed it is perhaps in this area, more than any other, that the researcher has been able to work on his own terms, relatively free from questions pre-formulated by public, establishment and broadcasting organizations. Given this freedom, the researcher responds by emphasizing the viewer as active in certain social and individual processes; a consequence of this emphasis on the viewer, rather than viewing or the effects of viewing, is that television itself is more likely to be placed in the broader context of mass media, or even treated as but one element in the child's immediate environment. Thus both Brown and von Feilitzen focus on the 'uses and gratifications' or 'functions' of television relative to other media. Similarly Dembo and McCron, in a study of working-class adolescents, treat television as one facet of the early teen-ager's on-going experience. They also utilize the uses and gratifications approach in presenting a theoretical analysis of the ways in which the adolescent reacts to and adapts to his immediate culture. Howitt and Cumberbatch consider in detail the relationship between young viewers and mass media characters. Their chapter draws on a study of the factors influencing children's desires 'to be like' certain television characters in order to clarify the related concepts of identification and attractiveness. The remaining two chapters feature the family as both the social environment in which most viewing takes place and a potentially powerful influence on the child's experience of television. Brown and Linné describe two investigations which are distinctively different in approach, but have a shared objective of exploring the process by which the family may modify the effects of television on younger children. The influence of family environment on the adolescent viewer is analysed by McLeod and J D Brown; they present results from a number of studies which indicate the importance of interpersonal communication in determining the influence of television and its use by adolescents. Further analysis of their results shows that the nature of interpersonal communication within the family is, itself, heavily influenced by the family's position in the broader social fabric. The six chapters are largely concerned with the psychology and sociology of young people's viewing; in their individual ways they elaborate the notion of the child as an audience member, and in so doing further the argument originated in Part I. Whilst the earlier chapters undermined the notion of viewing as random behaviour accompanied by mental passivity, these chapters indicate the complexity of the processes which determine the child's exposure and orientation to television.

5

The Functions Served by the Media: Report on a Swedish Study

Cecilia von Feilitzen

To understand the relationship between children and television we need knowledge of children's 'reality' and of their subjective experience of that reality. The present article deals with an aspect of this experience; it is based upon an empirical study (*von Feilitzen,* 1972) of the functions served for children by the mass media, or, in other words, children's experience of need fulfilment as a consequence of exposure to the mass media. The child's experience of reality influences his behaviour; what children themselves consider important about television, radio, books, etc., explains, in part, how and why they use them.

HOW DO SWEDISH CHILDREN USE TELEVISION?

In Sweden, as in other industrialized Western countries, the mass medium most used by children is television. A rough sketch of how Swedish children watch television at different ages also shows how the international viewing pattern agrees on many other points. The majority of Swedish children start to pay real attention to television at the age of three. Before that they look at the set from time to time and also show an interest in specific items, but this interest is short-lived. Once they have acquired a concentration, half of the pre-school children (three to six years of age) watch every day, and few view less often than three days a week. They devote, on average, around one and a half hours a day to viewing (*von Feilitzen* and *Linné* 1969a; *Henningsson* and *Filipson*, 1975). The scale of viewing then successively increases, reaching a peak at the age of twelve. As this peak is built up and then levels out, we can say that ten- to fourteen-year-olds constitute the heaviest TV consumers. This intensive viewing period involves, in Sweden, some fourteen hours' viewing per week. Thereafter viewing falls off fairly sharply, and it is not until adulthood that any major interest in television returns. But on no subsequent occasion is television viewing as extensive as around the age of twelve years (*Linné*, 1965; *Wactmeister,* 1972).

What, then, do children watch? One frequently encounters the misconception that children only watch children's programmes. It is true that Swedish three- to six-year-olds watch 'their own' programmes most, and like them best. But it is also common for them to see and like many adult programmes. It has been found, for example, that three-quarters of all Swedish pre-school children saw a popular Western series on television, and that half of them were regular viewers. The absolute majority reacted to the programme with great interest or enthusiasm, or enthusiasm mixed with fright. Even more pre-school children have seen the evening news programmes, although their viewing is here more sporadic and their involvement comparatively slight (*von Feilitzen* and *Linné*, 1969a).

From about the age of eight onwards, however, the child begins to acquire a more genuine interest in different adult programmes (*Wikström*, 1970). He or she still, admittedly, sees quite a lot of programmes specifically produced for children. But the main attractions are now entertainment shows, comedies, family series, feature films, detective series, spy-thrillers, Westerns and the like. On the other hand, children avoid adult news and information programmes, a trend that became particularly marked following the division into two channels in 1969. The children then acquired — and exploited — the opportunity to select and tack between preferred programmes (*Härenstam* and *Wikström,* 1971).

What is given above is a sketch of how matters stand. The majority of countries that have performed any research on the individual and the mass media have collected similar data as a starting point, and the patterns of viewing established among children are, as already indicated, much the same in most Western countries. One can point, of course, to certain cultural differences. Swedish children between ten and fourteen, for example, watch for about fourteen hours per week, while children of corresponding age in the United States watch more than twice as much. This is due partly to the circumstance that Swedish television, with the exception of some children's programmes in the afternoon, broadcasts mainly in the evenings, while American television broadcasts also during the day. But the overall similarities between the mass media systems and the mass media outputs in the West are more striking than the differences. Indeed 50 per cent of all the programmes seen on Swedish television are imported material, predominantly from Western Europe and the United States. Besides, the purpose of the present article is not to underline the cultural differences, but to present data that can promote a greater understanding of what is common to children's television viewing in the West.

When some sort of answer has been obtained to the question 'How do children watch television?', the question that originally motivated research comes to the fore: 'What consequences can viewing have?' And here it has proved more difficult to provide any clear answers. Research into the effects of television on children is discussed in other chapters of this book. It is sufficient for our purposes to note that researchers were soon obliged to abandon a faith in the direct effects of the all-powerful mass media that characterized empirical research in the 1920s and 1930s. We know now that television and other mass media have effects, both 'positive' and 'negative', but that this applies mainly under certain circumstances and to certain children.

Great efforts have been made to find out what circumstances and which children. And since it has been established that this depends largely upon what the child brings to television, i.e. the properties of the child even before he or she watches, much of the research has concerned the questions 'What circumstances cause children to watch television' and 'Which children primarily watch?' A supplementary question to 'How do children watch television?' has thus become 'Why is it so?', and it is to this last question that the present article will try to provide a partial answer. One approach has been to explain television viewing by studying such background variables as age, sex, place of domicile and socio-economic status. That age has a bearing on children's television viewing was indicated in the introductory sketch. Sex, too, plays its part. This is noticeable, however slightly, even among pre-school children: Swedish boys and girls between the ages of three and six watch roughly the same amount of television, but there is a difference in *what* they watch, in that boys watch adult programmes more often than girls, and are more interested in them. Mothers have also observed that boys are influenced more frequently by the adult programmes in their games and behaviour (*von Feilitzen* and *Linné*, 1969a). After the pre-school age, however, the sex-role pattern is clearly established: boys then watch more television in general than girls, with particularly marked difference in the case of sports, news and the more hard-boiled programmes such as detective series, spy-thrillers and Westerns (see, for example: *Brolin*, 1964; *Linné*, 1965; *Schyller*, 1968). With respect to place of domicile, the differences are small; it seems, however, that children living in the country watch somewhat more television than those in town (*Brolin*, 1964). Further, we know that children of fathers with little education watch television to a greater extent than children of fathers with higher education (*von Feilitzen* and *Linné*, 1969a). But on reflection, one realizes that age, sex, place of domicile and socio-economic status explain, in themselves, fairly little of the circumstances governing children's television viewing. We are still faced by the question 'Why is it so?'.

Age, for example, represents in a general sense the child's development. No research has been performed on how the child's development is directly connected with television viewing at different ages. But it seems reasonable, on the face of it, to observe that certain 'critical' ages in the development of viewing fit certain 'critical' ages in the child's cognitive development: at eight years, when the child begins to acquire a more genuine interest in various light adult programmes, is also the point at which the child, according to Piaget and others, leaves the 'pre-operational stage', which is characterized, among other things, by egocentric thinking. At this point the child enters the 'stage of concrete operations', and is now able to shift between his own view and those of others (*Flavell*, 1963). This change thus facilitates an identification with programmes in which older children and adults act heroically in various ways (*von Feilitzen* and *Linné*, 1974). The age of twelve, when the viewing peak is reached, is also that at which the child enters the 'stage of formal operations', ie when thinking begins to resemble adult thinking as regards the ability to abstract and solve problems. That the child has previously avoided adult news and information programmes to a greater extent than adults would thus appear to be due partly to the degree of difficulty involved in these programmes.

But age is not simply a measure or symptom of the child's development; it also tells us something about the child's social situation. For the most part, a child of pre-school age is in contact primarily with the family. And studies have shown, as documented elsewhere in this book, that the parents have a great influence on the child's mass media choices, both directly in the form of prohibitions, and — perhaps more important — indirectly. Children's television viewing is largely a matter of learning the family's television behaviour. They follow to some extent the family's habits, and also seem to learn what the family likes (*von Feilitzen* and *Linné*, 1969a). The influence of the family thus partly explains why pre-school children watch certain adult programmes. But this is not all. It also helps us to understand to some extent the differences in viewing that exist between boys and girls, between children in the country and in town, and between children of different socio-economic status. It is namely the case that corresponding differences in viewing apply among adults (eg *Wactmeister*, 1972).

We have thus been able to distinguish two factors that seem essential in explaining children's television viewing: the development of the child and the behaviour of the family. Not even these two factors, however, offer any exhaustive explanation. We can ask, once again, 'Why is it so?' Why, for example, do adult men watch more television than adult women? Here, of course, one factor is time. It has already been mentioned that Swedish television is broadcast mainly in the evenings, a time when women more than men are traditionally tied to other activities in the home — cooking, washing up and taking care of the children. That men then watch more sports, news, and the 'hard-boiled' type of programme is bound up also with their experience and interests. And the reasons why male and female living habits, leisure activities, experience and interests often differ are to be sought, after all, in the society's system of norms and values.

NEEDS AS AN EXPLANATORY FACTOR OF TELEVISION VIEWING

Trying to explain why children watch television is, it seems, like opening a Chinese box, only to find that it contains another box, and that this in its turn contains yet another. Even so, the explanatory factors quoted above are by no means a complete list. It is possible — and this indeed is what characterizes most research — to go on indefinitely, continually eliciting new factors. We are forced, ultimately, to realize that instead of lining up more and more individual explanatory factors, we should start at the other end. We must assume that the total situation plays a role, and consider the interplay or the tensions existing between *all* factors. Then we should assess the importance of different factors in relation to each other. We should recall that the reason for trying to explain children's television viewing by means of these individual factors — and, similarly, their cinema going, or comic reading — was not *primarily* to explain their TV viewing as such, but rather to establish under what circumstances and for which children the media have 'positive' and 'negative' effects. The fundamental question was thus: 'What do the mass media do with the individual?'

Parallel, however, with this research into effects, another approach in mass communications research has asserted itself, although to a markedly lesser degree. With this approach, the question is rather: 'What does the individual do with the mass media?' This is a converse approach, in which the active role is assigned to the individual, and not to the mass media. Investigations of this kind have been dubbed 'uses and gratifications' studies, in that they are based on the assumption that the individual, by his use of the mass media, obtains a reward in the form of needs gratification. The individual is selective and chooses (more or less consciously) mass medium and mass medium content on the basis of the functions, or the meaning, which the medium and the content have for him, and the availability of functional alternatives. The functions are steered by the individual's needs, which are dependent in their turn upon both psychological factors existing in the individual (eg sex, age, development, personality, intelligence, experience and interests) and the more social factors (eg place of domicile, socio-economic status, relationships with family and peers, living habits, leisure activities and the society's system of norms and values). Thus mass media effects do not occur unless the individual himself chooses to use the mass media in a certain way (*Edelstein*, 1966; *von Feilitzen* and *Linné*, 1972; *Klapper*, 1963; *Maletzke,* 1963).

The first uses and gratifications studies were performed in the 1940s, and the approach has been adopted in a number of investigations of children. Schramm, Lyle and Parker (1961), for example, formulated this approach in their study of children and television. They rejected 'the favourite image of children as helpless victims to be attacked by television', believing a more adequate picture to be that of television as a 'great and shiny cafeteria from which children select what they want at the moment ... A child comes to television seeking to satisfy some need. He finds something there, and uses it.' It should be added that the child not only chooses between different television programmes, but also between television and other activities, the functional alternatives, which may meet his needs as adequately. It is possible that the child will enter instead the adjoining restaurant or go to the icecream stall outside.

The picture of the independent, active child is undeniably attractive. But the studies on children in England and Sweden that have applied the uses and gratifications model in recent years, have used the model in a more differentiated way. The research results reported above are sufficient for us to understand that the child cannot, in all reason, be so fully active and rational. The influence of the family, for example, on the child's viewing was mentioned as a restricting factor. And, if we considered the picture at large, the type of society also played a role here. Other essential factors which we have hardly touched upon relate to the structure and content of the mass media, ie broadcasting times, the division into channels, type of programmes and so on. What is shown on television constitutes, after all, a limited supply, and it reflects a biased selection of norms and values, depending on the more or less conscious policy of the producer, and the organization within which he works. Content analyses have shown, for example, the existence of large 'white areas on the map' in the world commented upon by news programmes (*Nordström* and *Thorén*, 1972-3). Similarly, we know that many entertainment programmes present a stereotyped picture of people as regards occupational roles, sex roles and minority groups (*Huston Stein*, 1972). Finally, our own experience tells us that children's access to different mass media and their actual opportunities to meet friends and pursue other leisure activities are often limited.

The conclusion is thus that the uses and gratifications model admittedly offers an advantage, in that it does assume that the total situation plays a role. Since the needs of the individual are assumed to be shaped by all his psychological and social characteristics, we can also assume that by studying his needs we will already have allowed for the various circumstances that influence children's television viewing and the relative importance of these circumstances. In this way, we have roped in, as it were, the many separate explanatory factors. But at the same time, we must not accord excessive emphasis to the individual's needs. That the psychological and social factors, including the mass media system, and type of society, are channelled through the needs structure of the child implies, after all, that the child does not have unlimited freedom of choice. The child is selective, admittedly, but it is a selectivity which operates *within the framework* of all these conditions. For example, certain needs must be seen as having been created by the television output. Why a child watches television is thus to some extent a question of the interplay between supply and demand (*von Feilitzen* and *Linné*, 1972).

The needs structure of the child and the functions of the mass media are consequently dynamic phenomena; they can be altered if other factors, for example, the programmes, change character. The meanings of mass media for the individual must thus be seen in an ongoing process; they vary at different times, in different environments, and with different mass communication systems (*von Feilitzen*, 1972).

It is also important to point out that the future goal of uses and gratifications studies should not be limited to exploration of the functions of mass media, but should include the consequences of the use of the mass media and their functions to the individual, to his social groups and to the society at large. For the uses and gratifications model to be meaningful in the long term, the question that it must ultimately answer must, as with the traditional effect models, relate to the influence of mass media (*Klapper*, 1963).

THE FUNCTIONS SERVED FOR CHILDREN BY THE MASS MEDIA

With this more differentiated picture of the uses and gratifications model in mind, we shall now consider a selection of results obtained in a Swedish survey of what needs the mass media satisfy in the case of children. The survey thus tries to answer the question 'Why is it so?' in the alternative manner described above. It does not, however, offer a complete answer. The intention was to plot the general functions of all the mass media — ie TV, radio, cinema, books, newspapers, magazines, comics and records — for three- to fifteen-year-olds in Sweden.[1] The question of what needs television satisfies among different groups of children was also studied to some extent. On the other hand, the survey does not tell us what needs are satisfied by different mass media *contents*. Nor was it the intention to deal with effects, ie to say what effects the mass media have on children for whom the media satisfy different needs. Examples of the questions considered are: 'What do children get out of watching television?', 'What is more important for young people listening to the radio: that the programmes are good, or that radio provides an opportunity to withdraw for a while?', 'Which mass media compete with each other in the sense of being functionally similar?', and 'Does television serve similar functions for both children who are heavily exposed to it and those who are infrequent viewers?'

It would be beyond the scope of this article to consider in any detail the different ways in which one can delimit and measure needs/functions. We will simply note that uses and gratifications studies delimit functions by applying a subjective definition.[2] What are reported here are, therefore, the functions that children experience the mass media as having, or the needs they experience them as satisfying.[3] In order to measure needs/functions the survey applied the theory of motivation.[4] If, for example, one of the motives for viewing is that 'you get information about what is happening in the world', then television has an informative function. All motives incorporated in the survey have been formulated by children, and consist of words and expressions that children actually use and understand.[5]

THE FUNCTIONS THAT CHILDREN EXPERIENCE TELEVISION AS HAVING

The first striking result obtained by the study is that the mass media have more than thirty different functions for children. For the sake of clarity, we shall group them under five headings. At the same time, we shall consider how far they are valid in the case of television. In the public debate mass media are often said to have two functions: to entertain and to inform. These two expressions, however, proved irrelevant to children. And even if we have allowed ourselves to incorporate them in two of the headings, we are aware that they are both diffuse and schematic concepts. The terms 'entertainment' and 'information' cover a whole succession of subsidiary aspects.

Entertaining or Emotional Functions

Three motives for viewing emerge as being by far the most important and were mentioned by practically every three- to fifteen-year-old in Sweden: I watch television because 'the programmes are good', 'the programmes are fun', and 'the programmes are exciting'. These motives show a high internal correlation. A further three functions come into this group: I watch because 'it's a bit of relaxation', 'I don't have anything else to do for the moment', and 'you can see things that don't happen for real'. Apart from programmes being *good, amusing* and *exciting*, television viewing can thus mean *relaxation, passing the time,* and *fantasy orientation*. And indeed not only can mean, but usually does mean, since these functions are reported by a large majority of children.

Informative or Cognitive Functions

Even if children on average place television's entertaining functions in the foremost place, television meets informative needs with almost equal frequency. The majority of both younger and older children (three to six and seven to fifteen years of age respectively) give all of the following functions: 'You see things that happen in real life', 'You learn a lot', 'You find out what is happening in the world', and 'You get new thoughts and ideas'. Almost equally often they say they watch because 'You learn how to do things', 'TV shows what is right and what is wrong', and 'I want to try everything'.

The informative needs that television satisfies for children can be described as *reality orientation, general knowledge, information on current events* and *stimulation of fantasy*. They can also be the needs for *practical information and advice, norms* and *curiosity*.

Social Functions

In addition to TV's entertaining and informative functions, there emerges a group that is often of equal importance: television meets a large number of social needs on the part of children. The children actually report eleven such motives. Four are mentioned by the majority of both younger and older children. They watch because 'you "get inside" people and events', 'You get to be a sort of friend with some of the people on the screen', 'I'm used to it', and, 'You talk about the programmes with other people'.

Television's most important social functions are thus that one can *identify* with and obtain *an almost real contact* with people on television (an idea which was discussed by *Horton* and *Wohl,* 1956, and which they labelled 'Para-social interaction'), that viewing has become a well-established *habit,* and that the programmes provide *topics of conversation.*

Two functions are mentioned by a majority of the older children: 'I want to know as much as other people', and 'You get the feeling you want to talk about the injustices of the world'. These functions could be termed *status* and *social commitment.* The remaining five fit certain children, but less than half of either the younger or the older group. These are, in the order given: I watch because 'you meet other people at the same time', 'it makes me feel calm and secure', 'it feels as if you were really doing something', 'I feel alone', and 'it makes you feel older'. Television thus sometimes makes possible: *contact with others in the actual viewing situation, security, performance, distraction from loneliness* and yet another form of *status.*

Non-social or Escapist Functions
The fourth group of functions is by no means as prominent. It contains only two motives, and these are mentioned by a minority of both younger and older children: I watch because 'you dream yourself away', and 'you can be in peace then'. Television can thus from time to time, but not particularly often, meet a need for *escapism,* and a need to *get away from the people around.* It is reasonable perhaps to call both motives escapism. While the first is related primarily to the programmes, the second relates more to the actual act of viewing.

In connection not only with escapism but all the functions listed above, it is important to emphasize that while some have to do with the actual *content* of the mass medium, others have to do with the *act* of viewing, listening and/or reading.

Mode of Consumption or Medium Level Functions
It is not always easy to decide whether some functions are associated with a particular type of programme or with the act of watching television. There is, however, a clearly defined group of functions which are associated with the mode of consumption and the non-content characteristics of the medium. These functions are connected with the form of the mass medium in question, both in terms of its technical properties and the context of use. For

example, must the child watch, listen or read? Is it possible to do something else whilst using the medium? Can the medium be used at any time, or only during defined periods? Can the medium be used anywhere, or only in a special environment? And is it possible for the child to re-use specific content at will, or must it be accepted when given? As will be seen, this category of function is often extremely influential in determining which medium the child turns to at any particular time. In the case of television, the majority of children say they choose it because: 'TV's got both picture and sound' and 'you can watch TV at home'.

Summarizing Comments

Five main groups of needs satisfied in children by the mass media have emerged: entertaining (or emotional) functions, informative (or cognitive) functions, social functions, non-social (or escapist) functions, and mode of consumption (or medium level) functions. Apart from the interest of each individual function *per se*, the results obtained provide a basis for *inter alia* a more general argument.

On average, children consider the most important functions of television to be its 'entertaining' functions, closely followed by the 'informative' functions. One may have been led to believe that it is television's 'entertainment programmes' that meet the need for 'entertainment', and its 'informative programmes' the need for 'information'. This, however, is far too simple a conclusion. In the light of what we know about children's interest in different programmes, the informative functions would then have come very much farther down the list, at least in the case of the older children. And, after all, if it were that easy to link a specific function to a specific type of programme, research into the functions would be unnecessary.

One of the reasons for this sort of conclusion may be the common conception of entertainment and information as opposing poles. But it is more reasonable to suppose that every programme and every message in a communication contains, basically, a certain measure of information which is more or less entertaining, depending on the manner of presentation. With such an approach, one can understand why children tie the motive 'the programmes are good' to 'the programmes are fun' and 'exciting'. It does not necessarily follow that children think informative programmes are poor, but rather that children are positive about what is

communicated in an entertaining manner. In this context it is worth
noting that television, in spite of the children's comprehensive
consumption of entertainment programmes, is the mass medium
that constitutes their most important source of knowledge. In the
long run, learning is in this way 'indirect', ie it is primarily the adult
entertainment programmes that broaden children's sphere of
experience. The information they acquire from television is not
simply an acquaintance with current events, but is perhaps more a
sort of 'reality orientation' in the adult world. Television's
contribution to this reality orientation has been shown to relate less
to the family and peers, with whom the child is anyway familiar,
and more to values and concepts concerning occupations, status,
and people's roles outside the home and the schools (*Capecchi* and
Livolsi, 1973; *Himmelweit, et al*, 1958).

In the light of empirical evidence the assumption that particular
forms of content are monofunctional — entertainment programmes serving solely to entertain, information programmes to
inform — can no longer be maintained. For example, in spite of the
fact that adults view news broadcasts with great interest, the
audience member's understanding of news is often exiguous,
but functional studies have shown that for many viewers, and
especially those who are alienated, the primary function of news is
not informational. The news broadcast, apparently, is more closely
related to habit; it also affords the individual feelings of security
and social contact (*Nordenstreng,* 1969).

If we consider for a moment the earlier studies of children and
mass media functions conducted in other countries, we find that
they have often concentrated, apart from on entertainment and
information, on children's need for escapism. In fact, the uses and
gratifications studies had their historical origins in precisely this
line of thinking. Attempts were made to test the assumption that a
high degree of attention to such entertaining content in the mass
media as affords an unrealistic picture of the world, implied
escapism on the part of the individual. It was assumed that this in
its turn could lead, for example, to an impaired capacity to deal
with the problems of real life, and to physical, mental and social
passivity. Over the years frequent voices have also been raised in
the public debate to warn us that children's interest in stereotyped
television entertainment serves an escapist need.

The results of the Swedish study among children, however, do
not support this assumption in respect of television. The non-social

or escapist functions are the group that children, in relation to television, mention least frequently of all. It is possible that we are faced here with discrepancies of definition. Escapism, as indeed entertainment and information, is a vague and overused concept (*Katz* and *Foulkes*, 1962). If one gives the term a very wide interpretation and assumes that it covers, in addition to flight from reality, such factors as relaxation, passing time, identification and contact with people on the screen, then it will apply, as shown above, to the majority of children. But if one means escapism in the sense it is used here, to denote social withdrawal, then it actually applies only to a minority of children. A possible objection that the children in the study have not mentioned escapism for reasons of language or prestige can easily be met. As we shall see later, children mention the escapist functions fairly frequently in regard to certain other mass media. And, ignoring the mass media entirely, the great majority admit a tendency to escapism from time to time. In addition recent research in England and Japan indicates that television viewing by children does not usually involve escapism (*Brown et al,* 1973; *Furu,* 1971).

Instead of putting the emphasis, perhaps too one-sidedly, on children's need for TV escapism, one should therefore adopt a perspective corresponding to that applied in the studies on adults and news programmes quoted above. We should look in the other direction and focus on what has so far attracted relatively little attention in research and debate, namely the many-faceted social functions which television has for children. It is this group that the children themselves experience as the third most important. When one looks at the social functions a bit more closely, they fall into one of two categories. First it seems as if television viewing can mean a social relationship *per se* (cf, for example, the findings that television permits identification, contact with television person-alities, distraction from loneliness, and security). Secondly, children consider television as a source of information on the social environment, or of information that they can use in their social environment (cf that TV means topics of conversation and social commitment, that viewing signifies status and performance).

One should remember that mass communication is a form of communication, an interaction between two or more persons. And one can therefore ask whether the social functions of mass media are not in fact the most fundamental of all. If this assumption is correct, then the argument pursued in the last few pages could be summed up as follows: Why do children watch television? Children want information from television, preferably presented in an entertaining manner, because they want social contact *per se*, and because they want in various ways to improve their real social contacts. Sometimes, but not in the majority of cases, this is coupled with escapism.

THE FUNCTIONS THAT CHILDREN EXPERIENCE OTHER MASS MEDIA AS HAVING

Why, then, is television the mass medium that children use most? For the purposes of comparison, the use of other mass media by Swedish children is illustrated in Figure 5.1. The curves show how many children of different ages usually listen to the radio, read books, read comics etc. once a week or more, as indicated by their answers to the question 'How often do you usually listen to the radio?' etc., a type of question that often produces an overestimate of the true consumption. Even if the percentage of children given may thus be too high, the figure does permit comparisons between different mass media in different age groups.

Radio listening increases with age. Since the television peak has no counterpart in radio listening by children and young people, the radio acquires particular importance for those in their teens. What children listen to most is the special programmes for children and young people, and light music (*von Feilitzen* and *Linné*, 1967). Magazine reading and record playing are on a lesser scale than radio listening, but they increase in a similar way. The curve for newspapers, however, rises more sharply, and in the ten to fifteen age bracket newspapers are the third most frequent medium, after television and radio. But the reading is limited. What children read most are the strip cartoons and the time schedules of the television programmes, followed by news in the form of accidents and crime (*Schyller*, 1968). The curves for comics and books are different. The interest in comics reaches a peak in the seven to twelve year bracket. Books (school books excepted) are most popular up to and including the age of nine, after which their popularity begins to fall. One-quarter of Swedish thirteen- to fifteen-year-olds say they never, or hardly ever, read books. Cinema-going is most common between the ages of seven and fifteen.

Why is it so? It is easy to realize that this scenic railway-type pattern in children's use of the mass media at different ages reflects

FIGURE 5.1
Percentages of children in Sweden using different mass media at least once a week

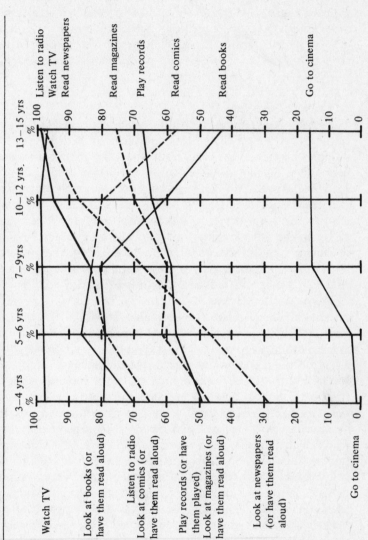

a complicated interplay of all explanatory factors involved in the total situation. Even if we take the short cut of saying that use of the mass media is governed by the children's needs, it is difficult to provide any exhaustive explanation. Since small children do not use any mass media so often, we shall restrict ourselves to a brief account of the functions served by the above-mentioned mass media for seven- to fifteen-year-olds.

Functions of the Radio

The needs structure of the individual can be conceived as having its counterpart in an activity pattern, in which certain activities satisfy different needs and thus, generally speaking, may 'complement' each other. Other activities satisfy the same needs; they are functionally equal and thus may 'compete' with each other. When two media are functionally equal, the individual presumably chooses the one which he thinks satisfies him best. When this is repeated, the other medium will gradually be used less and less. Such a medium, if it is to 'survive', must be changed, in respect of its form for instance. This is what happened with radio when television was introduced. Radio listening first declined, but then recovered to some extent. This recovery was doubtless related to certain changes in radio, for example: provision of broadcasts when television was not available, the introduction of new channels and the production of car radios and portable transistor radios.

The overall impression as regards the entertaining, informative, social and non-social functions of radio for Swedish seven- to fifteen-year-olds, is that they are similar to those of television, but not identical. Children listen somewhat more often to the radio because they feel alone, and in order to get some peace. But on the whole radio and television are functionally similar and can thus be said to be in a competitive situation. Furthermore, the children consider that television better satisfies their needs. This means that children, generally speaking and other things being equal, prefer television to radio. When they listen to radio, the reason is often to be sought in the medium-level functions. What the majority of children consider to be good about radio, but not television, is that you can listen at any time, that you can do something else at the same time and that you can listen to radio wherever you please.

Functions of Magazines

Perhaps more surprising, but no less interesting, is that children of these ages also consider that magazines satisfy their needs for entertainment and information, as well as their social and non-social needs, in the same way as television. Magazines, like television, are often accused of inviting escapism. (Perhaps this is a case of adults projecting their own use of magazines on to children.) However, when it is possible to watch television, the child will choose to do this rather than to read a magazine, since, as with radio, television satisfies these needs better. Again, as with radio, it is the medium-level functions that play a decisive role for children's magazine reading. The advantages they ascribe to magazines but not to television are that you can read them at any time and anywhere.

Functions of Books

Children experience books as more escapist than television, radio and magazines. Again this may not be what many adults would expect, since books have acquired a culturally positive image in the public debate. Apart from the escapist functions, children find that books serve the entertaining, informative and social functions, but the last two categories are found less often than is the case with television. Books are considered to stimulate the imagination rather more than television, and to give a sense of security to a slightly greater extent. And, predictably, books have two medium-level functions that are lacking in television: they can be read at any time and several times over.

Functions of Comics

The two non-social or escapist functions are also characteristic of comics. Further, they have, according to the children, entertaining and social functions, but seldom informative ones. Even so television is considered to fulfil the needs of entertainment and the social needs better, with the reservation that comics are more fantasy-orienting. Medium-level or mode of consumption properties of comics, as distinct from television, are that they can be used at any time, anywhere and several times.

Functions of Gramophone Records

The third medium that children often use for non-social or escapist reasons is recorded music. Like comics, records provide entertainment and meet social needs, but only in a couple of cases do they do so better than television: in respect of relaxation and one form of status (that you feel older when you play records). The medium-level advantages of records over television are that you can play them at any time and several times, and you can do something else at the same time.

These results are supported by an intensive study among fifteen-year-olds in Stockholm, which revealed that the main functions of pop music for them were precisely of entertaining, social and non-social character. The three functions least ascribed to pop were information about what is happening in the world, social criticism and social commitment. This may evoke some surprise, depending upon degree of familiarity with 'pop' music, but it is worth noting that quite a lot of pop is 'serious' in as much as its messages might be expected to make the listener aware of prejudices, injustices, current events and also his own emotions and experience. It also emerged that the young people who listened to pop a lot emphasized the majority of functions — but above all identification and escapism — more often than those who listened relatively little. The young people who preferred 'serious' pop also stressed the majority of functions — and again primarily identification and escapism — and they did so *more* than the devotees of non-serious pop (*von Feilitzen* and *Linné*, 1969b).

Functions of the Cinema
Children go to the cinema mainly for entertainment and for social reasons. The only respects in which the cinema is more important than television are that you meet other people when you go there and, to some extent, the opportunities offered for escapism. For the majority of children the cinema does not appear to have any formal advantage over television.

Functions of Newspapers
Children's motives in reading newspapers have to do with entertainment, information and social needs, but seldom with non-social needs. Compared with all the other mass media considered, it is the informative functions that predominate. In spite of this, television still fulfils the informative needs better. And since television is at the same time more entertaining and social, it is highly probable that children in a situation of choice prefer television. As with certain other mass media, the child's reading of newspapers will thus be decided only by medium rather than content functions: these are the two mentioned in connection with

magazines and comics, namely that they can be read anywhere and at any time.

SUMMARIZING COMMENTS

In answer to the question why television is the mass medium most used by children, we can, by way of summary, draw the following conclusions. To begin with, children find that television satisfies the most needs, ie it is the least specialized medium. Second, they find that it satisfies these needs best. No other medium is experienced as being at the same time so entertaining, informative and social as television. This is partly bound up with the fact that television has both picture and sound. Also television has the advantage that it is easily accessible, since it is there in the home. Other mass media do have entertaining, informative and social functions to varying degrees, but not as extensively and/or intensively as television. The needs that these mass media satisfy better than television among seven- to fifteen-year-olds are instead usually of a non-social or escapist nature. Additionally different media provide their individual medium-level or mode of consumption functions. Television fails to compete with other media on the following grounds: they can be used at any time, in any place and several times over, and they often allow the user to indulge in some other activity at the same time.

Some important questions still remain. How are we to explain the television peak and the sharp fall-off in the interest in television after the ten to fourteen bracket? And why does radio acquire such importance instead? It is not uncommon for the radio now, with certain attractive programmes (programmes for young people, especially pop), to be able to outcompete similarly attractive evening television programmes such as quiz games and entertainment series (*von Feilitzen* and *Linné*, 1967).

Looking at the replies given by the oldest children in the study, we find that television no longer meets their needs as well. When they watch, it is no longer as actively and intensively as before; the only two TV functions that are now more important than previously are relaxation and passing the time. The radio, on the other hand, suddenly satisfies several needs better than television. Apart from the two escapist functions, these are mainly social: young adults listen to radio because it means security and habit, because they feel a 'personal' contact with those taking part in the programmes, and it is a distraction from loneliness; finally, it provides topics of conversation and confers status. They also strongly emphasize that you can do something else while you listen. One interpretation of these results is that television, as children reach the teens, comes to represent the family from which they are increasingly inclined to withdraw. In its place the radio meets other, now more prominent social needs.

DISCUSSION

By studying what children feel to be important about the mass media, we seem to have acquired a deeper understanding of why and how children use them. The conclusions drawn are, among others, that children want information from television, preferably in an entertaining manner, because they want a social contact *per se*, and because they want to improve their real social contacts. On the other hand, TV viewing does not very often imply escapism. Other mass media also serve entertaining, informative and social functions to varying degrees, but none at the same time as extensively and intensively as television. Instead several of these mass media satisfy escapist needs more frequently than television. Earlier studies, by emphasizing escapism to the detriment of other motivations, have apparently presented an unbalanced picture of television's functions, a conclusion also drawn by other researchers presently working in this area.

But research must not stop here. The subject matter of the present article has been the functions of the mass media in general. The picture may alter if, for example, we focus on the functions that specific individuals experience the mass media as serving. We can also consider the differences in functions found by children who view television in distinctive ways: for example, it seems that the majority of functions are reinforced for those children within a given age who are heavily exposed to television and also for those who seek out adult entertainment programmes.

As emphasized earlier, perhaps the most important task now is to study children's different social needs in more detail. We already have evidence which suggests that children who watch a lot of television, and particularly entertainment programmes, are often emotionally insecure, and have often unsatisfactory relationships with parents, peers and other adults in their immediate surroundings. Moreover research indicates fairly clearly that an influence of television is less probable when there is a good, stable relationship with other groups, and where programmes are also discussed. If the child is unsatisfied, insecure and isolated, however, the probability is that television becomes more influential (*Linné*, 1969; *Television and Growing Up*, 1972). At the same time, we know that a high consumption of television also means a high consumption of many other mass media, and that the individual's taste as regards the content of one mass medium usually seems to agree with his taste in respect of other media (*Himmelweit et al.*, 1958).

How great, then, is the social significance of this process, in which different mass media seem to operate in the same direction, when personal contacts are weak? And what, in its turn, does this imply? Mass communications, after all, are not a system in which all people, with the help of different media, communicate with each other. Mass communication, unlike personal communication, is, in the main, a one-way process. In order to understand this, we must see mass communications as a minor part of the individual's total communications pattern and realize that the mass media are only some out of all the possible means of satisfying needs; even television has its rivals, including the child's real social activities (*Himmelweit et al.*, 1958; *Brown*, 1976).

What we must do is study whether what children consider important about the mass media, and other means of satisfying their needs, can assist us also in acquiring a deeper understanding of the effects process, deeper than is acquired by studying the many separate explanatory factors. It was pointed out above that the functions of mass media for the individual are conceptually distinct from the effects of mass media. But by studying what needs the mass media (and the social and physical environment) satisfy for children who use the media in different ways, one may also perhaps have studied, in an alternative manner, the conditions for the occurrence of different mass communication effects. Such effects can be both 'positive' and 'negative'; they may relate to the individual himself, the groups of which he is a member, or society at large. What we know on the subject 'Why is it so?' should thus be combined with the question 'What consequences can use of the mass media have?'

A further point should be re-emphasized, namely that the functions of the mass media can and do change; they are not given once and for all. The fact that children do not experience any other mass medium as being at once so entertaining, informative and social as television does not imply that television is a perfectly developed medium. From the results obtained in the Swedish study among children, we can see that not even the children themselves consider that television fully meets their informative and social requirements. More children, for example, consider they are interested in getting thoughts and ideas, and learning things, than the number who use television for these purposes.

The existing empirical data cannot tell us what needs the mass media theoretically might satisfy. How many of the functions mentioned by the children are concerned, for example, with self-confidence and identity, with a sense of collaboration and responsibility for others, with awareness of problems and critical thought, or with the possibility of surveying and influencing one's situation? Rarely did children hint at such functions, and yet these are only a few examples to be found in discussions of the potentials of mass media.

As indicated in the introductory remarks, we must combine our knowledge of how children experience reality with our other knowledge of that reality. Thus, we should ask which of the child's psychological and social properties — including the mass media system and the type of society — are most important in influencing the mass media functions children mention, as well as the consequences mass media have. Certain of these properties, such as the child's development, are largely beyond control, but others are more subject to change. In part these are related to children's actual terms of social existence. They are also connected with the picture of reality given by the mass media, and, ultimately, those who control and shape that picture.

Finally, then, it is not enough to answer the questions: 'How do children use the mass media?', 'Why is it so?' and 'What consequences can use of the mass media have?' We must go on to ask: 'Is the situation desirable?' If the answer is no, the next questions are: 'How can things be otherwise?' and 'What alternative solutions to the problems exist?'

NOTES

1 Data were collected in 1970 by a mail questionnaire sent to a sample of some 1,800 children, representative of all three- to fifteen-year-olds in Sweden. Non-response was c. 5 per cent. Parents answered the questionnaire on behalf of the three- to seven-year-olds, while the eight- to fifteen-year-olds completed their own questionnaires during school hours.

2 'The functions of the mass media are the specific meaning the media have for the individual as an acting and experiencing subject.' (Maletzke, 1963). Some authors have tried to make a list of needs or functions on the basis of an objective approach (e.g. Merton, 1957; Wright, 1960). These lists inevitably vary according to the researcher's premises. It would seem more reasonable to describe that approach as normative.

3 We must therefore be more cautious when interpreting the results obtained in respect of the younger children, in that we are here obliged to rely on information from the parents.

4 The behaviour of the individual is a constant attempt to satisfy his needs. When a need is directed, by means of learning, towards a given goal, a motive arises which activates and steers the individual's behaviour. Achievement of the goal entails a reward in the form of needs-gratification. The functions are thus defined as motives (need + goal) for a certain action. For the sake of simplicity, however, the terms 'TV's functions for the individual', 'the individual's motive for viewing' and 'the individual's need to watch television' are used here as equivalent.

5 These wordings emerged in a previous pilot study, in which children produced answers to open-ended questions on their mass media and other leisure activities. In the main study, the children were asked to consider the same motives for each mass medium, each motive representing a function. Thus, the motives incorporated in the main study covered functions that are not associated primarily with the mass media, but excluded those which were never associated with media in the pilot study.

REFERENCES

Brolin, H (1964a), *Barnpublikens storlek och reaktioner under radio-och tv-veckan, 8-14/3 1964* [The Size and Reactions of the Child Audience during the Radio and Television Week, 8-14/3 1964]:

Brolin, H (1964b), *Tvs Kvantitativa och kvalitativa roll i tonaringars massmediaut-veckling* [The Quantitative and Qualitative Importance of Television for Teenagers' Mass Media Development], Sveriges Radio Audience and Programme Research Department, Stockholm.

Brown, J R, Cramond, J K and Wilde, R J (1973), '*Children's Use of Mass Media: A Functional Approach*', paper presented to the British Psychological Society.

Brown, J R (1975), 'Children's uses of television', this volume.

Capecchi, V and Livolsi, M (1973), *The Socialization Process in Pre-adolescent Children*, Radiotelevisione Italiana, Servizio Opinioni, Rome.

Edelstein, A S (1966), *Perspectives in Mass Communication*, Einar Harcks Forlag, Copenhagen.

von Feilitzen, C and *Linné, O* (1967), *Children, Youth and Radio, March 10-16, 1966*:

von Feilitzen, C and *Linné, O* (1969a), *Living Habits and Broadcast Media Behaviour of 3-6 year-olds*:

von Feilitzen, C and *Linné, O* (1969b), *Barn, ungdom och etermedia* [Children, Youth and the Broadcast Media], Sveriges Radio Audience and Programme Research Department, Stockholm.

von Feilitzen, C (1972), 'Om etermediernas funktioner' [On the Functions of the Broadcast Media]:

von Feilitzen, C and *Linné, O* (1972), 'Masskommunikationsteorier' [Mass Communication Theories], in *Radio och tv möter publiken* [Radio and Television meet the Audience], Sveriges Radios Förlag, Stockholm, 291-322 and 15-65.

von Feilitzen, C and *Linné, O* (1974), *Children and Identification in the Mass Communication Process*, Sveriges Radio Audience and Programme Research Department, Stockholm.

Flavell, J H (1963), *The Developmental Psychology of Jean Piaget*, Van Nostrand, Princeton.

Furu, T (1971), *The Function of Television for Children and Adolescents*, Sophia University Press, Tokyo.

Henningsson, R and *Filipson, L* (1975), *3-8 åringars tv-tittande* [Television Viewing of 3-8 year-olds], Sveriges Radio Audience and Programme Research Department, Stockholm.

Himmelweit, H T, Oppenheim, A N and *Vince, P* (1958), *Television and the Child: An Empirical Study of the Effect of Television on the Young*, Oxford University Press, London.

Horton, D and *Wohl, R* (1956), 'Mass Communication and Para-social Interaction', *Psychiatry*, XIX, 215-29.

Huston Stein, A (1972), 'Mass Media and Young Children's Development', in Gordon, I J; *Early Childhood Education, II*, The University of Chicago Press, Chicago.

Härenstam, M and *Wikström, P* (1971), *Tv-tittandet oktober 1970* [Television Viewing October 1970], Sveriges Radio Audience and Programme Research Department, Stockholm.

Katz, E and *Foulkes, D* (1962), 'On the Use of the Mass Media as "Escape": Clarification of a Concept', *Public Opinion Quarterly*, XXVI, 377-88.

Klapper, J T (1963), 'Mass Communication Research: An Old Road Resurveyed', *Public Opinion Quarterly*, XXVII, 515-27.

Linné, O (1965), *Barn och etermedia 23-29/10 1964* [Children and the Broadcast Media, 23-29/10 1964]:

Linné, O (1971), *Reactions of Children to Scenes of Violence on TV*, Sveriges Radio Audience and Programme Research Department, Stockholm.

Maletzke, G (1963), *Psychologie der Massenkommunikation*, Hans Bredow Institut, Hamburg.

Merton, R K (1957), *Social Theory and Social Structure*, Free Press, New York.

Nordenstreng, K (1969), 'Comsumption of Mass Media in Finland', *Gazette*, XV, 249-59.

Nordström, B and *Thorén, S* (1972-3), *Studier kring nyhetsutbudet vid Sveriges Radio* [Studies of the Content of Swedish News on Television and Radio], Audience and Programme Research Department, Stockholm.

Schramm, W, Lyle, J and *Parker, E B* (1961), *Television in the Lives of our Children*, Stanford University Press, Stanford.

Schyller, I (1968), '8-16 åringars mediavanor' [Media Habits of 8-16 year-olds], in SOU 1968:48 *Dagspressens situation* [The Situation of Newspapers], Allmänna Förlaget, Stockholm, 41-5.

Television and Growing Up: The Impact of Televised Violence (1972), Report to the Surgeon General's Scientific Advisory Committee on Television and Social Behaviour, US Government Printing Office, Washington.

Wactmeister, A (1972), 'Televisionens publik' [The Television Audience], in *Radio och tv mötor publiken* [Radio and Television meet the Audience], Sveriges Radios Förlag, Stockholm, 141-73.

Wikström, P (1970), *Barnintervjuer den 10-14 April 1970* [Interviews with Children April 10-14, 1970], Sveriges Radio Audience and Programme Research Department, Stockholm.

Wright, C R (1960), 'Functional Analysis and Mass Communication', *Public Opinion Quarterly,* XXIV, 605-20.

6

Children's Uses of Television

J R Brown

William Fisher, hero of Keith Waterhouse's novel, *Billy Liar*, regularly escaped into his own fantasy land of Ambrosia. It was a land fit for heroes, each one played by William Fisher, and it was a land which gave Billy the freedom, authority and 'goodies' which were denied him in his daily life. It is well to remember that escapism can be a creative activity. Billy, for example, takes the mediated images and values of war-torn Europe and uses them in order to build Ambrosia. Significantly, Billy aspires to become an author. It is often maintained that escape into fantasy is a negative, dysfunctional activity, but it seems at least equally likely that it has positive values: giving respite; allowing a new perspective on problems; and, where the dynamics of fantasy are linked to the escapist's problems, sometimes leading to their solutions. Furthermore the fantasy itself can be of value to others. Mark Twain and Edgar Poe produced much of their work as a consequence of the pressures which existed in their day-to-day lives; in a sense they were escapist writers (although not necessarily writers of 'escapist' literature). Many people 'throw themselves' into their work in order to escape from other issues; society often rewards the escapist.

Escapism, then, need not necessarily be the deadening, passive state which is usually assumed when the term is applied to children's use of television. In fact recent studies tend to suggest that television is less of an escapist medium than most suspect. However, earlier investigations were often couched in terms of escapism almost to the exclusion of other uses or functions of television. In part this was because of the methods used in the 1950s. Researchers who wished to comment on the functions of television for children used one of two techniques. They either recorded the activities displaced by television and then explained this displacement by assuming that television served the same function as the displaced activity, or they compared audience characteristics with the characteristics of their favourite television content and interpreted these empirical findings in terms of functions or satisfactions. Both procedures involve a degree of subjectivity on the researchers' part and it is not surprising that their conclusions were in line with prevailing assumptions concerning children's use of media. Nevertheless these early studies are of considerable importance, especially those which exploited the opportunity to study the onset of television (*Himmelweit et al,* 1958; *Schramm et al,* 1961). Both studies are reviewed elsewhere in this book (*Cramond,* 1975), but some comments are relevant here.

Himmelweit is the more rigorous of the two. Rarely nominating satisfactions, she prefers to postulate an explanatory principle which suggests that television displaces other media to the extent that they serve similar functions as television. Schramm is prepared to chance his arm in inferring specific functions from displacement as assessed by comparisons of children in two towns, one with television, the other without.

He outlines three main uses of TV by the child:

1 The passive pleasure of being entertained, living a fantasy and escaping real-life boredom. His evidence for this is that children are committed to favourite programmes and sit with absorbed faces.

2 Information: for example, how to dress, behave, play sport.

3 Social utility: watching in mixed company, he argues, gives both an excuse for young men and women to sit close together, and a topic for conversation.

He suggests that the process of maturation, with its difficult experiences and frustrations, leads the child to escape from his conflicts, to seek aid for his problems, or, if he gives up 'the challenge of life', to use television as entertainment and escape from boredom. There are, he suggests, two kinds of television content: reality and fantasy. He outlines the two types of content and what they offer: fantasy material is used vicariously to solve problems, as a distractor, and as wish-fulfilment; reality material provides information. He believes that 'it is clear that the primary function of television for children is its contribution to fantasy behaviour'; it is clear, because 'when children talk about gratifications they get from television, the fantasy gratifications come out first and in much greater number'. Furthermore, fantasy-type programmes outnumber reality-type programmes when children are asked to list their preferences. Schramm argues that a child is fantasy-oriented because he or she likes programmes which Schramm classifies as fantasy.

Schramm 'tested' his hypothesis by considering the displacement effects of television. Using Himmelweit's principle of functional similarity, television, a fantasy-oriented medium, should only displace other fantasy-oriented media. He predicts and records decreases in the use of comics, radio and film, since these are, he argues, predominantly fantasy-oriented media. On the other hand, exposure to books and newspapers, being reality-oriented, is not changed.

It is not difficult to criticize this type of circular argument. Even if the strict fantasy-reality dichotomy is accepted, the classification of children's books as reality-oriented is extremely questionable.[1] But, more importantly, the dichotomy itself, when applied to media content, is of dubious validity and demonstrably difficult to use: one man's fantasy *is* another's reality.

The basic weakness in Schramm's analysis of the satisfactions children find in viewing television is that it depends upon his personal reading of the content provided by television and other media. Another researcher (*Bailyn*, 1959) had a far stronger basis for inference. Bailyn was primarily concerned to explore the effects of viewing on the child's cognitive processes, but in order to do this she found it necessary to suggest certain intervening factors, one of which was the function of exposure to television. In addition to the characteristics of media, Bailyn considered the characteristics of children. For example, she classified the children under study according to the intensity of their problems associated with self, friends and family. She found that whilst the presence of such problems was not related to overall exposure to television, comics and films, it was negatively related to radio listening and book reading: children with many problems apparently spent less time listening to radio and read fewer books than their trouble-free contemporaries. Her next step was to ask whether children with differing characteristics would have different patterns of content preference rather than different rates of exposure to media as such.

Here she found that in general the presence of problems was not related to content choice. However, more detailed analysis showed that amongst boys with problems who were also highly exposed to mass media there was a significant deviation from the general pattern of preferences. Such boys showed a marked preference for 'aggressive-hero' content: Westerns, crime, spy, war and science fiction programmes.

On the basis of this result, and certain other audience/programme relationships, Bailyn concludes that 'for certain children, under certain conditions, the mass media serve one function in particular — that of escape'. Her argument is that use of television for escape assumes a desire to escape; children with problems necessarily have this desire; their preferred content also reflects this need to escape. She points out that 'aggressive-hero content' tends to feature environments and times which are divorced from the child's first-hand experience; such a distancing is a prerequisite of escapist material. Bailyn's study and her conclusions were not unique; other researchers published comparable conclusions (eg *Riley* and *Riley*, 1951; *Maccoby*, 1954) based on similar findings.

It would seem then that relevant studies in the 1950s produced a rather consistent picture of television viewing as a form of escapism for at least some children. But, of course, there is still the strong element of culture-bound subjectivity to contend with. The studies often emphasized children with problems of interpersonal relationship; no wonder findings were interpreted in terms of escapism. Television programmes themselves were assessed subjectively and in terms of surface content. From recent work on content analysis (*Watt* and *Krull*, 1974) it can be argued that Bailyn's aggressive-hero content would also be 'information rich', that is it would contain a high proportion of action, changing camera angles, exciting background music and so on. Its appeal might have been related to arousal rather than the production of suitable fantasy environments. Even the most rigorous studies were open to counter-interpretation, and the concept of escapism itself was soon to be assessed and its overtones reshaped in an important article by Katz and Foulkes (1962).

Some years before the first attempts to investigate the motivations of child viewers, Herzog (1940: 1944) studied the 'uses and gratifications' of certain radio programmes. Herzog's approach, when compared with the investigations outlined above and the recent studies of adult audience gratifications,[2] was almost naively straightforward (and for some has yet to be improved upon; see, for example, *Elliott*, 1974). Basically, she asked fans what satisfactions they derived from radio listening. Herzog's respondents, given the opportunity to explain their preferences, suggested that a wide range of uses and gratifications were to be found in such 'escapist' material as radio soap opera and quizzes. During the forties, fifties and early sixties studies of the adult audience for mass media rarely featured 'uses and gratifications', functions or satisfactions, but the last seven years have produced a 'renewed surge of activity' which not only represents 'an alternative to the difficulties of studying effects, but at the same time it reflects an intrinsic interest in media gratifications as such, as well as a recognition of their role as intervening variables between media messages and effects' (*Katz et al*, 1973). Although based upon different techniques, particularly in their use of multi-dimensional statistical analysis, the results of these latter-day investigations were in line with Herzog's conclusions in that they too suggested that the audience member found a range of satisfactions in his or her media use. The results of one of the earlier British studies (*Blumler et al*, 1970; *McQuail et al*, 1972) encouraged the researchers to suggest a typology of uses and gratifications, or, as the authors preferred to call them, 'media-person interactions'. Whilst including escape functions the typology elaborates them and adds three more categories of satisfaction:

1 *Diversion*
(a) Escape from the constraints of routine
(b) Escape from the burdens of problems
(c) Emotional release

2 *Personal Relationships*
(a) Companionship
(b) Social utility

3 *Personal Identity*
(a) Personal reference
(b) Reality exploration
(c) Value reinforcement

4 *Surveillance*

An important assumption common to these investigations is that when the television is switched on the viewer is not switched off: 'He brings certain expectations and responds in line with these, and he derives certain affective, cognitive and instrumental satisfactions'. (*McQuail et al*, 1972.) In other words, the audience member is seen as a manipulator of media, as well as, or rather than, the prior view of the media as manipulators of the audience member. Amongst the new studies were a number which were directed towards the functions of media for children (*Furu*, 1971; *von Feilitzen*, 1972, 1976; *Brown et al*, 1973; *Dembo*, 1973; *Dembo* and *McCron*, 1976; *Greenberg*, 1974). Like the investigation of adult audience satisfactions, these studies suggest that use of television is more than 'mere escapism'.

The Leeds study of media functions used a simple data collection technique produced on the basis of discussion with researchers, time spent with Leeds school children, and trial and error. Perhaps the most difficult aspect of questionnaire design involves ensuring that the questions encompass the respondent's range of experience, and that they are couched in terms recognizable to him. Many other problems can be solved by applying formulae or rules of thumb, but in writing the final questionnaire there is no substitute for prolonged contact with the types of people who will have to answer the questions. This problem is exacerbated when the respondents are children, especially if the researcher requires a wide age range. There are two general approaches: either write different questions tailored to specific age groups, or write standard questions which are meaningful to the younger child without patronizing the older child. The latter approach was used in Leeds. The basic instrument was originally produced in order to test Himmelweit's hypothesis concerning the displacement by television of functionally equivalent activities. The instrument was used in a study of the onset of television in a small community in the north-west of Scotland (*Brown et al*, 1974). During the summer and autumn of 1972 the instrument was expanded and converted into a self-completion questionnaire for use in school classrooms. The final form was administered to over 1,000 Leeds school children aged seven to fifteen years. Seven-year-olds were interviewed individually; older children completed the questionnaire in their school classrooms under the supervision and direction of a researcher. A major part of the study involved the children in selecting from pictorial representations of eight media, plus solitary and accompanied play,

---

FIGURE 6.1
Functions or use statements

Which of these lets you know how other people live? (DIFFERENT PEOPLE)

Which of these do you do if you want to find out about things that happen in different places? (DIFFERENT PLACES)

Which of these tells you about things you don't learn in school? (NOT IN SCHOOL)

Which of these tells you what it's like to be grown up? (GROWN UP)

Which of these makes you think about things? (THINK ABOUT)

Which of these do you talk about most with your friends? (TALK ABOUT)

Which of these do you do if you're sad and want to be cheered up? (SAD)

Which of these helps you to forget about something unpleasant/nasty? (FORGET)

Which of these do you do when you feel lonely? (LONELY)

Which of these do you do if there's no one to talk to or play with? (NO ONE)

Which of these do you get so lost in that you're not interested in anything else when you're doing it? (LOST IN)

Which of these do you find the most exciting? (EXCITE)

Which of these do you do when you're bored and want to pass the time? (BOREDOM)

---

those activities they 'usually' turned to under a range of conditions. The response sheet showed: television, radio, comics, magazines, books, records, newspapers, cinema, solitary play and accompanied play. Figure 6.1 lists the statements to which children responded. Inconsistencies in format (for example, 'Which of these things lets you know ...' against 'Which of these things do you do ...') resulted from pilot work with children.

From the total sample a carefully defined analysis group of 800 children was selected such that age, sex and social class were fully balanced. The findings are in terms of children's beliefs as to the *frequency* of certain uses of particular media rather than *duration*. This feature of the study should be kept in mind when considering the data which follow.

Before turning to age trends in children's uses of television it is as well to see uses of television in the general setting of all available media. The results are shown in Table 6.1. The table presents frequency distributions expressed as percentages; each column is

TABLE 6.1
Choice of media for each of thirteen uses
(Percentages to nearest whole number N's = 800)

	Different People	Different Places	Not in School	Grown up	Think About	Talk About	Sad	Forget	Lonely	No-One	Lost in	Excite	Boredom
TV	47	38*	32	29	37*	49**	18*	23**	26***	31**	30**	25	37*
Records	1	1	6	3	10*	21**	31**	23**	20**	26*	13***	12***	23*
Books	5	6	11	9	16	4	4*	12	10	16*	25**	6*	15**
Others	5	1	6	7**	3	13**	18	19**	23	1	10*	31*	8**
Self	–	1	1	4*	3	1	2	3*	8*	12	4**	1	4
Radio	6	8	8	3	4	2	8	5	6	7*	2	1	5**
Comics	1	1	4	–	2	1	10*	6	4	5	5	2*	4*
Cinema	1	3	6**	5	6	7	8	7	3	1	7	20	2*
Newspapers	31**	42*	22	25	18	1	–	1	–	–	2*	1	1
Magazines	4*	1	4	14**	2	1	1	1	1	1	2	–	–

Sex and class differences indicated by asterisks above or below entry respectively *, P .01 **, P .001

based on the responses of all 800 children. Any particular column indicates the percentage frequency that each medium or activity was a first choice reaction to the statement which heads it. Thus, when asked 'Which of these lets you know about different people?', 47 per cent selected television, 1 per cent selected records, 5 per cent books, 5 per cent others, and so on. For nine of the thirteen functions statements television receives more choices than any other medium. On only two occasions do less than 25 per cent of the children select television; these two uses are *sad* and *forget*. Presumably they approximate to the notion of escapism and it is of considerable interest to note that relative to its other reported uses, television does so badly in this area. Of course this finding does not discount the earlier studies; they often isolated children with problems. Furthermore, it will be recalled that the present study is directed towards incidence of use rather than duration. Nevertheless the low use of television for escapism (mood control is a preferable expression) has important theoretical implications which are discussed later.

The first four columns of Table 6.1 represent informational uses of media and a large majority of children select either television or newspapers. Only the fourth use, 'tells you what it's like to be grown up', deviates from this pattern; here magazines are selected by 14 per cent of the sample. As with escapism, or mood control, the children's reports of informational uses of media fail to reinforce the predominant assumptions of the 1950s. Another trend to note concerns the uses of records, clearly of importance for mood control. They are also topics of conversation (cf. *Dembo* and *McCron*, 1975), and sources of companionship and relief from boredom.

A few comments on sex and social class differences are warranted. Where a percentage is accompanied by an asterisk it means that there is a statistically significant difference between the responses of boys and girls, or working-class and middle-class children. Within the limits of this study it seems that sex produces more variations in media use than does social class (thirty-one significant differences as against twenty-five). Apart from a few exceptions, informational uses hold steady across sex and class; certainly television's use as a source of information does not depend upon these biological and economic distinctions. However, in the remaining uses there is evidence of heavy patterning. In general, boys are more likely to turn to television as a source of satisfactions than girls (cf sex differences in exposure: *Greenberg,* 1976). It is usually the case that girls turn to records. Working-class girls are more likely than their middle-class counterparts to turn to records for: *talk about, sad, lost in*, and *excite*, and working-class children are more likely to use television for *think about, forget,* and *lost in*.

The picture which emerges from Table 6.1 is of television as a multi-functional medium, a source of varied satisfactions for most children. In addition there is an indication that the sex and class characteristics of the child are influential in shaping his or her functional orientation to media. In fact the same general conclusions are equally suited for the findings from studies of the adult audience members' use of media.

Just as exposure to television varies with age, so do the satisfactions children seek from television. Table 6.2 shows the percentage of children in each age group who selected television as their first choice as a source of the various listed uses or satisfactions; the first line of figures shows that 26 per cent of seven-year-olds selected television as a source of information about different people, 52 per cent of nine-year-olds, 51 per cent of eleven-year-olds and so on. The most striking feature of these age distributions is their consistency; with the exception of *boredom*, the age trends follow a similar pattern, relatively low incidence at seven years, followed by an increase, and then a drop in the teens.

Although there is a noticeable tendency for the distributions to start low and end low, there are consistent deviations. Information uses are internally consistent: the most marked increase in use occurs between nine years and eleven years, whereafter the use is more or less consistent until there are indications of a decline at fifteen. The other uses share a similar step between seven years and nine years and then a more gradual decline which, in the majority of cases, leads to lower incidence at fifteen years than at seven years. The definite misfit is use of television to relieve boredom; here, it seems, there is little variation in use as the child grows older. Although there is evidence of a slight decline from nine years onward (42 per cent falling to 34 per cent), it seems that just over a third of children of all groups regard television as the most useful antidote to boredom. Again it should be remembered that the data do not reveal the duration of exposure as a reaction to boredom. It is quite possible that a totally different age distribution best describes duration of use. Of course the assumption of a period of exposure being

TABLE 6.2
Age trends in reported uses of television
(Each cell entry is a percentage. Base = 160)

	7 years	9 years	11 years	13 years	15 years
Different people	26	52	51	58	49
Different places	27	44	33	42	41
Not in school	17	32	34	41	36
Grown up	26	36	33	30	21
Think about	31	48	41	35	29
Talk about	42	65	57	51	31
Sad	17	29	24	15	7
Forget	20	32	29	20	12
Lonely	19	35	31	22	21
No one	20	44	34	34	20
Lost in	32	39	36	29	14
Excite	28	40	29	19	7
Boredom	39	42	35	33	34

maintained by a single gratification does not underlie this study, or uses and gratifications studies in general. It is generally assumed, for example, that whilst a child might turn to television as a reaction to boredom, the viewing experience itself will provide a range of different satisfactions dependent upon the child's previous experience and prevalent state of mind.

In addition to distribution over age, Table 6.2 shows the incidence of different uses within each age category. In absolute terms the table shows that selection of television for the two mood control uses (*sad* and *forget*) never exceeds 32 per cent for the five age groups, whilst the social function (*talk about*) never falls below 31 per cent. But it is probably more meaningful to consider the data in relative terms by noting, for example, the top five satisfactions for each age group. At age seven, children peak on the following uses: *think about, talk about, lost in, excite* and *boredom*. Two years later, at nine, two information uses appear: *different people, different places,* in addition to *think about, talk about* and *no one.* At eleven years the top five are: *different people, think about, talk about, lost in* and *boredom*. At thirteen: *different people, different places, not in school, think about* and *talk about*. Finally, at fifteen years the list reads: *different people, different places, not in school, talk about* and *boredom*. Informational uses apparently become more salient as the child develops; only *talk about* consistently appears in the top five, but *think about* and *different people* appear in four out of the five lists. *Sad, forget* and *lonely*, never appear amongst the most salient uses of television.

Talk about, sometimes referred to as the 'coin of exchange' function, involves the use of television material in order to initiate or maintain conversation. It is a delayed use which is apparently as important to children as it is to adults and which doubtless, in part, gains its significance from the near universality of television (like rain it falls on ...). The age distribution for this coin of exchange function follows the characteristic pattern: rapid increase and gradual decline. The technique for eliciting these data ensured that all children nominated a medium for each function, therefore a decline in the use of one medium is of necessity accompanied by an increase in the use of at least one other medium. Figure 6.2 illustrates this complementarity in the case of *talk about* with reference to television, records and peers (others). The figure shows television as the most frequent choice during the early years; thereafter the gradual decrease in selection of television is accompanied by increases in records and others. By the age of fifteen there is a roughly equal probability that the topic of conversation will be television, pop music, or, other people.

Figures 6.3 and 6.4 show the age trends for television, records, books and others in the context of mood control uses. The two figures have certain marked similarities; television shows a very similar profile for both uses and so do books. However, whilst both records and others increase with age, their relative position varies across the two uses. Records are more likely than peers to be used by the teenager to cheer himself or herself up, but the peer group is apparently better able to blot our unpleasant thoughts (significantly, the age distribution for 'others' as a source of excitement runs from 14 per cent selection of 'others' by seven-year-olds to a high of 66 per cent selection by fifteen-year-olds).

Some of the findings presented so far are readily recognizable as fitting everyday experience whilst others are rather unexpected; relatedly, some are amenable to *post hoc* explanations whilst others

FIGURE 6.2
Talk About

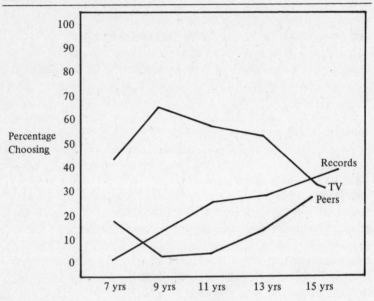

FIGURE 6.3
Sad

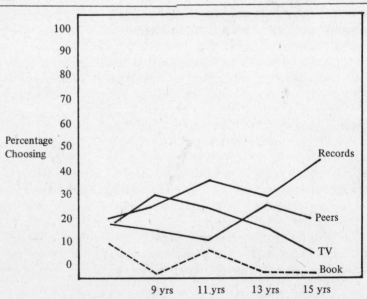

FIGURE 6.4
Forget

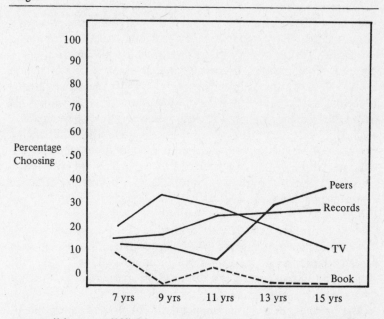

are possibly more difficult to explain. However, it is more useful to produce a general hypothesis which more or less fits than to produce a convincing explanation for a particular finding (especially since all research is subject to some degree of error and, therefore, some individual findings are likely to disappear if the study is replicated). A hypothesis of this type has been suggested elsewhere. It is based upon the general assumption that 'media use may be regarded as adaptive behaviour characterized by an on-going process of reorganization, the dynamic of which is provided by changes in the communications environment and developments in the audience member's unfolding experience' (*Brown et al*, 1974). The data presented in tables and figures illustrate the outcome of a process of reorganization. Children's uses of media are not constant from child to child, nor are they constant from age to age; in order to explain these variations it is necessary to consider the interactions of child characteristics and medium characteristics. Whereas the earlier studies inferred functions on the basis of child and medium characteristics, it is now possible to introduce child-centred measures of function into a description of the process that links child with medium.

Functions or uses of media can be regarded as if they are requirements which the child aims to satisfy during daily interaction with his environment. There are several ways of classifying such requirements. For example, they can be labelled cognitive, emotional, social; at a different level they can be ordered into a typology along the lines of that suggested by adult studies (*McQuail et al,* 1972); it is also possible to attempt to classify them by reference to the media content which is their prime source of satisfactions (cf Schramm's fantasy and reality needs which are satisfied by fantasy- and reality-oriented media). For present purposes the requirements can be positioned on a continuum running from those requirements which are more or less ever-present to those which are spasmodic. The distinction to be borne in mind, then, is between continuous requirements and spasmodic or cyclical requirements (an analogy can be drawn: in relative terms, man has a continuous requirement for oxygen intake but cyclical requirements for food and sleep). Informational requirements can be regarded as continuous; the child is ready to process information throughout the waking day. On the other hand, mood control is a rather more spasmodic requirement — a source of satisfaction is either needed or not.

The basic distinction has implications for the characteristics of media which make them more or less likely to be sources of satisfaction for particular requirements. Informational require- ments of a continuous nature ('tells me about different places/ people, what it's like to be grown-up', and so on) are adequately served by a medium which presents a wide range of suitable content. Only when the requirement is spasmodic does the child need more than wide-ranging, suitable content, and then he obviously needs a high degree of control over the selection of that content. Considering the presently available media it is clear that they vary, not only in the type of content they provide, but also in the amount of control the child has in making selections from that content. Television, radio and books probably present the widest range of content, but books allow a high degree of control over selection whilst television, until cassettes are commonplace, is a take it or leave it medium.

So far it has been suggested that requirements may be continuous or spasmodic and that this distinction relates to the degree of control the child must exercise in his selection of the content presented by various media. Media which present roughly equivalent ranges of content can be grossly different in terms of the user's ability to select suitable content. Additionally, media differ in range of content; for example, specialist magazines and comics present a limited range whilst books, radio and television present a broad range. A further factor that is influential in the child's functional orientation to media is most obvious in the case of the printed word; in order to gain the potential satisfactions offered by books the child must be able to read. There are equivalent constraints on the uses of other media. The child must learn some of the conventions of television and radio; he needs certain interpretative and evaluative skills. And in order to make maximum use of, for example, television or records, he requires basic manual dexterity, not to mention persuasive or coercive skills.

The four factors — nature of requirement, suitability of content, control over selection, ability to 'read' the medium — taken together are the basic elements for a simple model of change in children's media use. Should any of the four elements change, the consequence will be a reorganization of the child's functional orientation to media. Thus the introduction of a new medium encourages a complex redistribution of satisfactions, as does a change in the range of available content, or the provision of greater control over its selection. However, developments of this type are relatively infrequent, and findings discussed so far cannot be explained in such terms since the data were collected at the same time. It follows then that differences between age groups, and also those differences attributable to sex and social class, are a consequence of differential salience of requirements and differential abilities to read or manage various media (including, of course, the availability of the medium itself).

Differences in media use between different socio-economic groups are likely to be based upon the availability of media and family influences on the freedom children are allowed in terms of selection and duration of exposure. It can also be argued that children from different social classes require different types of content in order to satisfy the same requirement. The argument is stronger when applied to sex differences; many books, comics and magazines are produced specifically for boys, others for girls, but this division is not maintained in the newer media. Table 6.1 shows seventeen significant sex differences in uses of television, records and radio, but only seven for books, comics and magazines. The majority of sex differences are found in children's uses of television and records: in terms of satisfaction television is a boys' medium, pop music a girls' medium. Searching for sex bias in media content is an increasingly popular activity and the assumption that television shows males in a more glamorous light is given some backing by the sex differences appearing in Table 6.1. The same reasoning cannot be applied to the other commonly voiced assumption, that television has a middle-class bias. Table 6.2 shows that working-class children are likely to gain more satisfactions from television than their middle-class counterparts. Sex differences can also be accounted for by differential salience of requirement. It is generally accepted that girls develop more rapidly than boys. They become emotionally volatile and, therefore, spasmodic requirements will feature at an earlier age for girls than boys. Girls, then, will seek mediated experience which allows mood control; essential to such spasmodic, or peaking, requirements is control over selection of suitable content — a characteristic of records not shared by television. It seems likely that the distinctive sex differences in uses of records and television result from both differences in salience of requirements and differences in media content.

One aspect of age differences is implicit in the discussion of sex differences; the emergence of mood control requirements in early adolescence is almost certainly related to the decline in uses of television which is a general feature of Table 6.2. The importance to the child of particular requirements will vary with age, therefore a medium which has given general satisfaction at one age will start to lose out to some other form of stimulation; this in turn influences duration of exposure to specific media.

The period during which children find exposure to television increasingly satisfactory coincides with the 'latency period', a stage of development sandwiched between the last throes of infant emotionality and the turbulence associated with puberty. During this period the child masters language and learns many of the mores, values and attitudes which will define his or her 'place' in society. By and large his learning is unsystematic and, therefore, television is an ideal source of stimulation: the mixture of information, excitement, humour and opportunities for identification ensure that television becomes an extremely attractive facet of his environment. But puberty understandably upsets the child's hierachy of requirements and therefore encourages a reorganization of his uses of media.

Ability to read or manage the medium is also involved in

age-based changes in media use. Consistent peaking at nine to eleven years for uses of television can also be regarded as an indication that, prior to nine years, children are unable fully to 'read' television. Such an assumption is not at all unlikely. Television content embodies quite complex devices and conventions of communication which must be correctly interpreted if the viewer is to understand its content. 'Action replay' can be a cause of confusion for the young child, and the inclusion of flashbacks or thoughts can be confusing to older children and to some adults. (Not long ago flashbacks, or a character's thoughts, were introduced by gradual undulation of the image. This convention is now rarely used. Instead the viewer is expected to recognize such a sequence by its relationship to the plot, or a cue is given by showing, for example, a look of stony immobility on the character's face.) Changes in time, essential to understanding some drama, are indicated pictorially by showing a clock, someone returning from work, a leafy tree previously bare, or other comparable devices. Such straightforward visual cues are accompanied by quite complex conventions, often rooted in technology. For example, lighting can be used in order to decrease or increase the apparent realism of a sequence; documentary has characteristic camera shots which are sometimes used in drama to the same effect. Without necessarily being aware of these devices the viewer responds to them as he or she 'reads' the medium. It seems reasonable that these, and other skills, are based on viewing experience and therefore take time to develop.

The concepts introduced in the preceding paragraphs, especially the general, functional reorganization hypothesis, emphasize the dynamics or process aspects of media use. It is necessary that this feature of media use is emphasized since the usually employed survey research carries its own biases towards a rather arid structural representation of 'what people get out of media'. This tendency is unfortunate but can be counter-balanced in the interpretation of survey data, and, perhaps more importantly, by the application of research techniques that are suited to the investigation of process rather than structure, particularly longitudinal studies and field or laboratory experiments.

Early studies of children's uses of media shared a tendency for the researcher to impose his or her culturally-bound subjective inferences, and unavoidably the assumptions which shaped these influences also shaped the studies themselves. The present round of investigations has tended to shift the element of subjectivity back to the child, and in so doing creates problems previously avoided. In particular the present studies are open to the criticism that children will respond to questionnaires in a socially acceptable or stereotyped manner. Hopefully future studies will overcome this potential problem. Another criticism of the direct questioning approach to studying children's media use is that the child lacks insight and is therefore incapable of giving valid answers. Again experimental studies in which, for instance, the requirement is manipulated and changes in exposure are recorded, should overcome that criticism. Also experience with children negates the criticism. Given the opportunity to communicate, children often reveal impressive insight into the nature of their relationship with media content. Unfortunately such opportunities are often missing in survey and experimental investigations. The researcher's desire for data amenable to numerical presentation and statistical analysis usually results in an image of media use which lacks the richness and idiosyncrasies often apparent when the individual is given freedom to talk about his or her personal experience. Exploratory interviews prior to survey can reveal specific uses of media which for different reasons the survey cannot encompass. Some examples taken from wide-ranging interviews with young children in Scotland illustrate the inability of surveys to catch the richness of media use. They also reveal the insight of young children.

'Before we had television I always wanted to go live in a big city; now I'll stay where I am because I've seen what cities are like on telly,' Statements of this type, made by a nine-year-old girl, are reduced to 'tells me about different places'. A seven-year-old boy explained that television not only gave him something to block out the sound of his parents 'yacking', but that the parents themselves had been less likely to argue since they became viewers. Another boy of the same age described how he 'just pretended to be Tarzan', and this enabled him to climb a garden tree which had always been beyond his confidence, if not his strength. (This apparent potential of role play and identification for overcoming personal 'limitations' is confirmed by a study in which children increased their scores on a test of divergent thinking by completing the test in the assumed role of 'John McMice — the well-known artist who is an uninhibited, rather Bohemian figure'. The experiment was conducted by *Hudson*, 1968.) The same boy explained how he and his friend acted sequences from televised war films. In this way their games of 'war' were improved by the introduction of agreed roles or rules. Before they adopted this procedure the game was usually a failure because 'whenever I shot him Richard would say "You missed," and sometimes I'd make an ambush and he'd go the wrong way'.

The numerical results presented in this chapter reveal that there is more to children's use of television than 'escapism'. But the preceding anecdotes emphasize that there is much more to children's uses of television than can be communicated in tables and graphs. Researchers who believe they have succeeded in quantifying experience have simply produced an arid Ambrosia, but then it is well to remember that escapism can be a creative activity.

NOTES

1 Books offer a wider range of subject and treatment than any other medium. Whilst recording the totality of Western knowledge, they also reflect myth, folk-lore and fantasy. It seems odd that Schramm should classify children's books as reality-oriented; the range of available content rather suggests that books could be 'used' in several different ways. In a recently published article (Brown *et al.*, 1974) it is argued that whilst the onset of television has little effect on the *time* children spend on reading, it does produce a reduction in the range of *satisfactions* children find in reading.

2 For an overview of 'uses and gratifications' research see Katz *et al.*, (1973). A revised version is printed in Blumler and Katz (1974) along with numerous empirical and theoretical contributions to the study of audience gratifications. The numerous labels: gratification, use, satisfaction, requirement, function, have different shades of meaning when employed by different authors. In the present paper no attempt is made to define differences clearly. As a general guide 'gratification' and 'satisfaction' are roughly synonymous; 'uses' and 'functions' are also almost synonymous; 'requirement' refers to a state or process which directs the child (or adult) to certain activities hopefully to achieve satisfaction/gratification.

REFERENCES

Bailyn, L (1959), 'Mass Media and Children: A Study of Exposure Habits and Cognitive Effects', *Psychological Monographs*, LXXIII.
Blumler, J G, Brown, J R and *McQuail, D* (1970), 'The Social Origins of the Gratifications Associated with Television Viewing', mimeo, University of Leeds.
Blumler, J G and *Katz, E* (Eds) (1974), *The Uses of Mass Communications: Current Perspectives on Gratifications Research*, Sage, Beverly Hills.

Brown, J.R. Cramond, J K and *Wilde, R J* (1973), 'Children's Use of Mass Media: A Functional Approach', paper presented to the British Psychological Society, mimeo, University of Leeds.

Brown, J R, Cramond, J K and *Wilde, R J* (1974), 'Displacement Effects of Television and the Child's Functional Orientation to Media', in Blumler and Katz, *The Uses of Mass Communications.*

Cramond, J K (1976), 'The Introduction of Television and its Effects upon Children's Daily Lives', in this volume.

Dembo, R (1973), 'Gratifications found in Media by British Teenage Boys', *Journalism Quarterly,* L, 3.

Dembo, R and *McCron, R* (1976), 'Social Factors in Media Use,' in this volume.

Elliott, P (1974), 'Uses and Gratifications Research: A Critique and a Sociological Alternative', in Blumler and Katz, *The Use of Mass Communication.*

von Feilitzen, C (1972), 'Om Etermediernas Funktioner' [On the Functions of Broadcast Media], in *Radio och TV Möter Publiken,* Sveriges Radios Förlag, Stockholm.

von Feilitzen, C (1976), 'The Functions served by the Media: Report on a Swedish Study', in this volume.

Furu, T (1971), *The Function of Television for Children and Adolescents,* Sophia University Press, Tokyo.

Greenberg, B S (1974), 'Gratifications of Television Viewing and Their Correlates for British Children', in Blumler and Katz, *The Uses of Mass Communications.*

Greenberg, B S (1976), 'Viewing and Listening Parameters among British Youngsters', in this volume.

Herzog, H (1940), 'Professor Quiz: A Gratification Study', in Lazarsfeld (ed), *Radio and the Printed Page,* Duell, Sloan and Pearce, New York.

Herzog, H (1944), 'What do we really know about Daytime Serial Listeners?', in Lazarsfeld and Stanton, *Radio Research 1942-3,* Duell, Sloan and Pearce, New York.

Himmelweit, H, Oppenheim, A N and *Vince, P* (1958), *Television and the Child: An Empirical Study of the Effect of Television on the Young,* Oxford University Press, London.

Hudson, L (1968), *Frames of Mind,* Penguin Books, London.

Katz, E and *Foulkes, D* (1962), 'On the Use of Mass Media as Escape: Clarification of a Concept', *Public Opinion Quarterly,* LXII.

Katz, E, Blumler, J G and *Gurevitch, M* (1973), 'Utilization of Mass Communication by the Individual,' paper prepared for Conference on Directions in Mass Communication Research, Arden House, New York. Revised in Blumler and Katz, *The Uses of Mass Communications.*

Maccoby, E (1954), 'Why do Children watch Television?', *Public Opinion Quarterly,* XVIII (Fall).

McQuail, D, Blumler, J G and *Brown, J R* (1972), 'The Television Audience: A Revised Perspective', in McQuail (ed), *Sociology of Mass Communications,* Penguin Books, London.

Riley, M W and *Riley, J W* (1951), 'A Sociological Approach to Communication Research', *Public Opinion Quarterly,* XV.

Schramm, W J, Lyle, J and *Parker, E P* (1961), *Television in the Lives of our Children,* Stanford University Press, Stanford.

Watt, J H and *Krull, R* (1974), 'An Information Theory Measure for Television Programming', *Communication Research,* I. 1.

7

Social Factors in Media Use

Richard Dembo and Robin McCron

For much of its history, mass media research has focused its attention on the impact the media have on their audience. This line of inquiry, which traces its influence from the study of propaganda in the two World Wars, operates on the premise that the media *do* exert an effect, and that it is the task of research to locate what kind of influence this is and at what levels it is at work (*Brown*, 1970). The tradition of research following this theoretical interest is considerable, and embraces the disciplines of political, sociological and psychological science. The list of researchers from these subject areas who have made contributions to effects research includes such notables as Lasswell, Hovland, Lazarsfeld, Berkowitz and Bandura, and spans some forty years. Notwithstanding this impressive line-up of investigators whose work has enhanced the literature of media effects, impact studies have yielded little evidence to accord the media the all-pervasive powers attributed to them. Even the recent massive report of the US Surgeon General's Scientific Advisory Committee on Television and Social Behaviour (1972) confirms that the phenomenon of media impact is imperfectly understood, and the consequences of exposure, if any, remain unknown.

In retrospect, two negative findings stand out as being critically important in calling the effects model into question: (*a*) *The People's Choice* (*Lazarsfeld et al.*, 1944), because it was carried out by key figures in the media field, and was based on the premise that the media were influential in determining how people vote; and (*b*) the report of the UN educational campaign in Cincinnati, USA, in 1947-8 (*Star* and *Hughes*, 1950), because it represented a comprehensive and sophisticated attempt to use the media in an instrumental way to change people's attitudes and behaviour.

The People's Choice, a study of the voting behaviour of Erie County residents during the 1940 US national election, was a landmark in the survey research being carried out at Columbia University at the time, and failed to provide any support for the thesis that the media produce an independent effect on their audience. The findings, based on extensive interviews employing a panel design, showed that the people most interested in the forthcoming election decided soonest how they would vote; they also selectively exposed themselves to, and interpreted, media materials in a manner that was consistent with their intentions. Most of the people who were uncertain or wavering in their voting intentions eventually voted in a manner that was predictable from the social affiliations which they held.

The 1947-8 education campaign for the United Nations in Cincinnati was a more direct refutation of the effects model. This study involved a six-month campaign of information designed to enlighten the public about the nature and purposes of the newly-founded United Nations, and was carried out by the National Opinion Research Centre at the University of Chicago. A before-after design assessed public attitudes and behaviour with reference to the impact of literature that was distributed, newspaper and radio features, public speaking engagements, and hundreds of documentary films. The results showed clearly that the campaign had greatest impact on those persons who were initially interested in international affairs and the UN. It was these people who were reached by the campaign, and not the general public at whom it was directed.

It would be unfair to say that the effects model foundered in Erie County or in Cincinnati, but a strong argument can be made that these research findings represented a turning-point in a tradition of media research. The key finding of the Erie County study, that the determination of voting patterns was more interpersonal and less media-related than had been commonly supposed, led Lazarsfeld and his associates to explore further the process by which personal influence came about (see: *Katz* and *Lazarsfeld,* 1955; *Merton,* 1968). Both studies provided a basis for the stress Freidson (1953) and Riley and Riley (1951) laid on assessing the social situation and reference groups of individuals if one is to grasp the media relationships they establish, and how these experiences are put to use in their lives.

Growing disenchantment with the effects model led to an increased interest in what has come to be known as the uses and gratifications orientation to media research which has as its thesis that in order to understand how the media exert their impact, it is necessary to determine how people use these materials. The uses tradition can be traced to the research of Waples *et al.* (1940) into the reading behaviour of adults, the work of Fearing (1947) on the cinema, and the more notable research by Herzog (1944) and Warner and Henry (1948) into daytime radio serial listeners, among others (see also: *McQuail*, 1969). While the findings of these studies, suggesting that what the media do to individuals is a function of what these persons do with the media, emerged at the same time that research into media effects was being carried out, they were never really integrated into the effects tradition. There were both theoretical and substantive reasons for this neglect. Theoretically, the uses results could not be located within the notions of the mass society and alienated individual that underpinned the effects view so well articulated by Wirth (1948), because they implied a less anomic actor. In terms of subject matter, the phenomenon of uses was considered more of a psychological than a sociological issue, despite the fact that such a notable effects researcher as Berelson (1949) himself conducted a most interesting inquiry into the gratifications derived from newspaper reading, and it is perhaps indicative of this view that the important paper by Warner and Henry appeared in a journal of psychology.

The flowering of the 'structural-functional' sociological perspective in the US during the late 1950s and early 1960s led to an application of the concepts of this approach to thinking about the media (see: *Parsons,* 1951; *Merton,* 1968; *McQuail,* 1969; *Wright,* 1959). The functional stress on the manifest and latent utility of social behaviour and attitudes fitted quite comfortably with the uses orientation, and McQuail has shown how the two can be combined to provide an interesting programme of research in the middle range. This line of inquiry, focusing on the demographic correlates of the gratifications derived from the media, is developing in some fruitful ways, for example in recent work at the Leeds Centre for Television Research (*Blumler et al,* 1970; *McQuail et al,* 1972), by Katz and his associates in Israel (1973), and by Rosengren and his associates in Sweden (1971, 1972).

Unfortunately the functional orientation has a number of deep-rooted and, we believe, insoluble problems implicit in it. To begin with, the perspective requires for its analytic strength an assumption of basic needs that can be fulfilled by the media. We are in agreement with Chaney's argument (1972) that this necessity leads us to presume too much about the subjects of our research. The phenomenon of media impact, and of how individuals relate to and incorporate features of their media experiences, is not really made problematic, but is used as a point of reference to demonstrate their effectiveness against other alternatives for satisfaction. The research subject is not taken as a focus of inquiry in his own right, but is used heuristically to examine a presumed relationship, a point which Schutz (1962, 1963, 1966) repeatedly makes. This is not to say that the media do not influence individuals in the manner functionally-oriented media researchers posit, but merely to assert that we can never know if they do. We have glossed over too many assumptions to provide for this possibility. Functionalists must first establish that people behave in the rational manner their model assumes before they can clarify the way they conceive the media to relate to their lives.

AN ACTOR-ORIENTED MODEL OF THE MEDIA-PERSON RELATIONSHIP

An alternative to the functional approach which is equally at home with the uses interest is an actor-oriented view that places the research subject and the social context of his experience at the centre of its concern. Rather than treating the features of the individual's location in the social structure, such as his social class and type of home neighbourhood, as somehow eliciting certain kinds of behaviour from him, this approach stresses the creative relationship which exists between people and their environment. Interest in the creative relationship between the individual and structural aspects of his environment has often been subordinated to the study of the structural features, such as family, school and peer groups, in themselves. For example, although there has been considerable research on the influence of the family, school and peer groups on the development of 'personality', 'attitudes' and 'social skills' in childhood, there has been remarkably little on the perception of such influence *by the children themselves*. Nevertheless, relevant conceptualization and the results of some research that has been done point to the value of the actor-oriented approach.

The core of the actor-oriented view is the idea that individuals strive after unity and consistency. We believe this assumption is necessary to offset the notion that behaviour can be understood in terms of a simple stimulus-response model, which sees the individual as merely reactive to discrete external stimuli. The actor view sees the individual as a purposive, *active* person. A corollary of our assumption is the existence of a cognitive factor, which is often labelled 'the self'. This notion is in itself contentious but, following Hall and Lindzey (1957), we conceived of the self as having two aspects: (*a*) that of self-as-object, denoting the person's attitudes, feelings, perceptions and evaluations of himself, and (*b*) that of self-as-process, consisting of groups of dynamic processes such as thinking, perceiving and remembering; this position parallels G H Mead's 'me' and 'I' (1934). The two aspects of self are in fact closely interrelated, and in terms of our assumptions of striving after unity, the self-as-process operates to maintain the unity of self-as-object. This conception of self is by no means new. Prescott Lecky (1945 and 1969) argued that all behaviour is directed towards the ultimate aim of maintaining self-consistency: 'The point is that all of an individual's ideas are organised into a single system, whose preservation is essential. The nucleus of the system, around which the rest of the system revolves, is the individual's idea or conception of himself. The individual sees the world from his own viewpoint, with himself at the centre.' Carl Rogers acknowledges the influence of Lecky's work in the development of his own personality psychology, and in fact the idea of the individual striving to maintain his self-conception is basic to Rogers's theory (1947, 1959, 1964).

One of the theoretical problems associated with the self-concept lies in addressing its development during the life span. One of the properties that Rogers attributes to his conception of the self is that it develops out of the individual's interaction with the environment, a view which again parallels Mead's work, in his fundamental assumption that the self is 'a social structure, and it arises out of social experience'. While psychological self theorists such as Rogers and G W Allport (1961) are in general sympathetic to Mead's formulations, they have misgivings about his lack of a concept of motivation. However, the two approaches are not incompatible, and Mead's emphasis on the social nature of the self acts as a necessary antidote to the excessively individualistic approach of the personality psychologists.

A major criticism of the use of the self concept is that it is often based on a naive type of phenomenology which underplays the possible influence of unconscious factors in motivation. Rogers has relied on self report techniques in most of his work, though he seems to have increasing reservations about this method, and to be willing to accept that the person should be studied from various 'perceptual vantage points', only one of which should be from within the consciousness of the person himself. Hilgard (1967) has proposed a more conscious conception of the self, and a mode of study which circumvents the problem of accepting all self reports at face value. He uses the term 'inferred self' which he sees as being a more inclusive self concept than a simple 'self-as-awareness' (or in the terms we have used, self-as-object). His approach is 'to infer a self from the data open to an external observer, to construct a self which will give a coherent account of motivated behaviour'.

Hilgard suggests three hypotheses which must be supported in determining the adequacy of any 'inferred self', and which provide a useful basis for empirical work:

1. The organization of motives and attitudes that are central to the self is one which persists and remains recognizable as the person grows older.

2. Motives unlike in their overt expression may represent an underlying similarity.

3. The important human motives are interpersonal both in origin and in expression.

Although Hilgard makes little explicit reference to it in his treatment of the inferred self, it can be seen from these hypotheses that he allows for the possibility of the self as a maintainer of unity. Our empirical approach to motivated action resembles that of Hilgard more than the Rogers school of thought, in that we construct self-pictures from responses to questions about various areas of behaviour and attitude. The present study is unable to illuminate the first of Hilgard's hypotheses, because of our lack of a longitudinal perspective, but we believe that the remaining hypotheses are of interest in discussing some points arising from the study.

Self-orientation is often explored in a piecemeal fashion to probe particular research problems. For example, we learn how delinquents and non-delinquents differ in their self-images and social behaviour (*Jensen*, 1972), or how self-esteem relates to social participations. However, we have failed to fulfil the promise of this approach if we do not develop a strategy which takes explicit account of the social and cultural features of people's environment, and the purposeful manner in which they relate to them (see: *Hudson*, 1968). The following comments articulate some of the major assumptions and approaches of research incorporating the self as a critical concept.

The first step in the analysis involves uncovering those features of the life experience of different, socially-locatable groups of people which serve as guides to understanding their behaviour. This involves demographic analyses to outline the characteristics of the life experience to which behaviour and value adjustment are made, and the location of sub-cultural value systems. Economic and social status characteristics provide a backdrop for closer study of the factors of motivation and purpose underlying adjustment to the environment; they do not themselves represent explanations for action. The essence of the approach lies in tracing these environmental features to their manifestations in the behavioural displays of individuals. The premises of this approach can be generalized as follows:

1. We must locate the social and demographic life circumstances of the people we are studying.

2. We must locate the cultural and social values and behaviour that are important to them.

3. We must see how the first two factors relate to purposive behaviour, including in this case the use of the media.

Obtaining information of this kind permits us to uncover the systems of social relationships and patterns of meaning available to individuals and groups in specific settings. It provides insight into the stocks of knowledge held by them, and the relevance of particular features of their life style for them — essential ingredients in understanding how and why they engage in meaningful action.

A RESEARCH EXAMPLE

Some results from a recent study of aggression and media use among working-class youths living in the North-east of England illustrate the research approach we are advocating.[1] The research examined the relationship between the media and violence by detailing the life experiences, values, social behaviour and media use patterns of ninety-nine boys aged twelve to fifteen who were rated by their school peers as being either aggressive or non-aggressive. All of the forty-nine aggressive and fifty non-aggressive youngsters lived in a 'problem' neighbourhood, were low educational achievers, drawn from the same school classes, and not officially labelled as delinquent. The research data were derived from interviews with the youths and their parents.

Both groups of youngsters described the extent of their aggressive behaviour in a manner that was consistent with the judgements made of them by their peers. Aggressive and non-aggressive boys defined themselves differently, and selectively incorporated features of their environment that reflected their images of themselves. They also preferred different friends. Aggression and non-aggression were important ways of summarizing the self-identifications and behaviour of the two samples. For example, aggressive youngsters valued the display of physical prowess; they saw success in such activities as fighting, sports and getting on with girls as confirming the picture they wished to present of themselves. On the other hand, non-aggressive youths were less concerned with affirming themselves in physically aggressive ways; they were more interested in the content of their school experience, and their involvement with their friends was based on different criteria (*Dembo,* 1973).

Before going on to examine the media involvements of these youths in the light of their differing relationships to their social experience, a comparison of some results from the present study with those of Hargreaves (1967) will show the utility of the actor-oriented approach in avoiding over-simplistic explanations of research data on sub-cultural groupings.

In his research into the social values and behaviour of youngsters in a secondary modern school, Hargreaves posited the existence of two sub-cultures, which he labelled 'academic' and 'delinquescent', and which were seen to represent alternative modes of adaptation to the school. 'Academic' youths were relatively successful in school, and enjoyed the school experience. They engaged in out-of-school activities that reinforced their classroom experiences, and valued upward social mobility. 'Delinquescent' boys were negatively disposed to school, their values being in the direction of delinquent concerns, such as the display of aggression and the desire for immediate gratification.

FIGURE 7.1
Behaviour choice character descriptions

BOB is the sort of bloke who gets on well with everyone. He can take a joke, and he always shares things with his mates.

MICK feels that most of the things you do in school are a waste of time. He is always mucking around in class and being cheeky to the teachers. He can't wait to start work.

JOHN gets good marks at most things and usually comes top in at least one subject. The teachers like him because he always pays attention in class. John wants to stay on and pass some exams.

ANDY is pretty good-looking. He never has any trouble picking up girls and spends a lot of his time taking them out.

PHIL is naturally good at sports. When he is not playing for his team he usually goes to a match or watches sport on the television.

CHARLIE is never stuck for things to do or places to go. He is a natural leader and the rest of the group usually follow him.

PETE never comes on top in anything but he works hard and always does the best he can. On the whole he enjoys lessons.

GEORGE spends most of his time out with his mates just mucking around doing nothing in particular.

PAUL is a keen pop fan. He spends a lot of time listening to the radio or playing his own records. He always knows what's in the Top Ten and can usually say whether a new record will be a hit or not.

JASON is a hard guy and enjoys proving how really tough he is. He is the kind of guy you can depend on in a fight.

The present study incorporated a role-model question, adapted from previous research by Murdock and Phelps (1973), which

comprised descriptions of ten youth types. The youngsters were
asked to indicate their similarity or dissimilarity to each of these
character descriptions along a five-point scale (the character
descriptions are given in Figure 7.1). The intercorrelations of the
ten descriptions were rotated to varimax criterion by factor
analysis, and two main clusters emerged. One was highly loaded on
Bob — the good friend, Paul — the pop fan, Andy — the lover,
Charlie — the natural leader, and Jason — the hard guy, and did
not load at all on John — the school achiever, and Pete — the
schoolwork plugger. It seemed to show an orientation to the street
groupings that were characteristic of the neighbourhood where the
research was conducted, and was called *street culture orientation*
(SCO). The second cluster was highly and positively weighted on
John — the school achiever, and negatively weighted on Mick —
the school rejector, George — the muck about, and Jason — the
hard guy. This factor was labelled *educational orientation* (EDO).
Table 7.1 summarizes these results.

TABLE 7.1
Loading of role model items on the two varimax factors*
(Decimal points omitted)

Behaviour choice item	I	II
Bob – a good friend	50	49
John – school achiever	05	74
Phil – sportsman	26	−08
Pete – plugger	−06	11
Paul – pop fan	67	−21
Mick – school rejector	35	−71
Andy – the lover	75	13
Charlie – natural leader	72	24
George – muck about	09	−55
Jason – hard guy	63	−43
Per cent of total variance explained	23.8	19.3

All roots greater than unity

On the surface these clusters seem to duplicate the two culture idea of Hargreaves, but it would be incorrect to see them as wholly confirming his argument. While there are parallels between 'academic' and 'delinquescent' subcultures and EDO and SCO respectively, Hargreaves's research makes assumptions of his subjects that his data cannot support. In arguing for the rejection of school, he sees lower-stream youths as representing 'double failures' of the educational system, in that they lack the motivation and/or ability to get into grammar school, and are also low placements in their present school. He then argues that their realization of this is the basis for rejection of school, but in doing so he assumes a feeling of relative deprivation on the part of the boys which he does not substantiate. More fundamentally, his thesis presumes a middle-class value system as a point of reference against which the youths gauge their values and activities, though he fails to demonstrate the validity of this assumption. Hargreaves adopted the theoretical standpoint which Cohen (1955) used in his study of delinquent boys, and attempted to make his data fit the theory. This is a major difficulty in Hargreaves' work. Cohen's version of anomie theory[2] assumes that a major factor responsible for the commitment to conforming or delinquent behaviour is the acceptance or rejection of the middle-class value system represented by the school. Boys in the low-achieving streams of secondary modern schools are thought to be subject to status frustration. They wish for but cannot achieve the middle-class status to which they aspire, and their inability to do so leads them to reject the school. If this argument is to be accepted, however, it should be subjected to empirical test, and not made an *a priori* assumption. This can only be done by investigating how the structural aspects of the school and out-of-school situations of these youngsters impinge on them, as Hargreaves himself eventually acknowledges; such an inquiry would also help clear up several anomalies in Hargreaves's work. For example, he found that the behaviour of boys in the second top stream often more closely approximated that of youths in the bottom stream than the activities of top streamers. In addition, a number of bottom-stream youths did not opt for a delinquescent solution to their situation, as Hargreaves' theory would predict.

A key weakness in Hargreaves's model is its use of a 'disjunctive value' paradigm which neglects to deal with the motivational basis for attachment to either the 'academic' or 'delinquescent' sub-culture. The actor approach precludes this difficulty by assuming that behaviour must be seen as acts of the individual in response to and in line with the maintenance of a developing self-concept. Considerations of such terms as societal values, role and status become important only through their mediation in the individuals we study. It is appreciated that the development of the self is a dynamic process which is influenced by and indeed wholly dependent on the individual's social perceptions, and that this experience cannot be fully grasped in non-longitudinal research, but the approach allows for variability in the extent and kind of behaviour that is denied by conventional theories of conformity and deviance. The present research provides clear evidence of the strength of the model used. The project concentrated exclusively on the bottom streams of a school, where, following Hargreaves or Cohen, one might expect uniform rejection of the school experience. Our analysis shows that the situation is far more complex than they would have us believe.

The results presented in Table 7.1 show the cultural and social features which the North-east youngsters perceive to exist in their community. The fact that we found both groups of youngsters to perceive their behaviour as being appropriate to their environment argues that they see their neighbourhood in different ways, and forces our attention to the value and behavioural possibilities that the boys feel are provided for them to identify with and act out. An important division of these perceived possibilities is provided by examining the association of SCO and EDO with some of the self-image, attitude and social behaviour data that were gathered.[3] As Table 7.2, which presents these results shows, there is a strong, consistent clustering of SCO and EDO relationships covering a wide range of beliefs and action. These figures express more strikingly than words the large number of factors associated with the cultural options the youngsters saw as existing in their neighbourhood.

The results in Table 7.2 argue that the street culture and educationally oriented youths were purposively adjusting to the varying possibilities they saw their environment as offering them. Both groups were using the social and cultural resources of their neighbourhood in a manner that was consistent with their individual capacities and interests. In this sense both groups were 'achievers' in their community, its culture providing for expression of *both* modes of adjustment, school values and street culture.

TABLE 7.2
Correlations (r) between behaviour, personal perception, street culture and educational orientation.

Attribute	Correlation with street culture orientation (N=99)	Correlation with educational orientation (N=99)
Peer nominated aggression	.30***	−.18*
Self-reported anti-social behaviour[a]		
Factor I — interpersonal aggression	.24**	−.18*
Factor II — property-damage, theft	.06	−.34***
Factor III — interpersonal aggression	.25**	−.09
Factor IV — property damage, theft	.16	−.30***
Factor V — home problems	.09	−.06
Factor VI — interpersonal aggression	.10	−.15
Self-image		
I am a hard guy	.45****	−.26**
I like to be good with my fists	.34****	−.24**
I like to pick on nippers	.18*	−.28***
I like being cheeky to teachers	.27***	−.40****
I carry a chip on my shoulder (that is, act cocky or tough)	.38****	−.26**
Interpersonal relations		
I begin to fight when others try to get me to do something I don't want to	.24**	−.21**
If someone doesn't treat me right, I fight back	.30***	−.33***
I pick fights or argue with my parents	.22**	−.29***
These days my parents really help out; they don't let me down	.03	.27***
I get on well with my parents	.10	.33***
Commitment to school[a]	−.21	.40****
Parent-peer orientation[a]		
Preferences for peers as a source of fashion and spare-time companions	.25***	−.13
Valued activities		
Hard guys are good guys to be with	.33****	−.28***
It is important to be good at some form of sport	.23**	.00
It is important to be the person in the group who is best with the birds (or girls)	.53****	−.19
I like to do exciting things	.25**	−.01

TABLE 7.2 continued

Attribute	Correlations with street culture orientation (N=99)	Correlations with educational orientation (N=99)
View of their environment		
You've got to be tough to get on around here	.27***	−.01
People my age in my neighbourhood get into fights	.24**	−.10
You've got to be tough to get ahead in life	.24**	−.14
I like to be on my own and be my own boss	.24**	−.21**

[a] *These factors were results of varimax factor analyses of twenty self-report behaviour items, seven attitudes toward school and ten parent-peer orientation questions, respectively.*

Two tailed test significance levels:
* .10 > P > .05
** P < .05
*** P < .01
**** P < .001 (correlation probabilities below this level are not recorded)

Aggressive values must be seen as reflecting the general culture of the North-east community in which the youngsters lived, and not *in themselves* regarded as a sufficient way of summing up the environment of the boys. Table 7.2 tells another interesting story. Aggression correlates with SCO and EDO at the 0.30 and −0.18 levels respectively; there is a significant tendency for aggressive youths to be committed to the values of the street culture and negatively oriented to the school experience, but SCO and EDO can claim the attachment of both aggressive and non-aggressive youngsters. This being the case, our analysis of the media relationships established by boys of differing street culture and educational orientations will take their aggression into account, where indicated.

Because the youngsters were asked to indicate how similar or dissimilar they felt they were to each of the role model descriptions, SCO and EDO are also measures of self-image. The large number of correlations among SCO, EDO and the youths' values and behaviour suggest that the boys would be inadequately understood by simply focusing on them as individuals or on the social values prevalent in their neighbourhood. Only as neighbourhood values become internalized into the youngsters' perceptions of themselves and their activities do they become important in learning about them.

SCO, EDO AND MEDIA EXPOSURE

Examination of the relationship between SCO, EDO and exposure to eight media (books, cinema films, comics, magazines,

TABLE 7.3
Correlations (r) among SCO, EDO and exposure to eight media

	Exposure Mean[a]	Correlation with SCO (N=99)	Correlation with EDO (N=99)
Books	2.8	.07	.19*(.18*)
Cinema films	3.9	.20**(.19*)[b]	.04
Comic books	4.4	.02	.02
Magazines	1.8	.08	.02
Newspapers	4.3	.08	.15
Radio	4.5	.16	−.34***(−.38***)
Records	3.6	.41***(.40***)	−.22**(−.20**)
Television	5.0	.00	.00

a Mean exposure figures are based on the following operationally defined frequencies:

Books (5) 1 or more a fortnight (4) 1 a month (3) 3 to 6 a year (2) 2 a year or less and (1) never

Cinema films (5) 1 time or more a fortnight (4) 1 time a month (3) 3 to 6 times a year (2) 2 a year or less (1) less often (0) never

Comic books and magazines (5) 1 or more per week (4) 1 per fortnight (3) 1 a month (2) 3 to 6 a year (1) less often (0) never

Newspapers, Radio, Records and Television (5) several times a week or more (4) 1 or 2 times a week (3) 1 time a fortnight (2) 1 time a month (1) less often (0) never

b Partial correlations controlling for peer-rated aggression.

Two-tailed test significance levels:
*   .10 > P > .05
**   P < .05
***   P < .001 (correlation probabilities below this level are not recorded)

newspapers, radio, records and television) provides some interesting results in line with the thesis of this paper. These findings,
shown in Table 7.3, indicate the predictive power of street culture
orientation and educational orientation in understanding a number
of the media involvements of the youths in the study.

The boys showed a low level of interest in books. Book reading
frequently was the second lowest of the media exposure categories,
a finding which is predictable and understandable in view of the
lads' low educational placement. They have little motivation to
acquire the literary interests associated with educational progress.
A majority of the boys read fewer than two books a year, and
about a quarter claimed *never* to read books other than for school.
This low interest in books is paralleled by that of their parents.
When interviewed, the parents of the youngsters claimed to read
fewer than six books a year. Despite this, EDO is predictive of
frequency of book reading, showing the insight this factor provides
into understanding the involvement the boys had with books.
Controlling for aggression makes no difference in this relationship.

The significant correlation between SCO and cinema attendance
is consistent with previous research (*Pfuhl*, 1960). Movie going has
been found to be associated with aggression and delinquency,
though the long implied causal relationship between the two is
extremely doubtful, and masks the social nature of the cinema
experience. Boys with street culture values participate in many
group activities, including attending the cinema. Thus it can be
argued that it is their social interest rather than their aggression
which accounts for their cinema going. This inference is borne out
by the results. The original relationship between SCO and
frequency of cinema attendance still holds when the correlation is
controlled for aggression. Examination of the films the youths
claimed to have seen during the three or four months preceding the
interview revealed a mixed bag of favourites, with Westerns, war,
and spy films high on the list. This action-oriented content is quite
consistent with the assertive character of SCO.

Since the boys' favourite records and radio programmes, which
we shall soon discuss in detail, were almost exclusively 'pop', these
media are best discussed together. Most interest centred on
mainstream pop, those ever-changing Top Twenty tunes. Little
involvement was shown in 'deeper' underground music. In spite of
the similarity in content of pop music preferences, there are
consistently significant differences in the amount of exposure to

pop between the SCO and EDO groupings. Boys high on the street culture factor have more contact with pop than those low on SCO, as we would expect. This finding is reversed when pop exposure is examined in relation to the boys' school orientations. Aggression makes no difference to these relationships; when aggression is controlled, the original correlations remain significant. Further analysis suggested that one particular group accounted for most of the variance in exposure to pop. While street culture orientation was not related to exposure to pop for aggressive boys, non-aggressive boys who were street culture oriented claimed more frequent exposure to pop than non-aggressive boys who were low on street culture orientation. This suggests that non-aggressive, high SCO boys selectively use pop music to gain acceptance and popularity from their friends. Street culture oriented aggressive boys who have the physical prerequisites to gain status for their physical prowess can rely on these sources of esteem among their peers, and need not use pop music as a coin of social exchange. Pop music is thus seen to occupy an important place in the lives of the non-aggressive street culture keen adolescents.[4]

There is a positive relationship between EDO and newspaper reading (although the correlation does not reach significance). Taken together with the correlation between EDO and book reading, this relationship suggests a general interest in print media among boys who value the school experience, as one would expect.

There are no simple relationships between SCO and EDO and exposure to comics, magazines and television. In the case of magazines this lack of correlation is understandable in that the mean exposure figure in Table 7.3 indicates that the youths had little contact with them. The comic and television exposure figures show that these two media were so often used that the response categories were not sensitive enough to detect differences in exposure between the groups.

Further insight into the media relationships of the boys is provided by analysing the uses and gratifications they derived from their media experiences. We now turn to these results.

MEDIA USES

The procedures used to probe the youths' uses of the media were simple. Boys claiming frequent exposure to each of the media were asked a number of detailed questions about their experience with these media. These questions applied to all boys (*a*) claiming to read three or more books a year, or going to the cinema as often, (*b*) reading one or more comics or magazines a month, and (*c*) reading newspapers, listening to the radio or records, or watching television once a fortnight or more. The number of boys questioned varied for each of the media, but there were no significant differences in the numbers of high or low SCO or EDO boys responding for any of the media.[5]

1. Each boy was asked to name a few of the books he had read during the preceding six months; films seen at the cinema during the previous three or four months; comics and magazines read during the previous month; newspapers, radio and television programmes he read, listened to or watched regularly; and favourite records at the time of the interview. No limit was placed on the number of items to be recalled, but owing to the limits of interviewing time, it was decided to stop probing at three.

2. For each item mentioned, the boys were presented with a card listing eleven uses-gratifications (Figure 7.2). These covered the experience implied by the typology of Blumler *et al.* (1970), and were supported by pre-testing. As can be seen, these uses-gratifications encompass a wide range of media-person interaction. The boys were asked to indicate those feelings on the list that came closest to how they felt when watching, listening to, or reading these media items.

3. After indicating their uses-gratifications from the list, and being given an opportunity to volunteer any others not listed, the boys were asked questions probing 'why' they mentioned the uses-gratifications they did, and 'how' their experiences with these materials made them feel the way they said they did.

Responses were recorded as near as possible verbatim, and the interviewer attempted to clarify any problems of meaning in the answers.

Books
Analysis of the uses-gratifications derived from book reading showed that twenty-four (or 27 per cent) of the ninety books mentioned were of the classic schoolboy variety (*Tom Sawyer,*

FIGURE 7.2
Listing of the eleven uses-gratifications

Helps me to get away from the humdrum of things

Helps me to forget my worries for a while

Felt relaxed

Helps me to have some company

Would be able to talk to my friends (or mates) about it

Fancied myself in it

Helps me understand other people

Reflects the way I feel about things

It's exciting

Keeps me in touch with what's going on

Would be able to talk to my parents about it

Oliver Twist, Black Beauty, etc). While most boys read books such as these at some time during their school career, it is interesting that high EDO youths were more likely to have these classics among their reading fare (33.3 per cent) than were their less educationally interested peers (20.5 per cent) (statistically significant: $p < .10$). There was no difference in the number of classics read by high and low SCO boys. The rest of the books mentioned covered a wide range of content areas, though books on sports, animals, hobbies and annual comic books were especially favoured. No best sellers or recent best sellers were mentioned.

The 'It's exciting' category of uses-gratifications was the most frequently mentioned of the one hundred gratifications given, and these centred on adventure and action. While the data do not permit a full description of the kinds of relationships the boys established with books, they emphasize that printed matter plays a limited role in their lives. However, even here high EDO boys seem oriented towards a particular type of book fare.

Magazines

Magazines also had little popularity, but here again content preferences clearly reflected selectivity and purposiveness. Sports material was highly represented in the magazines the boys claimed to have read during the month preceding the interview. In fact one-third of all magazines mentioned were of this type, with football magazines predominating, and this reflects strongly the keen sports interest which was uncovered in another part of the study. Boys with high or low SCO had similar preferences in magazines, but those with high and low educational orientations differed significantly in the content they favoured. Only three of the twenty-eight (10.7 per cent) magazines mentioned by the high EDO youngsters concerned sports, whereas twelve of the twenty (60.0 per cent) magazines mentioned by the low EDO boys were of this type ($p < .001$). High EDO boys were more interested in hobby, news, family and radio/TV magazines. Controlling for aggression makes no difference to this result.

The uses-gratifications associated with magazine reading centred on 'keeping in touch' and in providing information about established interests. Sports magazines can be seen as playing a complementary role to newspapers in keeping the boys informed about sports activities. While newspapers, which we shall soon discuss, were relied upon to provide information on team changes and league tables, sports magazines provided more detailed stories about star players and their teams, putting the newspaper into greater relief.

Records and Radio

Study of the data gathered on the uses-gratifications associated with pop music provides more insight into the results from the section on exposure to pop. A majority of SCO and EDO youngsters claimed to have a favourite pop star, although we were unable to uncover any indication that the youths were deeply involved in the world of pop. This suggests that there is a selective commitment to pop. Pop tunes seemed to be regarded as of momentary interest, subject to conversation for a brief period, soon to be replaced by the emergence of new hits; almost all the favourite records were at the top of the charts during the three-month period in which the interviews were completed.

The relaxing aspect of record listening was stressed in the uses-gratification listings of boys in both the SCO and EDO groups. Other gratifications, including the 'exciting' category, are given only minor emphasis. There is no difference in the gratifications given by the two groups.

Thus far our discussion has centred on the youngsters' commitment to pop and the personal gratifications derived from record listening. Another aspect of pop which we have not yet discussed is that of knowledge of pop music. It is here that the radio listening behaviour of the boys becomes insightful in the analysis. Following up the earlier finding that non-aggressive high SCO boys used pop music knowledge as a coin of social exchange, we argued that this group should be significantly more likely to have learned of their favourite records from the radio — the fastest means of contact with new tunes — than from such slower sources as purchase, friends or siblings. When we compared the mean ratio of favoured records learned from the radio among high and low SCO boys, controlling for aggression, the results strongly supported our inference. Non-aggressive high SCO boys exploit the quickest means of keeping up with the swift changing top-of-the-pops world, thus their ability to keep their friends informed of the chart placings of favourite records and of the emergence of new hits. Once again the social exchange value of pop music knowledge for non-aggressive high SCO boys was confirmed.

Newspapers
Newspapers were quite popular, with 87 per cent of the SCO and EDO groups claiming to read at least one or two newspapers a week. Each boy was asked about the sections he turned to in reading newspapers, and ten categories emerged. Three referred to specific content areas (sports, non-sporting news, and cartoons and jokes), three to information (television programmes, adverts for the cinema and adverts for jobs), and two to physical features of the papers (pictures and headlines). An 'other' category included a few unclassifiable items, and a 'just go through' category was uncovered as an important feature of the way the youths 'read' newspapers.

The uses nominated showed a similar pattern *within* regional daily, national daily and Sunday national newspaper groups, and there was no difference between high-low SCO and EDO boys on this score. This uniformity of usage suggests that different types of newspapers were perceived to provide different sorts of knowledge or entertainment. For example, national daily and Sunday national papers were preferred for sports news, whereas regional papers were favoured for television programme information. Non-sports news was obtained from all three types of paper. A first priority in newspaper reading was sports news, regardless of street culture or educational orientation. This is consistent with our findings that sports, and especially football, were the major leisure activity of the North-east boys.

The fact that almost all the boys obtain sports information from their newspaper reading, and that SCO boys read more sports magazines than those high on EDO gives more evidence that while sports was a popular spare-time activity among all the boys, success in this pursuit is more critical to the self-concept of SCO than EDO boys. In addition to showing that the boys read newspapers purposively, the results suggest that current affairs news is of secondary importance, and again there is no important difference between high-low SCO boys. Few boys in either group claimed to read a specific news section, and among the small proportion of SCO and EDO youths who did read the news, human interest material outweighed local, national and international news. Again, these findings indicate that the boys' newspaper reading fits their everyday interests. News material and features that relate to activities they value, such as sports and television viewing, are stressed in their reading.

The Pictorial Media: Cinema, Comics and Television

Examination of the uses-gratifications derived from the cinema, comics and television provide insight into the multi-purpose place these media occupy. Because of the large number of cinema, comic and television items, and because the boys gave many responses to questions about their reactions to these materials, two adults who did not know to which samples the boys were assigned were asked to code these responses separately. The codings agreed 95 per cent of the time, and the few differences were resolved by mutual agreement. These convincing results of inter-rater reliability permitted a detailed analysis of the boys' experiences with these media.

Cinema films were fairly popular. The films the boys had seen in the three or four months prior to the interview were tabulated and sample comparisons were made. The results showed that there was a close similarity in the films the SCO and EDO boys mentioned, as might be expected in view of the nature of the film distribution system.

Deeper insight into the cinema experience of the boys was obtained by examining the uses-gratifications they claimed to derive from their essentially similar film fare. One impressive finding was the wide range of gratifications offered, which covered twenty-six categories. The distribution of these gratifications shows that neither high or low SCO or EDO boys can be said to be getting a limited range of things from these films. Indeed a whole spectrum of experiences were reported, including relaxation, excitement and conversation, though there are particular gratification emphases which we shall report shortly.

No less than six categories of 'exciting' (adventure, aggression, suspense, solving of crime, action without mention of aggression, and 'others') were uncovered. On the basis of these results, we can say that 'exciting' means a number of different things to the boys, and that only one of these refers to the display of violence. Comparison of the uses-gratifications supplied by boys of different SCO and EDO found no strong differences, and in no way suggested that they were getting fundamentally different things out of cinema films. In general, the boys stressed the exciting features of their cinema experiences (37 per cent of the total uses-gratifications), while conversation (18 per cent of the total) and relaxing, getting away from the humdrum and forgetting one's worries (15 per cent) were given secondary emphasis. One interesting difference did develop. Earlier results showed that the non-aggressive boys claimed to talk about films with their friends more than did the aggressive boys. When this finding was elaborated, using SCO, suggestions about the social utility of cinema viewing emerged. The non-aggressive high SCO boys were the keenest cinema conversationalists in the study. There was no significant difference in cinema discussion among aggressive and non-aggressive low SCO boys. As in the pop music findings, non-aggressive SCO boys were again found to be media conversationalists.

Comics were very popular among the boys, with a total of forty different comics being mentioned some 220 times. The titles were tabulated, and a comparison made of those receiving three or more nominations by high or low SCO or EDO boys. The results showed that there was a close similarity in the comics favoured by both groups.

The uses and gratifications the youngsters claimed to derive from reading comics covered a wide range of twenty-two categories. However, no strong differences were found in these gratifications among boys with varying SCO and EDO. The six-member 'exciting' group is once more represented, though the total of these responses, and the aggressive aspect of this category comprise much smaller proportions than they do for the cinema film material. On the other hand, relaxation and getting away from the humdrum of things were proportionately more highly represented than for cinema films. If the responses suggesting the humorous aspect of comics (the 'funny' category) is added to this group, a further 13 per cent of all the comic uses-gratifications are accounted for. These data indicate that a stress on the feeling of well-being and pleasure is associated with reading comics.

All the boys claimed to watch television several times a week or more. There were no differences between SCO and EDO groups' programme preferences. The uses-gratifications offered are extensive and revealing. Twenty-five categories emerged, with the six-member 'exciting' group taking up a larger proportion of the total gratifications than was the case for either cinema films or comics (38 per cent, 37 per cent and 19 per cent respectively). However, the aggression-exciting category covers a smaller proportion of television gratifications than for cinema films (9 per cent vs 16 per cent). The de-emphasis in television aggression is partly taken up by an increase in the information function of television ('keeping in touch with what's going on', and 'learning things', centring on the programme *Blue Peter*) which comprise 12 per cent of all television gratifications, but less than 2 per cent of cinema and comic responses. The boys get more and different things out of television viewing than they do from the cinema or comics.

There is no difference in the pattern of gratifications for boys of differing EDO, but an interesting difference in television use emerged when the responses of high and low SCO youngsters were examined. High SCO boys stressed adventurous aspects of their favourite programmes more often than those boys low on the SCO factor. This is not surprising in view of the fact that the SCO factor is highly weighted on items reflecting physical prowess but when we pursued this result by controlling for peer-rated aggression, the non-aggresive high SCO boys were seen to be the group most oriented to television adventure ($p < .02$). There was no significant difference between high and low SCO aggressive boys on this score. Consistent with the findings on pop exposure and learning source, and cinema conversation, the non-aggressive high SCO boys are seen to be a highly media-involved group.

COMPARISON OF THE USES-GRATIFICATIONS DERIVED FROM CINEMA FILMS, COMICS AND TELEVISION

Examining the uses-gratifications of high and low SCO and EDO boys is important, and documents the fact that in general they all obtain similar things from their cinema, comic reading and television experiences. While a few significant differences emerge, there is no evidence to suggest that these media are put to fundamentally different purposes. However, a comparison of this kind needs to be accompanied by a study of uses-gratifications *across* the pictorial media, if we are to be able to see the varying way in whch these experiences fit into the boys' lives. When this was done, a very interesting picture of uses-gratification emphasis across the three media develops. Combination of those gratification categories which seemed to reflect similar experiences lead to the isolation of five main clusters:

1. 'Helps me to get away from the humdrum of things', 'helps me to forget my worries for a while' and 'felt relaxed': labelled RESPITE.

2. The six 'exciting' categories (adventure, aggression, suspense, solves crime, action, and other) were treated as one EXCITING category.

3. 'Keeps me in touch with what's going on', and 'learn things': labelled INFORMATION.

4. 'Would be able to talk to my friends (or mates) about it', and 'would be able to talk to my parents about it': labelled CONVERSATION.

5. 'Funny', 'makes me laugh': labelled FUNNY.

Table 7.4, which presents data for these five categories, shows that (*a*) they comprise a majority of all the gratifications obtained, and (*b*) there are differences in emphasis among cinema films, comics and television. The findings presented are for high and low SCO boys only, but they parallel closely those obtained for high and low EDO boys. Respite is more associated with comics than with cinema or television viewing. Excitement is clearly favoured among cinema films and television. Information is most salient in the use of

TABLE 7.4
Distribution of RESPITE, EXCITING, INFORMATION, CONVERSATIONS and FUNNY uses-gratifications for cinema films, comic books and television among high and low SCO youths

		Medium		
Gratifications/Group		Cinema	Comics	Television
1 RESPITE	Hi SCO*	17.3%	27.6%	9.1%
	Lo SCO	12.6%	24.1%	9.5%
	Total	15.2%	25.9%	9.3%
2 EXCITEMENT	Hi SCO	38.7%	17.9%	38.5%
	Lo SCO	35.5%	21.7%	39.2%
	Total	37.2%	19.7%	38.8%
3 INFORMATION	Hi SCO	2.0%	2.5%	12.6%
	Lo SCO	1.4%	1.2%	12.2%
	Total	1.8%	1.9%	12.4%
4 CONVERSATION	Hi SCO	17.7%	6.1%	11.5%
	Lo SCO	18.7%	8.7%	15.7%
	Total	18.2%	7.3%	13.4%
5 FUNNY	Hi SCO	17.7%	6.1%	11.5%
	Lo SCO	16.0%	10.7%	6.1%
	Total	10.6%	13.5%	5.8%
Total gratification accounted for by RESPITE, EXCITEMENT, INFORMATION, CONVERSATION and FUNNY categories. (Totals 1-5)**		83.0%	68.3%	79.7%

* *Defined as high or low depending upon whether the factor score was above or below the median for the score distribution.*
** *A number of youths gave more than one mention in categories 1-5*

television. Both cinema films and television have a fair degree of conversational stress, with comics least; and comics and cinema are more likely to be regarded as funny than television.

CONCLUSION

Collectively considered, the results reported in this paper show a coherent thread uniting self-conception, attitude, behaviour, media exposure and uses-gratifications. The findings suggest that the boys we studied prefer media activities which are consistent with their self-concepts, and that media inolvement must be treated as a factor dependent on their orientations to critical features of their environment.

We can now offer at least in outline fashion some treatment of the results in terms of the hypotheses about the self-concept suggested by Hilgard which we mentioned earlier. The importance of aggression in the life styles of the boys has been noted elsewhere, and this evidence also shows the value attached to aggression in the North-eastern community we studied. Factor analysis of the role model data showed that two dominant value frameworks emerge in the boys' experience, namely street culture orientation and educational orientation. In terms of our analysis, the interactions between these factors, aggression and media use provide insight into the self as an organizer of social experience. The findings strongly suggest that behaviour is purposive, with the aim of maintaining a certain conception of the self. This was most evident in the case of non-aggressive high SCO boys, whose media behaviour seems to be directly geared to maintaining acceptance with other SCO boys, who, because of their physical characteristics, have less need of the media as a coin of social exchange. Media knowledge was a key factor in the experience of non-aggressive high SCO boys, and this is a thread that integrates much of their separate media experiences. Similar mechanisms operate in the case of boys oriented towards educational achievement. They purposively use their media experiences to confirm their self-conception in their chosen mode of social adaptation.

In general, media preferences and uses can be seen as one means of maintaining consistency in a social environment which, despite its apparent homogeneity, provides for several modes of adaptation. It is suggested that these findings are consistent with the two hypotheses regarding the 'inferred self' which the present research was capable of addressing.

It remains for us to incorporate these results into research of a longitudinal kind, tracing social and media-use histories over time, and establishing in greater detail how media preference patterns develop. This was not possible in the present study, which has merely scratched the surface of these issues. Nevertheless, following a research strategy such as the one we suggest may permit us to engage in some exciting media gratification work. Although examinations of the demographic correlates of media use are initially necessary, they must give way to more subtle attempts to delineate the value frameworks underlying particular preference patterns if we are to learn 'how people of different ages and from different cultural and educational backgrounds process, retain and internalise the information that is presented to them by the mass media' (*Halloran*, 1970). It is undoubtedly useful to establish the demographic factors relating to programme preferences, but it is analytically necessary to relate these variables to the media experience through the value orientations of their audience. To study the media in isolation from these concerns is to bring into question the relevance of any research in illuminating these issues. The social mapping paradigm represents a research programme to meet this task. The model, and the socio-cultural concerns that its use implies, constitutes a challenge for media research in the 1970s.

NOTES

1 R. Dembo (1972). The second author of this paper was field interviewer for the study. We are also grateful for the assistance of Tom Woolley, who helped gather the ratings of aggression, and Mrs Peggy Gray for clerical assistance in the tabulation of our findings.
2 For a fuller discussion of anomie theory, see: R K Merton, 'Social structure and anomie' and 'Continuities in the theory of social structure and anomie' in Merton (1968) and Hirschi (1971).
3 This analysis was accomplished by using each student's SCO and EDO varimax factor scores. Since the samples were not probability samples, the use of the statistical model, strictly speaking, does not apply. However, the model was used for heuristic purposes as a basis of comparison of the results with that of a random model to assist in locating significantly appearing relationships and patterns. Owing to the exploratory nature of the study, two tailed statistical test significance levels were used. The factor-analysed question sets are reported in Dembo (1972). The attitude toward school items were adopted from Murdock and Phelps (1973).
4 This finding converges with the results of other research. See for example: Brown and O'Leary (1971), Murdock and Phelps (1973) and Howitt and Cumberbatch (1971).
5 The one exception to this is the case of radio listening, where 33 high EDO and 48 low EDO youths were involved. However, because almost all of these programmes were of the mainstream pop music variety, and the boys' uses-gratifications with records in general were probed, this difference does not affect our reported findings. The number of high-low SCO and EDO boys

in the 'sometimes' or more often use categories for each of the media are:

	Books	Cinema	Comics	Maga-zines	News-papers	Radio	Records	TV
High SCO	23	44	45	14	44	47	44	49
Low SCO	20	35	44	15	41	44	37	49
High EDO	26	39	44	16	43	33	38	49
Low EDO	18	40	45	14	42	48	46	49

Median SCO and EDO score cases have, of course, been excluded from the chart.

In several instances, boys claiming exposure to one or more of the eight media 'sometimes' or more often did not mention any specific materials for uses-gratifications analysis and/or did not respond to all questions asked for each medium. However, there were no significant differences in the non-reporters, or specific question non-respondents, in the high or low SCO or EDO groups.

REFERENCES

Allport, G W (1961), *Pattern and Growth in Personality*, Holt, Rinehart and Winston, New York.

Berelson, B (1949), 'What Missing the Newspaper Means', in Lazarsfeld and Stanton (eds), *Communications Research 1948-9*, Duell, Sloan and Pearce, New York.

Blumler, J G, Brown, J R and *McQuail, D* (1970), 'The Social Origins of the Gratifications Associated with Television Viewing', mimeo, University of Leeds.

Brown, R L (1970), 'Approaches to the Historical Development of Mass Media Studies', in Tunstall (ed), *Media Sociology: A Reader*, Constable, London.

Brown, R L and *O'Leary, M* (1971), 'Pop Music in an English Secondary School System', *American Behavioural Scientist*, XVII.

Chaney, D (1972), *Processes of Mass Communication*, Macmillan, London.

Cohen, A K (1955), *Delinquent Boys*, Free Press, New York.

Dembo, R (1972), 'Aggression and Media Use among English Working Class Youths', unpublished report, University of Leicester.

Dembo, R (1973), 'A Measure of Aggression among Working Class Youths', *British Journal of Criminology*, XIII, No. 3.

Fearing, F (1947), 'Influence of the Movies on Attitudes and Behavior', *Annals of the American Academy of Political and Social Sciences*, CCLIV.

Freidson, E (1953), 'Communications Research and the Concept of the Mass', *American Sociological Review*, XVIII.

Hall, C S and *Lindzey, G* (1957), *Theories of Personality*, Wiley, New York.

Halloran, J D (1970), *Mass Media in Society: The Need for Research*, UNESCO Report on Mass Communication, Paris, LIX, 15.

Hargreaves, D (1967), *Social Relations in a Secondary School*, Routledge, London.

Herzog, H (1944), 'What do we Really Know about Daytime Serial Listeners?', in Lazarsfeld and Stanton, *Radio Research 1942-3*, Duell, Sloan and Pearce, New York.

Hilgard, E R (1967), 'Human Motives and the Concept of the Self', in Lazarus and Opton (eds), *Personality*, Penguin Books, London, 253.

Hirschi, T (1971), *Causes of Delinquency*, University of California Press, London.

Howitt, D and *Cumberbatch, G* (1971), *The Ethnology of Imitation,* mimeo, University of Leicester.

Hudson, L (1968) *Frames of Mind,* Methuen, London.

Jensen, G F (1972), 'Delinquency and Adolescent Self-conceptions: a Study of the Personal Relevance of Infraction', *Social Problems,* XX, No. 1.

Katz, E, Gurevitch, M and *Haas, H* (1973), 'On the Use of Television for Important Things', *American Sociological Review,* XXXVIII, 164-81.

Katz, E and *Lazarsfeld, P* (1955), *Personal Influence,* Free Press, New York.

Lazarsfeld, P F, Berelson, B and *Gaudet, H* (1944), *The People's Choice,* Duell, Sloan and Pearce, New York.

Lecky, P (1969), *Self Consistency,* Anchor Books, New York.

McQuail, D (1969), *Towards a Sociology of Mass Communications,* Collier-Macmillan, London.

McQuail, D, Blumler, J G and *Brown, J R* (1972), in McQuail (ed), *Sociology of Mass Communications,* Penguin Books, London.

Mead, G H (1934), *Mind, Self and Society,* University of Chicago Press, Chicago.

Merton, R K (1968), 'Patterns of Influence: Local and Cosmopolitan Influentials', in Merton, *Social Theory and Social Structure* (Enlarged edition), Collier-Macmillan, London.

Murdock, G and *Phelps, G* (1973), *Mass Media and the Secondary School,* Macmillan, London.

Parsons, T (1951), *The Social System,* Glencoe, Illinois.

Pfuhl, Jr, E H (1960), 'The Relationship of Mass Media to Reported Delinquent Behavior', Ph. D., Washington State University.

Riley, M and *Riley, J W* (1951), 'A Sociological Approach to Communications Research', *Public Opinion Quarterly,* XV.

Rogers, C R (1947), 'Some Observations on the Organisation of Personality', *American Psychologist,* II.

Rogers, C R (1959), 'A Theory of Therapy, Personality, and Interpersonal Relationships, as Developed in the Client-centred Framework', in Koch (ed), *Psychology: A Study of a Science,* III, McGraw-Hill, New York.

Rogers, C R (1964), 'Towards a Science of the Person', in Wann (ed), *Behaviorism and Phenomenology,* University of Chicago Press, Chicago.

Rosengren, K E and *Windahl, S* (1971), 'Mass Media Consumption as a Functional Alternative', in McQuail (ed) op. cit.

Schutz, A (1962), *Collected Papers,* I, Nijhoff, The Hague.

Schutz, A (1963), *Collected Papers,* II, Nijhoff, The Hague.

Schutz, A (1966), *Collected Papers,* III, Nijhoff, The Hague.

Star, S A and *Hughes, H M* (1950), 'Report of an Educational Campaign: The Cincinatti Plan for the United Nations', *American Journal of Sociology,* LV.

Television and Social Behavior (1971), Report to the US Surgeon General's Scientific Committee on Television and Social Behavior, US Government Printing Office, Washington DC.

Waples, D, Berelson, B and *Bradshaw, P R* (1940), *What Reading Does to People,* University of Chicago Press, Chicago.

Warner, W L and *Henry, W E* (1948), 'The Radio Daytime Serial: A Symbolic Analysis', *Genetic Psychology Monographs,* XXXVII.

Wirth, L (1948), 'Consensus and Mass Communication', *American Sociological Review,* XIII.

Wright, C R (1959), *Mass Communications: A Sociological Perspective,* Random House, New York.

8

The Parameters of Attraction to Mass Media Figures

Dennis Howitt and Guy Cumberbatch

The notion that during exposure to fictional materials, in particular at the cinema or on television, the viewer identifies with one or more of the characters involved is a common theme running through much of the concern with the effects of the mass media on young people. However, little empirical research has been carried out in this connection and the precise implications of the act of identification have never been formulated. In many instances, the concern has centred around the effects of 'heroes' using violent means to achieve their ends. This is incorporated, for example, in the British Broadcasting Corporation's (1962) code on violence: 'The main danger points are: ... d) Bad habits in "good" characters; for example, chain-smoking, hitting below the belt' (p.61).

Here the suggestion is that the 'good character' (that is, the one for whom there is likely to be a high positive effect) can influence children to adopt 'bad habits'. A more sophisticated approach would be implied by the following: 'Worries have ... been expressed about the effect on aggressive children of seeing television heroes who, although on the right side of the argument, still use violence to solve inter-personal problems and themselves take on the punishing of the "bad guy".' (*Halloran*, 1968 p.25). Schramm, Lyle and Parker (1961) turn this worry into a formal statement of 'fact': 'There is no doubt that the child can more easily store up behaviours and beliefs which he has imaginatively shared with the character with whom he identifies' (p.78). This statement is based on a study of the recall of movie content (*Maccoby* and *Wilson*, 1957) in subjects identifying with film characters. It does not, however, indicate that the observational learning is in fact put into operation. Opinion rather than empirical research, seems to have dominated the area. For example, Freeman (1961) wrote:

'Psychopathic youngsters, whose identification with meaningful adult figures has been seriously impaired, whose self censoring and self governing mechanisms are defective, are likely to be shallow and transitory in their relations with others. Poised to rebel, unsure of their own image, distant in their relationships, they may use the television criminal as their model of rebellion and be precipitated and guided by him' (p.192).

Glucksmann's (1971) assessment of the current state of knowledge in this area is quite accurate: 'It has not been proved that all the hero's activities tend to be "carried out" by the young viewer. It is possible that imitative identification with the star remains limited to secondary aspects of behaviour related to fashion (clothing, superficial relations between the sexes).' (p.42) Gluksmann also makes the following point which has been readily forgotten: 'Admiration for the hero does not seem to imply, *ipso facto* imitation in real life.'(p.41)

This statement makes it clear that 'identification' is not necessarily a bad thing in that attraction towards a mass media character does not automatically result in the imitation of that character. Halloran (1967) makes a similar point: 'The full significance for moral development of ... ideal person choice patterns is not known, although it could be hypothesized that young people are likely to have strong sentiments towards those they use as models, and that these sentiments are likely to become sentiments for what the people believe in or stand for.' (p.125) However, the hypothesis about the influence of identification on moral development suggests a mechanism for influence even though the author expresses dissatisfaction with the state of present knowledge in this area. Klapper (1960) has given expression to an attitude which defines a rather different hypothesis to the above: 'A large number of psychiatrists and psychologists interviewed by the present author in 1953 held that vicarious identification with the media character could serve children as an outlet for aggression which might otherwise be socially manifested'. (p.143)

Thus where one hypothesis suggests that identification is likely to have a beneficial influence on real life aggression, the hypothesis described by Halloran allows for the possibility that identification could have adverse effects. The vast bulk of the available research on identification has been concerned with the latter hypothesis, but there is some evidence bearing on the catharsis hypothesis and identification. Ancona and Fontanesi (1967) found that on their measures of aggression (derived from the Thematic Apperception Test) it was the subjects who were more active in their places during the film *Mondo Cane* who became 'less aggressive' following the film. To the extent that activity can be expected to correlate with positive involvement in the film and a positive attraction for certain of the film characters, these results can be taken as support for the view articulated by Klapper. However, the difficulty here is that the evidence depends very much on projective measures of hostility and on the fact that any interpretation of the meaning of bodily activity during the viewing of a film can be, on the basis of current knowledge, inferential only.

Both Halloran, Brown and Chaney (1970) and Noble (1971) have compared the identifications of delinquents and matched samples of non-delinquents. Halloran *et al.* asked their respondents two main questions referring to identification. The first of these was to name the persons who they would like to be like and the second was to name the people that they best like on television. Interestingly enough, probationers were less able to state the names of people they would like to be like, they did not identify more with characters from serials, and their favourite people on television were much the same as those of the non-delinquents. On the other hand, when asked to state the reasons for liking their favourite television programmes, the probationers did mention the hero more often than controls. The significance of this is not to be overestimated since the delinquents preferred 'exciting' programmes (those likely to contain a hero) more than controls. Noble's work was somewhat different in that it adopted a less direct measure of the importance of aggressive heroes to the child. He used the perceived similarities between the child and various media characters and family members as his measure of identification. Paralleling Halloran *et al.*'s results, Noble found no tendency for the delinquent boys to perceive themselves as being more similar to the aggressive hero than did the control group. However, delinquents perceived much less similarity between themselves and their fathers than did controls and on this basis Noble puts forward the very tentative argument that the aggressive hero is much more salient for the delinquent than the non-delinquent. Certainly a simple model of the effects of identification can be rejected on the basis of these findings.

Perhaps much more conclusive is the formal experimental work of Cumberbatch and Howitt (1971) and Howitt and Cumberbatch

(1972) which concerns the effect of affective feeling for a mass media character on attitudes towards violence. Fundamentally, the design employed over a series of studies was to have subjects rate the degree to which they were attracted to a mass media model and then to have them rate their attitudes towards an act of violence performed, in one experimental treatment, by that model or, in the other treatment, by a character with whom the subjects had no opportunity to form affective bonds. The design was completed by dividing subjects according to their attraction for the mass media model as measured by the initial questionnaire. Over the series of four studies, no evidence was found that the degree of attraction to a mass media model influenced attitudes towards aggression. It was therefore concluded that identification is not an important parameter in the effects of mass media portrayals of violence.

This, of course, is not to say that identification as a concept is not important to mass communication research nor is it to say that identification away from the media cannot influence behaviour (all of the above studies were concerned with violence and delinquency which may be a special case). Bandura and Huston (1961) have demonstrated that a nurturant rewarding model has a greater power to induce imitation in the child than does a more cold and distant model. Since in this experiment the model was always nearby, these findings could be the result of the child's desire to please the model and so maintain the warm relationship. In the film situation the child is in no position to benefit further by imitating the model's behaviour. This distinction between the situations of attraction to a mass media model and to a real-life model goes a long way to help in the understanding of how identification might be a useful concept for real-life interactions, but of no help in understanding the relationship between mass media models and the viewer. Erving Goffman (1963) adds a further dimension to this: 'The phrase "to identify with" ... has two common meanings: to participate vicariously in the situation of someone whose plight has caught one's sympathy, to incorporate aspects of another in forming one's own ego identity.' (p.106)

This distinction of two meanings of the term identification illustrates that powerful attractions for mass media models are possible without necessarily influencing the individual to adopt the behaviour patterns of the model. Stated simply, the sum total of the research would suggest that identification does not seem to influence the viewer to adopt the behaviour of the model. On the other hand, most of the relevant research has been confined to violence and delinquency which may be exceptional to the general rule. It might be observed that there are plenty of instances in which the clothes and mannerisms of an admired media personality are adopted by the young viewer which contradict this statement. In reply, it should be remembered that these very attributes of the media personality may have a positive attraction quite independent of the attraction for the personality *per se*.

There is an alternative approach to the topic of identification with mass media characters which does not stem directly from the concern with the effects of the mass media on real-life violence. Himmelweit, Oppenheim and Vince (1958) gave some indication of the need for a different approach when they wrote: 'We know as yet too little about the importance and meaning to children of the different personalities who appear on television. What we do know is that no one individual, and no one type of personality, was named as the favourite by more than a small minority of the children.' (p.405)

Clearly then, there is a profound need for investigations into the affective relationships between the young viewer and media personalities and characters. For this reason, an exploratory study of mass media identification was planned which placed particular emphasis upon aggressive heroes.

Given that some children and adults have profound attachments to various media figures, the consequent questions abound. What functions do attachments to mass media figures serve? Are they substitutes for strong relationships with other people? What sorts of children idenfity with what sorts of media figures? What are the consequences of identification both at the personal and societal level? Of course, few of these questions will be answered in this paper which is essentially concerned with two broad matters:

children have a somewhat different pattern of attraction to mass media characters from younger children? What effect does family structure have upon identification? Does identification cross sex boundaries? Of course, the possible background variables associated with identification are virtually limitless, and only a small number may be dealt with in this study.

The design was based heavily upon the factorial approach.

METHOD

Subjects
The subjects were eleven- to fifteen-year-old students from a Leicestershire comprehensive school. After unusable questionnaires had been discarded, the questionnaires from 202 children were used in the study at the factor analysis stage and, of these, 104 were from boys and 98 from girls. Because of incomplete background data on two of these subjects, only 200 were used in the final correlations of background variables with factor scores, of which 96 were from girls.

Procedure
The questionnaires were administered to class groups of children to be self-completed.

Questionnaires
The first part of the questionnaire required the child to record his name, sex, school class, date of birth, age, father's job, mother's job, whether he had any brothers and sisters, the number of siblings, the number of brothers older than himself, the number of sisters older than himself, and the number of hours of TV watched each week. This last question was not coded because of the high number of omissions. The second part of the questionnaire was concerned with identification choices and was preceded by the following instructions:

> Please say how much you would *like to be like* the following people. You can do this by putting a tick in one of the boxes against each person's name.

Each name was followed by five columns labelled from *Like very much* to *Dislike very much* to be like that particular personality or character. The subject had to tick the appropriate column. Further instructions were given to indicate how to fill in the ratings.

Analysis

The correlation matrix of the identification ratings was computed; this was then factor analysed by the method of principal components, all of the roots greater than unity were rotated to the varimax criterion and on to the promax criterion. The factor scores on the varimax analysis were computed for each individual and correlated with the following background and derived variables — age in months, sex, social class (middle or manual), whether the child was first-born or only-born, and the number of siblings the child possessed.

RESULTS

The factors

The fifteen factors extracted in the factor analysis were as follows:

Factor 1 Highly loading on this factor were Mick Jagger, John Lennon, Jimmy Saville, Peter Townshend, Kenny Everett, Simon Dee and Paul McCartney. All of the figures have to do with the pop music world. All, with the exception of Jimmy Saville, Kenny Everett and Simon Dee are performers in pop groups. The three exceptions are disc jockeys. All seven have in common that they are male, non-establishment figures, with connections with the pop music world. It is interesting to note that they seem to be those most likely to be rejected by the adult establishment in that they do not conform to expected standards of behaviour. This view is supported by the fact that such performers as Tom Jones and Cliff Richard, although themselves pop singers, do not have the same sort of unconventional life style and do not load highly on this factor. Richard, in fact, propounds Christian attitudes. The female pop personalities (for example, Cilla Black, Julie Felix and Bobby Gentry) do not load at all heavily. However, it is not clear whether it is because of their sex or because they lack the same unconventional image. Any further analysis might usefully include unconventional female pop singers. Likewise, it is not known whether the associations between these figures and the pop music world is merely fortuitous or whether pop associations are important in this factor. The factor may provisionally be called *Unconventionality*.

Factor 2 Bobby Gentry, Julie Felix, Cilla Black, Steve Temple and Cliff Richard all load on this factor. The first three — all female pop singers — have by far the highest loadings. On the basis of these the factor might be described as one of female singers but this does not explain the Steve Temple and Cliff Richard loadings. Sex could explain the factor if it were not for the Cliff Richard loading. The loadings of Steve Temple and Cliff Richard are probably the result of incomplete rotation to simple structure since they are both reduced by the promax rotation. The preferred description is therefore *Female 'Pop' Singers*.

Factor 3 Superintendent Barlow, Robin Day, Dixon of Dock Green, David Frost and John Watt all load heavily upon this factor. This cluster certainly suggests that attractions to television characters and personalities cross reality-fiction dimensions. All of the fictional characters have in common the fact that they are policemen but this cannot explain the factor. All of the personalities are English but this, also, cannot explain the structure. One common element between them is pugnacity. Robin Day and David Frost are very aggressive interviewers when the occasion arises. Superintendent Barlow and John Watt are both verbally aggressive, given the chance. Dixon of Dock Green, although portrayed as a benevolent father figure, often appears a rather crotchety old man. All of these figures are representatives of power in one form or another and they are all of a rather elderly appearance, although Frost, in terms of age, is a rather young man. However, within the list of personalities and characters included in this study there are others having similar age attributes which do not appear on this factor. For this reason the factor is best labelled *Verbal Aggressiveness*. Physical aggressiveness, although occasionally arising, is not a common attribute of the characters and personalities forming this cluster. Also, physically aggressive characters such as McGill (*Man in a Suitcase*) are not included on this factor.

Factor 4 John Steed from *The Avengers*, Jason King from *Department S*, Richard Barrett of *The Champions*, and Cliff Richard have the high loadings over .400, Richard having the lowest loading. Apart from this the factor consists of aggressive heroes, modern and stylish and mature. The Cliff Richard loading is probably error due to an incomplete rotation to simple structure and a promax rotation indicates that it declines with a better approximation to simple structure. Again, there are aggressive heroes who do not load on this factor (for example, The Virginian and McGill) and it may be that a touch of humour is specific to the characters forming this cluster. Tentatively it might be termed *Sophisticated Aggressive Heroes*.

Factor 5 With Dr Who and Captain Kirk having by far the largest loadings on this factor, it might be considered to be one of space serial characters. Unfortunately, there is a moderate loading on Ironside which obstructs this interpretation. It might be that this loading is error or it may be that the interpretation of the factor is incorrect. All three of these characters have the attributes of powerful leadership. Dr Who often decides the fates of his many colleagues; Captain Kirk has the responsibility for a 'Starship'; and Ironside directs detective work from his wheelchair. A further alternative explanation is that the characters are in bizarre settings — two of them are space adventurers and the third is a crippled detective. However, because of the great disparity between the loading of the space characters and Ironside, 'the preferred description of the factor is one of *Space Heroes*.

Factor 6 This loads highly on Ray Langton and Elsie Tanner, who are both characters in the television serial *Coronation Street*. The factor may thus be defined by the parameters of this programme. Whether or not the strong working-class nature of these characters is responsible for their association on this factor is not ascertainable from the evidence at hand.

Factor 7 Sergeant Lynch of *Z Cars* and Bernie Winters of the comedy team Mike and Bernie Winters load heavily on this factor. Ostensibly, Superintendent Barlow of *Softly, Softly* also loads moderately but the promax rotation reveals that this is due to an incomplete rotation to simple structure and consequently this loading can be ignored. At surface level, this factor is difficult to interpret since there is no similarity in role between the two persons. However, both do seem to have a similar physical appearance (ill-formed and chinless) and something of a buffoonish manner at times. The factor therefore may be termed *Physical Appearance*.

Factor 8 The Virginian and Trampas, both characters from the Western series *The Virginian*, load most heavily and McGill (from *Man in a Suitcase*) has a moderate loading. All of these characters are physically aggressive and all of them are American. They are all superficial with little personality elaboration in the plot and they all lack sophistication, and this might distinguish this factor from Factor 4. It might usefully be termed *Unsophisticated Aggressive Heroes*.

Factor 9 Best friend, Mother and Father all load heavily on this factor. Clearly the factor is one of identification with 'local' models rather than media models.

Factor 10 Bobby Moore and Peter Shilton are the heavily loading personalities. Both are footballers and the factor is probably best described as *Football Heroes*. Jackie Stewart, the racing driver, loads only .386 but it may be an indication that the factor is one of sporting personalities rather than the more restricted football heroes. Without a greater number of different sorts of sport personalities included in the rating scales, this cannot be finally decided.

Factor 11 John Steed and Simon Templar (*The Saint*) both load highly on this factor. Each one of these is an 'aggressive hero' but no suggestions can be offered further about the nature of this factor.

Factor 12 My teacher, Steve Temple and Dr Liz McNeil all load heavily on this factor. Clearly the child's teacher may have been male or female and in some respects it is curious that he should be attracted to his teacher in a similar way as he is to fictional characters. However, the Steve Temple loading is probably the result of incomplete rotation to simple structure since in the oblique solution this factor loading is substantially reduced. This does not apply to Dr Liz McNeil from the television series *The Doctors*. A likely explanation of this factor is that it represents attraction to the role of the middle-class professional. The teacher is a middle-class professional and likewise Dr Liz McNeil's lifestyle is middle class and she is a doctor by profession. Attraction to the role of the teacher is thus functionally very different from that of friends and parents and seems to be oriented towards the professional status of teacher. The factor might thus be termed *Professional Orientation*.

Factor 13 Since David Coleman, the sports commentator, has the only high loading, this factor needs little discussion. The loading of Jackie Stewart suggests the concern with sport but there is little justification for offering any other interpretation than *Sports Commentator*. It must be realized, however, that this title is merely a description of the personality and it is not necessarily a complete interpretation of the factor.

Factor 14 Prince Charles and Bob Monkhouse, the comedian, load highly on this factor. No interpretation offers itself.

Factor 15 Vincent, a character from *Manhunt* (a World War II escape series), is the only high loading, so little in the way of interpretation can be offered because of this.

Correlations with background variables
There were a number of significant correlations between identification factors and background variables.

Sex: Aspiration to the role of the female pop singer (Factor 2) was associated with being female; aspiration to the role of the space hero (Factor 5) was greater for boys; aspiration to the roles of the working-class characters of *Coronation Street* was greatest in girls; boys aspired to the role of the sports commentator more than girls; and girls aspired to the role of Vincent more frequently than did boys. The fact that boys reject the role of the female pop singer is not surprising in view of the nature of sex-typing in boys. The boy's permitted role behaviour does not include femininity. Since it is not socially taboo for girls to dress and behave in a somewhat masculine manner, the lack of correlation of Factor 1 (which contains several male popular singers) with sex is not surprising. Although one might expect that boys aspire to the role of the sports commentator more than girls since it is an almost exclusively male domain, the complete lack of a relationship between sex and aspiration to the role of a football hero is unexpected. Whether it would equally be true that there would be no sex differences in aspirations to the roles of lady athletes is debatable. Certainly, there are many girls who attend football matches and are interested in the game but, alongside this, there is little active participation in

TABLE 8.1
Correlations between scores on each aspiration choice factor and certain background variables

Factor Number	Background Variable				
	Sex	Age	Class	Number Siblings	Birth Order
1	−.08	−.12	.01	−.03	−.06
2	−.35	.25	.13	.01	−.16
3	−.04	−.01	.02	−.06	−.05
4	−.02	−.10	−.11	−.05	−.02
5	−.27	.00	−.01	−.05	.12
6	−.24	−.01	.18	−.07	−.12
7	−.17	−.11	−.13	.03	−.01
8	−.13	−.06	.01	.03	−.09
9	−.13	.19	−.01	−.06	−.01
10	−.24	−.01	.18	−.07	−.12
11	−.17	−.11	−.13	.03	−.01
12	.30	−.25	.01	−.01	.05
13	−.38	−.10	−.12	.12	−.06
14	.11	.15	.06	−.03	.05
15	.21	.17	−.01	−.05	.03
Sex	−				
Age	−.10	−			
Class	−.06	.04	−		
Number Siblings	−.23	−.11	.16	−	
Birth Order	.12	−.02	−.18	−.02	−

the sport by females. Girls are more attracted than boys to the roles of the working-class characters of *Coronation Street*. This may be due to a general lower level of ambition in the female sub-sample. Most interesting of all, from the point of view of the concern with violence in the mass media, is the lack of sex differences in aspiration to the roles of the aggressive hero. Only in the case of the space heroes (Dr Who and Captain Kirk) was there any hint that boys preferred the fictional hero. Since Dr Who is perhaps only marginally in the category of aggressive hero (his actual involvement in the use of force is absolutely minimal), it would be unwise to use this one correlation as argument in favour of the hypothesis that boys prefer aggressive heroes. The character

Vincent's role was more highly coveted by girls than by boys. The reason for this is clearly unrelated to a male preference for aggressive models and a possible explanation is that this character is highly protective in nature and that this is particularly attractive to girls.

The preference of girls, on Factor 12, for the individuals unified earlier under the heading of 'professional orientation', of course, could be claimed to be simply the result of the tendency of males to reject aspiration to roles occupied by females. It is unreasonable to presume that the level of professional aspiration in girls is greater than in boys. However, it should be remembered that the professions concerned (teacher and doctor) are amongst those most readily available to girls.

Age: Although the age range of the sample was limited to roughly a three-year span, a number of correlations between aspiration choices and age were found. Older children were more inclined to aspire to be like the female pop singers (Factor 2) than younger children. This might reflect the change from childhood to adolescence and greater involvement in the media specifically aimed at this age group. However, this does not offer an obvious explanation of the lack of a significant correlation between age and Factor 1 (Mick Jagger,John Lennon, etc). This might be explained on the basis that although Factor 1 individuals obviously are concerned with pop music, their extreme behaviour and appearance might serve to alienate the adolescent who has not pulled free of his family environment. Factor 14 and 15 personalities are aspired to most by younger children.

However, the most interesting age correlation is that personal acquaintances (friends, father and mother) are most aspired to by the younger child. If adolescence is, in part, a period of rebellion against the home and family, then the rejection of parents with increasing age can readily be understood. Unfortunately, this does not explain why aspirations to be like a best friend should decrease. Perhaps a better interpretation in the light of this would be to argue that adolescence is a period of self-assertion, of freeing oneself from dependence upon others. This would explain why aspiration to be like a friend as well as like parents should decline with age.

Social Class: Social class might be expected to relate strongly to aspiration choices. It might be expected that working-class children

— since they are more likely to experience overt violence than middle-class children — would tend to identify more with the aggressive hero, etc. Virtually all such expectancies were disconfirmed except that there was a tendency for working-class children to aspire to the roles of the *Coronation Street* characters as defined in Factor 6. It is not surprising that it is the working-class children who aspire to the roles of these characters since one would not expect that the middle-class child would be overly keen to engage in downward class changes. None of the other characters and personalities are so obviously working-class. Of course, some footballers, pop singers, and policemen are of working-class origins but in attaining these roles they have pulled themselves out of this rigid class category, and for this reason it might be expected that class and aspiration to this sort of role are not related.

Family structure: Family size did not correlate significantly with scores on any of the factors. Birth order (whether first-born/only-born or later-born) correlated significantly with just one factor. The later-born child tended to aspire to the status of the female pop singer more. This was partly due to the fact that there tended to be more later-born girls than boys in the sample since when sex was partialled out the correlation diminished to —.130 from —.165. It might be suggested that the older sibling may meet much more resistance to the introduction of pop-relevant materials (for example, records, photographs and magazines) into the home than the younger sibling who has the advantage that his older sibling may have overcome some of this resistance and that he need not be fighting a lone battle.

DISCUSSION AND CONCLUSION

It can be confidently stated that attraction to the roles of aggressive mass media characters is not solely due to their aggressiveness. Factors 3, 4, 5, 8 and 11 are all concerned in part with the mass media aggressive hero, but each factor has its own particular characteristics. For example, Factor 3, which reflects both real persons and fictional characters, seemed to concern verbal rather than physical aggression. The differences in factor interpretation imply strongly that there is no general 'aggressive' hero which is attractive to children.

Factor 3 is also interesting because it suggests that in some circumstances the variance in identification with mass media figures is shared by real-life and fictional individuals. Not that this suggests that the child viewer cannot perceive the difference between reality and fantasy as has been implied many times (for example, Schramm, Lyle and Parker, 1961), but simply that some real-life individuals and some fantasy characters share the defining characteristics of the factor. The question of whether children confuse reality with fantasy is a different one, further complicated by the problems involved in trying to define what is fantasy and what is reality. For example, in some ways certain of the naturalistic crime series are more relevant to real-life than quiz games, but the quiz game is real while the crime series is fantasy. The view of life reflected by the quiz game — if adopted — would be equally, if not more unacceptable. The fact that the real-life personality and the fictional character share characteristics does not mean that the child considers that there is no difference between the two.

The relationship between age trends and rejection of personal or local models, in Chaney's (1970) terminology, is important from the point of view of the relative importance of the mass media to the child. Noble (1971) has argued that because delinquents did not perceive themselves to be more like male television heroes than a control group but wanted to be less like their fathers and best friends than a control group, the television hero is a more salient identification figure for the delinquent than the non-delinquent control. The argument being not that the delinquent identifies more with the mass media hero but that he identifies less with his family and friends. If this argument has any validity then it suggests that since in the present study the older children become the less they are dependent upon personal models, mass media models are more salient for the older adolescent. On the other hand, only aspirations to the role of the female pop singer increased with age. Certainly, the earlier argument about the effects of identification on real-life violence would tend to support this conclusion.

Maccoby and Wilson (1957) hypothesized that the amount and kind of material a viewer learns from a movie is in part a function of his choice of a character in the movie with whom to identify himself. They found that viewers identified themselves with the like-sexed leading character and were more likely to choose the protagonist whose social class corresponded with the viewer's aspired social class than his actual social class. More of the character's actions were remembered if the character was identified with. Although these results come from fairly simple laboratory studies, they do accord fairly well with the present findings. On the other hand, this study suggests that the results may be better understood in slightly different terms. There was some evidence to suggest that the working-class characters of *Coronation Street* were identified with more by the working-class viewer than by the middle-class viewer. This supports Maccoby and Wilson's findings. Unfortunately, the reverse is not true. The many factors which are associated with essentially middle-class characters (for example, Factors 4 and 11) are not associated with class to any significant degree. Thus the middle class do not prefer middle-class characters but they reject working-class characters. This suggests that class is influential only in so far as the middle-class child will reject working-class characters. The same sort of argument applies to sex differences in preference for identification figures. Girls were attracted to both male and female characters and personalities whereas boys were only attracted to male personalities. It seems that boys are likely to reject opposite sexed heroes, but girls did not make such a discrimination. Clearly these findings extend those of Macoby and Wilson.

There is plenty of scope for repetition and extension of these findings. Interpretation at times was made difficult by the lack of sufficient variety in the mass media figures used. This has already been discussed. Careful and systematic attention needs to be paid to sorting out relevant mass media figures to overcome the problem.

Finally, the results of this study offer some suggestions for improvements in research into mass communications. It is clear that identifications with mass media characters and personalities are rather more subtle than has been implied by previous research. Certainly there is more than one kind of aggressive hero although researchers have often treated them in much the same manner. This is partly a consequence of there being a very gross view of the relationship between the media and real-life aggression. Aggression is frequently regarded as being a unitary thing and as a consequence aggressive heroes are regarded as being the same. Perhaps the present research will lead to a more sophisticated approach.

REFERENCES

Ancona, L and *Fontanesi, M* (1967), 'Analisi delle relazioni dinamiche tra effetto catartico ed effetto frustrante di uno stimulo cinematografico emotivo', *Contributi dell' Istituto di Psicologia*, XXVIII, 30-48.

Bandura, A and *Huston, A* (1961), 'Identification as a process of incidental learning' *Journal of Abnormal and Social Psychology*, LXIII, 2, 311-18.

British Broadcasting Corporation (1962), 'Violence in television programmes', *Television Q*, I, 61-3.

Cumberbatch, G and *Howitt, D* (1971), 'The effects of film hero identification on the moral values of adolescents', mimeo, Centre for Mass Communication Research, University of Leicester.

Freeman, L (1961), 'Daydream in a vacuum tube', in Schramm, Lyle and Parker, *Television in the lives of our children*, Stanford University Press, Stanford.

Glucksmann, A (1971), *Violence on the screen*, British Film Institute, London.

Goffman, E (1963), *Stigma*, Prentice-Hall, Englewood Cliffs, NJ.

Halloran, J (1967), *Attitude formation and change*, Leicester University Press.

Halloran, J (1968), *The effects of mass communication*, Leicester University Press.

Halloran, J, Brown, R and *Chaney, D* (1970), *Television and delinquency*, Leicester University Press.

Himmelweit, H, Oppenheim, A, and *Vince, P* (1958), *Television and the child*, Oxford University Press, London.

Howitt, D, and *Cumberbatch, G* (1972), 'Affective feeling for a film character and evaluation of an anti-social act', *British Journal of Social and Clinical Psychology*, XI, 102-8.

Klapper, J (1960), *The Effects of Mass Communication*, Free Press, New York.

Maccoby, E and *Wilson, W* (1957), 'Identification and observational learning from films', *Journal of Abnormal and Social Psychology*, LV, 76-87.

Noble, G (1971), 'Some comments on the nature of delinquents' identification with television heroes, fathers and best friends', *British Journal of Social and Clinical Psychology*, X, 172-80.

Schramm, W, Lyle, J and *Parker, E* (1961), *Television in the lives of our children*, Stanford University Press, Stanford.

9

The Family as a Mediator of Television's Effects

J R Brown and O Linné

Viewing has at least three facets to its context: temporal, physical and social. For the child most viewing takes place in the early afternoon and evening, although Saturday morning is becoming increasingly popular as a time to view. Most viewing takes place in the child's own home, usually in a ground-floor room which also serves as the general 'living room'. And the social context of viewing is usually formed by other family members.

In fact the usual temporal and physical contexts of viewing tend to maximize the family as a most dominant element in the social context and this is important because both the family and mass media, of which the most salient is television, are recognized agencies of socialization.[1] How do they influence the child? We argue, and present evidence to support our argument, that the family acts as a filter to the child's experience of television. Furthermore, this filtering process actively affects the type of influence television has on the child.

Before considering the interaction of family and television, and its resultant influences upon the child, it is worth outlining some of the attributes and influences of the family and television. In most cultures the family plays a dominant role in socializing children. Essential to the infant is human support. Equally essential, if the child is to become an adult acceptable to 'society', is a rigorous training period which 'shapes' his behaviour in a most general sense so that it 'fits' a particular culture of society. Since usually the child is born into a family there is now a certain inevitability that the family unit becomes both the location for and the main instrument of training during this period. Members of the nuclear family are able to monitor the child's progress, using both positive and negative reinforcement to ensure that he or she keeps on the 'right lines'. They can also to some extent monitor and control the stimulation and information available to the child.

Television programmes provide a wide range of stimulation and information: models of behaviour, attitudes, opinions, accents, etc. It is understandable that television is often blamed for the child's bad behaviour since it can be seen as a fifth columnist, sitting in the very centre of the family and giving out messages and suggestions which may conflict with family objectives. Thus there is, and has been for some time, concern expressed about the effects of television upon children, and the effects of television upon the family. In spite of this the majority of families in Western industrialized society (roughly 93 per cent of households in the United Kingdom) have opted for ownership. Having introduced an independent agency of socialization into the home, the family makes adaptations. At one extreme we hear of parents who supposedly hand over *in toto* their socializing role.[2] At the other extreme parents attempt deliberately to use television as a tool in the training process which they, as parents, mastermind.

Research into mass media has many foci; the audience is only one. And audience research is now underpinned by a desire to describe more clearly the effects process as the outcome of a complex interaction between the individual and the medium. Early effects studies showed a tendency for the family to make adjustments to television which did not drastically influence the overall pattern of family interaction. For example, a British study (*Belson,* 1967) revealed that the amount of time a family spent together was not changed by television, but it was reorganized.[3] Recently Bronfenbrenner argued that television has produced an overall decrease in meaningful conversation between children and parents:

> The major impact of television is not the behaviour it produces, but the behaviour it prevents. When the television set is on, it freezes everybody; they're all expressionless, focused on the image on the screen, and everything that used to go on between people — the games, the arguments, the emotional scenes, out of which personality and ability develop — is stopped. So when you turn on television, you turn off the process of making human beings human. (*Bronfenbrenner,* 1973)

We disagree with this rather stark presentation. The 'frozen', 'expressionless' viewer is a stereotype applied to others but not oneself. Perhaps more importantly, we disagree with the notion of television 'turning off' the socialization process. Bronfenbrenner himself has outlined the formidable power brought to bear on the child when all agencies of socialization act in concert (*Bronfenbrenner*, 1971), but this certainly does not justify the assumption that conflict between agencies negates the process. In fact his own evidence indicates that when agencies conflict the result is a wider range of 'personalities', 'abilities', and, particularly, a wider range of attitudes to authority in all its embodiments. Whether one favours the outcome of a rigorous unidirectional socialization process or an admittedly more confused and confusing process is, of course, a matter of personal values.[4]

Perhaps the last word should be given to Weiss who, after assessing all earlier studies of television's effects upon the family, concluded that: 'Television is more likely to reinforce or bring to the surface existing family relations than to create new ones.' (*Weiss*, 1969) In other words television, at most, pushes families in the direction they were clearly going.

An alternative question to 'How does television affect families?' is 'How do families use television?' From this perspective the family is seen as active, making decisions based upon evaluation of content and individual reactions to it. In research terms this reorientation leads to many specific questions. How are decisions about television taken within the family? What satisfactions are gained from family viewing and how do they differ from those gained from individual viewing? At a more sophisticated level of conceptualization we can begin to consider the functional relationship which exists between family and television, in particular the manifest and latent functions of family viewing from the perspective of socialization.[5] And this leads us to explore the influence of, for want of a better term, family ethos, and family socialization objectives upon the child-television relationship: that is, mediation of the effects process by the intervention of certain aspects of the child's family experience. The question, 'How does the audience member use television?' does not mean that we are no longer interested in the effects process, a mistaken view held by some opponents of this approach. It is rather a step towards understanding that process, one which gives the viewer status as an active element rather than a pawn who is nudged around by a series of forceful directives.

So far we have suggested that television and family are agencies of socialization which often act upon the child at the same point in space and time. Furthermore, they intermesh although they may be in varying degrees of conflict with each other. We have briefly considered the influence of television upon the family and the way the family uses television.

In order to assess the outcome of family and television interaction in socialization we must specify quite clearly a model of the interaction process and then consider the operations of the model and how far the model fits the 'real world' of family life and child-rearing. We suggest a very simple model which has a long history of use in the behavioural sciences. This is the 'Stimulus'-'Intervening Variable'-'Response' model in which a particular stimulus is associated with a particular response, but the nature of the response is modified by some third feature of the process: a third variable, or set of variables, is said to 'intervene' in the process.

In our application of the S-IV-R model television is the stimulus. (Television can only stimulate, unlike family and child which can both stimulate and respond to stimulation.) The family is represented as a complex of intervening variables and the child responds, experientially or behaviourally, at varying time intervals during and after stimulation. Of course, we could argue that S should be the family, passing out directives, the effects of which are influenced by the intervention of television. Both models would perhaps fit. But since family intervention is under more direct control of the individual parent than is television and its content, it seems reasonable to select a model which, if successfully applied, allows the individual not only an understanding but some degree of control over the process. Additionally it is arguable that since the family can respond to the medium and its content, and can also monitor the child's behaviour, the family is potentially the greater source of influence on the child. And, of course, for those who argue that in some cases the family plays no role we can adapt our model by giving the intervening variable a zero rating, that is, the intervention has no observable effect upon the SR process.

The kind of conceptualization outlined above encouraged us both, independently, to study the family context of children's viewing. One of us has been concerned to study the family in an attempt to isolate measurable features of it which might be expected to act as intervening variables. The other has conducted a study of the effects process which can be seen as an application of the S-IV-R model outlined above. Both studies have been reported in detail elsewhere (*Linné*, 1971: *Brown et al.*, 1974; *Brown*, 1974(*a*)) and only general findings can be described in the present paper.

The Leeds study was not primarily concerned with the effects of television upon the child. Its main objective was to produce a set of measuring instruments relevant to the family's 'intervening' role, an assumption being that these instruments could then be used in effects studies.

Even if we simply sit back in our chairs and think about how the family can intervene, many possibilities present themselves; for example, the amount of freedom the child is allowed in selecting programmes, the general or specific rules parents impose on their children's viewing, the frequency of discussion and comments on the programmes. And overriding these specific factors there is a more general, amorphous, feature; the family ethos. By this we mean the 'feel' of the family which, presumably, is generated by the interplay of each facet of family life. Just as numerous hypotheses present themselves, so there are numerous routes towards producing objective measures of family influence. Each method has its limitations and advantages. The Leeds research group decided to use a small-scale survey based upon detailed qualitative research.[6] After the initial qualitative stage, which gave a realistic orientation to the problems and a grasp of the language mothers use to discuss children and television, a list was produced of 300 statements about children and television. The items were reduced, first subjectively, and then by piloting them on two groups of fifty mothers. Fifty-seven statements which were fairly independent of each other were included in a final inventory. They represented as nearly as possible all points of view expressed by mothers.

Questions about viewing habits, attitudes to other media, and family social background, were included in a questionnaire along with the list of statements to which mothers would be asked to express their reaction. Interviews were conducted with 450 mothers of nine-year-old children selected so that they were representative of women in this category. The Leeds team were looking for measures of intervention in terms of matenal attitude. Maternal attitude might be expected to embody not only specific features of intervention, control, rules, etc, but also the more amorphous notion of 'ethos'.

By statistically analysing[7] the mothers' degree of agreement they explored the dimensions involved in the mothers' attitudes to and understanding of children's television use.

Six distinct dimensions emerged from this study. Descriptions of the dimensions are given in Figure 9.1.

FIGURE 9.1
Mothers' Attitudes to Children and Television

Dimension I   Suggestive of a protective attitude to the child, consistent with the view that television is often unsuitable for a young audience.

Dimension II   Suggestive of a belief that children easily become 'addicted' to television.

Dimension III   Suggestive of a liberal approach, allowing the child to select his own viewing pattern.

Dimension IV   Suggestive of a positive attitude to television as a medium providing entertainment, relaxation and information for children.

Dimension V   Suggestive of a positive attitude to television as a medium which stimulates the child and encourages him to consider the realities of life.

Dimension VI   Suggestive of the deliberate use of television in socializing the child, a cluster which represents frequent evaluation of content by parents in the child's presence.

The attitude clusters were converted into measuring scales which can be used in future research. Also, each mother was given a score on each scale and two further sets of analyses were conducted. Firstly the research showed that the scales related to other features of family behaviour and background. For example, Scale VI measuring a fairly deliberate use of TV content in order to socialize the child, has some interesting relationships. Although unrelated to the amount of television viewed by the child or the mother, VI is clearly related to the amount of the child's viewing which he does in the company of his mother. Those who have a protective attitude to the child (Scale I) tend to discuss programme content when the programme is over, whilst lower scorers on this scale discuss the programme during and after its airing. Numerous relationships of this type indicate that the scales are sensitive to those aspects of medium, content and family which interact to create the child's experience and understanding of television.

Of course, what the Leeds research does not show is that these measures of maternal attitude, even though they are related to viewing behaviour, child content preferences, etc, will influence the effects process. We feel that they are extremely suitable candidates for inclusion as intervening variables in effects studies (*Brown*, 1974b). Whether our assumptions are justified, and maternal attitudes do work in this way, must depend upon the outcome of further research.

The second study to be described was designed by Linné and financed by Sveriges Radio (*Linné*, 1971). Whereas the Leeds team decided to approach the effects process gradually, undertaking a range of studies (*Brown et al.*, 1972-4) directed towards exploring the child's experience of television and producing measuring instruments for manipulation as intervening variables in a further sequence of effects studies, Linné's choice was a direct investigation of the effects process as such. The study was small-scale in terms of sample, thirty-four children and their mothers, but covered a wide range of variables. The point of contact between the two studies is not method or approach to the problem, but a shared desire to explore the utility of the S-IV-R model as a basis for effects studies. This is also the basis for our present collaborative paper. Linné's exploration of the family as an 'intervener' involved a totally different research approach to that used in Leeds. We now describe the Swedish study and then attempt to draw conclusions from the combined outcomes of both studes.

In the spring of 1968 the Audience Research Department of Sveriges Radio conducted a study of the social habits and media behaviour of three- to six-year olds (*Feilitzen* and *Linné*, 1968). Their sample of 700 children was representative of that age group in Sweden; data were collected by intensive questioning of their mothers. During the late sixties and early seventies researchers became aware of an increasing concern that televised violence is linked to aggressive anti-social behaviour amongst children. Many studies were undertaken in American and Europe in an attempt to throw light on this socially important question. The Swedish study also explored the question of a linkage between violent content and aggression. By exploiting the 1968 survey a small but well-defined group of five- to six-year-old children was located which might be used in a further exploration of the violence-aggression question. The 1968 study provided a wealth of information about the social and family background of the children. Thus by experimenting with this small, select sample it was possible to explore the influence of family variables upon the effects process as if they were intervening variables.

The study may be described as semi-experimental. In the outline of research design given below, the experimental part is marked off by the inner rectangle. Remaining parts of the design are ascribable to the intensive study.

FIGURE 9.2

Low-exposed children	High-exposed children	Mothers
1 Knowledge test and rating test	1 Knowledge test and rating test	1 Questionnaires on Exposure to TV
2 Rating test	2 Rating test	2 Attitude test on developing children's TV tastes
3 Agression test (half the group)	3 Aggression test (half the group)	3 Questionnaire on receiving situation for for *High Chaparral*
FILM together with mothers	*FILM* together with mothers	*FILM* together with children
4 Aggression test (other half of group)	4 Aggression test (other half of the group)	
5 Comprehension test	5 Comprehension test	4 Comprehension test
		5 Questionnaire on background variables

All of the children lived in Stockholm; girls and boys were equally represented in the various groups. Low-exposure children had seen half or less of the *High Chaparral* series; high-exposure had seen 75 per cent or more of the series. An advantage of working with the five- to six-year-old is that, in Sweden, he or she is still not open to the influence of school. Also, his diet of violent material is very much limited to television; books, cinema and comics have yet to intrude. The children and mothers arrived in groups ranging from two to five pairs. Tests were administered to the children individually in separate rooms located near the room where the mothers were. After the first tests the children were taken back by their interviewers to this room, where children and mothers could watch the film together. Following the film each child returned with its interviewer to the first room to complete the testing procedure. In that way none of the children could communicate with and be influenced by one another or by their mothers.

The film shown was a sequence about fifteen minutes long taken from an instalment of *High Chaparral* which Sveriges Radio had not telecast. Though short, it had continuity of action: Victoria Cannon, wife of one of the series' main characters, John Cannon, was kidnapped by a Confederate officer after he had shot down her brother, Manolite Montoya. The sequence, which was put together from cuts, was considered by the test management to be representative of the series.

Various tests indicated in Figure 9.2 are briefly described below:

Children

1 *Knowledge test* Stills of the main characters in *High Chaparral*. The children were asked to name characters and pick those they liked most and least. The test was designed to find out how much the children had learned about the characters.

2 *Rating test* Stills of Indians and cowboys. The children were asked to evaluate them. The object of this test was to measure what effect *High Chaparral* may have had on the shaping of norms.

3 *Aggression test* Drawings of a child in three situations. The subject children were told a story about how a boy/girl had been given a bicycle but shortly thereafter robbed of it by another boy/girl. They were asked to choose between three given behaviours to indicate preference for how the child in the story should resolve this conflict situation. Choice of aggressive solutions could be related to exposure data and experimental condition.

In this way the tests can be analysed from a short-term effects perspective or a long-term effects perspective.

4 *Comprehensive test* Five stills from the film. The children were asked to arrange these in the chronological order in which they appeared in the film. The test provides a measure of the child's ability to recreate the plot of this type of film.

Additional to the data from these instruments were the results from the 1968 survey which, it will be recalled, had provided initial contact with mothers and children.

Because of the various background variables this study provides many clues to the role family can play in influencing the effects process. However, before considering these findings we summarize the study's primary findings on long- and short-term effects.

In the experimental part of the study the objective was to measure whether children who watched a programme containing 'justifiable' fictional violence were more inclined to choose aggressive behaviour to resolve a conflict situation than children who had not watched the film. This short-term effects experiment produced no significant[8] difference between the two groups. Hence the exposure to the violent content did not produce short-term effects in the form of an increased tendency to choose an aggressive solution to a conflict situation.

Summarizing the data on possible long-term effects of the *High Chaparral* series produces the following picture.

By comparison with the low-exposed children, a greater proportion of the high-exposed selected the more aggressive behaviour in the conflict situation covered by the test. Further, the high-exposed were familiar with more main characters in the series and were also more emotionally attached to them. On the other hand, the two exposure groups did not differ on the other rating questions concerned with Indians and cowboys. Both groups regarded the cowboy as a nicer person than the Indian. In addition, they believed an Indian shoots more than a cowboy and, lastly, they felt that the cowboy held 'the right to shoot'.

So far, then, the study has shown that the high-exposure child has a greater tendency to select an aggressive solution to the conflict test. How do the two groups of children differ on other variables? Firstly, they do not differ on comprehension. Both groups produced low scores on the comprehension test. Similarly, their mothers produced uniform, although considerably higher, scores on the comprehension test. Both groups, on the mothers' accounts, had shown the same number of fear reactions to the programmes. However, as we move towards the family influence variables differences begin to emerge more clearly. The high-exposure group are also more highly exposed to television as a whole than is the low-exposure group. Their mothers are also more highly exposed and more favourably disposed towards television Westerns. The mothers of high-exposure children impose fewer restrictions on their children's viewing, believing that television is fairly harmless and that the child should have the freedom to range over its content.

A striking finding is that the high-exposure child keeps track of *High Chaparral* broadcasts, whilst the low-exposure child tends to view them by chance or is told about the programme by other members of his family. However, the family context becomes clearest when analyses are conducted on the time that the child views and its consequences. At the time of this study *High Chaparral* was aired in the evening and repeated during the afternoon. Not only did high-exposure children view the pro-gramme in the evening more often than low-exposure children, they tended to watch the programme both times it was broadcast. This finding amply validates the high-low exposure groupings, but what of its implications? Mothers were asked what their children did immediately after watching *High Chaparral*. The majority of low-exposure children played with friends or talked about the programme; none of them went to bed. And yet the majority (ten out of eighteen) of high-exposure children went to bed immediately after viewing the programme. A further question shows that eleven of these children had already been washed and changed, ready for bed, prior to watching *High Chaparral*.

We have seen that the high-exposure child, in this study, tended to select an aggressive solution to the conflict problem. What feature of the high-exposure group's background discriminates between those choosing an aggressive solution and those choosing a non-aggressive solution? It is, in fact, whether or not the child is sent to bed immediately after his exposure to the programme. None of the high-exposure children who selected a non-aggressive solution to conflict were washed and in pyjamas before watching the programme. Almost all of the aggressive solution children were.

Even if this finding was replicated using very large groups of children, it would not prove a causal relationship. However, it clearly demonstrates the way a finding can be made more understandable (and more pronounced) by considering family variables. Again, the mechanism at work might be not so much direct family influence as an indirect influence. Both groups of children have been frightened by the programme. The low-exposure children and the high-exposure children who choose non-aggressive solutions have been given the opportunity to dissipate this fear through play or talk. Those who selected aggressive solutions were not given that opportunity. Thus one hypothesis which explains the finding depends upon dissipation of arousal through play and talk, rather than direct family influence as such. However, it is clear from the study that the opportunity to dissipate arousal is under the control of the child's parents and family.

Detailed linkages between the two studies are beyond the scope of this paper. However, some surface relationships are of interest. Linné has shown that a number of family background variables can be linked directly, or through exposure, to a relationship between viewing a programme containing violent scenes and choosing an aggressive solution to a conflict problem. That is, family background can be regarded as a set of variables which mediate between content and effects. Here results also show that the family can facilitate or inhibit the effects.

Not only does the Swedish study reveal the potential influence of clearly behavioural aspects of the family — Who viewed what? When was it viewed? Did the child go straight to bed after viewing? — it also shows that these features are related to more general aspects of the family. In a sense the child can be seen as if following a family pattern which is largely established by the parents. The child who is a frequent viewer of *High Chaparral* (and hence heavily exposed to television in general) is usually embedded in a family where the mother is positively disposed towards *High Chaparral* and is generally non-restrictive in terms of the child's viewing. Similarly the six dimensions of maternal attitude revealed by the Leeds study are significantly related to features of the child's family background, including rules about viewing, bedtimes, whether and when programmes are discussed within the family, whether television causes conflict at mealtimes and bedtime, and several other features of family life. Clearly then both studies show relationships between attitudes and behaviour within the family and, in addition, Linné's work has already revealed the potential of creating family variables of both types as mediators of the effects process.

In summary we have argued that the family can act as an intervening variable in the effects process. We have presented results from one study which demonstrates that factors under the control of parents are capable of mediating the effects of television on younger children. Furthermore, we have suggested that these factors and other features of the family context of viewing are correlates of the mothers' attitudes to children and television. Therefore, we predict that mothers' attitudes can be usefully incorporated into future effects studies as intervening variables.

One further point should be made. We have already suggested that parents have more control over the atmosphere in which children view than they do over television content. Naturally this does not negate the broadcaster's responsibility for his programme and its consequences. However, it is possible that if television does have avoidable negative consequences we can learn how to control them more quickly by investigating the role of the family. Whilst studies of televised violence and its relationship to aggression were being conducted, evidence began to emerge that televised violence might be a special case of a much more prevalent form of content which itself could be equally clearly related to youthful aggression. This type of content is 'information rich', that is, it consists of rapid action, movement, changes in camera angle etc. The report to the Surgeon General (1972) states:

> If generalized arousal is verified either as the single or as a contributing factor, the interpretation of many findings as reflecting exclusively the instigating effects of aggressive content would have to be modified. However, what can now be said specifically about the capacity of violent or aggressive content to instigate aggressiveness would not be greatly affected. Instead such effects of such content to a greater or lesser degree would become a special case of a more general phenomenon capable of more varied effects.

This new orientation considerably opens out the question of television's effects. We are, it seems, only beginning to understand the process by which television influences our children. Focus on the family might enable us to control the process before we have a detailed explanation of how it works.

NOTES

1 Socialization is a name for the process by which a child becomes shaped into an adult, ie he gains a stock of information, attitudes, values, opinions, habits, social and individual behaviours. The four dominant forces or agencies in this process are thought to be: family, peer group, school and mass media.
2 Behaviour which is quite impossible unless the parents abandon the child and, paradoxically, even this presents a clear and impressive example of adult and parental behaviour.
3 One exception to this finding was that the teen-age family member did spend less time with his family after the onset of television. Of course, other cultural factors were at work but it is intriguing to note that this change in teen-age behaviour coincided with the introduction of the label 'teen-ager'.
4 Unless, of course, you are the result of a unidirectional process in which case it is almost meaningless to refer to personal values as distinct from cultural or societal values since, by definition, when the process is working well, all values are consistent with those of authority.
5 The fairly clear conceptual tools of functional analysis have become confused in their application to media studies. Here we use 'manifest' and 'latent' to mean conscious deliberate use of media with a particular goal in mind (socialization) as against non-conscious non-deliberate sources of influence on the socialization process. Thus although the parents' comments on, say, an election broadcast are quite conscious and deliberate they could be serving a latent function in the socialization process.
6 Qualitative research involves the exploration of ideas and language in the absence of 'hard' numbers. In this case the qualitative stage of the study consisted of several group discussions with mothers. Six or seven mothers constituted a group. They would meet in a house similar to their own and be encouraged to talk about their children and television. Discussions lasted from one and a half to four hours. Each discussion was recorded on audio-tape for later analysis.
7 The procedure used was McQuitty's Elementary Linkage analysis (*McQuitty*, 1957) followed by cluster refinement towards the optimization of cluster reliability (Coefficient Alpha) and average intercorrelation between cluster items (*McKennell*, 1970).
8 Statistically significant, that is the results did not differ from chance. In the normal non-statistical sense of the word this finding is quite significant.

REFERENCES

Belson, W A (1967), *The Impact of Television*, Crosby, Lockwood, London.
Bronfenbrenner, U (1973), in Clayre, *The Impact of Broadcasting*, Compton Russell, London.

Bronfenbrenner, U (1971), *Two Worlds of Childhood: USA and USSR,* Allen and Unwin, London.

Brown, J R, Cramond, J K and *Wilde, R J* (1972-4), Children and Television Project, Progress reports, mimeo, University of Leeds.

Brown, J R, Wilde, R J and *Cramond, J K* (1974), 'Television in the Family Context: A Study of Maternal Attitudes and Influence', paper presented to the British Psychological Society.

Brown, J R (1974 a), 'Children and Television: Interpersonal and Intrapersonal Features of the Effects Process', mimeo, University of Leeds.

Brown, J R (1974 b), 'Child Socialization: The Family and Television', *Proceedings of the IXth General Assembly of the International Association for Mass Communications Research,* Karl Marx University, Leipzig.

von Feilitzen, C and *Linné, O* (1968), 'The Living Habits and Media Behaviour of 3-6-year-olds', Sveriges Radio Report.

Linné, O (1971). 'Reactions of Children to Violence on TV'. Sveriges Radio Report, Project 13/68.

McKennell, A (1970), 'Attitude Measurement: Use of Coefficient Alpha and Factor or Cluster Analysis', *Sociology*, IV. 2.

McQuitty, L L (1957), 'Elementary Linkage Analysis', *Educational and Psychological Measurement*, XVII, 207-29.

Rubinstein, E G Comstock, G and *Murray, J* (eds) (1971), *Television and Social Behavior*, Report to the Surgeon General's Scientific Committee on Television and Social Behavior, US Government Printing Office, Washington.

Weiss, W (1969), 'Effects of the Mass Media of Communication', in Lindzey and Aronson (eds), *The Handbook of Social Psychology,* V, 2nd Ed, Addison-Wesley, Reading, Mass.

10

The Family Environment and Adolescent Television Use

Jack McLeod and Jane Delano Brown

'*Twixt twelve and twenty are the years of confusion and doubt, We all have fears twixt twelve and twenty ...*' This quotation is from 'Twixt Twelve and Twenty', words and music by Aaron Schroeder and Fredda Gold, 1959 Spoone Music Corporation, and is reprinted by permission. It was a hit record of the late fifties recorded by the then top pop singer Pat Boone. Alas, the record is a collector's item today and was uncovered only after extensive sleuthing by musicologist-communication researcher Dean Ziemke. Mr Boone is to be seen most frequently today advertising jockey shorts (men's underwear) and children's laxatives on television.

It is paradoxical that most of the research on television and its effects has looked at two apparently contradictory outcomes for two different audiences: while it investigates the possible harmful effects of violent content on young children it has also been searching for the potentially beneficial effects on adult learning through news diffusion and public interest advertising. Perhaps in fairness we should reverse the emphasis by looking for positive effects on children and negative ones for older adults. At any rate, the result has been that communication research has neglected the study of adolescents, those between the ages of twelve and eighteen who are no longer children but who are also not yet adults.

The reasons for this neglect are not hard to find. According to the psycho-analytic doctrines of Freud and his followers of decades past, the child was pretty much a fixed quantity by the age of six. When it was later found that the 'latency' period between the ages of six and puberty that Freud had seen as a period of static quiescence was not so latent after all, attention shifted upward to late childhood. Psychological and child development research of the post World War II era focused on childhood and it was not surprising that communication research, being largely a borrowing field, followed their lead in the research of the 1950s. The child of twelve rather than the six-year-old became the fixed product. More recently, studies of intellectual and political development and change have suggested that socialization continues beyond puberty into adolescence and early adulthood.[1] As part of this trend, communication research has begun to investigate changes in television use during adolescence.

As Kurt Lewin observed many years ago, a phenomenon is best understood if it is studied while it is changing (*Lewin*, 1951). The rapid change associated with adolescence thus makes it an attractive arena for the study of communication behaviour. It is a period when the child anticipates the expectancies of adult roles and reacts to and sometimes adopts adult values and behaviours. Some of these values may have their origins in television content and, indeed, some communication behaviours may be a functional part of the process of moving from childhood to adulthood. Although still an empirical question, we should expect that these adolescent communication behaviours and their effects may have relatively long-term consequences for later adult behaviour.

The changing theoretical perspectives of communication research evidenced in the last decade have also increased the potential importance of studying adolescent television behaviour. The older stimulus-response models of communication effects implied the receiver was a relatively passive recipient of media messages; the helpless young child was a perfect example. More recently, however, communication research has moved away from such a simple model in the face of mounting evidence of its inadequacy. The focus on 'what media do to people' has given way to 'what people do with media'. Included in new models of communication processes are the orientations of people in the form of gratifications sought, attitudes toward the media, and so forth. The major point of communality in the new models is that they view audience members as *active* participants in the communication process, selecting and reacting to the content they receive. The activity of the adolescent is clearly more compatible with this view of the audience than is the more passive image of the young child.

Recent communication research has exhibited changes in the nature of effects studied that provides an additional basis for the focus on adolescence. While earlier research was limited in its concern with attitude change and at most to anti-social aggressive behaviour among children, the new research has broadened the outlook to include indirect and more subtle effects such as information processing, changing perceptions of reality and causality and occupational and sex-role stereotyping. While these effects can be effectively studied among younger children, it is during adolescence that these processes begin to show the serious consequences that will affect their adult lives.

DEPICTION OF ADOLESCENCE

Even though the period of adolescence between the ages of twelve and eighteen varies considerably for persons growing up in different societies and for those in different locations within the social structure of any given society, there are certain themes of adolescent development that are common to writers and researchers viewing adolescents in these various situations. First, the dependence on parental authority the child felt earlier will give way to greater freedom and independence as the parents begin to 'let go' during the adolescent years. There is a parallel increase in sociability with increasing interest in peer relationships that presumably shift the sources of influence on the adolescent away from the family. Thirdly, a rather rapid alteration of the adolescent's time budgeting occurs during these years, with more time being spent outside the home with age-mates. Along with this change comes a rejection of childish activities and the adoption of semi-adult values in recreation and life style.

Of course, the changing views regarding his or her occupational future will vary considerably across societies and classes. For most adolescents in most societies of the world the person's occupational future will be sealed with the ending of education and the start of work life before the end of adolescence. Most of the American youths whose behaviour we report here will finish secondary school and continue on to college during the adolescent period. For them, the realities of the occupational world will be delayed but at the same time they will be anticipating their future careers and making various accommodations to the expectations of the adult world. Whatever the situation, the adolescent years entail the development of a personal identity, through answering the classic question 'Who am I?" and through the selection of role models within or external to the family. The resolutions to these identity problems are probably determined by the forces of increasing differentiation between and within sex and social class boundaries. These social-cultural constraints become more salient as reality factors which operate to adjust and sometimes scale down the aspirations of early adolescence. It is pertinent to examine the role of the mass media in setting these aspirations and to investigate whether there are distinctive communication behaviour patterns associated with the various ways of 'settling' personal identity and future life style problems.

The adolescent period is usually as stressful for the parent as it is for the child. The parents are forced to adopt some kind of strategy to cope with the conflicts and changes evident in their adolescent. To ignore the problems and do nothing is one type of strategy. Other alternatives include the attempt to impose parental values on the child or, conversely, to encourage the child to explore and give encouragement for finding his or her own course of action. The effectiveness of these strategies is a major research question for all areas of socialization including the development of media use patterns.

RESEARCH QUESTIONS

The research on adolescent television behaviour we report here was developed from a socialization perspective which has as its key assumption that to understand human behaviour, we must specify its social origins and the processes by which it is learned and maintained (*McLeod* and *O'Keefe*, 1972). This demands the study of the socializing agent as well as the adolescent being socialized. In this case, we have examined the family as the focal point of the research, although the role of peers, siblings and schools may be other important sources of influence in developing the communication patterns of the adolescent.

This socialization perspective suggests the following set of questions regarding adolescent media behaviour:

1 Are there systematic changes in the media behaviour of youth during the years of adolescence? If there were no changes, of course, then all subsequent questions would be meaningless.

2 What learning models, if any, account for the emerging media patterns found for adolescents? Some experts have advised parents that 'example is the best teacher' for influencing children's media

behaviour, thus implying that imitative modelling is a sufficient condition for effect. However, reinforcement and other learning mechanisms may also account for adolescent media behaviour.

3 Do parents continue to have effects on their children's media behaviour beyond childhood into middle and late adolescence? If parental influence does decline during adolescence, which among these other agencies constitute the major source of influence? What part do other socialization agencies such as peers, schools and the media play in affecting media behaviour?

4 What are the effects of adolescent learning experiences and media patterns on other types of behaviours? While the study of adolescent media behaviour can be defended as legitimate in its own right, there is an implicit assumption that these patterns have some important consequences for the immediate situation and for later adult roles.

5 What is the relationship between adolescent media behaviour and the social-structural constraints that operate to shape the adolescent's intellectual, political and social development? What is the connection between the location of the adolescent's family in the social structure and the learning experiences of the adolescent? If we assume that the constraints of social structure (eg, growing up poor, black and female in an unjust society) impose reality upon the aspirations of youth, then we may investigate the possible relationships of such reality experiences to media behaviour. Various types of television exposure might either heighten or ameliorate the effects of reality confrontation, or conversely, the adolescent's media behaviour might be shaped by these experiences.

STUDY DESIGN

These questions have been examined as part of a media and youth change research programme at the Mass Communication Research Center of the University of Wisconsin. The data from three of these studies are reported here. The first, called the 'Political Socialization' study, was carried out in five Wisconsin cities varied in socio-economic level and ranging in population from about 17,000 to nearly 70,000.[2] The data consist of an interview with a parent

selected randomly from each of 1,292 families along with two
questionnaires completed six months apart by one of the children in
the family. About half the youth sample was twelve or thirteen
years old and the other half was fifteen or sixteen years old. Since
school attendance is mandatory for both age groups, the two age
levels were quite comparable on a number of demographic
characteristics.[3] As a precaution, however, appropriate controls
for socio-economic status (SES) and intelligence were introduced.

The second study, which we call here the 'Television Use' study,
combines data from two samples reported in the US Surgeon
General's Television and Social Behaviour series that investigated
the relationship between televised violence and anti-social
aggressive behaviour.[4] Adolescents in two different parts of the
United States filled out questionnaires that included information
about media exposure and reactions to television; included were
230 younger adolescents (twelve to thirteen years old) and 243 older
adolescents (fifteen to sixteen years old) from eight state-
supported schools in Prince Georges county, Maryland, and 68 and
83 adolescents of these ages in Middleton, Wisconsin. In the latter
sample, personal interviews were conducted with the mothers of
each of the adolescents. The two samples are combined for this
paper.

In order to extend our analyses beyond late adolescence into
early adulthood, a third set of data was extracted from our 'Young
Voter' study that includes 223 personal interviews with potential
first-time voters between the ages of eighteen and twenty four years
in Madison, Wisconsin.[5] Figure 10.1 shows the characteristics of
the samples from all three studies.

DEVELOPMENTAL CHANGES IN ADOLESCENT TELEVISION USE

Our first set of analyses attempted to establish whether there were
any systematic changes evident between early and late adolescence,
or, on the other hand, whether the pattern set down in childhood
would simply continue through adolescence. Ideally, longitudinal
data studying individual changes over a period of years would be
used. Our own data were limited to independent samples of two age
levels, thus making inferences more tentative and controls of greater
necessity. Differences between the early (twelve to thirteen year
olds) and middle (fifteen to sixteen years) adolescents are shown in

FIGURE 10.1
Description of Studies

	Political Socialization	Television Use Maryland	Wisconsin	Young Voter
Sample size and characteristics				
Early adolescents (12-13 yrs)	641	230	68	
Middle adolescents (15-16 yrs)	651	243	83	
Early adults (18-24 yrs)				223
Total N	1,292	473	151	223
Mothers Fathers	sampled randomly		151	
Population locale	Wis cities selected for SES and political diversity	Washington, DC suburb	Madison, Wis suburb	Madison, Wis
Population studied	state-supported school systems within five cities	eight state-supported schools	both state-supported schools in city	registered voters in city
Study design	longitudinal panel (two waves) self-administered questionnaire	self-administered questionnaire	longitudinal panel (two waves) self-administered questionnaire (child) interview (mother)	longitudinal panel (three waves) interview
Data reported here	T_2:Nov 1968	April 1970	T_2:October 1970	T_1:October 1972

Table 10.1. In order to make the results comparable across the two studies among the various television use measures, standard scores

have been used whereby each age and sex group's mean level of use is expressed as a departure from the grand (all groups) mean divided by the standard deviation for all respondents combined. The +40 for young adolescent boys, for example, indicates they are four-tenths of a standard deviation above the mean for all respondents on time spent with television.

TABLE 10.1
Adolescent's use of television (standard scores) by sex and age level

Television Use Index		*Political socialization study*			*Television use study*		
		Early Adoles-cents	Middle Adoles-cents	diff	Early Adoles-cents	Middle Adoles-cents	diff
Adolescent's	Boys	+40	−27	−67	+13	−05	−18
TV time	Girls	+36	−46	−82	+19	−27	−46
Adventure-	Boys	+29	−01	−30	+26	−09	−35
drama	Girls	+08	−28	−36	+07	−24	−31
Westerns	Boys	+21	−01	−22	+30	−14	−44
	Girls	+05	−24	−29	+08	−24	−32
Crime-	Boys	−	−	−	+36	+07	−29
detective	Girls	−	−	−	−01	−40	−39
Situation	Boys	+18	−19	−37	+15	−62	−77
comedies	Girls	+28	−24	−52	+64	−16	−80
Variety-	Boys	−	−	−	+21	−11	−32
comedy	Girls	−	−	−	+22	−29	−51
News-public	Boys	+14	+09	−05	+28	+14	−14
affairs	Girls	−17	−05	+12	−30	−11	+19
(Number of	Boys	(343)	(287)		(160)	(138)	
cases)	Girls	(298)	(364)		(150)·	(176)	

NOTE: Standard score entries are weighted cell means, setting the overall mean at zero and the standard deviation at one, for all four cells in each sample. Scores are calculated to two decimal places; decimals are omitted for simplicity. Statistical significance (.05 level) for differences between grades is: political socialization study, ± 16 or greater; television use study, ± 23 or greater.

Substantial decreases in viewing time from early to middle adolescence are shown for both the political socialization and television use youth samples in Table 10.1. This corroborates other research findings by Lyle and Hoffman (1971) in the United States and by Greenberg (1973) in Great Britain. There is also some evidence of increasing differentiation of television use by sex. While young adolescent boys and girls spent about equal amounts of time with television, the older girls watched television much less than any other group. This may indicate more rapid female maturation away from less sophisticated commercial television fare or it may merely mean they have stronger demands on their time away from the home television set.

Changes in specific programme types are also shown in Table 10.1. (Certain categories were not used in the political socialization study.) While a decline from early to middle adolescence is found in almost all comparisons, the greatest loss is shown for situation comedies and variety comedy shows. The only category to exhibit an increase is news and public affairs, and then only for girls. The deviation from other types of viewing preferences is significant, however, in that other analyses of these same studies, not shown here, have also found a clear, although small, increase in newspaper news reading among the middle adolescents.

Controls for socio-economic status and intelligence test scores do not alter the findings of Table 10.1. Adolescents with high IQ scores and, to a lesser extent, those from middle-class homes do watch less entertainment television and more public affairs content than the others, but these control variables do not differ in level in our two age samples so as to affect the results substantially. While the amount and kind of television used appear to undergo marked changes during adolescence, the internal responses to its content also undergo changes. The television use study adolescents were asked to indicate their reactions to 'television programmes with lots of action and adventure, like Westerns and crime shows'. Four types of cognitions were measured: perceived learning of aggression (learn how to get back at people; copy things I see people do); linkage of television violence to real life (tell about life the way it is; just like people I meet in real life); involvement in violent programming (I get carried away; sometimes forget that characters are just actors); and identification with violent characters (person most like to be, most like to see at movies, scored by degree to which actor is associated with aggression in roles).

Table 10.2 indicates standard scores for these cognitive reactions. Less reaction among the older adolescents is found on all four dimensions, but particularly in the perception of learning of aggression from television. Heightened sex-role differentiation is also evident in the table as girls are increasingly less likely to see television as a source of aggressive learning, or as a link to real life and they are less frequently identified with a violent actor. On the other hand, the older boys were even less likely than girls to report involvement in violent programming.

TABLE 10.2
Adolescent's level of cognitive reaction (standard scores) to television violence by sex and age (Television use study)

Reaction measure	Sex	Early Adoles-cents	Middle Adoles-cents	Diff.
Agrees that TV presents chance to	Boys	+36	+03	−33
learn anti-social behaviour	Girls	+19	−48	−67
Sees close similarity between	Boys	+14	−06	−20
TV violence and real life	Girls	+12	−17	−29
Becomes involved with characters	Boys	−09	−32	−23
and stories of action TV shows	Girls	+27	+14	−13
Identifies with violent	Boys	+54	+34	−20
TV character	Girls	−21	−62	−41
(Number of cases)	Boys	(160)	(150)	
	Girls	(138)	(176)	

NOTE See Table 10.1 note for explanation of standard scores. Statistical significance (.05 level) for differences between age levels is ± 23 or greater.

Other research, however, indicates that the motives for using television do not change very much over the adolescent period. Lyle and Hoffman show that both young and middle adolescents turn to television for entertainment, relaxation and relief from loneliness; neither age group is likely to seek television when the person is angry or when his feelings are hurt. Listening to music is a more likely outlet for these emotions. We can conclude, however, that there is sufficient evidence of systematic changes in television use and content preferences through adolescence to merit going further to study the origins of these developmental patterns.

LEARNING MODELS

The socialization perspective argues that it is necessary to specify the learning mechanisms involved in development if we are to understand fully the chain of functional relationships between social structural forces, socializing agents and the emerging behaviour of the person being socialized. We have chosen to use the term 'learning mechanism' rather than 'child-rearing practice' because the latter implies a conscious influencing effort by the socialization agent. Our research and that of others indicate that few parents make strong efforts to influence their children's television use. 'Learning process' not only allows for less conscious influence but it also places a more appropriate focus on learning rather than on teaching. While many types of learning may be posited, our work has involved but three types to date: *modelling, reinforcement* and *social interaction*.

Modelling

The simplest explanation of learning is that of modelling: through imitation the child adopts the behaviour of the parent or other socializing agent either through conscious attempts to emulate or simply because the agent's behaviour is the most salient pattern available. Unfortunately, modelling is easier to invoke than demonstrate. The early studies of children and television, for example, used the correlation between the child's media behaviour and that of the parent as evidence that 'parental example' has a direct influence on the child (*Schramm et al.,* 1961). It is logically unwise to consider parent-child correlations sufficient to establish causality of the modelling process. Such correlations are necessary, but are certainly not sufficient. Various third variables, such as the common social class of the parent and child, may account for the correlation. Another possibility is reverse causation — the child's behaviour may affect the parent's viewing.

Parent-child correlations for television use are shown in Table 10.3. The number of cases in the television use study is considerably smaller than in earlier tables because we interviewed mothers in the Wisconsin sample but not in Maryland. In neither state did we contact fathers. The results are somewhat equivocal in that the level of association is much stronger in the television use study than in the political socialization study. This may reflect that the former study used single categories of programmes. Part of the correlations in the television use study, then, may reflect

TABLE 10.3
Parent-child television use correlations by sex of parent and child

Television Use Index		Political socialization study		Television use study
		Fathers	Mothers	Mothers
Adolescent's	Sons	.14	.15	.12
TV time	Daughters	.09	.18	.13
Adventure-	Sons	.11	.13	.23
drama	Daughters	.02	.13	.27
Westerns	Sons	.19	.29	.19
	Daughters	.19	.25	.42
Crime-	Sons	–	–	.26
detective	Daughters	–	–	.24
Situation	Sons	.07	.13	.25
comedies	Daughters	.01	.09	.24
Variety-	Sons	–	–	.30
comedy	Daughters	–	–	.33
News-public	Sons	.11	.07	.18
affairs	Daughters	.14	.17	.28
(Number of	Sons	(297)	(333)	(119)
cases)	Daughters	(301)	(361)	(106)

NOTE Cell entries are Pearson rs, and differ from zero at the following significance levels:

political socialization study	television use study
$r \geq .12, p < .05$	$r \geq .19, p < .05$
$r \geq .14, p < .01$	$r \geq .25, p < .01$

conjoint watching rather than modelling. The television time measures were more comparable and very similar results are shown.

If modelling involves the anticipation of future adult roles by the child and television behaviour is part of that imitative process, then we would expect higher father-son and mother-daughter combinations than for the cross-sex parent-child comparisons. The political socialization study results shown in Table 10.3 indicate that mothers are more important sources of influence than fathers for both sons and daughters and there is only a very slight tendency for the same-sex correlations to be higher than those shown for opposite-sex parent-child combinations. But these findings are not consistent and they could be accounted for by general sex-role-linked male and female content preferences rather than direct imitation. This is hardly compelling evidence for modelling as the key learning process.

The possibility of *reverse modelling*, the child's television use influencing that of the parent, remains tenable. Indirect evidence from other studies indicates that this direction of influence is at least as strong as that from parent to child.[6] Another threat to the modelling interpretation is the opportunity to watch, the fact that one person has the set on may restrict the viewing choice of the second person. While our earlier research found no difference in parent-child correlations between homes with one television set and those with more than one in the political socialization study, a control for specific programmes watched conjointly in the television use study did reduce the correlations by about one-third. A final alternative is that some combination of third variables common to both parent and child television behaviour accounts for the 'modelling' correlation. Control for socio-economic status, for example, does reduce the parent-child correlations in Table 10.3, but they do not disappear altogether. Given the fact that the correlations are only low to moderate to begin with and acknowledging the potential of several alternative explanations to account for them, modelling does not seem to be a very potent explanation of adolescent communication behaviour.

Reinforcement
The use of direct rewards and punishment to influence television behaviour may be an unlikely alternative to modelling explanations

in that the number of parents who attempt to control their child's television behaviour is never high and declines markedly from early to middle adolescents.[7] There is some previous evidence supportive of a reinforcement explanation, however. Jeffres (1968) found that explicit parental rewards such as book giving and taking the son to the library did have an effect on the child's newspaper reading. Maccoby (1951) indicates that in middle-class families over-severe reaction and to a lesser extent underreaction to the child's aggressive behaviour leads to increased television viewing.

Our political socialization and television use studies included reinforcement measures relating to general parental treatment of the child rather than to specific influence attempts regarding television use. One reward measure (frequency of parental affection) and three punishment indices (physical, verbal and restrictive — taking away privileges, etc) were used. In neither study did we find the expected relationship between affection and low levels of viewing of violent television content. In fact, there were tendencies in the opposite direction. Physical and verbal punishment showed low positive correlations with violence viewing, but the relationships were inconsistent across sex and age categories. Restrictive punishment showed strong and more consistent positive correlations with violence viewing. It also showed low positive associations with other types of entertainment viewing and low negative relationships with exposure to news and public affairs media content. Overall, there is only a rather meagre amount of evidence making a connection between reinforcement learning mechanisms and adolescent television use.

Interaction

The social interaction view of the learning process is less specific as to the exact mechanism involved. This explanation asserts that the key source of learning is the characteristic social norms guiding and restricting the person's interactions with relevant other persons. These interactions are neither random nor structurally similar across all segments of the society. What is learned is a series of complex interpersonal relationships (*Brim* and *Wheeler*, 1966). To understand the person's learning situation and predict his behaviour, then, we must conceive of measurable dimensions that capture the variability in human relationships. For almost a decade the University of Wisconsin's Mass Communications Research

Center has conducted a programme of research studying family communication patterns. The basic data for the measurement of family communication is obtained from self-report responses of the adolescent and one of his parents. From sixteen to twenty items are used, each on a five-point scale ranging from 'frequently' to 'never'. In many different studies in a variety of settings, we have rather consistently found that there are at least two uncorrelated dimensions of communication structure in families.[8]

The first dimension, *socio-orientation*, involves parental expectations that the child should be deferential to his elders, maintain harmonious personal relationships and withhold his feelings. The second dimension we call *concept-orientation*, because it involves positive constraints to stimulate the child to develop her or his own views about the world, and to consider more than one side of an issue. For example, the parents may encourage the child to weigh all the evidence before reaching a conclusion, or may expose her or him to counter arguments — either by differing openly on an issue, or by discussing it with visitors to the home. The child learns to cope with the world in terms of these family structural constraints and they serve as a cognitive map to guide her or him in situations outside the home. Use of media is one manifestation of the child's coping style.

The social origins of these orientations appear quite complex. Working-class homes show some tendency to stress socio-orientations, while middle-class families give more attention to concept-orientation. The differences are not that strong, however, and the orientations have relationships to cognitive processes that do not seem explainable as simple products of social class.

We have found it useful to describe these relations in terms of Newcomb's A-B-X paradigm (1953). As shown in Figure 10.2, we interpret the paradigm by making A the child, B the parent, and X the concept or idea that is the focus of communication. Rather than retain Newcomb's assumption that all three relations among A, B and X are present and equally prominent, we have adopted the alternative assumption that each relation is variable in strength, and that any one could dominate the relationship. A socio-oriented pattern emphasizes A-X relations. Although each dimension is measured by a set of items that form a continuous distribution, it is easier to analyse the model if we dichotomize each dimension as either high or low. A four-fold typology of family communication is formed as a result (Figure 10.2).

Laissez-faire families are characterized by a lack of emphasis on either socio- or concept-oriented relation. For the most part, there is simply little parent-child communication; the more intentional form of 'true permissiveness' does not seem to be a very common pattern. The child in the *laissez-faire* family appears to be relatively more influenced by non-family settings such as peer groups.

In the *protective* family, obedience and social harmony (A-B) are valued and there is little concern with conceptual matters. 'Protective' indicates the goal, not the outcome of this structure. In fact, experiments have shown that the child from a protective home is highly susceptible to influence from external persuasion (*Stone* and *Chaffee*, 1970). This may be due in part to a lack of knowledge of effective counter-arguments and in part due to a lack of practice at argumentation.

FIGURE 10.2
Family communicative pattern typology interpreted by relations from Newcomb's A-B-X paradigm

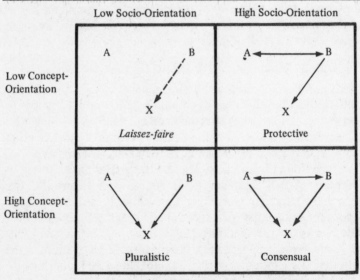

Key A = the child; B = the parent; X = the topic
Arrows indicate relations stressed in particular family type

The *pluralistic* pattern is the exact opposite of the protective home. The pluralistic environment encourages open communication and discussion of ideas (A-X) without the accompanying social (A-B) constraints. The emphasis seems to be on mutuality of respect and interests; the combination of positive impetus to self expression in combination with a lack of social constraints should foster both serious communication and competence.

Consensual families, as implied by the label, seem to be built on pressures toward agreement. The child in this family is faced with an incompatible set of combined A-B, A-X and B-X constraints. She or he is encouraged to take an interest in the world of ideas, yet to do so without disturbing the family's hierarchy of power and internal harmony. These conflicting pressures may induce the child to retreat from the parent-child interaction. But to the extent that such interaction is maintained, the child can meet both the socio- and concept-oriented constraints simultaneously by a simple strategy; he can learn what his parents views are and adopt them in shallow form.

Television use among adolescents from the four types of families is shown for the political socialization study data in Table 10.4. It is clear that adolescents from protective homes spend more time with television than any other group, although their avid viewing of entertainment fare does not generalize to their viewing of news and public affairs programming. One interpretation is that the protective adolescent watches a heavy diet of television in order to escape from the strictures of the strong A-B relation emphasis. However, it should be pointed out that their parents also watch far more television than the average parent.

Adolescents from pluralistic homes present a striking contrast to the protectives. While they generally spend far less time with television than does the average child, their attention to news and public affairs programmes is quite high relative to others. They show even higher standard scores on total public affairs media, indicating their above average public affairs newpaper reading as well as their attention to similar television content. Their news exposure might have been even higher were they not also very busy youngsters. Other analyses have shown that they are very active in school and other activities outside the home.

Apparently the strategy in *laissez-faire* homes of letting the child develop his own interests does not lead to any 'natural' interest in public affairs. The *laissez-faire* adolescent seems relatively uninterested in entertainment television as well. The consensual youngster tends to be about average in the viewing of entertainment programmes, and somewhat above the mean in public affairs

TABLE 10.4
Adolescent's media use (standard scores) by family communication patterns, age and sex (political socialisation study)

Media use index	Age		Laissez-faire	Protec-tive	Plural-istic	Consen-sual
			Family communication pattern			
Adolescent's	Early	Boys	00	29	−38	02
TV time		Girls	−09	27	−30	12
	Middle	Boys	11	28	−32	−03
		Girls	01	24	−13	−05
TV adventure-	Early	Boys	−24	07	17	−06
drama		Girls	−16	09	−01	09
	Middle	Boys	−02	31	−23	00
		Girls	−14	02	03	12
TV Westerns	Early	Boys	04	10	−33	10
		Girls	−10	28	−13	−02
	Middle	Boys	−14	13	−09	13
		Girls	−14	09	04	−10
TV news-public	Early	Boys	−08	−26	12	17
affairs		Girls	−17	−06	22	04
	Middle	Boys	−21	08	22	−07
		Girls	−23	−08	15	16
Total public	Early	Boys	−22	−33	29	04
affairs media		Girls	−15	−32	24	22
(newspaper and	Middle	Boys	−15	−03	18	00
television)		Girls	−31	−11	17	25
(Number of	Early	Boys	(78)	(81)	(70)	(114)
cases)		Girls	(82)	(65)	(68)	(83)
	Middle	Boys	(81)	(61)	(77)	(68)
		Girls	(104)	(70)	(102)	(88)

NOTE Standard score entries are weighted cell means, setting the overall mean at zero and the standard deviation at one, for all four cells in each row. Scores are calculated to two decimal places; decimals are omitted for simplicity. Statistical significance (.05 level) for differences between a given cell and the total of all other cells in that row ranges between 17 and 22 depending on the size of the cell and the other cells in the row.

television viewing and news reading. But other analyses have shown that these adolescents are clearly below average in their knowledge of politics. It appears that the gain in knowledge is not commensurate with the time they invest in public affairs media.

Data from the television use study are presented in Table 10.5. Since parental reports were obtained for the Wisconsin but not the Maryland sample and the family communication patterns are most reliably measured with both the child's and parent's report, only the Wisconsin data are shown. Because only 147 cases are available, the two ages and both sexes have been combined. The adolescents from protective homes are again extremely high television users, in terms of total TV exposure, violent programme viewing, and the watching of the cartoon shows that saturate American television on Saturday morning. They are also the most likely group to say that television presents a chance for them to learn behaviours that the adult world considers anti-social. Again, the pluralistic adolescent has an opposite pattern in being below other groups in television viewing time and is less likely to watch violent programmes and see television as a source of anti-social learning.

Laissez-faire adolescents from this Wisconsin sample appear to be extremely light television users. They also show a surprisingly contrasting pattern in seeing little similarity between television and real life, but conversely reporting greater involvement with the characters on action shows. The consensual youngsters, perhaps responding to the cross-pressures they face in their family situation, watch heavy dosages of violent content and are the most likely group to see similarity between what they watch and the world around them.

Our analysis of family communication patterns is by no means the only approach to studying interaction as a learning model influencing adolescent television use. A close relationship between the amount of discussion of a topic and its parallel use in the media has been noted by several researchers.[9] Others have found that the youngsters lacking in integration in a peer group showed a preference for action and violence in the media, (*Riley* and *Riley*, 1951; *Schramm et al.*, 1961), although our own television use study did not replicate this finding and found instead a positive correlation between the number of friends in their peer group and the viewing of violent content. In a series of studies, Clarke (1971) has shown that various aspects of congruency, the perception that

TABLE 10.5
Adolescent's television use and reactions (standard scores) by family communication patterns (television use study)

Television Use/ Reaction Index	Family communication pattern			
	Laissez- faire	Protec- tive	Plural- istic	Consen- sual
Adolescent's TV time	−23	+40	−22	+08
TV violence viewing	−14	+25	−41	+32
Saturday morning TV viewing	−31	+21	−31	+42
Agrees that TV presents chance to learn anti-social behaviour	−04	+19	−29	+14
Sees close similarity between TV violence and real life	−27	−02	−06	+33
Becomes involved with characters and stories of action TV shows	+24	−11	−02	−07
(Number of cases)	(34)	(40)	(34)	(39)

NOTE Standard score entries are weighted cell means, setting the overall mean at zero and the standard deviation at one, for all four cells in each row. Scores are calculated to two decimal places; decimals are omitted for simplicity. Statistical significance (.05 level) for difference between a given cell and the total of all other cells in that row is 29 for *Laissez-faire* and Pluralistic groups and 27 for Protective and Consensual groups.

another person shares interests and views, has important consequences for media behaviour. Our television use study found that the lack of agreement between mother and child on goals of education was strongly related to the viewing of violent content. It would seem that, in general, studies of interpersonal interaction are the most promising of the three types of learning models studied to date.

STABILITY OF PARENTAL INFLUENCE

It is a truism that the parents are the crucial socialization agents in the development of the child. That truism is backed by surprisingly little research evidence when media behaviour is the criterion of development. There is, nevertheless, some evidence at least that the parents do play an important role for younger children. It is less clear that the strength of this role continues through adolescence when the youngster begins striving for independence and has increasing contact with peers and other socialization agents outside the home.

Our political socialization and television use studies provide data regarding the stability of parental influence from early to middle adolescence. This stability can be indexed by the magnitude of the correlations between family learning variables and the media behaviour for the mid-adolescent sample compared to the younger sample. When we broke down the modelling comparisons shown earlier in Table 10.3 by the age level, we found that the average parent-child correlation in the political socialization study was .16 and .14 for the younger and older groups, respectively. The television use study that used listings of the names of shows for modelling data showed an average modelling correlation drop from .28 among the younger adolescents to .22 among those three years older. To the extent that there is any evidence for modelling, it seems to decrease only a moderate amount over the three-year period. The decline seems to be non-random in that it decreases more for boys than for girls, more for comedy and adventure shows, and not at all for news and Westerns.

Since the reinforcement measures produced only weak associations with adolescent television behaviour, the relative size of these correlations may not be a very sensitive criterion to use for comparing family effects in the two age groups. It does appear, however, that the magnitude of these generally low correlations does not show any decline from early to middle adolescence. In fact restrictive punishment, the best and most consistent variable in the reinforcement set, actually shows slightly stronger family effects in the older group. A better test is provided by comparing the early and middle adolescent groups in the family pattern analyses of Table 10.4. The standard scores, averaged (not shown here) across the four family types and first four dependent variables of the table, give a rough indication of the predictive strength of the family communication patterns in the two age levels. The mean for boys is 15.2 and 14.8 for the younger and mid-adolescents; a somewhat larger drop from 13.4 to 10.8 is found for girls although neither decline seems extraordinary in comparison to the very large changes taking place during these years in the levels of these same variables as shown in Table 10.1.

From these and other analyses of non-media effect variables, it appears that family influences do not decline substantially up through the middle of adolescence. In fairness, we should mention one alternative interpretation: that the parental influence has already declined before the onset of adolescence and that it remains at a low ebb through the adolescent period studied here. Although this is doubtful, we don't have comparative data to test this proposition.

TABLE 10.6
Early adults' TV use, gratifications sought and reasons for avoiding political TV content (standard scores) (young voter study)

TV use, gratifications, avoidances	Family communication pattern			
	Laissez-faire	Protective	Pluralistic	Consensual
Television use				
TV exposure	−11	−01	+04	+29
Public affairs TV exposure	−01	−01	−02	+01
TV entertainment exposure	07	−05	−16	+45
Gratifications				
Vote guidance	−16	+17	+01	−06
Reinforcement	−24	+34	−23	+19
Surveillance	−12	+24	−08	+22
Excitement	−20	00	00	+34
Ammunition	−16	+17	−16	+24
Avoidances				
Alienation	−19	+14	−07	+67
Partisanship	−08	+08	+08	−17
Relaxation	−20	−03	−01	+36
(Number of cases)	(53)	(68)	(70)	(32)

NOTE Standard score entries are weighted cell means, setting the overall mean at zero and the standard deviation at one, for all four cells in each row. Scores are calculated to two decimal places; decimals are omitted for simplicity. Statistical significance (.05 level) for differences between a given cell and the total of all other cells in that row is greater than $\pm$ 24 for *Laissez-faire*, $\pm$ 20 for Protectives and Pluralistics and $\pm$ 32 for Consensuals.

While it is theoretically understandable why parental effects would be evident throughout the period when the adolescent is still living in the home, it becomes more problematical whether to hypothesize that these influences would continue on into late adolescence and early adulthood. We have attempted to look at this question of long-term stability of family effects with our young voter study data, although there are some design and measurement limitations that require us to make our inferences with great caution. The data involve looking at media use and the gratifications sought from political television by young adults (ages eighteen to twenty-four) classified by their recollection of the family communication practices that operated when they were twelve to sixteen years old. The use of recollective data, involving looking backward an average of seven years, is a somewhat doubtful procedure. Then too, only half as many items were used and reports were not obtained from the parents of these young adults. These limitations should be kept in mind in looking at the late adolescent-young adult data in Table 10.6.

These young adults whose recollection of the communication practices of their families during adolescence classified them as *laissez-faire* tend to be infrequent users of television and to be low endorsers of various gratifications sought from political communication. On the other hand, they tend not to avoid such communication and are actually the best informed of the four groups regarding politics. While the adolescent protective group was shown to be heavy users of television in Table 10.4, the young adult protectives are only average on all exposure measures. They are distinguished by their use of political television for reinforcement ('to remind me of my candidate's strong points') and for surveillance ('to judge what political leaders are like', etc.). Their desire for reinforcement is consonant with their strong A-B origins that stressed consistency of belief.

The young adult pluralists represent something of a departure from their adolescent counterparts. While they do tend to be light users of entertainment like the younger group, they lack the emphasis on public affairs that characterized that family type in all previous research. Other analyses not shown here indicate that they are also only about average on newspaper public affairs reading and on knowledge of political affairs. They tend not to use political television for reinforcement or for ammunition in discussions with others. The former follows expectations but the latter does not. The young adult consensuals are more in line with previous expectations, being heavy entertainment viewers and using political television for reinforcement or for ammunition in discussions with others. The former follows expectations but the latter does not. The young adult consensuals are more in line with previous expectations, being heavy entertainment viewers and using political television for excitement ('enjoyment of the excitement of an election race', etc.), for surveillance and for ammunition in arguments. They are also the most likely to avoid political television with expression of feelings of alienation (eg, 'you can't trust what politicans say on television') and need for relaxation ('I prefer to relax when watching television'). Other analyses not shown indicate that they, like their younger counterparts, are the least politically informed group.

The extension of the family communication pattern typology to young adulthood, then, produces a mixed bag of results. The earlier adolescent patterns by no means are carried over intact, but there is sufficient patterning to suggest some residual validity. The question becomes: is it a measurement problem of shifting recall, insufficient reliability and lack of parental perspective, is it a theoretical problem that the long-term effects of family influence are contingent upon the young adult entering into a compatible environment after he leaves home? Weak design and measurement is clearly a factor, but we do notice some evidence for the latter theoretical point. It is those young adult pluralists who did not go on to college who show the greatest departure from the high public affairs pattern characteristic of younger pluralists; the college-educated pluralists continued to exhibit such a pattern.

To test adequately the stability of family communication influences, it would be necessary to use a panel design that would obtain adequate measurement of communication practices from both children and their parents during adolescence and then four or five years later remeasure the then young adults to study media behaviour and other effect variables. Another useful approach is to study other possible socialization agents as potential sources of growing influence. The normative communication patterns of peer groups, teaching classrooms, and occupational groups are plausible targets of future research. As originally conceived the socio- and concept-constraints were designed to be applicable to any social interaction situation, ie, the peer group, the classroom, the dorm floor. Most of our research has been restricted to family interaction settings, although we have recently begun to investigate peer group interactions. In this research we have attempted to characterize the communication norms of college student peer groups along dimensions similar to those found in families. Early evidence suggests that these norms do exist and relate to effects such as changing perceptions of sex roles, development of citizenship values, and changing particularism of religious beliefs.

CONSEQUENCES OF COMMUNICATION BEHAVIOUR

This chapter has focused on identifying antecedents of adolescent television use, treating the latter as a kind of end state. For those with intrinsic interests in communication research, this is an entirely satisfactory activity; however, most other people have interests in youthful television use patterns largely because of their potential consequences for the adolescent's current or future behaviour. There is surprisingly little convincing evidence that the customary media behaviour of the child or adolescent does have such consequences. At least three characteristics of much of the past communication research may account for this: researchers have been rather cavalier about the way they measure communication, treating time spent, content exposure and gratifications sought as if they were equivalents; they have been preoccupied with looking for unlikely effects like attitude conversion and criminal behaviour rather than the more likely consequences such as information gain or cognitive change; and they have most often relied on non-experimental research designs which use measurement at only one time point which presents problems regarding the proper causal ordering of media and 'effect' variables.

The problem of causal ordering was investigated by Chaffee and others (1971) using cross-lag correlation techniques with our political socialization study data. They looked at the prediction across time of political knowledge and activity by public affairs media exposure and the reverse. The results represented fairly strong evidence that for adolescents the main causal flow is from public affairs media exposure to increased political knowledge and activity across the six-month campaign period studied. Lefkowitz *et al* (1971) used similar cross-lag techniques with a ten-year interval in a panel of youngsters first interviewed at age eight. The correlation between violence viewing at age eight and aggressive behaviour ten years later was +.31; the reverse lag correlation of aggressive behaviour at eight to violence viewing at eighteen was +.01. Appropriate base-line and reliability controls did not eliminate the viability of the inference that violence viewing caused later aggression, although there are enough ambiguities in the data to retain reservations about making generalizations. In both cases (public affairs and violence viewing), there is considerably more supportive than non-supportive evidence from non-longitudinal research if we confine our search to the studies using adequate measurement procedures. At least there is sufficient evidence for both hope and concern regarding the effects of television on children and adolescents.[10]

The examination of effects has moved away from an almost exclusive focus on persuasion to the more likely but also more subtle types of effects in recent years. The focus is more on studies of information gain and cognitive change and the research question has shifted from simple discovery of such effects to trying to identify the conditions under which they are manifested (see, for example: *Douglas et al.*, 1970; *Mendelsohn*, 1973; *McCombs* and *Shaw*, 1972). Blumler and McLeod (1974) in a panel study of young adult voters in the 1970 British General Election, found three different paths through which communication behaviour stimulated or depressed voter turnout on election day. Similarly, our research has linked family communication patterns not only to television behaviour but also to a host of effects such as: sensitivity to information and source expertness in a message; cognitive differentiation and development; political competence; and number of school activities.[11]

While the development of adequate communication designs and measurement of effects are apt to remain complex problems, it is difficult to understand why communication research has paid so little attention to the measurement of communication exposure. Few distinctions are made among some very different concepts: time spent with a medium, exposure to particular types of content, and the gratifications sought from the content. Time spent is probably the least satisfactory measure for most purposes since it subsumes some very different kinds of exposure to a type of content; and the gratifications sought in viewing that content should not be confused.[12] In a study of the political campaign effects of television, McLeod and Becker (1974) found that neither the amount of exposure to public affairs content nor entertainment viewing was highly correlated with five types of gratifications sought from political television content. Likewise, neither type of exposure was strongly related to three dimensions of reasons for avoiding political broadcasts. More importantly, exposure and gratification-avoidances independently predicted significant amount of variance in a variety of political effect measures among the older adolescent-young adult voters.

Regardless of weaknesses in design and measurement, it does appear that the various patterns of adolescent television use do have important consequences for behaviour.

IMPACT OF SOCIAL-STRUCTURAL CONSTRAINTS

We have attempted to use data to portray the television behaviour of the adolescent as being shaped by the learning processes of her or his immediate interpersonal environment. This is not to imply, however, that these interpersonal patterns and their accompanying modelling, reinforcement and interaction processes are somehow random or independent of the culture, social structure and social roles of the adolescent and his family. Rather, it is important to the socialization model of media behaviour to identify these social forces which constrain the learning processes and their outcomes in the behaviour of the child, adolescent and adult.

Our data are very incomplete on these matters and our interpretation is necessarily quite speculative. However, we can postulate that the influence of social class on child development should be maximal during the first half of childhood, after which the child will begin to lessen her or his dependence upon her or his parents by gradually widening contacts with peers outside the home and through the world of television (see *Douvan* and *Adelson*, 1966). Since a relatively homogeneous image of the world is available on the television screen, this exposure could be expected to lessen the impact of social class differences in the home environment and have the effect of reducing the variance in the 'social reality' of the young adolescent. The youth of all social classes to some extent share in the dreams, fantasies and aspirations expressed in the common youth culture fostered partly by television.

Since we don't have our own data for childhood, we can only make rough comparisons with the childhood data other research presents, and make comparisons with our early adolescent, middle adolescent and young adult samples. It does appear, however, that the predictive power of social class is at a low ebb during the early adolescent years.[13] This set of stratification variables all but drops out of our regression analyses when family communication and other parental treatment variables are introduced in analyses of viewing behaviour and its effects. Working-class adolescents do watch more entertainment and violence and less public affairs programming than do those from middle-class homes, but the relationship is not strong even before other variables are considered. Himmelweit and Swift in a longitudinal study of 365 young British men, interviewed when they were adolescents (thirteen to fourteen years old) and again as young adults (twenty-four to twenty-five years old), have reported similar findings. They show that quality of home life, as distinct from its social and educational level, affects both media usage and 'taste'.

To the extent that modelling does take place, it has the effect of sharpening these television uses differences in that parents in each social class share the entertainment and public affairs patterns of their children. Middle-class families are also more concept-oriented and less socio-oriented in their communication practices, but this is by no means a highly deterministic relationship. Other factors may also affect family communication practices. For example, parents affiliating with religious groups that emphasize hierarchical constraints and devotionalism differ from others in their family communication practices (*Elliott*, 1972).

Coterminous with the growing independence of the middle adolescent years is a growing confrontation of the youth's aspirations and the realities of his or her position in society (*Stendler,* 1949). The anticipation of playing adult roles is restricted by the constraints of financial resources, previous school performance and the growing differentiation of sex-role and class distinctions. Our data indicate that the predictive power of family social class increases markedly from early to middle adolescence in the ability to predict level of political competence and other manifestations of acceptance of citizenship roles. To a lesser extent but nevertheless consistently, the prediction of television use and other media behaviour also becomes stronger during middle adolescence. But our data from Tables 10.3, 10.4, 10.5 and 10.6 indicate that parental impact declines somewhat during this period, which may mean that social class is operating more directly on the child, rather than indirectly through family influences. This speculation is upheld by the finding that the expectation of going to college is a strong predictor — stronger than family social class — on the middle adolescent's media behaviour. Himmelweit and

Swift also found that an adolescent 'success orientation' in British males was predictive of adult liking of technical literature, especially for those young men who had been educationally disadvantaged at school.

The middle adolescent period, then, is characterized by an educational tracking process that has as one of its major consequences the occupational situation of the young adult. Its side-effects are differential media behaviour and possibly subsequential varying performance in citizenship and other social roles. This education tracking process, of course, varies among societies as to the age at which it begins, the extent of social class determination and the severity of its effect. Yet it is present in all modern societies. A study of the effects of English school stratification found, not unexpectedly, that grammar school boys had higher aspirations and expectations than secondary modern school boys (*Liversidge*, 1962). Within the American system, additional tracking of a more subtle nature occurs within the college environment as working-class youths go into more technical-vocational fields and as females are deterred from training for 'masculine' professions.

Late adolescence and early adulthood also have varying consequences depending upon the person's status and role in the society. In American society, this differentiation is sharpest between those who have completed four or more years of college or university and those who have immediately entered the world of work after their stint of mandatory education. Our young voter data indicate sharp differences between the college and non-college groups not only for political participation and competence but for media behaviour as well. The college group is much more likely to watch news and public affairs material and less likely to view various kinds of entertainment content. These differences by education levels are considerably greater than those found for the family social class and anticipation of college measures in our adolescent studies. In other words, media patterns seem to be part of the person's occupational-educational role and not simply manifestations of earlier differences in ability. Himmelweit and Swift's British data substantiate this interpretation: they show that tastes for 'highbrow' literature were highly related to educational attainment regardless of family background. Although we do not have conclusive evidence, it seems possible that these media patterns will, in turn, have an effect on other social differences such as political activity and knowledge.

Another source of tracking which may operate in early adulthood stems from the traditional social roles of women, especially those who become homemakers before or after college rather than entering the occupational domain. Panel studies (*Trent* and *Medsker*, 1967) using change scores from before and after adoption of homemaker or occupational roles have found a decline among homemakers in such areas as autonomy and social maturity and a gain in authoritarianism and thinking-introversion that were not evidenced by women going into occupations, where any differences were in the reverse direction, ie, college-career women changing toward more autonomy, etc. It is very likely that media use patterns follow along these same lines, but no evidence is available on this point.

We have tried to make a strong argument for greater research attention to media processes and effects during adolescence and early adulthood. These are dynamic years, as sharp changes take place and crucial decisions about future life styles are made. The family's role is by no means an insignificant one during this period but it seems characterized less by the direct learning of childhood and more by the subtle processes of interpersonal interaction. These processes have considerable importance for the theoretical understanding of the mass media. The adolescent is in a position to be influenced by a host of socializing agents. And during this period her or his media behaviour is probably least determined by structural constraints, such as accessibility, lack of time or differences in educational levels. These factors should make adolescence an attractive target for researchers investigating the influence of television and other media on an audience needing information to make important decisions.

The informational needs of adolescents also should be of increasing concern to television producers. The traditional dichotomies of entertainment *versus* serious content and children's *versus* adult programming have been disfunctional for the adolescent whose needs for information tend to be ignored by most broadcasting organizations. Research clearly indicates that intellectual development does not end with childhood; instead some of the most crucial of life decisions are made during that period. This decline of attention to television noted in mid-adolescence should not be used as an excuse to ignore this age group; perhaps the lack of programming catering for them helps to account for their apparent decline in interest. After all, the advertising messages of commercial television do not spare this group and there is sufficient evidence to suggest that more socially-significant content would be beneficial to the adolescent.

NOTES

1 While research on adolescent intellectual development has expanded rapidly in recent years, its impact has been blunted by the lack of a theoretical paradigm comparable to Freud's stages of psycho-sexual development or Paiget's cognitive stages in the development of formal thought, both of which ended before adolescence. Kohlberg's moral stages also ended in early adolescence, although his most recent work (1973) suggests that changes in intellectual functioning continue through adolescence and into early adulthood. Erickson's rhetorical 'theories' of human development (*Erickson, E, Childhood and Society*) do include a formal description of adolescence with its central problem being the conflict between identity and role diffusion, but this clinical accounting gives little indication of the kinds of relationships we should expect regarding changes in adolescent television use and its antecedents and effects.

2 The study was conducted under a grant from the National Science Foundation to the senior author and Professor Steven H. Chaffee (Grant GS-1874). Others aiding in this research included Daniel Wackman, George Pasdirtz, Garrett O'Keefe and Jane Engels. Other aspects of the study have been reported elsewhere: *Chaffee* and *McLeod* (1971); *Chaffee et al.* (1970b); *Chaffee et al.* (1970a); *McLeod* and *Chaffee* (1972).

3 Other demographies were not as similar, however. Owing to a much heavier enrolment in Roman Catholic and Lutheran-affiliated schools during the early adolescent years, our samples, taken only from state-supported schools, include substantially more Catholics and Lutherans at the middle adolescent age level (when church-affiliated students generally transfer to the state-supported schools). Also, within the state-supported school systems, school district boundaries were not always the same for the early adolescents' schools and the middle adolescents' schools.

4 *McLeod et al.* (1971a) and *McLeod et al.* (1971b). Both reports describe studies supported by a contract (HSM 42-70-77) with the National Institute of Mental Health. Jack McLeod and Steven Chaffee were co-principal investigators. Charles Atkin, now at Michigan State University, was the study director. Others aiding in the data analysis were William Elliott, William Engels, Kenneth Sheinkopf and Catherine Willette.

5 This study was supported in part by grants from the John and Mary R Markle Foundation and the Social Science Research Council of Great Britain. Parts of it have been described in two reports: *McLeod* and *Becker* (1974); *McLeod et al.* (1974). All three studies received preliminary support from grants from the University of Wisconsin Graduate School.

6 *Clarke* (1963); *Bottorf* (1970); *Schramm et al.* (1971); *Chaffee et al.* (1970a).

7 *Greenberg and Dominick* (1969); *Lyle* and *Hoffman* (1971); *McLeod et al.* (1971).

8 *Chaffee et al.* (1966); *Eswara* (1968); *McLeod et al.* (1967); *McLeod et al.* (1969); *Wackman* (1968).

9 *Lyle* and *Hoffman* (1971); other researchers have found that the media may also affect the way a person orders topics of the day. The 'agendas' may in turn affect the content of interpersonal discussion. (*McCombs* and *Shaw*, 1972).

10 For a discussion of the logic of these inferences and a summary of available evidence see: *Chaffee, Steven H*, "Television and adolescent aggressiveness (Overview)", *Television and Social Behaviour, op. cit.*, III, pp. 1-34. Needless to say, controversy continues regarding the causal connection between televised violence viewing and aggressive behaviour. It is doubtful if any further experimental or non-experimental evidence will change the minds of those committed either to a yes-effects (see the polemics of Dr Frederic Wertham in *Seduction of the Innocent,* (1954), or the no-effects position (see *Dennis Howitt*, 'Comment on Leo Bogart's warning' (1973-4).) Rather than directing more research to the question of whether there are such effects, it would be more useful to examine what production decisions and family and school intervention techniques and strategies can be utilized to reduce the likelihood of undesirable consequences.

11 *Stone* and *Chaffee* (1970); *Chaffee et al.* (1973); *Wackman et al.* (1970); *Chaffee et al.* (1966); *McLeod et al.* (1967).

12 Dembo's research 'Gratifications found in media by British teenage boys', (1973) is a recent example of confusion of exposure and gratifications sought in the study of effects. He cites British data, showing no correlation between aggression-seeking as a television *gratification* and aggressive behaviour, as evidence for non-replication of US aggressive behaviour. Of course, this comparison is meaningless. The null finding does become important if and only if we assume that the only effects of media exposure are those consciously intended by the receiver. However comforting such a rational and controlled world might be, we cannot eliminate the possibility of unintended consequences for human behaviour.

13 *Greenberg* and *Dominick* (1969); *McIntyre* and *Teevan* (1971); *Stein et al.* (1971).

REFERENCES

Blumler, J G and *McLeod, J M* (1974), 'Communication and Voter Turnout in Britain', in Janowitz (ed), *Sociological Theory and Survey Research,* Sage, Beverly Hills.

Bottorf, A (1970), 'Television, Respect and the Older Adolescent', Master's Thesis, University of Wisconsin.

Brim, O G and *Wheeler, S* (1966), *Socialization after Childhood: Two Essays,* Wiley, New York.

Chaffee, S H 'Television and Adolescent Aggressiveness (Overview)', in Rubinstein, Comstock and Murray (eds), *Television and Social Behavior,* US Government Printing Office, Washington DC, III, 1-34.

Chaffee, S H and *McLeod, J M* (1971), 'Adolescent Television Use in the Family Context', *Television and Social Behaviour,* III, 149-72.

Chaffee, S H, McLeod, J M and *Atkin, C K* (1970a), 'Parental Influences on Adolescent Media Use', *American Behavioral Scientist,* XIV. 3, 323-40.

Chaffee, S H, McLeod, J M and *Wackman, D B* (1966), 'Family Communication and Political Socialization', paper presented to Association for Education in Journalism, Iowa City, Iowa.

Chaffee, S H, McLeod, J M and *Wackman, D B* (1973), 'Family Communication Patterns and Adolescent Political Participation', in Dennis (ed), *Socialization to Politics,* New York.

Chaffee, S H, Ward, L S and *Tipton, L P* (1970), 'Mass Communication and Political Socialization in the 1968 Campaign'. *Journalism Quarterly,* XLVII (Winter), 647-59, 666.

Clarke, P (1963), 'An Experiment to Increase the Audience for Educational Television', Ph.D. Dissertation, University of Minnesota.

Clarke, P (1971), 'Some Proposals for Continuing Research on Youth and the Mass Media', *American Behavioral Scientist,* XIV. 3, 313-22.

Dembo, R (1973), 'Gratifications found in Media by British Teenage Boys', *Journalism Quarterly,* L, 517-26.

Douglas, D F, Westley, B H and *Chaffee, S H* (1970), 'An Information Campaign that changed Community Attitudes', *Journalism Quarterly,* XLVII (Autumn), 479-87.

Douvan, E and *Adelson, J* (1966), *The Adolescent Experience,* Wiley, New York.

Elliott, W R (1972), 'Religion, Family Communication and Political Socialization', doctoral dissertation, University of Wisconsin.

Erickson, E (1950), *Childhood and Society,* Norton, New York.

Eswara, H S (1968), 'An Interpersonal Approach to the Study of Social Influence: Family Communication Patterns and Attitude Change', doctoral dissertation, University of Wisconsin.

Greenberg, B S (1973), 'British Children and Televised Violence', paper presented to the Association for Education in Journalism, Fort Collins, Colorado.

Greenberg, B S and *Dominick J R* (1969), 'Race and Social Class Differences in Teenagers' Use of Television', *Journal of Broadcasting,* XIII (Fall), 331-44.

Himmelweit, H T, Oppenheim, A N and *Vince, P* (1958), *Television and the Child,* Oxford University Press, London.

Himmelweit, H T and *Swift, B Adolescent and Adult Media Use: A Longitudinal Study,* Mimeo, London School of Economics.

Howitt, Dennis (1973-4), 'Comment on Leo Bogart's Warning ...', *Public Opinion Quarterly,* XXXVII (Winter), 645-6.

Jeffres, L W (1968), 'A Study of Similarities in the Use of Print Media by Fathers and Sons', master's thesis, University of Washington.

Kohlberg, L (1973), 'Continuities in Childhood and Adult Moral Development Revisited', in Baltes and Schaie (eds), *Life-Span Developmental Psychology,* Academic Press, New York and London, 180-204.

Lefkowitz, M M, Eron, L D, Walder, L O and *Huesmann, L R* (1971), Television Violence and Child Aggression: A Follow-up Study', *Television and Social Behavior,* III, 35-135.

Lewin, K (1951), *Field Theory in Social Science,* Harper, New York.

Liversidge, W (1962), 'Life Chances', *The Sociological Review,* X, 17-34.

Lyle, J and *Hoffman, H R* (1971), 'Children's Use of Television and Other Media', *Television and Social Behavior,* IV.

McCombs, M E and *Shaw, D L* (1972), 'The Agenda Setting Function of the Media', *Public Opinion Quarterly,* XXXVI, 176-87.

McIntyre, J J and *Teevan, J J* (1971) 'Television Violence and Deviant Behavior', *Television and Social Behavior,* III, 383-435.

McLeod, J M, Atkin, C K and *Chaffee, S H* (1971a), 'Adolescents, Parents, and Television Use: Adolescent Self-Report Measures from Maryland and Wisconsin Samples', *Television and Social Behavior,* III, 173-238.

McLeod, J M, Atkin, C K and *Chaffee, S H* (1971b), 'Adolescents, Parents, and Television Use: Adolescent Self-Report and Other-Report Measures from the Wisconsin Sample', *Television and Social Behavior,* III, 239-313.

McLeod, J M and *Becker, L B* (1974), 'Testing the Validity of Television Gratifications and Avoidances through Political Effects Analysis', in Blumler and Katz (eds), *The Uses of Mass Communications: Current Perspectives on Gratifications Research,* Sage Publications, Beverly Hills.

McLeod, J M, Becker, L B and *Byrnes, J E* (1974), 'Another Look at the Agenda-Setting Function of the Press', *Communication Research* I.2.

McLeod, J M and *Chaffee, S H* (1972) 'The Construction of Social Reality', in Tedeschi (ed), *The Social Influence Process,* Aldine-Atherton, Chicago.

McLeod, J M, Chaffee, S H and *Eswara, H S* (1966), 'Family Communication Patterns and Communication Research', paper presented to Association for Education in Journalism, Iowa City, Iowa.

McLeod, J M, Chaffee, S H and *Wackman, D B* (1968) 'Family Communication Patterns and Adolescents' Responses in Role Conflict Situations', doctoral dissertation, University of Wisconsin.

McLeod, J M, Chaffee, S H and *Wackman, D B* (1967), 'Family Communication: An Updated Report', paper presented to Association for Education in Journalism, Boulder, Colorado.

McLeod, J M and *O'Keefe, G J* (1972), 'The Socialization Perspective and Communication Behavior', in Kline and Tichenor (eds), *Current Perspectives in Mass Communication Research,* Sage Publications, Beverly Hills, 121-68.

McLeod, J M, O'Keefe, G J and *Wackman, D B* (1969), 'Communication and Political Socialization during the Adolescent Years', paper presented to Association for Education in Journalism, Berkeley.

Maccoby, E (1951), 'Why do Children watch Television?' *Public Opinion Quarterly,* XVIII, 239-44.

Mendelsohn, H (1973), 'Some Reasons why Information Campaigns can Succeed', *Public Opinion quarterly,* XXXVII, 50-61.

Newcomb, T M (1953), 'An Approach to the Study of Communication Acts', *Psychological Review,* LX, 393-404.

Piaget, J (1954), *The Construction of Reality in the Child,* Basic Books, New York.

Riley, M W and *Riley J W* (1951) 'A Sociological Approach to Communication Research', *Public Opinion Quarterly,* XV, 445-60.

Schramm, W J, Lyle, J and *Parker, E B* (1961), *Television in the Lives of our Children,* Stanford University Press, Stanford.

Stein, A H, Friedrich, L K with *Vondracek, F* (1971), 'Television Content and Young Children's Behavior', *Television and Social Behavior,* II, 202-317.

Stendler, C B (1949a), *Children of Brasstown: Their Awareness of the Symbols of*

Social Class, Univeristy of Illinois Press, Urbana.
Stone, *V A* and *Chaffee, S H* (1970), 'Family Communication Patterns and Source-Message Orientation', *Journalism Quarterly*, XLVII, 239-46.
Trent, J W and *Medsker, L L* (1967), *Beyond High School,* Center for Research and Development in Higher Education, University of California, Berkeley.
Wackman, D B (1968), 'Family Communication Patterns and Adolescents' Responses in Role Conflict Situations', doctoral dissertation, University of Wisconsin.
Wackman, D B, McLeod, J M and *Chaffee, S H* (1970), 'Family Communication Patterns and Cognitive Differentation', unpublished paper, University of Wisconsin.
Wertham, F (1954), *Seduction of the Innocent*, Rinehart, New York.

Part III
Processes of Influence and Some Effects of Exposure to Television

In this final selection we turn to the vexed question of television's effects on children. Over the years television has been accused of encouraging, or causing, various unseemly habits amongst young people. The nature of some television content, the sheer amount of exposure to television and the assumed consequences of exposure exercise public concern. And the fear that television is detrimental to society, because of its influence on children, has shaped the researcher's approach to the technically difficult problem of studying the nature of that influence and its consequences. As McQuail suggests, media researchers are more often asked for facts than theories, but theories are essential if we are to *understand* the processes by which television can influence children. Moreover, theories can further the public debate by encouraging more systematic research which might reveal effects of equal or greater social significance than those which presently attract interest. The probability that exposure to television has dramatic short-term effects, as yet unrevealed, is low, but it is likely that the daily ingestion of televised material over long periods influences our perception of social reality and has ramifications which have so far evaded the attention of researchers and public alike. If the reader is left with a vague uneasiness, it is a feeling shared by many researchers. Effects research still has a long way to go. On the other hand the study of television's effects on children has been by no means unfruitful. The following chapters document a large number of investigations that have contributed to an impressive and expanding body of knowledge. In its totality, effects research encompasses several different approaches and foci, and this diversity is reflected in the present contributions. Whilst Kniveton details the rigorous and largely laboratory-based studies of imitation and social learning, Cramond reviews the major survey studies of television's onset and their conclusions concerning the activities displaced when children became viewers. Murray discusses the outcome of studies on violence and viewing conducted for the Surgeon General, and Scott Ward reviews exploratory work on children and advertising which formed part of the report to the Surgeon General. In the penultimate chapter Howitt highlights the complexity of the problems faced by media researchers and justifies his plea for improved methods and theory by turning to areas where some researchers can be accused of barking up the wrong tree, whilst others sit silently beside the right one. Finally, McQuail analyses various concepts and theories which are implicit in effects research, and argues that they fall into four alternative conceptualizations of the process of influence. His assessment of the strengths and weaknesses of the four basic theoretical models draws on their past use and their potential to provide satisfactory guidelines for future research.

11

Social Learning and Imitation in Relation to Television

Bromley H Kniveton

One method of learning is to watch how someone else behaves and then to copy, or imitate, his behaviour. However, for an individual to change his own behaviour to coincide with that of someone else there is a need for him to feel that the change is worthwhile. This is only likely to occur if for some reason the actions of the person being observed are more attractive to the viewer than those he can think of for himself. All types of behaviour between two or more people involve social learning. However, as the aim of this book is to examine the effects of television on children I will concentrate on those studies which can be related to this, and in particular, in view of recent concern, to those which highlight the effects of violence on television.

Many researchers have demonstrated that a viewer can and does base his behaviour, under certain circumstances, on that of a model. The term model is used here in its broadest sense, referring to a character in a film or television programme or a child's parents, or indeed anyone whose behaviour a child has an opportunity of watching. The factors which influence why one individual bases his or her behaviour on that of another are the main concern of the first part of this chapter. Later in the chapter the extent that television itself influences social learning will be examined.

DO CHILDREN IMITATE THE BEHAVIOUR OF MODELS?

Numerous studies of children's reactions in play situations indicate that, under certain circumstances, children watching another person will subsequently act in the same or a similar manner. Everyday experience encourages us to reach the same conclusion: the readiness with which children imitate the behaviour of their

parents, washing up like mummy being one of many possible
illustrations. That children do imitate there can be no doubt.
Therefore experimental studies are not concerned to demonstrate
imitation as such but to assess the factors which influence what
decides whether imitation will occur in various situations.

Possibly one of the most important features of the imitation
process is the distinction drawn by Bandura (1971) between the
learning and retention of the model's behaviour and the
performance of that behaviour by the observer. As Stein *et al.*
(1972) state:

'Learning is thought to be partially a function of attention to the
stimulus and of capacity to cognitively code and retain the
stimulus material. Performance of the observed behaviour is
affected by reinforcement and punishment of the model, status
of the model, similarity between the model and the observer,
and subsequent reinforcement and punishment of the observer.
Other variables affecting performance involve interpersonal
contact between model and subject.'

The experiments to be discussed in the first part of this chapter
merely illustrate the processes involved in the imitation of a
model's behaviour. The experimental situations are inevitably
contrived and although the behaviour to be modelled is usually (not
always) aggressive behaviour, this is often directed towards
inanimate objects in a play situation.

Considerable care must be exercised in any attempt to relate the
findings directly to the effects of violence on television.
Furthermore, there are many methodological inadequacies in this
type of research. Techniques in this area have improved considerably, but for the benefit of the reader who may wish to delve
more deeply into the literature, or even follow up experimentally
some of the issues raised, a brief review of the deficiencies may be
useful.

METHODOLOGICAL INADEQUACIES OF RESEARCH INTO MODELLING PROCESSES

The research paradigm employed by many of the experimenters
investigating modelling effects has invariably and almost inevitably
involved the imitation of a model by an observer. For purposes of

this discussion an imitated event is defined as one in which new responses occur, or the characteristics of existing response repertoires are modified, as a function of observing the behaviour of others, without the modelled responses being overtly performed by the viewer during the exposure period. In the light of this definition, when demonstrating imitation it is necessary to employ a non-response acquisition procedure, in which a subject simply observes a model's behaviour, but does not copy whilst the model is performing. Any learning that occurs under these limiting conditions is purely on an observational or covert basis. This is the paradigm, which, with important modifications, forms the basis of many of the experiments mentioned in this review.

The experimental design usually involves the presentation of a model, performing in a specified manner. An opportunity is then provided for the observer, in a period of free expression, to imitate the model. Whilst this technique demonstrates that the observer does or does not copy in whole or part the behaviour to which he has been exposed, there are a number of deficiencies about the design which need mentioning. A brief description of an experiment would perhaps clarify.

Bandura *et al.* (1961) included seventy-two children in their study, thirty-six of each sex, with ages ranging from just over three years to just under six years. The models used were an adult male and an adult female. Subjects were divided into eight experimental groups of six subjects each and a control group of twenty-four subjects. Half the experimental subjects were exposed to models that were subdued and non-aggressive in their behaviour and half to more active aggressive models. These groups were further sub-divided into male and female subjects. Half the subjects in the aggressive and non-aggressive conditions observed same-sex models, while the remaining subjects in each group viewed models of the opposite sex. The non-aggressive model was seen to assemble some 'tinker' toys in a quiet manner. The aggressive model began by assembling the 'tinker' toys and, after approximately a minute had elapsed the model turned to a Bobo doll (an inflatable toy which when knocked over bounces back up again), and spent the remainder of the period aggressing towards it. The control group had no prior exposure to either model and was tested only in the generalized situation. This was a playroom furnished in a very similar manner to the room where the model had been. A nursery-school teacher and the experimenter, both of whom were well acquainted with the children, rated each of them on a variety of five-point scales which were intended to measure the readiness with which they initiated aggressive modes of behaviour. Control and experimental groups could therefore be matched on an individual basis, one control with two experimental subjects, one of the latter being presented with a non-aggressive model, the second with an aggressive model. In the experimental condition each subject was taken individually to an experimental room where he was seated with a task to occupy him. The model was then placed in another part of the room where he could be observed by the subject and was seen to behave in either an aggressive or non-aggressive manner. The aggressive behaviour included a variety of verbal and non-verbal acts directed against an inflated Bobo doll, and the non-aggressive behaviour included subdued assembly behaviour with 'tinker' toys. Subjects were then taken from the experimental room and frustrated by being shown some attractive toys which they were not permitted to play with. This procedure was adopted as Bandura suggested that children normally display aggressive behaviour when they have a reason for doing so. It was presumed that the frustrating experience would have the effect of providing the necessary encouragement. This justification is, however, suspect in the light of other research findings. Kuhn *et al.* (1967) reported that rather than encourage aggressive behaviour, frustration had the effect of inhibiting it, and Maccoby *et al.* (1956) failed to note any increase in retention of aggressive material after subjects had experienced frustration.

Subjects were then taken to a second experimental room and left to play. Their behaviour in this test for delayed imitation was then observed and classified into a number of categories. It is worth noting that each category — aggressive imitation, for example — contains a number of very different behaviours and therefore subjects acting in different ways would receive similar scores for aggressiveness. For example, hitting the Bobo doll with a mallet was scored the same as tossing it in the air aggressively. Are both behaviours equally aggressive? Imitation of a model could be assessed more satisfactorily if greater detail of the individual behavioural components were presented, and greater attention given to their relationship to the model's behaviour.

The manner in which the findings are usually presented prevents judgements of the extent to which the children's behaviour reproduces specific expressive motor patterns of the model. More detailed information about the relative incidence of the physical and verbal components of the children's behaviour would allow a more clear-cut decision on whether they reflect imitation or the subjects' prepotent dispositions. The actual observation techniques customarily provide generalized approximations of the subjects' behaviour, the observers merely indicating, on categorized sheets, the activity at which the child was engaged: the category 'striking the Bobo doll with the mallet', for example, would include the highly aggressive act of vicious striking and also a relatively gentle exploratory tap. If the model had been doing the former, a subject doing the latter could hardly be considered to be imitating.

Records of the subjects' activities are divided into five- (*Bandura et al.* 1961), and sometimes ten- or even fifteen-second intervals, with the consequence that to examine the time spent on any particular activity, and this is an important test of the extent of the influence of the model, errors of approximation may become large. Information concerning the number of incidents of imitation are of little value without details of their duration. That some experimenters do report their findings in a generalized manner is probably beyond dispute. Rosenkrans and Hartup (1967), who reported that children sometimes reproduced relatively unusual observed acts of aggression toward a clay figure, unfortunately did not specifically indicate the incidence of these acts.

An important criticism of the techniques used to demonstrate the effect of a model concerns the use of control groups. First, when a non-aggressive model is used as a control for an aggressive model there is usually a difference in the level of activity between the two films: the non-aggressive model being the less active when such conditions do obtain, it could be that level of activity is the important variable rather than the aggressive behaviour. Secondly, a group of subjects are exposed to a model and the amount of imitative behaviour they display is then compared to the behaviour spontaneously emitted by a comparable group of subjects who did not observe the model. It is assumed that the occurrence of imitation will be obvious when the subject reproduces the model's behaviour, and it is novel with respect to what might be expected to be normal. This can, of course, be estimated by means of reference to the control group. In the case of most experiments, it is reasonable to assume that the children would not spontaneously emit much of the behaviour which they show, if they had not first been provided with cues by a model. The use of different children as a control is, however, not very satisfactory. In many experiments the number of children used is small, and therefore the behaviour of each child is important. As children vary considerably in their behaviour, it is not really satisfactory to state that because one child does not do something it is unlikely that another will do it.

A more satisfactory method of providing a control on which to base an estimation of the effect of the model would be to use each child as his own control by comparing his behaviour before and after the exposure experience. One experiment is reported to have done this (*Kuhn et al.*, 1967) using a pre-observational base line of behaviour to estimate the amount of imitation elicited. This experiment, however, can be criticized on the grounds that the five-minute period allowed was insufficient to permit the child to do more than explore the novel environment. In another experiment (*Kniveton* and *Stephenson,* 1970) a longer pre-observational baseline was included in the design. However, this proved to be a variable in itself: playing in the situation before seeing the film model, the children learned various methods of playing which later affected how much they were influenced by the model. Stringent investigation of experimental control techniques is therefore very necessary.

Goranson's (1970) review does, I feel, answer satisfactorily the most frequently expressed criticism of all, which is that experiments of this type do not relate to real life. He suggests that if enough experiments produce similar findings using varying experimental designs, and if enough different groups of subjects, whether they be children or university students, are used in these experiments, it is reasonable to use the consensus of the finding to predict behaviour. There has been a considerable amount of research conducted on modelling effects and, I feel, the findings warrant consideration. The analysis of experimental weaknesses does not apply to every experiment; some have few failings. Therefore I am able to restrict the discussion to areas where a number of different experiments produce consistent findings and where it is possible to be reasonably confident that the conclusions reached are applicable to the social learning situation.

CHARACTERISTICS OF THE MODEL

Experimental studies of the modelling process have been concerned with the differing effects of a variety of models on the imitative behaviour of the viewer. The findings predictably revolve around the basic psychological principle that the more attractive or the more rewarding the model appears to the particular viewer, the more likely he is to imitate its behaviour. A brief review of some results may clarify the relative influences of some typical models.

It is demonstrable that when the model is rewarded for his actions, the child observers imitate more than when the model is punished. (*Bandura et al.,* 1963a; *Bandura* and *McDonald* 1963; *Bandura* and *Whalen,* 1966; *Rosenkrans* and *Hartup,* 1967; *Walters et al.,* 1963). Furthermore, research shows that it is the punishment which has a suppressive effect on the observer's behaviour and is, therefore, a more influential feature than the reward. Children who observe behaviour that is followed by no particular obvious consequences engage in the same behaviour almost as much as do those who have observed the rewarded consequences of the behaviour. (*Bandura,* 1965; *Walters* and *Parke,* 1964; *Walters et al.,* 1965.)

Other researchers (*Rosenbaum, et al.,* 1962; *Henker,* 1964) have shown that a highly competent model in the viewers' eyes is likely to result in children displaying a higher degree of imitation than a less competent model. Rosenbaum and Tucker (1962) expanded on this by showing that high and low competent models produced a higher degree of imitation than those of mediocre competence. Other variables related to high competence have also been shown to enhance the influence of the model. Age (*Bandura* and *Kupers,* 1964; *Hicks,* 1965), sex (*Bandura et al.,* 1963b; *Rosenblith* 1959), social power (*Mischel* and *Grusec,* 1966) and ethnic status (*Epstein* 1966), which are generally associated with predictable reinforcing outcomes, likewise influence the degree to which social attitudes and behaviour will be reproduced by others. This has similarly been shown with models who are purported experts (*Mausner,* 1953) or, with adults, celebrities (*Hovland et al.,* 1953), and those who possess symbols of socio-economic success (*Lefkowitz et al.,* 1955).

Bandura and Kupers (1964) reported that adults served as more powerful modelling stimuli than peers in transmitting self-reinforcing responses. Nicholas *et al.,* (1971) largely support this finding. These studies suggest that because of differential competencies, adults are likely to exhibit more successful and rewarding responses than peers and, therefore, to the extent that children are differentially rewarded for matching adult and peer models, adults would usually become the most powerful modelling stimuli. In contrast, however, Hicks (1965) found that children imitated an aggressive peer model more than an adult model. In one of my own studies (*Kniveton* 1973a) I hypothesized that these conflicting findings could be accounted for by social class differences in identification with adult models. It was anticipated that middle-class children would be more likely to imitate an adult than a child model and that the reverse would be the case with working-class children. This did not happen. There was, however, a tendency for the adult model to have a greater effect on total imitation than the peer model. The relative influence of adult and peer models needs further clarification, probably in the area of role expectations; for example, adults behaving in an adult manner, it may be assumed, will prove a more attractive model to the viewing child than will adults behaving in a juvenile manner.

Bandura and Huston (1961), working on the assumption that identification is a process of incidental learning, investigated the hypothesis that children should imitate the behaviour of individuals with whom they feel an affection more than those they do not. Prior to the test situation children were placed with a model who bahaved in either a 'warm' (affectionate) or a 'cold' (not affectionate) manner. Children who were exposed to the 'warm' model patterned their behaviour more on that of the model than those exposed to the 'cold' model. Aggressive behaviour, however, was imitated irrespective of which model was observed. This experiment demonstrates that the characteristics of the model, although important in determining its influence, are not independent of the type of behaviour observed. The relationship between model and observer in this situation does not affect aggressive imitation, but does affect the other experimental measures, namely, discrimination in a learning situation and constructive behaviour.

A number of studies explored the extent to which the viewer is able to relate the model's behaviour to his own. There are two ways in which this factor has been investigated by researchers: first they have considered the closeness with which the model resembles real life, and secondly the relationship between the stimuli observed and the stimuli available to the observer when he has an opportunity to re-enact the behaviour displayed by the model. Bandura (1965) suggests that children learn to imitate the behaviour of a model towards a stimulus by the contiguity of similar stimuli and mediation. This theory, stated more concretely, suggests that a child observes a model performing and retains images of this behaviour. At a later time, perhaps when the model is no longer present, the child, on entering a situation which is sufficiently similar to that in which the model performed, will associate the two situations and imitate some part or all of the behaviour displayed by the model. Imitation of the whole of the behaviour pattern of the model is unusual, but partial imitation may occur and other behaviour may show obvious signs of being inspired by that of the model. According to this theory there are two predictions upon which studies have thrown some light. Firstly it could be anticipated that the more similar the model is to the observer, in the observer's eyes, the greater the likelihood that the observer will imitate its behaviour. A number of studies have investigated this and although the findings are not too clear a definite tendency can be seen. Lovas (1961) and Siegal (1956) exposed children to films of animated cartoons depicting a large number of aggressive acts and both found that few of the subjects displayed the aggressive behaviour seen on the film. This suggests that animated cartoons are too far removed from real life for the children to consider them appropriate models. Alternatively it may be that a cartoon does not offer sufficient sanction to permit the child viewer to be aggressive in a manner which is not socially acceptable. Mussen and Rutherford (1961), on the other hand, present different findings. In their study, unlike those mentioned previously, the children were not assessed by their willingness to be aggressive in a social context, but were asked to answer questions in a relaxed permissive environment. Their answers reflected increased aggressiveness after watching aggressive cartoons. This demonstrated that it is not so much an inability to relate the aggressive cartoon to their situation which is the operative variable, but a reluctance to go against their own social mores with only the sanction of an animated cartoon. The obviously much needed follow-up experiment was conducted by Bandura *et al.*, (1963a) in which they presented to children either a live human model, or a film of a human model, or an animated cartoon. The results largely confirm that the more similar the model to real life, the more the influence on the child's subsequent behaviour. My interpretation is that with aggressive behaviour a child will willingly accept the sanction of seeing an adult commit taboo acts, but will not take the risk of accepting the sanction of an animated cartoon. Alternatively, the importance of identification with the model is examined in another experiment with a very different design. Rather than the stimulus being altered, the situation was investigated: three conditions were included. Meyerson (1966), after exposing children to a film of a model performing aggressively, placed them in a play situation with high, medium or low similarity to the observed setting. The results showed that the level of imitative aggression increased with increasing similarity between the film and the post-film settings.

INDIVIDUAL'S SUSCEPTIBILITY TO MODELLING INFLUENCES

Research into modelling processes has been preoccupied with the method of presentation of the model. Some of the variables which have been reviewed outline the importance of reinforcement and identification with the model; however, each viewer is an individual with his own past experience, expertise and motivations. This becomes extremely important in the context of television violence, for if television does have an anti-social effect, there is every reason to believe that some children and adolescents are more at risk than others. The question, therefore, is which children are more likely to be influenced in their behaviour?

Bandura (1971) argues that viewer characteristics cannot be considered to be divorced from the characteristics of the model for, as we have already seen, factors such as the status of the model, the competence of the model and the age of the model affect the extent to which imitation occurs. Each of these is obviously relative to the status, competence and age of the viewer. A model who appears competent to one viewer, in another viewer's eyes appears as a novice. I believe, however, that viewer characteristics can be isolated and if these are examined in a number of varied situations it is reasonable to assume that generalizations can be made as to which individuals are likely to be put at risk. Bandura (1971) himself suggests that a minimum cognitive development or skill development is necessary for a viewer to imitate a model's behaviour. The child who does not have the intellectual ability to comprehend the highly skilled actions of a brain surgeon is hardly likely to be able to imitate his behaviour. Similarly the child who is insufficiently well developed physically will be unable to imitate the behaviour of an older model (*Kniveton* 1974).

Kniveton and Stephenson (1970) hypothesize that children with few interests of their own are likely to be more susceptible to the film model's example than those children with other interests. In this experiment, middle-class children, who had prior experience with the toys to be seen in the film, imitated the behaviour shown on the film significantly less than those who did not have this experience. The authors suggest that pre-experience had provided the subjects with an opportunity to develop their own interests which 'inoculated' them against the film's influence. This concept of 'inoculation' will be examined in more detail later when the impact of television violence is considered on the social learning of young people. In a subsequent experiment (*Kniveton* and *Stephenson,* 1972) an interaction between social class and pre-experience was observed. Working-class children seemed less able to develop their own interests than did middle-class children. This was shown in an examination of the play behaviour of children from both social class groups over a period of time. The behaviour of middle-class children stabilized more quickly than working-class children and this was illustrated by a decrease in the amount of 'flitting' from toy to toy, and in the number of toys played with. The amount of imitation displayed by working-class children was greater than that shown by middle-class children, except when the amount of pre-experience was extended considerably. This social class difference was examined in relation to the development of interest in play (*Kniveton* and *Pike*, 1972). Intelligence was a second variable which interacted to affect the constructiveness of play, as did length of time in the play situation. Constructiveness decreased with time and this was taken to indicate increasing boredom. Working-class children reached an earlier boredom peak than middle-class children, but the fact that the children were restricted to the experimental situation complicated the issue, as there was little alternative to playing with the toys. The middle-class children soon exhausted other activities and returned to the toys. Their behaviour was accompanied by an appropriate change in verbalizations from non-toy to toy-related conversation. These results highlight the effects of social class and intelligence, with particular reference to length of experience in the play situation. The major effect of these variables seems to be upon the low-level constructiveness of play and on talking in the experimental situation. Lack of interest reflected in a low level of constructiveness implies vulnerability to influences.

Kniveton and Stephenson (1973) have demonstrated that the

tendency to imitate an aggressive film is a consistent behavioural characteristic. In this experiment children of both middle-class and working-class homes were exposed on two occasions to very different aggressive films. The two play experiences took place in different laboratories with an interval between sessions of at least four months. There was a highly significant positive correlation between imitative response to the two films. Children largely reacted aggressively to both or to neither film. In addition it was shown that increases in aggression occurred consistently over and above the initial tendency to behave in that way. Kniveton (1973b), with working-class children who were readily influenced, showed the effect of an aggressive film to be long lasting. Many months after seeing the film children were placed in the play situation again and still imitated as much as they did immediately after seeing the film.

Other researchers have reported factors which can be considered in relation to the vulnerability of the viewer. For example, Crutchfield (1955) outlined types of people who were unlikely to conform to group pressure: highly creative individuals were less likely to conform than less creative. Rosenbaum and de Charms (1960) showed that subjects with less self-esteem were more easily conditioned and more prone to imitate behaviour, and Lanzetta and Kanareff (1959) showed 'incompetents' to be more prone to imitate models. And children not attending nursery school imitate aggressive models less than those who do (*Kniveton* 1972).

Summary

From the studies outlined so far we can extract two general conclusions: first, some models are more influential than others and, secondly, some viewers are consistently more likely to be influenced by models than others. It has been suggested that the greater the breadth of experience available to the viewer, the less he will be affected by the model's example. This interpretation will be substantiated later with particular reference to the effects of television violence.

TELEVISION VIOLENCE AND AGGRESSIVE SOCIAL BEHAVIOUR

There has been a great deal of literature published concerning the social consequences of watching aggressive television, and a number of recent studies will be discussed which demonstrate the variety of techniques that are used to reveal effects on the viewers' social behaviour. For example, correlational material (*McIntyre* and *Teevan*, 1972) shows an association between exposure to aggressive television and various measures of aggression among children and adolescents. Correlational studies show that children who are aggressive watch more aggressive television than children who are less aggressive. However, they do not provide any proof that it is watching violent television that makes them aggressive. It could equally be that because they are already aggressive they choose to watch violence on television, or that both activities are linked to some third causal factor. Many other studies have found correlations between preference for television violence and children's aggressive behaviour (*Eron,* 1963; *Baker* and *Ball*, 1969), but no relation of aggressive behaviour to overall frequency of television viewing. The fact that aggressive children claim they watch a great deal of violent television could be explained by Pfuhl's interpretation (1970) that delinquents will be only too eager to deflect blame from themselves on to the shoulders of the film producers.

Some recent experimental work has attempted to come to grips with the problem of filmed material and aggressive behaviour in interpersonal situations. Researchers have tried to show that children who watch violent films will behave in an aggressive manner with other children after seeing the films. In some experiments (*Leifer* and *Roberts,* 1972) children are exposed to aggressive films and then asked which of various alternate acts they would commit against another child. Children who saw the aggressive film selected more violent verbal responses than those not shown the aggressive film. Of course, it should be remembered that what the child *says* he would do will not necessarily predict what he actually *would* do. In other experiments (*Leibert* and *Baron*, 1972) children were encouraged, after exposure to an aggressive film, to take part in a task which supposedly allowed them to help or hurt another child in a separate room. The form this procedure took was that the child was told that the subject in the other room was playing a game and that whenever a white light came on on his own control panel he was either to press a green button and help the other subject, or a red button which would make a handle the other subject was holding hot and thus hurt him. The buttons were clearly labelled 'help' and hurt'. Results from this experiment show that seeing the violent film makes the children more willing to 'hurt' another child than children who saw a neutral film. These studies certainly suggest that television violence may affect social behaviour, but they do not take into account the social and moral constraints which operate in a real face-to-face encounter, nor do they examine the suggestion that children learn specific aggressive acts from films, that is, imitate.

Stein and Friedrick (1972) conducted one of the few field studies showing a strong link between watching aggressive films and a heightening of aggressive behaviour. They included in their sample four- to five-year-old boys and girls, and exposed them to a series of aggressive, pro-social, or neutral films over a series of days in the school setting. The children's behaviour in daily play situations was observed during a two-week period after seeing the film series. They found that aggressive programmes increased the aggressive behaviour of children who were already relatively high in aggression. At the same time, self-controlling behaviour, particularly tolerance for minor frustrations, declined for all children exposed to the aggressive condition. This reduction in self-control was accompanied for children from higher social class groups by increased social interaction that was primarily co-operative. It appears, therefore, that the aggressive programmes had a general stimulative effect on the children from higher social class groups that led to higher social interaction and lower levels of self-control. It must be noted, though, that this study demonstrates not that violence on television encourages the viewer to be violent, but that it encourages the viewer who typically displays a high level of aggression to be violent. This study will be referred to again below. As a field study it avoids many of the inadequacies of experiments already mentioned and its contribution to our understanding of the effects of television is, in my view, rather important.

Milgram and Shotland (1973) in a series of experiments attempted to show the effects of anti-social behaviour on television in a naturalistic setting. Unlike almost all other experimenters, they were involved in the preparation of a programme in a series which was shown by an American television company (which, incidentally, sponsored the project). The experimental manipulations were complex, however; the basic outline was that in the programme a character was seen to be frustrated by being removed from his job. He then telephoned a charity organization and threatened to steal from and then destroy their charity boxes.

He was then seen to be doing this and according to the experimental condition was either rewarded (by escaping) or punished (by being caught). A variety of methods was used by the experimenters to select samples of viewers who had seen the programme, and these were asked to complete questionnaires which concerned the programme generally. As an inducement to co-operate they were offered transistor radios for their assistance. These had to be collected from distribution centres where the subjects were in some conditions frustrated by being informed that the radios were not available. At this stage, they were faced with charity boxes similar to those shown in the television film and their behaviour was observed for evidence of imitation of the behaviour of the character shown on the film. The findings of the project failed to produce any evidence which supported the view that anti-social acts on television encourage the viewer to behave in an anti-social manner. The authors suggest many reasons why the results could have been negative. However, there are a number of serious criticisms of the study that they failed to mention. Perhaps the most important of these is that viewers are exposed to violence on television on a daily basis and it is the effects of this long-term experience which is of concern. It seems naive, to say the least, to present on one occasion a specific violent act and expect viewers to imitate it at the first opportunity. In addition, the violent behaviour selected by Milgram and Shotland was really most inappropriate as an assessment of the effects of violence on television on viewers' behaviour. Breaking into charity boxes is a particularly anti-social type of behaviour which the average citizen would probably find broke too many taboos. On the other hand, the hardened delinquent is unlikely to find the behaviour either attractive or novel. It is the researcher's responsibility to select acts which people actually do, and then in his study demonstrate an effect of television by showing whether the incidences of that type of behaviour increase. In addition, *Medical Centre* may not have been a suitable programme to select for purposes of the research project, for it is not exceptionally violent and McIntyre and Teevan (1972) have shown that violent people do not watch non-violent programmes as much as they watch violent ones. It could be that Milgram failed to attract a violent audience.

In the light of these criticisms the study, in my view, contributes little to our knowledge of the effect of television violence. It does not give television violence the clean bill of health it appears to, because there is no evidence that the behaviour investigated is likely to be imitated, particularly in this one-off situation. The study has been mentioned as it is one of the very few cases where the media have co-operated in such a practical way with this type of research, but it is unfortunate that the experiment was so naive in its construction.

Summary

I have suggested that the experimental studies, of which those mentioned previously are simply a sample, do not demonstrate that watching violence on television will necessarily encourage the viewer to be violent. There is, however, no reason why some of them should not be considered to have their own intrinsic merit. It is the broad generalizations which are made from their very limited findings that are suspect. This experimental evidence does show quite clearly that under certain circumstances watching violent behaviour on films can result in the viewer having aggressive thought reactions to situations, although thinking aggressively is one thing and acting in an aggressive manner with another human being is a very different matter. Similarly it has been shown that children after being exposed to violent films will administer, by pressing a button, 'hurt' to other children under the direction of the experimenter. Here the situation is an extremely permissive one, and the target of the aggressive behaviour is somewhat remote. Noble (1973) provides support for this by demonstrating how aggressive behaviour varied with the remoteness of the target. He suggested that children became more anxious after seeing aggression filmed with the victim being clearly seen rather than when the victim was a considerable distance away. Extrapolating from this finding one could suggest that whilst a child will press a button to institute 'hurt' to a victim in a permissive atmosphere this is not evidence which shows that he will necessarily be prepared to hit or attack the victim personally in real life. Correlational studies show little more than that viewers who are themselves delinquent or violent watch violent television programmes more than people who are not delinquent; the evidence which can be considered appropriate to real life, that of Stein *et al.* (1972), only reports aggressive arousal after seeing aggressive films from people who are initially aggressive anyway. This finding is, however, particularly pertinent and is supported by other studies to be mentioned later. The aggressive individual is, one may assume, the one most likely to commit a violent anti-social act, and it is he who is most influenced by violence on television according to Stein's study.

THE CATHARSIS HYPOTHESIS

For a while, evidence suggested that violence and aggression on films and television had a therapeutic value — the catharsis hypothesis. Exponents of this theory suggest that the involvement in fantasy aggression may serve as a 'displacement', providing a harmless 'release' for children's hostile impulses, thus reducing the instigation to overt acts of aggression (*Albert*, 1957; *Dollard et al.*, 1939; *Emery,* 1959; *Kenny*, 1952; *Lovas*, 1961; *Siegal*, 1956). Feshbach (1955) produced experimental support for the catharsis hypothesis. He found that self-initiated verbal responses while writing TAT stories following the arousal of aggression led to a reduction in the amount of subsequent interpersonal aggression. (TAT: Thematic Apperception Test. The subject is asked to produce imaginative stories based on sets of ambiguous illustrations.)

The original formulation of the catharsis hypothesis, as a result of largely negative experimental findings has been revised by some theorists (*Buss,* 1961; *Feshbach*, 1961). They contend that the cathartic or drive-reducing function of aggressive modelling stimuli occurs only under certain, specified conditions. Witnessing the behaviour of aggressive models supposedly decreases subsequent aggression when the observer has been aggressively aroused at the time of exposure. If, on the other hand, the aggressive drive has not been activated whilst the film was being watched, such exposure increases ensuing aggressive responses. The revised catharsis theory thus presupposes that the functional properties of modelling stimuli are dependent upon transitory emotional states of the observer. However, an alternative explanation of many experiments which can be used to support the catharsis hypothesis is that exposure to aggressive films arouses anxiety in the viewer and consequently subsequent aggressive behaviour is inhibited. This view will be discussed in the next section.

VIOLENT FILMS AS INHIBITORS OF AGGRESSIVE BEHAVIOUR

There is a growing number of studies which demonstrate that for a variety of reasons many viewers are discouraged from being aggressive as a consequence of watching violent programmes. I hasten to point out that the studies to be discussed do not demonstrate that violent television does not encourage aggressive behaviour, but they do indicate that under certain circumstances some viewers are discouraged from being aggressive for reasons other than those put forward by the exponents of the catharsis hypothesis. Perhaps the obvious place to start is to refer back to the study by Stein *et al.* (1972). They found that children who were initially low in aggression did not behave more aggressively after seeing a violent film than did non-aggressive children who had seen a pro-social or neutral film. They suggest that these children, in the course of their socialization, had developed controls over their aggressive impulses which were sufficient to prevent aggressive behavioural effects, or alternatively, they may have more aggressive anxiety (ie feel anxious and uneasy when they see aggressive behaviour) than children who are typically highly aggressive, and this it is hypothesized would inhibit their violent behaviour. This latter explanation is supported by a study of my own (*Kniveton*, 1974) in an experiment in which very young children displayed fear whilst watching a film of a child model beating an inflatable doll. They subsequently refused to have any contact with any of the stimuli seen on the film. In addition, an experiment conducted by Noble (1970) provides further evidence to support the anxiety hypothesis. Six groups, each containing four six-year-old boys and girls, were shown a war film and a puppet film in random order. Immediately after exposure to each film the groups of children were observed during a twenty-minute play session in a room which contained stimuli similar to those seen on the two films. The results showed that a regression in play occurred after seeing the war film. In this context a regression means that the child's behaviour became typical of that of a child of a younger age; in particular it is less constructive. This means that instead of the child playing in complex and involved ways with the toys he played in a simpler manner. Freud (1933) and Barker *et al.* (1941) interpret a regression in behaviour as being symptomatic of anxiety reactions. When social class was controlled it was found that these regressive responses were apparent only for children of middle-class parentage. The findings of the study are interpreted by the experimenter in terms of anxiety reactions. He suggests that working-class children were less shocked by the war film (perhaps because they see more of such films, or because they were not encouraged by their parents to condemn this type of violence) than were the middle-class children in the sample. This interpretation is substantiated in part by other researchers. Newson and Newson (1968), for example, have shown that middle-class mothers claim to discipline their children by physical aggression less than working-class mothers and aggressive behaviour in working-class children is said to be tolerated more. An additional finding by Noble that there was a greater general reduction in the level of social interaction after seeing the war film than that which took place in the control groups supports the anxiety hypothesis. Children who feel anxious play with other children less.

A number of survey studies have shown that various types of aggression disturb children (*Himmelweit et al.*, 1958; *Schramm et al.*, 1961). These researchers found that realistically filmed aggression, portrayed in a ritualistic and stereotyped way, and aggression involving daggers and sharp instruments rather than guns have the effect of upsetting young children. Noble (1973) presents evidence in an experimental study which modifies this view somewhat. He suggests that it is the sight of the victim seen at close range, rather than the weapons involved, which determines the amount of anxiety induced in the child viewer. Four films were used in this study: one showed realistic aggression, the second stylistic aggression; both films showed aggression with sight of the victim. The remaining two films, again realistic and stylistic, showed aggression at a distance from the victim. The results supported the view that children play less constructively after viewing realistically filmed agression than after viewing stylistically filmed aggression. Again a decrease in constructiveness, or a regression in behaviour, is interpreted as a symptom of anxiety. This supports Himmelweit's finding. Noble also found that children play less constructively after seeing aggression filmed with sight of the victim rather than at a distance. Noble suggests that it is the sight of the victim that causes the most anxiety and not, as suggested by Schramm, that it is the type of weapon used that is the anxiety stimulus. In this experiment, incidentally, the children regressed more in their play when they had seen a film using guns as weapons than one using swords and knives. The greatest amount of anxiety was displayed when realism was combined with sight of the victim and the least when stylistic aggression was filmed at a distance. Incidentally, destructive play was rarely displayed by the children in this experiment. Hartmann (1965) demonstrated how exposure to the consequence of violence can reduce the aggressive behaviour of subjects. Subjects were shown one of three films of a vigorous but non-violent basketball game. Of the two experimental versions of the film one focused on the attackers' responses, the other on the victims' plight (the pain cues version). Half the subjects were angered before seeing the films by being allowed to hear a fellow subject (actually a confederate of the experimenter) make derogatory remarks about them, and the others heard the confederate making neutral statements about them. After observation of the films the subjects were given an opportunity in the context of a learning situation to administer electric shocks to the confederate. The effect of the aggressive film versions on the angered subjects was to increase the intensity and duration of the electric shocks (ie they were more aggressive), this being most marked in the pain cues version. With the non-angered subjects the effect of the pain cues film was to reduce the intensity and duration of the shocks they administered. These results suggest that these subjects (incidentally they were teen-age juvenile delinquents) were sensitized by seeing the consequences of violence, and hence, appreciating the significance of violent behaviour, their own aggressive reactions were inhibited. Presumably this was not the case with the angered subjects. The significant feature of this experiment is, however, that it demonstrated that the emotional receptivity of the viewer influences whether he will be influenced by violence on films. If he is not in an angered mood he is unlikely to exhibit aggressive behaviour. Vulnerability to the anti-social effects of films is dependent on transitory emotional states rather than being an enduring characteristic. This supports Stein's finding mentioned earlier and is really rather important. The very people who are most willing to cast aside the rules of society because of their emotional state are the ones most likely to be influenced by television violence.

Feshbach and Singer (1971) in an extensive naturalistic study managed to incorporate experimental controls over a six-week period. Varied samples of adolescent boys were exposed to a diet of aggressive or non-aggressive television programmes. The boys attended a variety of residential schools, and were randomly assigned to one of the viewing selections. This meant that the programmes they were permitted to watch were listed by the researchers. Various measures were taken to avoid difficulties which could occur when a child was not allowed to watch a programme he normally enjoyed. The behaviour of the boys in their schools over the period was observed along with a number of other measures. Within the restrictions of the sample characteristics, range of stimuli utilized, and duration of the experiment, the experimenters found that exposure to aggressive content in television does not lead to an increase in aggressive behaviour, and also that exposure to aggressive content in television seems to reduce or control the expression of aggression in aggressive boys from relatively low socio-economic backgrounds. They suggest that boys, who are already typically aggressive, have little to learn from the film as they have already acquired a repertoire of aggressive behaviour. They further suggest that non-aggressive boys were prevented from being aggressive as a consequence of their own socialized controls which restrict this type of behaviour. Against laboratory studies they argue that the experimenter gives approval for aggressive behaviour, whereas in the naturalistic situation there is no one to provide this sanction, and so the viewers' own inhibitions have more effect. Feshbach also maintains that violence in the form of fiction is much less likely to reinforce, stimulate or elicit aggressive responses in children than is violence in the form of news events. Relatedly the world of drama, play and imagination is not the same as the world of social interaction, work and factual communication.

CONFLICTING FINDINGS?

Stein, with normally aggressive children of between four and five and a half years of age, found that viewing aggressive films increased their aggressive behaviour. Feshbach, with children between eight and eighteen years found with normally aggressive children that they did not become more aggressive after watching aggressive television. It would, therefore, appear that the influence violence on television has on aggressive youngsters depends on the age range under consideration. It would seem likely that the socialized controls of the younger children are not sufficiently strong to prevent their indulging in violent behaviour whereas those of the older children are stronger, and as Feshbach suggests, they anyway have little to learn from aggressive films. Younger children on the other hand are still building up an aggressive repertoire and so the films provide them with more ideas. These explanations need investigating experimentally.

There is no reason to suppose that Hartmann's finding, that angered subjects (teen-agers) aggress more as a consequence of watching violent films, conflicts with this view. Hartmann angered a group of subjects; this was a transitory state, unlike Feshbach's subjects who were normally aggressive and so the two are examining different emotional states.

Summary

Taken together these studies suggest firstly, that aggressive fictional violence does not encourage the non-aggressive child to be aggressive (*Feshbach* and *Singer*, 1971; *Stein et al.*, 1972). Secondly, that real-life violence with the consequence clearly shown causes anxiety in the viewer and does not encourage him to be aggressive (*Noble* 1970 and 1973). Thirdly, that naturally aggressive young children are incited to be violent by watching violence on films but that with older children this is not the case. It would seem, however, that teen-agers, when angered, are likely to be encouraged to be violent after watching violence on television.

THE PRO-SOCIAL INFLUENCE OF TELEVISION

Whilst the preoccupation of researchers has been with the effects of violent television on young viewers there is some evidence that television does have a constructive and useful role to play in the development of children. If we refer back once again to the study by Stein *et al.*, (1972) there is some evidence that the pro-social programmes were most effective in helping the children to develop increased self-control and task persistence. This was most marked in children with relatively high levels of intellectual functioning. Overall it appeared that exposure to the pro-social programmes increased pro-social inter-personal behaviour, particularly co-opertion, for lower social class children. Exposure to the aggressive programmes resulted in increased pro-social behaviour for children of higher social classes. The researchers offer a tentative explanation for this finding, suggesting that the lower social class children had little expertise in pro-social behaviour and found the behaviour novel and hence rewarding. The higher class children may have found the aggressive film which they were not used to seeing exciting and, as they were already skilled in pro-social techniques, the generalized stimulation could have led to increased pro-social interaction. The heightening of activity level after watching a film was also observed by the present author (Kniveton, 1973a) in an experiment concerned with modelling in which the children were significantly more active in their general behaviour after watching an aggressive film.

In general, evidence suggests that children who are, for any reason, limited in their opportunities for getting experience in life will turn to television as a source. This applies to non-aggressive beahviour as much as to aggressive behaviour. Feshbach and Singer (1971) suggest that normally aggressive children have little to learn from aggressive television, and similarly Schramm *et al.*, (1961), in a study conducted when television was still a relatively new addition to our experiences, found that the children who were likely to learn from television had limited environmental experiences. The child living in a city flat, for example, is unlikely to know of the existence of cows and other rural features if he cannot read or has not been taken to the country by parents anxious to broaden his outlook on life. Schramm suggests that as children grow older television becomes less important as a source of information, since alternative more efficient means become available. Any learning that then takes place is really incidental, bits of information being picked up as and when they are presented in the course of programmes.

Schramm suggests that it is largely the factor of novelty (the absence of novelty was suggested by Feshbach and Singer (1971) to be a possible cause for the lack of violent behaviour with aggressive subjects) which attracts attention on the media, and hence it is with younger less well-experienced children that learning from television will have most effect. Very young children cannot tell reality from fantasy; therefore they are influenced as much by television as they are by all the new things around them. As they get older they realize that much television is fantasy and they feel less associated with it. Learning is influenced by the amount of identification that occurs with specific characters. A child can store up for future use the opinions and attitudes of these characters, just as they can store up the opinions and attitudes of parents, teachers and peers.

Brown *et al.*, (1973) also suggest that children use television as an information source. They are virtually always prepared to accept new information and the media present, over a period of time, a fairly wide range of information about people and places and things. They suggest, too, that when the information need is specific, television loses its importance in preference to other sources, because the child does not have control over when information is broadcast. With increased age the child's ability to select the most useful medium to acquire information improves and television becomes less important as a source.

The information value of television does, however, need to be kept in perspective in the view of Trenaman and McQuail (1971) who support the general point that people do receive information from television but found that the viewer managed to screen himself from direct persuasion in the short term. Hovland (1959) explains that whilst attitudes can be changed in the laboratory, in general campaigns conducted through the mass media are not successful in producing mass changes in attitude in the short term on any issue that people really care about and are involved in. The essential point about these notes of caution, however, is the emphasis on the short term. Exposure to television is a long-term experience and so changes in people's attitudes are going to occur, if they do, after many months or years of watching television. It is thus very difficult for the social scientist to monitor these changes and be able to attribute them to the effects of television as distinct from the consequences of any other of life's experiences.

INOCULATION AGAINST THE INFLUENCE OF MODELS

The significance of the finding that the child's own breadth of interests may serve to 'inoculate' him against the effects of a model is considerable. It suggests quite plainly that the child who will be most likely to be influenced for good or bad by models is the child who for some reason has been brought up in an environment where he is not encouraged to develop his own ideas and behaviours. The child whose parents encourage him to watch television, read books, talk about the programmes and discuss what they have read, who is taken for rides in the car and walks and is encouraged as he goes along to notice points of interest and ask questions about them, the child who is given toys and not just left to play but is encouraged by his parents to 'see what kind of new games you can play with it', this is the child whose breadth of experience will give him the confidence in a situation to think for himself. He is less likely to seek someone to show him how to behave. Firstly, he will have his own more considerable experiences to call upon and secondly he will be used to exploratory learning and finding out how to do things for himself. If he does turn to a model for guidance, and obviously there will be times when this child needs someone to demonstrate how to do something, the occasions will not be as frequent as for the child who has not been brought up in this type of stimulating environment.

The value of the viewer's own experience in inoculating him against any specific model's influence finds direct and implied support from a variety of experimental sources. This encourages me to extrapolate and suggest that the principle of inoculation applies also to television violence. For example, Schramm *et al.*, (1961) suggest that the influence of television material is closely related to the novelty value of that material, and hence if one assumes that a broadly experienced child will find less television material to be novel, it follows that he will be less likely to be influenced.

Baker and Ball (1969) state that pre-school children are thought to be especially susceptible because they are less able than older children to separate fantasy from reality, or to treat what they see as being something which is not relevant to themselves. Everything they see concerns them and so the younger the child the greater his vulnerability to the influence of a model. In addition, Feshbach and Singer (1971) suggest that fantasy stands as a protection between the internally aroused individual and his need to engage in behaviour which may be damaging to himself or others. Meltzoff, *et al.* (1953) and Singer (1960) consider fantasy to be a controlling mechanism which allows for delays in behaviour. Feshbach and Singer argue that since part of fantasy is cognitive, the more advanced the child the more able he will be to utilize fantasy in constructive ways. Singer (1966) indicates that variables such as higher intelligence, upper-middle-class family background, provision of books, and time alone, are productive of the ability to develop fantasy skills. Children of lower intelligence, lacking books, suffering impoverished stimulation and with no time to be alone or to think, have less ability to fantasize. From a very different theoretical viewpoint this supports the views already expressed based on experimental results. A child's vulnerability to be influenced by models depends to a considerable extent on factors involved in the socialization process such as social class, methods of upbringing and so on. Baker and Ball (1969) support this view by suggesting that children with a more limited repertoire of behaviours are more likely to adopt actions presented to them on television. They suggest that some children have a socialization 'void', whether it be for aggressive or non-aggressive behaviour. Yet another argument which finds support in the study by Stein *et al.*, (1972).

Psychologists are concerned not only with explaining behaviour but also with predicting an individual's responses in a situation. In this context it is possible that the concept of inoculation against the influence of a model is a useful one. There is a considerable amount of research in the child development literature (for example, *Mussen et al.*, 1970) which specifies the variables which influence whether a child is likely to be able readily to develop his own methods of behaving in a variety of situations, or whether strangeness presents a stressful and anxiety-producing situation in which any example which provides an acceptable pattern of behaviour is copied with enthusiasm.

Summary

Studies into social learning and imitation reviewed in this chapter show: firstly that children will imitate the behaviour of models if they see that behaviour as being more rewarding than actions they can think of for themselves. The better able the child to develop his own interests, and the broader his own experience, the less susceptible he will be to a model's influence, whether that model be parent, peer or television character. Secondly, that in experimental situations children and adults as a consequence of watching violent films can be encouraged to display aggressive behaviour in contrived situations, but it is doubtful whether one is justified in extrapolating from this that violent television makes the viewer aggressive. One study which is more closely related to the real-life television viewing situation shows an aggressive after-effect only for young children who are of an aggressive disposition anyway. In another study this is not shown to apply to older children and adolescents who are of a naturally aggressive temperament. Thirdly, studies show that when the horrific consequences of violence are shown the normally non-aggressive viewer is likely to become anxious and will certainly not behave in an aggressive manner.

Social learning is a complex, long-term process and it is difficult for the social scientist to attribute changes in behaviour and attitudes to any particular one of life's many varied experiences.

NOTE

I would like to thank a colleague, Tony Routledge, for his critical and helpful comments on an early draft of this chapter. He is, however, in no way responsible for any of the views and interpretations expressed.

REFERENCES

Albert, R S (1957), 'The Role of Mass Media and the Effect of Aggressive Film Content upon Children's Aggressive Responses and Identification Choices', *General Psychological Monographs,* LV, 221-85.

Baker, R K and *Ball, S J* (1969), *Mass Media and Violence: A Staff Report to the National Commission on the Causes and Prevention of Violence,* IX, US Government Printing Office, Washington DC.

Bandura, A (1965), 'Vicarious Processes: A Case of Re-trial Learning', in Berkowitz (ed), *Advances in Experimental Social Psychology,* II, Academic Press, New York, 1-55.

Bandura, A (1971), *Psychological Modelling: Conflicting Theories,* Aldine Atherton, Chicago.

Bandura, A and *Huston, A C* (1961), 'Identification as a Process of Incidental Learnings', *Journal of Abnormal and Social Psychology,* LXIII, 2, 311-18.

Bandura, A and *Kupers, C J* (1964), 'Transmission of Self Reinforcement through Modelling', *Journal of Abnormal and Social Psychology,* LXIX, 61-9.

Bandura, A and *McDonald, F J* (1963), 'The Influence of Social Reinforcement and the Behaviour of Models in Shaping Children's Moral Judgments', *Journal of Abnormal and Social Psychology,* LXVII, 272-81.

Bandura, A, Ross, D and *Ross, S A* (1961), 'Transmissions of Aggression through Imitation of Aggressive Models', *Journal of Abnormal and Social Psychology,* LXIII, 575-82.

Bandura, A, Ross, D and *Ross, S A* (1963a), 'Vicarious Reinforcement and Imitative Learning', *Journal of Abnormal and Social Psychology,* LXVII, 601-7.

Bandura, A, Ross, D and *Ross, S A* (1963b), 'A Comparative Test of the Status Envy, Social Power, and Secondary Reinforcement Theories of Identification Learning', *Journal of Abnormal and Social Psychology,* LXVII, 527-34.

Bandura, A and *Whalen, C K* (1966), 'The Influence of Antecedent Reinforcement and Divergent Modelling Cues on Patterns of Self-reward', *Journal of Personality and Social Psychology,* III, 373-582.

Barker, R, Demb, T and *Lewin, K* (1941), *Frustration and Regression: An Experiment with Young Children,* Studies in Child Welfare, XVIII, University of Iowa.

Brown, J R (1973), 'Children's Use of Mass Media: A Functional Approach', paper presented to the British Psychological Society, Mimeo, University of Leeds.

Buss, A H (1961), *The Psychology of Aggression,* Wiley, New York.

Crutchfield, R S (1955), 'Conformity and Character', *American Psychologist,* X, 191-8.

Dollard, J, Doob, W, Miller, N E, Mowrer, D H and *Sears, R R* (1939), *Frustration and Aggression,* Yale University Press, New Haven.

Emery, F E (1959), 'Psychological Effects of the Western Film: A Study of Television Viewing, 11. The Experimental Study', *Human Relations,* XII, 215-32.

Epstein, R (1966), 'Aggression toward Outgroups as a Function of Authoritarianism and Imitation of Aggressive Models', *Journal of Personality and Social Psychology,* III, 574-9.

Eron, L D (1963), 'Relationship of TV Viewing Habits and Aggressive Behaviour in Children', *Journal of Abnormal and Social Psychology,* LXVII, 193-6.

Feshbach, S (1955), 'The Drive-reducing Function of Fantasy Behaviour', *Journal of Abnormal and Social Psychology,* L, 3-11.

Feshbach, S (1961), 'The Stimulating versus Cathartic Effects of a Vicarious Aggressive Activity', *Journal of Abnormal and Social Psychology,* LXIII, 381-5.

Feshbach, S and *Singer, R D* (1971), *Television and Aggression,* Jossey-Bass, San Francisco.

Freud, S (1933), Republished in *The Standard Edition of the Complete Psychological works of Sigmund Freud,* XXIII, Hogarth Press, London (1964), and *New Introductory Lectures on Psychoanalysis,* Norton, New York (1973).

Goranson, R E (1970), 'Media Violence and Aggressive Behaviour: A Review of Experimental Research', in Berkowitz (ed), *Advances in Experimental Social Psychology,* Academic Press, V, 2-28.

Hartmann, D (1965), 'The Influence of Symbolically Modelled Instrumental Aggression and Pain Cues on the Disinhibition of Aggressive Behaviour', unpublished doctoral dissertation, Stanford University, Stanford.

Henker, B A (1964), 'The Effect of Adult Model Relationships on Children's Play and Task Imitation' *Dissertation Abstracts,* XXIV (11) 4797.

Hicks, D J (1965), 'Imitation and Retention of Film-mediated Aggressive Peer and Adult Models', *Journal of Personality and Social Psychology,* II. 1, 97-100.

Himmelweit, H, Oppenheim, A and *Vince, P* (1958), *Television and the Child: An Empirical Study of the Effects of Television on the Young,* Oxford University Press, London.

Hovland, C I (1959), 'Reconciling Conflicting Results derived from Experiments and Survey Studies of Attitude Change', *American Psychologist,* XIV, 8-17.

Hovland, C I, Janis, Z L and *Kelley, H H* (1953), *Communication and Persuasion,* Yale University Press, New Haven.

Kenny, D T (1952), 'An Experimental Test of the Catharsis Theory of Aggression'. unpublished doctoral dissertation, University of Washington.

Kniveton, B H (1972), 'Nursery School as an Inhibitor of Working-class Aggressive Imitation', *British Journal of Social and Clinical Psychology,* II, 295-6.

Kniveton, B H (1973a), 'Social Class and Imitation of Aggressive Adult and Peer Models', *Journal of Social Psychology,* LXXXIX, 311-12.

Kniveton, B H (1973b), 'The Effect of Rehearsal Delay on Long-term Imitation of Filmed Aggression', *British Journal of Psychology,* LXIV, 2, 259-65.

Kniveton, B H (1974), 'Age as a Factor influencing Imitation of an Aggressive Film Model', *Durham Research Review.*

Kniveton, B H and *Stephenson, G M* (1970), 'The Effect of Pre-Experience on Imitation of an Aggressive Film Model', *British Journal of Social and Clinical Psychology,* IX, 31-6.

Kniveton, B H and *Stephenson, G M* (1972), 'The Effect of Social Class on Imitation in a Pre-Experience Situation', *British Journal of Social and Clinical Psychology,* XII, 225-34.

Kniveton, B H and *Stephenson, G M* (1973), 'An Examination of Individual Susceptibility to the Influence of Aggressive Film Models,' *British Journal of Psychiatry,* XX, 566, 53-6.

Kniveton, B H and *Pike, C R* (1972), 'Social Class Intelligence and the Development of Children's Play Interests', *Journal of Child Psychology and Psychiatry,* XIII, 167-81.

Kuhn, D Z, Madsen, C H and *Becker, W C* (1967), 'Effects of Exposure to an Aggressive Model and Frustration on Children's Aggressive Behaviour', *Child Development,* XXXVII, 3, 739-46.

Lanzetta, J T and *Kanareff, V T* (1959), 'The Effects of Monetary Reward on the Acquisition of an Imitative Response', *Journal of Abnormal and Social Psychology,* LIX, 120-7.

Lefkowitz, M, Blake, R R and *Mouton, J S* (1955), 'Status Factors in Pedestrian Violation of Traffic Signals', *Journal of Abnormal and Social Psychology,* LI, 704-5.

Leibert, M R and *Baron, R A* (1972), 'Short-term Effects of Televised Aggression on Children's Aggressive Behaviour', in Comstock, Rubinstein and Murray (eds), *Television and Social Behavior, II, Television and Social Learning,* US Surgeon General's Scientific Committee on Television and Social Behavior, US, Government Printing Office, Washington DC, 181-201.

Leifer, D A and *Roberts, D F* (1972), 'Children's Responses to Television Violence', in *Television and Social Behavior, II, Television and Social Learning,* 43-180.

Lovas, O J (1961), 'Effect of Exposure to Symbolic Aggression on Aggressive Behaviour', *Child Development,* XXXII, 37-44.

Maccoby, E E, Levin, H and *Selza, B M* (1956), 'The Effects of Emotional Arousal on the Retention of Film Content: A Failure to Replicate', *Journal of Abnormal and Social Psychology,* LIII, 373-4.

Mausner, B (1953), 'Studies in Social Interaction: The Effect of Variation in one Partner's Prestige on the Interaction of Observer Pairs', *Journal of Applied Psychology,* XXVII, 391-3.

McIntyre, J J and *Teevan, J J* (1972), 'Television Violence and Deviant Behaviours', in *Television and Social Behavior, III, Television and Adolescents' Aggressiveness,* 383-435.

Meltzoff, J, Singer, J L and *Korchin, S J* (1953), 'Motor Inhibition and Rorschach Movement Responses: A Test of the Sensory Tonic Theory', *Journal of Personality,* XXI, 400-10.

Meyerson, L (1966), 'The Effects of Filmed Aggression on the Aggressive Responses of High and Low Aggressive Subjects', unpublished doctoral dissertation, University of Iowa.

Milgram, S and *Shotland, R L* (1973), *Television and Anti-Social Behavior,* Academic Press, New York.

Mischel, W and *Grusec, J* (1966), 'Determinants of the Rehearsal and Transmission of Neutral and Aversive Behaviours', *Journal of Personality and Social Psychology,* III, 197-205.

Mussen, P H, Conger, J J and *Kagan, J* (1970), *Child Development and Personality,* Harper and Row, New York.

Mussen, P H and *Rutherford, E* (1961), 'Effects of Aggressive Cartoons on Children's Aggressive Play', *Journal of Abnormal and Social Psychology,* LXII, 461-4.

Newson, J and *Newson, E* (1968), *Four Years Old in an Urban Community,* Allen and Unwin, London.

Nicholas, K B, McCarter, R E and *Hechel, R V* (1971), 'Imitation of Adult and Peer Television Models by White and Negro Children', *Journal of Social Psychology,* LXXXV, 317-8.

Noble, G (1970), 'Film-mediated Aggressive and Creative Play', *British Journal of Social and Clinical Psychology,* IX, 1-7.

Noble, G (1973), 'Effects of Different Forms of Filmed Aggression on Children's Constructive and Destructive Play'. *Journal of Personality and Social Psychology,* XXVI.1, 54-9.

Pfuhl, E H (1970), 'Mass Media and Reported Delinquent Behaviour: A Negative Case', in Wolfgang, Savitz and Johnson (eds), *The Sociology of Crime and Delinquency,* V.1, Wiley, New York, 509-23.

Rosenbaum, M E and *de Charms, R* (1960), 'Direct and Vicarious Reduction of Hostility', *Journal of Abnormal and Social Psychology,* LX, 105-11.

Rosenbaum, M E and *Tucker, I* (1962), 'The Competence of the Model and the Learning of Imitation and Non-Imitation', *Journal of Experimental Psychology,* LXIII.2, 183-90.

Rosenbaum, M E, Chalmers, D K and *Home, W C* (1962), 'Effects of Success and Failure and the Competence of the Model on the Acquisition and Reversal of Matching Behaviour', *Journal of Psychology,* LIV.2, 251-8.

Rosenkrans, M A and *Hartup, W W* (1967), 'Imitative Influences of Consistent and Inconsistent Response Consequences to a Model on Aggressive Behaviour in Children', *Journal of Personality and Social Psychology,* VII, 429-34.

Rosenblith, J F (1959), 'Learning by Imitation in Kindergarten Children', *Child Development,* XXX, 69-80.

Schramm, W, Lyle, L and *Parker, E B* (1969), *Television in the Lives of our Children,* Stanford University Press, Stanford.

Siegal, A E (1956), 'Film Mediated Fantasy Aggression and Strength of Aggressive Drive', *Child Development,* XXVII, 365-78.

Singer, J L (1960), 'The Experience Type: Some Behavioural Correlates and Theoretical Implications', in Ricker-Osiankina (ed), *Rorschach Psychology,* Wiley, New York.

Singer, J L (1966), *Daydreaming: An Introduction to the Experimental Study of Inner Experience,* Random House, New York.

Stein, A H, and *Lynette, K Friedric* (1972), 'Television Content and Young Children's Behaviour', in *Television and Social Behavior,* II, 202-317.

Trenaman, J and *McQuail, D* (1961), *Television and the Political Image,* Methuen, London.

Walters, R H, Leat, M and *Mezei, L* (1963), 'Inhibition and Disinhibition of Responses through Empathetic Learning', *Canadian Journal of Psychology,* XVII, 235-43.

Walters, R H and *Parke, R D* (1964), 'Influence of Response Consequences to a Social Model on Resistance to Deviation', *Journal of Experimental Child Psychology,* I, 269-80.

Walters, R H, Parke, R D and *Cane, V* (1965), 'Timing of Punishment and the Observation of Consequences to Others as Determinants of Response Inhibition', *Journal of Experimental Child Psychology,* II, 10-30.

12

The Introduction of Television and its Effects upon Children's Daily Lives

Joyce Cramond

Like most innovations television was, and still is, received with a healthy scepticism by those who regard themselves as guardians of the values of society. It is criticized for the supposed deterioration in cultural standards, for diminished critical thinking, for manipulating political and social attitudes, for encouraging conformity, replacing more worthwhile leisure pursuits, and most vociferously of late for encouraging violence and influencing sexual mores. There are several levels and types of effects which fall into one of two broad categories: (*a*) medium or displacement effects and (*b*) content effects. Displacement effects refer to the reorganization of activities which takes place with the introduction of television; some activities may be cut down and others abandoned entirely to make time for viewing. Content effects relate to the influence of particular types of broadcast material usually on attitudes, values, thinking, knowledge and behaviour. Of course, the two categories are not mutually exclusive, nor do they exhaust the list of potential effects of television. However, the categories provide a structure which is useful for describing some of television's effects.

When television is introduced into a society it becomes the most popular individual leisure-time activity, and it tends to reorganize patterns of leisure behaviour. This paper is concerned with such displacement effects of television in the lives of children and draws information from four major studies conducted during the last two decades.

MAJOR INVESTIGATIONS OF THE ONSET OF TELEVISION

Assessment of the effects of television on children's activities requires a situation in which the behaviour of children without television in the home can be compared with the behaviour of children in a similar situation in which television is available. Studies of how television influences behaviour have generally taken one of two forms: (*a*) The before-and-after study where measures of the behaviour of children have been taken before the advent of television and compared with those taken after the children have been exposed to it for a while. This type of study usually involves the use of a control group to show that any changes between the before-and-after testing is not due to other factors, eg difference in age. (*b*) A direct comparison of two groups, one of which was exposed to television, the other group, acting as controls, which was without television. Such studies normally require the matching of a member of the television group with his control at least in terms of social class and sex.

Several investigations of displacement effects have been conducted. All of them were conducted at a particular time of the year and therefore refer to behaviour and changes occurring at that time. Needless to say, different activities take priority throughout the year; for example, in winter children spend less time out of doors and this affects viewing.

England

Himmelweit *et al.*, (1958) reported the major British investigation. Part of the study was carried out in Norwich in the mid-fifties using a before-and-after design. Her questionnaire was completed by all the ten- to eleven and thirteen- to fourteen-year-olds in Norwich during May 1955 when hardly anybody had a television set. One year later, she compared changes in a group of children who had acquired sets with changes in a group who had not (there being 370 children in all). In addition to this before-and-after study she carried out a main survey in which she compared a group of children who had television with a group who had no television at home, matched for sex, age, intelligence and social background. The children for this study lived in London, Portsmouth, Sunderland and Bristol, providing a total sample of 1,854 matched viewers and controls, divided into two age groups: ten- to eleven and thirteen- to fourteen-year-olds. A problem in this latter study, which Himmelweit could not avoid, was the presence of pre-existing differences between families: non-viewers had chosen not to have television in the house and differed in several other ways from those who had chosen to have television, who, for example, were more dependent on ready-made entertainment, were more gregarious and tended to have lower and more limited aspirations. Despite this, however, Himmelweit produced some convincing results about the effects of television. She used two different methods of measuring the amount of time spent on various activities: (*a*) diaries and (*b*) ratings on frequency scales (eg number of books read per month). Diaries gave the more detailed picture of activity but the amount of information and complexity of scoring encouraged the researchers to concentrate on eighty-four viewers and their controls. Most of the data referring to media activities were provided by the questionnaires; other activities were based on diary entries.

North America
Schramm *ct al.*, (1961) carried out a comparative study in the spring of 1959 of a community with television (referred to as Teletown) and a community without access to television (Radio-town), both in Western Canada. This approach overcame the problem in Himmelweit's study because the inhabitants of Radiotown (the control group) had not chosen to be non-viewers and were therefore more likely to be comparable in other respects to the inhabitants of Teletown; they would not necessarily have the same attributes as the pre-selected control group in Himmelweit's study. The total sample was 913, representing three age groups: six-to seven, eleven- to twelve, fifteen- to sixteen-year-olds. Most of his analysis concentrates on the two older age groups. Although the towns were matched according to economic and demographic structure, individual children were not matched, the entire attendance of all classes within the grades being included in the final sample. Children were asked to report frequency of use of media in terms of number of books read per month, comics read per month, hours spent listening to radio per day, etc.

Norway
A third study was conducted in Finmark, Norway (*Werner*, 1971). She employed a before-and-after design. The first round was conducted in October 1967 before the introduction of television

and the second round during October 1969 after the introduction of television. Werner questioned 4,000 ten- to fifteen-year-old children about media behaviour and attitudes. Her data refer to increases and decreases in the percentage of children with a 'large consumption of different types of media'.

Japan
Furu (1971) reports a series of studies conducted in Japan. The first Shizuoka study was carried out in 1957 and compared a group of children whose families had television with a group who had not. The control group was selected by the individual matching method. At that time few families had television, so in 1959 a second study was conducted on the same sample in order to measure displacement effects. The sample was made up of two age groups: ten-year-olds and twelve-year-olds, and the time spent on activities was assessed by the diary method.

Although the afore-mentioned studies form a basis for our present understanding of displacement effects, each one has its own historical and cultural context. Firstly, television was a particularly novel phenomenon, whereas now it is accepted as part of the life and furniture of the home. Secondly, since the studies were conducted television itself has changed; new types of programme are broadcast, the number of channels and hours of viewing have increased and 'colour' is widely available. Furu (1972) reports a comparison of 1959 and 1967 viewing figures which show an increase over the eight years of one hour per day and he accounts for this by reference to more varied programmes and increased hours of broadcasting. Thirdly, children's activities themselves change over time. Sutton-Smith and Rosenberg (1971) have shown in an historical study of games that there is a changing emphasis in the types of games played. Over the last sixty years there has been an increasing preference for informal group activities and a reduction in time spent on formal games. This, they suggest, is more in accord with the social world of today, formal games being an aspect of an earlier, more hierarchically arranged society. Finally, there have been social, political, technological and cultural developments, which may or may not be related to television, such as changes in the education system, changes in parental attitudes, and increased urbanization. However, despite these reservations, the studies reveal the dynamics of displacement and thus some of the consequences of the introduction of television.

THE EFFECTS OF TELEVISION'S ONSET ON CHILDREN'S USE OF MEDIA

Some parents believe that were it not for television, children, and adults also, would be engaged in a varied selection of more worthwhile pursuits. Would this be the case? What kinds of things have children abandoned to make room for television? Each investigation reveals a rather similar picture: the activities most affected were use of other media and certain types of play; on the other hand, bedtimes and time devoted to homework were little affected. The viewers went to bed slightly later, although Himmelweit points out that their controls were more likely to read, play or write after going to bed; therefore there was little difference between the two groups in total sleeping time. The heavy viewers tended to stay up longest and perhaps these, if any, are the children whose sleep suffers. Children also gave themselves more time by cutting down on homework but the difference was so small as to give no cause for concern. Schramm reported a difference of fifteen minutes and Himmelweit an average difference of eight minutes among secondary modern and primary school children only; time spent on homework by grammar school children was unaffected.

Time given to viewing must therefore be taken from other activities and the activities most readily sacrificed were often those which were thought to satisfy the same needs or 'functions' as television. This is the principle of 'functional similarity' which has been widely accepted as an explanation of displacement. The principle states that functionally similar activities will be replaced; those which serve other functions will be unaffected by television's onset. It has now become apparent that there are numerous difficulties in the general acceptance of this principle. Firstly there is a problem in establishing what function a medium is serving. Whereas Schramm relied to a great extent on an assumption that the functions of children's viewing were limited to escapism and information-seeking, Himmelweit tended to avoid the pitfalls of labelling functions. Secondly, the principle assumes that a medium serves a function or set of functions which is similar to that or those served by another medium and that it is this function which is the dominant factor in shaping the child's behaviour. For example, the principle accounts for reduced comic reading by postulating that the child's comic reading was serving an escapist function which is now served better by television. This can be accepted only as a hypothesis, not as an explanation. There may well be other reasons why the child prefers to spend more time with television. Thirdly, it accepts that needs are finite, ie each child has a certain amount of need for, say, escapism, and if one medium takes over to some extent, the use of the medium previously serving that need will be reduced by that amount. But a Japanese study by Muramatsu (1970) found no reduction amongst heavy viewers of activities regarded as functionally equivalent. Similarly with light viewers there was no reduction. This suggests that either some children have a high need for escapism so that every possible medium which provides for it is used, or they watch television because it provides its own distinct satisfactions. In any event this result goes against the interpretation of displacement effects solely in terms of functional similarlity.

This principle proved limited, both in its formulation and application, and this led researchers to introduce additional explanations. Himmelweit suggested that marginal fringe activities, ie the more casual unstructured activities, are more likely to be displaced than organized and structured activities. A third principle, that of physical-psychological proximity was put forward by Furu to explain some displacement effects. Physical proximity refers to two activities which share the same physical content, for example, homework and viewing in the case of Japan where houses are open-plan. Psychological proximity can be given one or both of two interpretations: (*a*) phenomenological, applying to two activities that are experientially similar, and (*b*) the condition which obtains when the child can easily think of the satisfaction to be derived from some activity.

A more detailed discussion of the various principles of displacement can be found in Brown *et al.*, (1974), which assesses the concept of functional similarity as an explanation of displacement and suggests in its place a process of 'functional re-organization'. They write: 'The introduction of a new medium, instead of provoking a piecemeal displacement, creates a change in the communications environment to which the child reacts by a more comprehensive re-structuring of his functional orientations to media.'

In all studies the greatest decrease in use occurs with the cinema, radio and comics — media which might be regarded as having several characteristics similar to those of television. Television and cinema are both audio-visual media. Although, superficially, they seem alike, there are several differences in terms of context, availability and content. Television viewing takes place in the home where one can move around; it is freely available and provides a wide range of programmes. On the other hand, at the cinema there is no opportunity to move around, there are fewer distractions, visits must be planned within the available programme times, and some effort made to get there; also there is, in the main, only fictional content. Sometimes attendance at the cinema may be regarded as little more than a desire to have an evening away from home and family. There appear to be more differences than similarities between the two media although, of course, they may be similar enough to replace each other.

Television and radio are more alike in terms of context, availability and content. Radio has the added advantage of being portable and provides at any time a wider selection of programmes, a fact which will be discussed later in relation to the redefinition of the roles of media. The aspect which makes it less attractive, of course, is its non-visual form and it is perhaps for some consumers, particularly children, less absorbing.

Comics can be read at home, at will, and like television are a source of entertainment. The added attraction of comics is the opportunity to read what one likes at any time. Although television is available most of the time, the child has no real control over the selection of content. He has the choice to watch one or two programmes at a particular time or not, whereas, with comics, he has ready access to preferred content.

The fact that cinema, radio and comics are still available and used by children suggests that, for some at least, they are sources of satisfactions which cannot be provided by television. The displacement effects of television on each of these media are now discussed in more detail.

The Effect on cinema Attendance
There has been a general reduction in cinema audiences since television appeared and many cinemas have closed. This is largely a reflection of adults' behaviour, television being used as a substitute for cinema. Belson (1967) suggests that the decline of the cinema might not be accounted for solely by the arrival of television. Lawton's study (1950) in America indicated that there was a decline amongst non-viewers as well as viewers. Bogart (1956) reported

that in 1949 attendance was down in all parts of America, long before television was competing. Although there was a wartime increase in cinema attendance in Britain, a decline began before television re-started. Another study of the opinions of cinema goers suggested there was dissatisfcation with the industry which might have discouraged attendance. Nevertheless, Himmelweit, Schramm and Werner all report that cinema going was reduced with viewing. But the effect varied between different age groups and did not appear to be permanent. For example, although the older children's attendance at the cinema dropped, after a year with television the attendance had risen once again to its former frequency. This illustrates an influence which has been labelled as a 'novelty effect', ie television seems to have a strong immediate impact on children's other activities, while they are exploring and learning about this new medium. This effect wears off gradually as the child accustoms himself to television, begins to be selective and wants to revert to previous activities.

Among the young viewers, however, after three years of viewing there was no tendency to increase cinema attendance. Himmelweit explains this in terms of differing functional use of the cinema by different age groups. For the young age group, cinema provides entertainment and this, she argues, is as effectively served by television as by the cinema. For the older children, however, in addition to entertainment, the cinema is regarded as a social occasion on which they can be with their friends and away from family. Obviously television cannot serve this purpose and hence once the novelty effects of television have worn off the child reverts to his previous pattern of cinema attendance. Schramm failed to find this age difference, but in some ways the situation was such as to prevent such a difference from being expressed, since the cinemas in Teletown had closed down whilst the two in Radiotown flourished. Although the closure could be attributed to the coming of television, we cannot assume that the non-attendance would have been permanent had the children had an opportunity to attend. Werner's study reports a decrease over two years in her ten- to fifteen-year-old group, but we have no information about age differences.

Himmelweit also refers to the influence of intelligence on cinema attendance. The duller children reduced their cinema visits more than the brighter children. But as the brighter children went less to the cinema, before television, their visits still numbered fewer than those of the duller children. She reports that the duller children soon stepped up their visits again, and suggests a basic difference between bright and dull children: the former allows neither television nor cinema to encroach too much on his other interests, and the latter seems to have a greater appetite for ready-made entertainment. Apparently, then, this suggests that the appearance of a functionally similar medium, far from displacing the medium, will be assimilated according to the child's behaviour patterns. Should the medium serve a function particularly salient to the child, he will make it a heavy addition to his activities; if not, he will allow it to displace to some extent another medium serving this function.

The Effects on Radio Listening

As with cinema, a large decrease in radio listening has been reported amongst adults with the onset of television. The research on chidren's radio listening shows a similar influence. Himmelweit reported her controls to listen five times as much as viewers, even although future viewers were keener listeners than the controls before television arrived. Schramm found that the sixth- and tenth-grade children in Radiotown listened for 3 hours a day whereas the Teletown group listened for 1.3 hours a day. He identified a difference in amount between the age groups in Teletown but not in Radiotown; the sixth graders listened on average 57 minutes and the tenth graders 1 hour 51 minutes in Teletown, compared with about 3 hours for both groups in Radiotown. Radio possibly provides satisfactions for the older child which have little appeal to his younger counterpart. The most popular radio programmes in Teletown were pop music and news, interest in which increases with age. It seems that television has the effect of re-defining the role of radio, which becomes a source of music and news and frequnetly a secondary medium, ie an accompaniment to some other activity such as studying, reading or working. Himmelweit, however, found no comparable difference in her two age groups, the same amount of time in each group being spent with radio, which was used predominantly as a source of sports news, panel games and discussion. This may reflect different cultural factors, either in radio content or in children's interests.

In the mid-fifties there were three national programmes: Home, mainly a 'talk' station, Light for music and Third for culture. In addition, Radio Luxembourg provided pop music. The redefinition of the role of radio in response to television perhaps accounts for the appearance of the pirate radio stations providing continuous pop music and the subsequent reorganization of BBC radio into BBC1 for pop, BBC 2 for light, BBC 3 for classical and BBC 4 for news and discussions. Werner's study also reported a reduction in radio listening and on further analysis this was revealed to be in the category of programmes with speech only; no decrease in listening to programmes of pop music was recorded. All in all it would seem that these studies are in line with the prevalent assumption of today: for the younger audience, radio is a source of 'pop'.

The Effect on Comic Reading
Comic reading is another activity which is greatly affected by the appearance of television. Again all the studies report a decrease in the amount of time spent with comics, but some discrepancies appear in the results. In her Norwich study, Himmelweit reports that the future viewers differed from controls in that they read more comics. After a period of viewing they were reading slightly fewer comics than their controls. Although there was little difference between the two groups after the introduction of television, the viewers had in fact drastically reduced the number of comics read. No age differences were revealed in the change in the number of comics read but the diaries, in which details of daily activities were recorded, revealed the amount of time spent on comic reading to have decreased in the older age group of viewers well below that of the controls. The records of the younger age group showed viewers and controls to spend the same amount of time reading comics. These data pertaining to the older group are not inconsistent, suggesting either that the same number of comics are read but less thoroughly, or possibly in some other context, or as a secondary activity. Television has generally reduced children's need for comics except in the case of heavy viewers who read comics more often than occasional viewers. Again, two 'types' have been identified, those with an extensive need for ready-made entertainment who spend a lot of their time with television and comics and those who spend less time with both. There was no recovery in comic reading as there was with the cinema. The observed reduction amongst viewers was still evident after a number of years of viewing.

Schramm reports a similar trend but finds a much bigger difference between viewers and non-viewers in number of comics read per month. Whereas Himmelweit showed a decrease in the viewers' comic reading from previous level to that of the controls, Schramm showed the viewers to read half as many comics as the controls (3.6 in sixth and tenth grades in Teletown as opposed to 7.9 in Radiotown). This may be related to the fact that Radiotown was not a self-selected sample in the way that Himmelweit's control group was. Schramm found age differences, unlike Himmelweit, in the reduction of comics read. In the sixth grade, Teletown children read half as many comics as the Radiotown children; in the tenth grade, however, the viewers' comic reading was negligible, 0.1 comics per month as opposed to 8.2 read by the controls. Again, as with radio, television might well be implicated in new trends in comic publishing. Recent years have seen an increasing range of comics and special interest magazines. Comics themselves are now more likely to have letter pages and information sections. Some attention is given to this question of the interplay between media in Brown *et al.* (1974).

The Effect on Book Reading

The displacement of cinema, radio and comics by television has been demonstrated quite clearly in all the studies. The changes were mostly predictable by the principle of functional similarity and the result lent support to this principle. In the words of Schramm: 'If we know precisely what television replaces, we know something about what needs it is meeting ... If television were meeting what we call the fantasy need — that is the need for escape, for excitement, for wish-fulfilment, what activities should we expect it to replace? ... comics ... movie-going ... radio listening.' He goes on to consider books: 'If these services [of television] are chiefly the provision of fantasy experiences, then we should expect that television would not replace the reading of newspapers, books or general magazines.' This is acceptable in the case of newspapers and magazines but do books not comprise, especially amongst children, the kind of content which Schramm on other occasions classifies as fantasy, for example, adventure, fairy stories and Westerns? His prediction seems to be somewhat at odds with those he makes relating to other media. Surprisingly enough, however, it is borne out in his study. He records very little difference in the average number of books read per month between viewers and non-viewers (2.2 and 2.3 respectively). There is, all the same, an interesting age difference which is not referred to in the text.

Sixth-grade viewers read more books per month than their controls (2.5 and 1.8 respectively) but the tenth-grade children show a reversal, the viewers reading less than the controls (1.9 and 2.8 respectively), so that, on average, there is no difference between viewers and non-viewers. The difference in the older age group is consistent with those occurring with other media, that television has in fact displaced some book reading and is not in line with Schramm's prediction. The difference in the young group requires a more complex explanation. Parental and school influence may be stronger and more effective in combating the feared effects on the younger child's reading.

There is then some doubt about the no-effect result reported by Schramm. Himmelweit found that, a year after the onset of television, the older children were reading fewer books. Similarly in her main survey the older children cut down their book reading, particularly the boys and children of average intelligence. She suggests that it is those children who are perhaps in greater need of reading who are likely to give it up — those who read fewest books before having television were, it seems, the most affected by viewing. But this inroad into reading by television is short-lived. In her main study Himmelweit compared three groups of viewers: recent (one year of viewing), experienced (one to three year of viewing) and veteran (three to five years' viewing). The comparison revealed that the children who had been viewing for at least three years, ie the veterans, read as many books as the controls. She implies, then, that after three years' viewing, reading reverts to its pre-viewing pattern. But in the absence of data on the veteran viewers' previous reading behaviour, the inferences are limited, there being no control for other changes which have taken place over time. Himmelweit considers that the cause for concern lies in the implications of the drop in reading over two or three years rather than with any long-term decrease. Viewing, it can be argued, is too different from book reading to replace books according to functional similarity. The control over choice of content at any one time is greater with books, as is the range of avilable content itself. Also, it may be that once involved in a particular sequence of reading, involvement is less easily disrupted than involvement in television where people talk, move about and distract. Possibly children brought up with television will suffer long-term adverse effects. Himmelweit suggests that viewing may, in fact, act as a continuing stimulus to reading. The viewers in Norwich who had previously shown a relative lack of interest in non-fiction subjects, after a year's viewing were more interested in reading non-fiction than the controls were. Their range of fiction had also expanded, particularly those areas covered by television, especially thrillers, Westerns, horror and crime. This result was consistent across both parts of Himmelweit's investigation, viewers showing more interest in several fiction and non-fiction subjects. It applied most clearly to the less intelligent older age group and the most intelligent younger age group, suggesting that television extends the reading range of children at a particular mental age.

Although Werner reports a drop in the percentage of pupils who spend a large amount of time reading, her study spanned two years, and it is likely that the novelty effect of television was still operating. Thus all three Western studies are roughly in line. Furu, in fact, reported a drop in reading and explained it in terms of the principle of physical-psychological proximity.

As far as reading is concerned, television does have a displacing effect in the first instance, but this effect is short-lived and ultimately the children read just as much, if not more. Schramm's explanation that reading is not displaced because it does not provide fantasy material for escape is, however, unconvincing, since a large amount of children's reading matter includes material he would classify as escapist. His interpretation obtains only in the case of non-fiction. It is likely that reading is just too different from television for it to be abandoned in the same way that comics, cinema and radio are.

The Effect on Other Reading Material

Newspapers and magazines are available in most homes and children tend to spend some time with them; the amount of time is apparently unaffected by the presence of television. In Schramm's terms these are reality media which are not functionally similar to television, therefore not displaced. It is an arguable point; television provides news and documentaries but it is at least possible that children perceive television mainly as an entertainment medium. Himmelweit points out that unlike books, newspapers and magazines do not require prolonged attention, and can be referred to in odd moments or read while watching television.

THE EFFECTS OF TELEVISION'S ONSET ON SOCIAL LIFE AND PLAY

The other broad category of activities studied was the child's social life and play. Particular interest was directed to the effects on outdoor versus indoor activities, on organized as opposed to unorganized activities, and on solitary versus accompanied play. These categories are not mutually exclusive; there is some degree of overlap, eg accompanied play tends to be more organized and to take place out of doors, but Himmelweit, particularly, distinguished clear categories for comparison.

The viewers spent less time out of doors than the controls. The younger viewers revealed the greatest discrepancy, perhaps because they have less leisure time available, their waking day usually being shorter than that of older children. The differences were not great, 70 per cent of the younger children and 50 per cent of the older children spending at least one hour a day out of doors. (The data refer to a week of good weather in May.) Some outdoor activities were affected more than others: the unorganized activities such as walking and being out with friends were reduced more than such organized events as sport and watching sport. Sport is important to children, encouragement of the interest coming from several sources. Its essential competitive element, absent from solitary and unorganized activity, reflects dominant themes in our culture which may provide a continuing motive for interest and encouragement. Club attendance, another organized activity, was only slightly affected by television. Future viewers had revealed themselves to be more club-oriented than their controls, and this difference persisted after a year's viewing among the adolescents, both groups increasing their rate of attendance. The younger viewers reduced and the controls increased attendance very slightly so that for this age group the controls were the more frequent club members. As with cinema attendance an explanation in terms of social functions is perhaps adequate.

Werner reports similar results for clubs and sports. However, fewer children are involved in handicraft/carpentry and fishing, although playing musical instruments, stamp collecting and other hobbies remained unchanged.

Findings relating to friendship are somewhat complex. Diaries kept by the children in Norwich showed no difference between the young viewers and controls, but the adolescent viewer spent less time visiting friends than did his control. In absolute terms older children spend more time visiting, and in all forms of social interaction, but it seems that television delays the usual social development by keeping adolescent viewers at home. About a fifth of the children entertain friends at home, adolescent viewers as much as their controls, but the younger viewers do twice as much entertaining as their controls. This is in line with Belson's findings that viewers spent slightly more time at home than non-viewers (*Belson,* 1967). The nature of the entertainment is not quite clear and it may be that the friends are visiting in order to watch television. Other general social activities, such as wandering, talking, loitering with friends, reveal the same picture. Adolescents spend more time on this kind of activity and are more likely to reduce it when television is available. At a crucial time in social development, adolescents are avoiding the informal social situation in favour of second-hand experience. This may have further implications as regards sociability and the value placed on social interaction. There appears to be a tendency towards doing things with friends rather than just being with them: an emphasis on activity rather than interaction, a tendency towards valuing the world of television above the fluid world of people, and hence one detects perhaps the seeds of a 'dehumanization' process.

The Effect on Disorganized Activity
The other major aspect of the leisure displacement is the reduction in disorganized, aimless or, as Himmelweit names it, 'marginal' activity. The tendency is for the children to become busier and more organized with no time for 'day-dreaming'. This refers to time spent staring out the window, at the sky or any time when he is not actively concentrating on or involved in some activity outside himself. The busier a child is, the less time he will have to reflect, to think, and this may set a pattern, not necessarily desirable, for life. The value of such activity is difficult to assess and will vary between individuals. It gives the child an opportunity to contemplate his experience, to think about and try to understand things.

It may be that the child day-dreams some of the time while watching television and that objective measures of his activities do not reflect entirely what is going on in his head. If he is interested in a programme he may concentrate on it, but when his interest is not held his mind may wander. There may therefore be no reduction in time spent out of mind, simply a reorganization of it, but as yet we have no evidence to the contrary.

SUMMARY

It is quite clear that television does have displacement effects and the activities displaced have served as material on which to base explanations of the dynamics of this process. As regards certain media it seems that television can fulfil as well, if not better, some of the needs previously served by radio, cinema and comics, viz. the need for entertainment. In some cases the role of the previous medium has been redefined, eg radio is used now mainly for music and news. In the case of other media, especially books, which serve needs other than those served by television, although there is some equivalence, there tends to be little displacement. Any drop which does occur does so because television leaves little time for an activity requiring prolonged concentration, rather than the two activities being functionally similar.

The principle of functional similarity does not help to explain changes in activity such as play and social interaction. Formal and organized activities such as sport, attendance at clubs, seem unaffected. It is the less organized, marginal activities which decline. It is unlikely that television is serving the functions served by such activities because of its structured absorbing nature. The child may be taken out of himself by television, whereas aimless activity would tend to absorb the child with himself. Also television directs the child's thoughts and he has little control over input. Unstructured activity, on the other hand, allows the child to respond at will, to let his mind wander. The question of which is the more constructive process — the directed or the undirected — is at present mostly a matter of faith, there being supporters for both. But it is important to be aware of the possible implications in this change in the child's use of time.

Most of the changes reported here were observed several years ago when television was establishing itself as a major element in our lives. It is likely that changes in activities would have occurred irrespective of television as a reflection of ongoing changes in society, but it is not unreasonable to assume that the introduction of this medium has directed the change in some ways. The nature of the medium has also been transformed — longer hours of broadcasting, increase in number of channels, development in variety and quality of content — so the findings are set in a particular historical period and extrapolation to present-day conditions may be misleading. Nevertheless the studies, particularly those conducted by Schramm *et al.* and Himmelweit *et al.*, remain the classic works, to date, on children and television.

The recorded displacements of radio, comics and cinema are not simple. Rather they show subtle differences between children of different backgrounds, intelligence, interests and sex. Himmelweit reports the case of a boy whose leisure time was taken up with sport and television, at the expense of all other activities. Viewing and sport were two conflicting interests, sport winning slightly, but whenever this was not available, television took over. Another child was particularly interested in social activities and used television only as a stop-gap. A third child's life was dominated by television, participating in other activities only when there was no television to watch.

As television took over some of the functions of other media, those not served by television were emphasized to the extent that these media took on a different role, eg for many, radio has become a medium providing little more than music and news.

To sum up, it seems that television has had no drastic effect on the child's activities. Where some pursuit is important to the child, it will be continued and the majority of children are involved in varied activities. The effects reported are often short-lived. They may only occur on the introduction of television and can be regarded as novelty effects. But the child's life does become busier and more organized, usually around television, and it is the implications of this value of television over and above other activities and people and the absence of 'free time' which may be the greatest cause for concern.

REFERENCES

Belson, W A (1967), *The Impact of Television,* Crosby Lockwood, London.

Bogart, L (1956), *The Age of Television,* Crosby Lockwood, London.

Brown, J R, Cramond, J K and *Wilde, R J* (1974), 'Displacement Effects and the Child's Functional Orientation to Television', in Blumler and Katz (eds), *The Use of Mass Communications: Current Perspectives on Gratifications Research,* Sage, Beverly Hills.

Furu, T (1971), *The Function of Television for Children and Adolescents,* Sophia University Press, Tokyo.

Furu, T (1972), *Television and Children,* Mimeo, International Christian University, Tokyo.

Himmelweit, H T, Oppenheim, A N and *Vince, P* (1958), *Television and the Child: An Empirical Study of the Effect of Television on the Young,* Oxford University Press, London.

Lawton, S P (1950), *When TV Moves In: A Report of a Series of Studies of Changes in Living Habits in Homes when Television Sets are Purchased,* University of Oklahoma.

Maramatsu, T (1970), 'Television and Children's Life: How Heavy and Light Television Viewers spend their Time', *Monthly Bulletin of Japan Broadcasting Corporation,* September.

Schramm, W, Lyle, J and *Parker, E B* (1961), *Television in the Lives of our Children,* Stanford University Press, Stanford.

Sutton-Smith, B and *Rosenberg, B G* (1971), 'Sixty Years of Historical Change in the Game Preferences of American Children', in Herron and Sutton-Smith (eds), *Child's Play,* Wiley, New York.

Werner, A (1971), 'Children and Television in Norway', *Gazette,* XVII.3.

13

Television and Violence: Implications of the Surgeon General's Research Programme

John P Murray

The magnitude of television's involvement in our daily lives is rather impressive. Recent census figures estimate that 96 per cent of the households in the United States contain at least one television set; many have two or more. In families where there are young children, the television ownership rate approaches total saturation — 99 per cent. Moreover, the data available from broadcast rating services indicate that American television sets are turned on for an average of approximately six hours each day. The obvious implication of these rather dry statistics is that virtually every person in the United States has access to television, and some are watching for a considerable length of time. These facts, coupled with the common observation that our youngest citizens are among the heaviest users, have fostered serious concern about television's potential impact on the attitudes, values, and behaviour patterns of this vast audience. This concern has been expressed not only by legislators but also by parents, teachers, and a wide range of mental health professionals involved with the growth and development of children.

Throughout television's quarter-of-a-century broadcast history, various commissions and committees have questioned its impact. In the early 1950s, the National Association of Educational Broadcasters surveyed the programme content of stations in four major cities (Los Angeles, New York, New Haven and Chicago) and reported that 'crime and horror' drama accounted for 10 percent of all programming broadcast in these cities.

The first Congressional inquiry was launched in 1954 by Senator Estes Kefauver, Chairman of the Sub-committee to Investigate Juvenile Delinquency. As a result of testimony presented to this committee, it was concluded that televised crime and brutality could be potentially harmful to young children. Broadcasters were then urged to take appropriate action to reduce the level of violence portrayed in their programming. A subsequent survey of programme content, undertaken by the same Senate sub-committee in 1961, indicated an increase in the level of televised violence over that observed in the 1950s. An additional survey conducted in 1964 again indicated no diminution in the level of protrayed violence. As chairman of these later hearings, Senator Thomas Dodd noted: 'Not only did we fail to see an appreciable reduction of violence in the new shows, but we also found that the most violent shows of the 1961-62 season have been syndicated and are now being reshown on independent networks and stations.' (US Senate, 1964, p. 3731) The committee concluded that, despite its laudable achievement in the fields of education and entertainment, television has also functioned as 'a school for violence.'

In 1969, the Mass Media Task Force of the National Commission on the Causes and Prevention of Violence concluded on the basis of a review of existing research, that there was sufficient justification to call for a general reduction in the level of televised violence. The Commission particularly stressed the need to eliminate violence portrayed in children's cartoon programming. The Violence Commission also recommended continued evaluation of television programming, research on the long-term cumulative effects of viewing televised violence, and an analysis of the broad range of television's impact on society (*Baker* and *Ball,* 1969).

In response to this mounting concern, Senator John O. Pastore, Chairman of the Sub-committee on Communications of the Senate Commerce Committee, asked the Secretary of Health, Education and Welfare to request the Surgeon General to conduct a study of the impact of televised violence. In requesting the Surgeon General's participation, Senator Pastore noted the recent success of the Smoking and Health Study and indicated that he considered television violence to be a similar public health question. As a result of this request, the Surgeon General's Scientific Advisory Committee on Television and Social Behaviour, composed of twelve behavioural scientists, was appointed in June 1969. At the same time, $1 million was allocated for research funds, and a staff at the National Institute of Mental Health was appointed to coordinate the research programme. During the following two years, a total of twenty-three independent research projects were conducted by scholars at a number of universities and research institutes.

The resulting set of approximately sixty reports and papers was reviewed by the Advisory Committee during the late summer and fall of 1971, and the Committee's report, entitled 'Television and Growing Up: The Impact of Televised Violence', was presented to the Surgeon General on 31 December 1971. The Advisory Committee report and 5 volumes of research reports were published early in 1972.

The studies in this programme were focused on three major research questions concerning (*a*) the characteristics of television programme content: (*b*) the characteristics of the audience (Who watches what? For how long?); and (*c*) the potential impact of televised violence on the attitudes, values, and behavior of the viewer. Within this framework, let us turn first to the research findings that bear on the nature of the stimulus — the characteristics of television programmes viewed in American homes.

TELEVISION CONTENT

One study, conducted by George Gerbner (1972) at the Annenberg School of Communications, was addressed to an analysis of the content of prime time (7.30 — 10.00 p.m. on weekdays and 9.00 — 11.00 a.m. on Saturday) television programming broadcast during one week in October for the years 1967, 1968 and 1969. Observers recorded all instances of violence defined by 'the overt expression of physical force against others or self, or the compelling of action against one's will on pain of being hurt or killed'. The results indicated the following:

1 The level of violence did not change from 1967 to 1969. In each of the three years, violent episodes occurred at the rate of five per play or eight episodes per hour, with eight out of every ten plays containing some form of violence.

2 Lethal violence (killing) *did* decline over the measured years from two in ten leading characters involved in killing in 1967; to one in ten in 1968; to one in twenty in 1969.

3 The level of violence portrayed in programmes especially designed for children — cartoons (already the leading violent programme format in 1967) — became increasingly violent in 1969. As Gerbner (1972) pointed out: 'Of all 95 cartoon plays analyzed during the

three annual study periods, only two in 1967 and one each in 1968 and 1969 did not contain violence [p.36].'

On the average, in 1967, one hour of cartoons contained *three* times as many violent episodes as one hour of adult programming. However, in 1969, one hour of cartoons contained *six* times as many violent episodes as an adult hour.

A more recent study, conducted by F Earle Barcus (1971) at Boston University, was focused on the content of Saturday morning children's programmes during the 1971 season. Barcus reported findings that parallel Gerbner's: 71 per cent of all segments had at least one instance of human violence and three out of ten dramatic segments were 'saturated' with violence.

In one sense, these statistics are merely body counts, significant perhaps, but to 'understand' televised violence one must look at the qualitative aspects: the time, place or setting and the characteristics of the aggressors and victims. In the world of television, violence tends to *occur* in the past or future; in places other than the United States; and frequently in remote, uninhabited or unidentifiable areas. The means to commit violence are usually weapons, with guns being the most favored weapon. The agents of this violence are usually humans; however, the prevalence of non-human agents has increased each year from 1967 to 1969. The consequences of all this violence are almost negligible. Punching, kicking, biting, even shooting do not seem to result in much suffering. As Gerbner (1972) pointed out: 'Pain and suffering were so difficult to detect that observers could not agree often enough to make the results acceptable. There was no doubt that no painful effect was shown in over half of all violent episodes (p.41).'

Who commits all this mayhem? And who are the unlucky recipients? We noted earlier that the agents of most of the violence are humans; so, too, are the victims. But the aggressors and the victims, the powerful and the weak, the killers and the killed, do not share many common characteristics. Indeed, as Gerbner lyrically indicated: 'The shifting sands of fate have piled a greater burden of victimization on women.' (p.50) The aggressors are more likely to be male, American, middle-upper class, unmarried, and in the 'prime of life'.

Approximately 70 per cent of all leading characters studied by Gerbner were involved in some form of violence (either as an aggressor or a victim). Of those involved in killing, the odds are two to one in favour of the leading character being a killer rather than being the one killed. Moreover, the odds were also seven to one that the killer would *not* be killed in return.

How 'real' is this violence? Some researchers have suggested that, in a statistical sense, it is very *un*real. For example, content analyses show that violence in the *television* world occurs between total strangers, but crime statistics indicate that lethal violence in the *real* world is likely to be perpetrated by persons known to the victim. A study conducted by David Clark and William Blankenburg (1972) at the University of Wisconsin failed to find a clear relationship between the level of televised violence broadcast each year and an environmental crime index based on the FBI Uniform Crime Reports. What they were able to demonstrate is that the level of broadcast violence has fluctuated from 1953 to 1969 and seems to run in cycles reaching a peak every four years. In addition, if the audience applauded violent television programmes during one season, the viewers were likely to receive an increased dosage during the following season. Thus, Clark and Bankenburg were able to demonstrate a significant correlation between the number of high-violence programmes available during a given season and the average Nielsen rating of that type of programme during the preceding season.

What are the implications of these content analyses? Foremost is that violence is inherent in television drama and, according to Gerbner (1972), appears to be used to define power and status. In another study, conducted by Cedric Clark (1972) at Stanford University, the author concludes that some members of our society are regularly denied power and status by being continually cast in the role of the helpless victim. Indeed, Clark suggests that the portrayal of specific groups, such as blacks or women, in powerless roles is a form of violence against society.

The overwhelming conclusion that can be drawn from these content analyses is that violent behaviour is a common theme in many of the television programmes viewed in American homes. Keeping this fact in mind, let us turn next to the topic of viewing.

VIEWING PATTERNS

Who watches television? Virtually everyone does. It was noted earlier that some studies have estimated that the television set is turned on for an average of more than six hours each day. However, it would be a mistake to leave the impression that everyone views extensively. True, almost every home has a television set, but the patterns of use vary according to age, sex, and the family's socio-economic level. There are, of course, some general guidelines concerning the extent of viewing, such as younger children view more than older children; women more than men; and persons from lower income homes more than middle and upper income families. With regard to children, the developmental pattern is one of onset of television viewing at one and a half to two years of age, followed by extensive television viewing during pre-school and early elementary school years, which is followed by a sharp decline in viewing as the youngster approaches adolescence. Indeed, the extent and duration of viewing remain low from adolescence to early adulthood. For adults, the peak life-span viewing periods occur for persons in their late twenties through early thirties and the elderly.

An idealized curve demonstrating the extent of television viewing across all ages would identify three primary clusters of viewers: young children, young adults, and elderly persons. The most parsimonious explanation for these clusters is the lack of alternative activities: young children have limited physical mobility outside the home; young adults are more likely to be married and have families with young children; and elderly persons frequently report a restricted range of outside activities due to physical limitations.

Our research programme has been focused on only one of these three groups: young children. Although this seemed reasonable in terms of limited resources, future research should not neglect the elderly viewer. At present, one can only speculate about the experiences of a person who is physically separated from his or her family, alone and lonely, whose only regular visitor is Johnny Carson.

With regard to children's viewing, we have already suggested that they are among the heaviest users of television. Indeed, several studies (*Lyle* and *Hoffman*, 1972a, 1972b; *Murray*, 1972) have demonstrated that young children spend between two and three hours watching television each day, and they watch more on weekends than during the week. On the average, pre-schoolers spend approximately half of an adult's work week sitting in front of the television set.

What kinds of programmes do they watch? Universally, the youngest children prefer cartoons and situation comedies to other types of television fare. There is a definite sequence of change in preference patterns during childhood, beginning with cartoons and shifting to situation comedies (eg *I Love Lucy*) and child adventure (eg *Lassie*), and then to action adventure programmes (eg *Hawaii Five-O* and *Mod Squad*). It should *not* be assumed, however, that very young children are only exposed to relatively non-violent programming. Indeed, we have already noted that cartoons are among the most violent programmes on television. Moreover, the three studies cited above, which asked parents to keep a diary of the programmes viewed by their children, indicated that even pre-schoolers spent almost half of their viewing time watching action/adventure programmes such as *Mannix, Mod Squad* and *The FBI*.

IMPACT OF TELEVISED VIOLENCE

Given the fact that there is a considerable amount of violence portrayed on television and that large segments of our society are routinely exposed to such material, one may legitimately question the impact of such programming. In this regard, a considerable body of prior research on imitative behaviour (*Bandura*, 1969) as well as accumulated folk wisdom, has led to the conclusion that children *can* learn from observing behaviour of others. The 'others' may be their fellow playmates, parents, teachers, or the repairman who visits the child's home. Thus, the boy or girl who mimics the teacher's voice and the youngster who pretends to be the plumber who repaired the family's kitchen sink yesterday are generally considered living proof of this thesis. Can one extend this line of reasoning to include television as one of the 'others' from whom a child is likely to learn specific behaviours? (For recent reviews, see *Murray et al.*, 1972; *Weiss*, 1969.) We know that there have been isolated incidents in which a child has attempted to replicate behaviour he has just observed on television — occasionally with tragic consequences. But what about the youngster who is merely surly or inconsiderate toward his brothers and sisters, excessively aggressive or disruptive on the playground, or hostile and cynical about the value of trust and love in interpersonal relationships? Can these, too, be related to the behaviours the child has observed on the television screen? Perhaps. However, the basic question to which several studies in this programme were addressed was: Are children who view televised violence more aggressive than those who do not view such fare? With this question in mind, let us look at some of the findings.

One study, conducted by Aletha Stein and Lynette Friedrich (1972) at the Pennsylvania State University, assessed the effect of exposing pre-school children to a 'diet' of either anti-social, pro-social, or neutral television programming. The anti-social programmes consisted of *Batman* and *Superman* cartoons; pro-social programmes were composed of segments of *Misteroger's Neighborhood*; and neutral programming consisted of children's travelogue films. The children were observed throughout a nine-week period which consisted of two weeks of previewing, four weeks of television exposure, and three weeks of follow-up. All observations were conducted while the children were engaged in their daily activities in the nursery school. The observers recorded various forms of behaviour that could be described as pro-social (ie helping, sharing, cooperative play, tolerance of delay) or anti-social (ie arguing, pushing, breaking toys). The overall results indicated that children who were adjudged to be initially somewhat more aggressive became significantly more aggressive as a result of viewing the *Batman* and *Superman* cartoons. On the other hand, the children who viewed twelve episodes of *Misteroger's Neighborhood* became significantly more co-operative, willing to share toys and to help other children.

In another study, Robert Liebert and Robert Baron (1972), at the State University of New York at Stony Brook, assessed young children's willingness to hurt another child after viewing either aggressive or neutral television programming. The aggressive programme consisted of segments drawn from *The Untouchables*, while the neutral programme featured a track race. The main findings indicated that the children who viewed the aggressive programme demonstrated a greater willingness to hurt another child. The experimental setting provided a situation in which a child could press a button that would either HELP or HURT a child in another room. The youngest children who had viewed the aggressive programme presssed the HURT button earlier and for a longer period of time than did their peers who had viewed a track race. Moreover, when the children were later observed during the free-play period, those who had viewed *The Untouchables* exhibited a greater preference for playing with weapons and aggressive toys than did the children who had watched the neutral programming.

In a related study, Paul Ekman (1972) and his associates at the Langley Porter Neuropsychiatric Institute filmed the facial expressions of the children in the Liebert and Baron study and attempted to relate the child's emotional expression while viewing to later hurting or helping behaviour. The results indicated that young boys whose facial expressions depicted positive emotions of happiness, pleasure, interest or involvement while viewing *The Untouchables* were more likely to make hurting responses than were the boys whose facial expressions indicated displeasure or disinterest in such television fare.

An additional series of studies conducted by Aimee Leifer and Donald Roberts (1972) at Stanford University further explored the impact of televised violence in relation to the child's understanding of the motivations and consequences for the portrayed violent acts. The results indicated that as the child grows older, he is more likely to understand the portrayed motives and consequences, but such increased understanding does not seem to modify his postviewing aggressive behaviour. Indeed, when a number of variables were assessed, the best predictor of subsequent aggressive behaviour was the amount of violence portrayed in the programme viewed: children who had viewed the more violent programmes produced significantly more aggressive responses.

The several studies we have discussed thus far have demonstrated some immediate, short-term effects of viewing televised violence. But one may justifiably question the long-range cumulative impact of viewing violence. In this regard, a number of studies in this research programme attempted to relate the child's programme preference and viewing patterns to the viewer's perception of violence and attitudes concerning the use of violence or force to resolve conflicts. Bradley Greenberg and Thomas Gordon (1972) have suggested, on the basis of a series of studies conducted at Michigan State University, that watching violence on television sensitizes the viewer to perceive more violence in the world around him and increases the likelihood that the viewer will espouse attitudes favorable toward the use of violence as a means of resolving conflicts. Moreover, Steven Chaffee and his associates (*Chaffee* and *McLeod*, 1971; *McLeod et al.*, 1972a, 1972b) at the University of Wisconsin and Jennie McIntyre and James Teevan (1972) at the University of Maryland have noted that there is a consistent and reliable relationship between preference for and viewing of violent television programmes and engaging in aggressive or delinquent acts.

Perhaps the most crucial study in this regard was one conducted by Monroe Lefkowitz and his colleagues (*Lefkowitz et al.*, 1972) at the New York State Department of Mental Hygiene. This study is of particular importance because it was designed to investigate the development of aggressive behaviour in children by studying the same boys and girls over a ten-year-period, at ages eight and eighteen. Ten years ago, the investigators obtained several measures of each child's aggressive behaviour and related these to his or her preference for violent television programmes (see *Eron*, 1963). Now, ten years later, when the subjects were one year out of high school, the investigators obtained similar measures of programme preferences and aggressive behaviour. For boys, the results indicated that preference for violent programmes at age eight was significantly related to aggressive and delinquent behaviour at age eighteen. For girls, this relationship was in the same direction but was less strong. Thus, one general interpretation of the results of this study is that preferring violent television at age eight is at least one cause of the aggressive and anti-social behaviour these young men displayed ten years later.

The conclusions that can be drawn from the results of this series of studies are threefold. First, there is considerable violence portrayed on the television screen. And such violence tends not to mirror societal violence, but rather is used as a dramatic punctuation mark — a definer or arbiter of power and status among the performers in each dramatic episode. Second, young children view a considerable amount of television, in the course of which they are exposed to a considerable amount of televised violence. Third, there are a number of studies which point to the conclusion that viewing televised violence causes the viewer to become more aggressive. Indeed, the Surgeon General's Scientific Advisory Committee on Television and Social Behavior (1972) summarized its interpretation of this point as follows:

> Thus, there is a convergence of the fairly substantial experimental evidence for *short-run* causation of aggression among some children by viewing violence on the screen and the much less certain evidence from field studies that extensive violence viewing precedes some *long-run* manifestations of aggressive behavior. (p.10)

Thus, the major implication of the results of this research programme is the clear need for a reduction in the level of violence portrayed on television. At the same time it is equally important to encourage broadcasters to modify the balance of programming in favour of prosocial content. Indeed, the recommendations stemming from this research programme are not merely negative sanctions against televised violence but rather a plea for more beneficial and useful forms of television content.

NOTE

This article was presented at the Current Issues in Mental Health Forum sponsored by the Mental Health Association of Oregon, Portland, 17 May 1972. Some of this material was also presented at a symposium, Violence in our Society, sponsored by the Washington Association for Mental Health, Seattle, 16 May 1972. The Author wishes to acknowledge the contribution of his colleagues at the National Institute of Mental Health, especially Eli A Rubinstein. Opinions expressed are those of the author and do not necessarily reflect the opinions or official policy of the National Institute of Mental Health.

REFERENCES

Baker, R K and *Ball, S J* (1969), *Mass Media and Violence: A Staff Report to the National Commission on the Causes and Prevention of Violence,* US Government Printing Office, Washington DC.

Bandura, A (1969), 'Social Learning Theory of Identificatory Processes', in Goslin (ed), *Handbook of Socialization Theory and Research,* Rand McNally, Chicago.

Barcus, F E (1971), *Saturday Children's Television: A Report of TV Programming and Advertising on Boston Commercial Television,* Action for Children's Television, Boston.

Chaffee S and *McLeod, J* (1971), 'Adolescents, Parents, and Television Violence', paper presented at the Annual Meeting of the American Psychological Association, Washington DC, September.

Clark, C (1972), 'Race, Identification, and Television Violence', in Comstock, Rubinstein and Murray (eds), *Television and Social Behavior,* V, *Television's Effects: Further Explorations,* US Government Printing Office, Washington DC.

Clark, D G and *Blankenburg, W B* (1972), 'Trends in Violent Content in Selected Mass Media', *Television and Social Behavior,* I, *Media Content and Control.*

Ekman, P, Liebert, R M, Firesen, W, Harrison, R, Zlatchin, C, Malmstrom, E.J and *Baron, R A* (1972), 'Facial Expressions of Emotion while watching Televised Violence as Predictors of Subsequent Aggression', *Television and Social Behavior,* V, *Television's Effects: Further Explorations.*

Eron, L (1963), 'Relationship of TV Viewing Habits and Aggressive Behavior in Children', *Journal of Abnormal and Social Psychology,* LVII, 193-6.

Gerbner, G (1972), 'Violence in Television Drama: Trends and Symbolic Functions', *Television and Social Behavior,* I, *Media Content and Control.*

Greenberg, B S and *Gordon, T F* (1972), 'Children's Perceptions of Television Violence: A Replication', *Television and Social Behavior*, V, *Television's Effects: Further Explorations.*

Lefkowitz, M, Eron, L, Walder, L and *Huesmann, L R* (1972), 'Television Violence and Child Aggression: A Follow-up Study', *Television and Social Behavior*, III, *Television and Adolescent Aggressiveness.*

Leifer, A D and *Roberts, D F* (1972), 'Children's Responses to Television Violence', *Television and Social Behavior*, II, *Television and Social Learning.*

Liebert, R M and *Baron, R A* (1972), 'Short-term Effects of Televised Aggression on Children's Aggressive Behavior', *Television and Social Behavior*, II, *Television and Social Learning.*

Lyle, J and *Hoffman, H R* (1972a), 'Children's Use of Television and Other Media', *Television and Social Behavior*, IV, *Television in Day-to-day Life: Patterns of Use.*

Lyle, J and *Hoffman, H R* (1972b), 'Explorations in Patterns of Television Viewing by Pre-school-age Children', this volume.

McIntyre, J and *Teevan, J* (1972), 'Television and Deviant Behavior', *Television and Social Behavior*, III, *Television and Adolescent Aggressiveness.*

McLeod, J, Atkin, C and *Chaffee, S* (1972a), 'Adolescents, Parents, and Television Use: Adolescent Self-report Measures from Maryland and Wisconsin Samples', *Television and Social Behavior*, III, *Television and Adolescent Aggressiveness.*

McLeod, J, Atkin, C and *Chaffee, S* (1972b), 'Adolescents, Parents, and Television Use: Self-report and Other-report Measures from the Wisconsin Sample', *Television and Social Behavior*, III, *Television and Adolescent Aggressiveness.*

Murray, J P (1972), 'Television in Inner-city Homes: Viewing Behavior of Young Boys', *Television and Social Behavior*, IV, *Television in Day-to-day Life: Patterns of Use.*

Murray, J P, Nayman, O B and *Atkin, C K* (1972), 'Television and the Child: A Comprehensive Research Bibliography', *Journal of Broadcasting*, XXVI.1, 21-35.

Stein, A and *Friedrich, L K* (1972), 'Television Content and Young Children's Behavior, *Television and Social Behavior*, II, *Television and Social Learning.*

Television and Growing up: The Impact of Televised Violence (1972), Report to the US Surgeon General's scientific Committee on Television and Social Behavior, US Government Printing Office, Washington DC.

United States Senate, (1964), Committee on the Judiciary, *Effects on Young People of Violence and Crime Portrayed on Television*, Part 16, *Investigation of Juvenile Delinquency in the United States, 30 July, 1964*, US Government Printing Office, Washington DC.

Weiss, W (1969), 'Effects of the Mass Media of Communication', in Lindzey and Aronson (eds), *The Handbook of Social Psychology,* (2nd edn), Addison-Wesley, Reading, Mass.

14

Effects of Television Advertising on Children and Adolescents

Scott Ward

Questions about the effects of television advertising on children have frequently been raised by television's critics. Surprisingly, little published research exists in this area. Investigators have examined the effects of television programming on children, but they have not been concerned with television advertising; conversely much research has examined effects of television advertising, but the focus has been on adults rather than on children. It would be naive to use these sources to derive hypotheses for research studies of effects of commercials on children. The content, structure and repetitive presentation of commercial messages are different from programming, so the effects on viewers should be different. Moreover, hypotheses about effects of television advertising on children cannot simply be derived from research with adults.

For these reasons, the overall purpose of the present programme of research was to provide exploratory baseline data on the effects of television advertising on children and teen-agers. The objective was to conduct studies in several areas which might suggest a range of effects of television advertising on children and teen-agers from five to eighteen years old. This research programme sought to stimulate future hypothesis-testing research rather than explicitly to undertake such research. Seven separate studies were undertaken for this project. Four concern effects of television advertising on pre-teen-age children; three concern effects on adolescents and are based on a survey in a Maryland school district. Four additional papers, summarizing various aspects of the data, reporting preliminary data, or dealing with related aspects of the research, are available. The purpose of this overview paper is to summarize the areas of research, the methodologies employed, and the major findings.

AREAS OF RESEARCH

Figure 14.1 presents a descriptive model of the various areas of research in this project.

FIGURE 14.1
Major variables in studies of effects of television advertising on youth

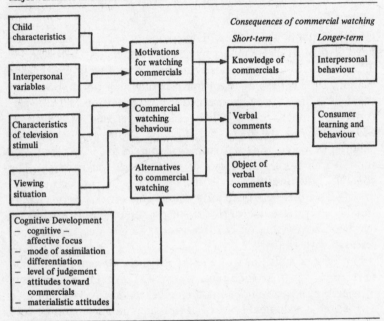

Three areas of research were of primary concern in the studies of young children (ages five to twelve): commercial watching behaviour, effects on cognitive development and effects on interpersonal behaviour.

Commercial watching is a necessary condition for learning from commercials; among young children, such learning presumably affects more complex learning during adolescence and early adulthood, when cognitive orientations and skills relevant to behaviour as consumers are acquired.

Our study of 'commercial watching' focuses on the degree of

children's attention to commercials and on the incidence of alternative or coterminous activities during commercial exposure. We also examine some determinants of watching behaviour and short-term consequences of commercial watching. Our concern is with child characteristics, characteristics of television stimuli, and the viewing situation as determinants of commercial watching. We examine verbal comments about the objects advertised in commercials or about the commercials themselves as one kind of short-term consequence of commercial watching.

The second area of research with younger children is the relationship between responses to television advertising and stages of cognitive growth. Four aspects of cognitive development interest us: (a) *cognitive-affective focus*, referring to the kind or quality of physical, emotional or intellectual stimuli which are most likely to affect children; (b) *mode of assimilation*, referring to the ways in which children recall and use the information they receive from television advertisements; (c) *differentiation*, referring to the degree to which children can discriminate fantasy from fact, products advertised from the advertisements themselves, and elements of commercials, and (d) *level of judgement*, referring to the stage of cognitive or ego development at which a child judges commercials, or is susceptible to commercial appeals.

The third area of concern is the effects of television advertising on interpersonal behaviour — specifically, the extent to which children attempt to influence parental purchasing. One study reports data from mothers of young children — their perceptions of the frequency with which television commercials influence their children to want advertised products, and the extent to which they yield to children's purchase influence attempts.

Among adolescents, television advertising is one influence on the process of 'consumer learning' — the process of developing attitudes, skills and norms relevant to consumption behaviour. We are concerned with the relative impact of television advertising on four aspects of 'consumption behaviour': attitudes toward advertising, materialistic attitudes, knowledge of commercials and buying behaviour. Additionally, we are interested in the motivations of adolescents to watch commercials and in the relationship of television advertising to intrafamily communication about consumption matters. Finally, data from adolescent samples are analysed by race, to determine whether television advertising differentially affects black and white adolescents.

To summarize, while much mass communication research is concerned with the role of mass media in persuasion, the focus of this project is on learning — what children and adolescents learn from television advertising. Moreover, the project attempts to relate television advertising to different kinds of learning which are relevant to different age groups. Among young children, we examine actual commercial watching behaviour as well as relatively simple aspects of learning from commercials. Among adolescents, television advertising is considered one input to more complex processes of acquiring skills and attitudes relevant to consumption behaviour.

METHODOLOGY

Three surveys and one clinical investigation were conducted during the course of this research project. The initial survey was conducted in April 1970 among 1,094 junior and senior high-school students in the Prince Georges County, Maryland, school district. During the following autumn, a subsequent supplementary survey was conducted in school districts with high proportions of black students. The purpose of this initial survey was to gather basic information about adolescent attitudes toward advertising and toward commercials, the nature and extent of intrafamily communication about consumption matters, the effects of commercials on buying behaviour, materialistic attitudes and so forth.

A second survey was conducted in spring 1971 in the Boston area. For this study 134 mothers of five- to twelve-year-old children were asked to observe one of their children watching television — and commercials — for six to ten hours during the child's normal viewing times over a ten-day period.

A third survey involved mail questionnaires completed by each of these 134 mothers. The objective of this study was to relate mothers' perceptions of the influence of commercials on their children to such interpersonal behaviour as the child's purchase influence attempts and parental yielding to these requests.

Finally, exploratory research was conducted with four groups of five children each, drawn from kindergarten, second, fourth, and sixth grades in a Boston area school. While sample size in this clinical examination was quite limited, the objective was to suggest some effects of commercials on young viewers, and to relate these

TABLE 14.1
Summary of studies, objectives, methodology in 'effects of television advertising on youth' project

Study	Objectives	Methodology
A Cognitive Developmental Study of Children's Reactions to Television Advertising (Blatt, Spencer, and Ward)	To gather exploratory data concerning effects of commercials on young children and to relate effects to stages of cognitive development	Four groups of five children each were exposed to a videotape recording of Saturday morning programming and commercials. The following day group interviews were conducted. Age groups were five to twelve, with children drawn from kindergarten, second, fourth, and sixth grades.
Children's Attention to Television Advertising (Ward, Levinson, and Wackman)	To examine determinants and short-term consequences of commercial watching; to examine degree of children's attention to commercials, and the incidence of alternative or coterminous activities during commercial exposure	134 mothers of five- to twelve- year-old children were recruited from service clubs sampled from various socio-economic areas of the Boston metropolitan area. The mothers were trained in the use of code sheets for unobtrusively observing one of their children watching television. Observation periods were scheduled according to a sample of each child's estimated normal viewing behaviour. Mothers observed for a minimum of six and a maximum of ten hours and were paid $10 each for their participation. Data from sixty-five mothers were coded in three age groups: 5–7 (n=29), 8–10 (n=18) and 11–12 (n=18). Data are based on a sample of one-fifth of the 6,465 commercials watched by sixty-five children during the ten day period.
Television Advertising and Intra-Family Influences: Children's Purchase Influence Attempts and Parent Yielding (Ward and Wackman)	To examine effects of commercials on children's attempts to influence mother's purchases; mother's responses to influence attempts; perceived frequency of commercial influence on children	The 134 mothers participating in the watching behaviour study received a self-administered questionnaire. Analyses are based on 109 returned instruments (81 per cent of the mothers)

TABLE 14.1 continued

Study	Objectives	Methodology
Adolescent Attitudes Toward Television Advertising (Ward and Robertson)	To examine the nature of attitudes towards television advertising among adolescents from different racial and socio-economic backgrounds; to examine predictors of attitudes, and to relate attitudes to other variables, e.g., intra-family communication, television use, aspirations, etc.	Self-administered questionnaires were completed by 1,094 adolescents (eighth to twelfth grades) in randomly-selected classrooms in the Prince Georges County, Maryland, school district. A subsequent survey gathered data from adolescents in predominantly black schools
Family and Media Influences on Adolescent Consumer Learning (Ward and Wackman)	To analyse the influence of demographic variables, motivations for watching commercials, quantity of media use, and intra-family communication, on four aspects of acquiring consumer skills and values: recall of advertising content, attitudes towards commercials, materialistic attitudes and buying behaviour	Subsequent analysis of Prince Georges County survey data, and supplementary data from primarily black districts.

effects to stages of cognitive development.

Table 14.1 summarizes the five major study areas, the objectives for each area, and the methodology employed.

It should be emphasized that this research relies upon cross-sectional rather than longitudinal data. Thus our research concerns age-related differences but not age-related change. Taken as a whole, the data suggest different effects of commercials on children in different age groups, but they are not meant to suggest an explicit developmental process. The division of studies into those concerning young children (ages five to twelve) and those concerning adolescents (ages thirteen to eighteen) is arbitrary.

FINDINGS: RESEARCH AMONG PRE-TEEN-AGE CHILDREN

Children's commercial watching behaviour

The study by Ward, Levinson and Wackman examined two aspects of commercial watching behaviour: degree of attention and types of behaviour at commercial exposure. Four determinants of watching behaviour were examined: 1. personal characteristics (age and sex): 2. characteristics of the viewing situation (time and day of viewing, who child views with); 3. characteristics of the viewing situation (duration of commercial, position of commercial, object of commercial — product category); 4. prior watching behaviour (degree of attention to programme just before commercial appears).

Analysis of marginal data indicates that children pay full attention to prior programming about 65 per cent of the viewing time, although somewhat higher incidence of full attention is found among younger children (under ten years old). Children make some verbal response at commercial outset about 25 per cent of the time. When such a response is made, it is most likely to be favourable ('here's a good commercial,' 'now watch this,' etc.).

Across all product categories, times of viewing, number of companions, and so on, all children exhibit a drop in attention during commercial exposure from attention to prior programming. The drop in full attention is least for the youngest children (five- to seven-years-old) and greatest for the oldest children (eleven- to twelve years old). Talking with others during commercial exposure — either a result of or an alternative to commercial watching — occurs during about 25 per cent of the commercial exposures for eleven- to twelve-year-olds, somewhat less for younger children.

Comments about the commercial and/or the product are made after about 20 per cent of commercial exposures. When comments are made, they are most likely to be made by younger children (under ten), and they are more likely to be about the product advertised than about the commercial. The incidence of comments about the commercial itself increases with age: when young children make comments after a commercial, they are most likely to be about the product advertised; among older children about half the comments are about the product, and about half are about the commercial.

No significant sex differences were observed, although girls in the oldest age group talked during 28 per cent of the commercial exposures, while boys in the same age group talked during 20 per cent.

The data are divided into two groups (that for five- to eight-year-olds and that for nine- to twelve-year-olds) for analysis of time of viewing as a determinant of commercial watching behaviour. Older children watch less Saturday morning television; when they do, they pay less attention to prior programming and less attention during commercial exposure than do young children. They are also more likely to make negative comments at commercial onset than at other viewing times, and are more likely to make such comments than the younger children.

Another aspect of the viewing situation is the other people who may be watching television with the child. Viewing with siblings and with father ('family viewing') increased with age (the mother was always present, *de facto*, observing the child's behaviour), but paying full attention to commercials during family viewing decreased with age; talking with others increased with age, suggesting that older children use the opportunity of commercial breaks for interpersonal communication with family members more than younger children do.

Characteristics of television stimuli are another class of determinants of commercial watching. One such characteristic is the length of the commercial. Regardless of commercial length, older children paid less attention to commercials than did younger children. Least 'full' attention was paid to ten-second commercials. With the exception of the youngest age group, most attention was paid to sixty-second commercials.

Another characteristic which may affect differential commercial watching is the position of a commercial within a 'block' of commercials. While children in all age groups had similar (and high) prior attention to programming, attention level decreased more rapidly during a sequence of commercials for the oldest children.

Attention was greatest to commercials at the beginning of programmes for all three age groups. Full attention among older children decreased as the programme progressed, while younger children showed little differences in full attention regardless of the commercial's position in programme context.

The product category of the advertising may also determine watching behaviour. Advertisements for food products were *a priori* designated 'relevant' to children. Advertisements for cleaning products, cosmetics and patent medicines were considered less relevant. The drop in full attention to commercials for relevant products is roughly equivalent for the three age groups. However, for commercials in the 'less relevant' product group, young children's attention actually increased slightly from prior attention to programming. As age increased, attention to the less relevant commercials decreased. It may be that children are so familiar with food products — through advertising exposure, direct consumption, and intrafamily influence attempts — that advertising for food products is actually less relevant than advertising for products associated with adult roles.

A final determinant of commercial watching behaviour is the watching behaviour of children just prior to commercial exposure. Among children paying full prior attention to programming, attention falls off during commercial exposure for all age groups. However, the drop in full attention is smallest for the five- to seven-year-olds; the greatest drop occurs among the eleven- to twelve-year-olds. Older children were more likely to engage in other behaviours — getting up, talking, etc. — than younger children. Among children paying no attention or partial attention to prior programming, increases to full attention were observed during only 12 per cent of commercial exposures, with slight age differences.

Reactions to television advertising and stages of cognitive development
In the exploratory study by Blatt, Spencer and Ward, eight categories of responses to commercials were identified and related

to stages of cognitive development.

1 *Reality* Children in all age groups could identify the term 'commercials', but kindergarten children exhibited confusion and judged the relationship between commercials and reality based on coincidental reasoning or affect.

2 *Purpose* While kindergarten students exhibited no understanding of the purpose of commercials, second-graders exhibited clear understanding that commercials are intended to sell goods, and fourth- and sixth-graders commented on techniques employed in constructing commercials.

3 *Discrimination between product and advertisement* The youngest children do not discriminate between commercials and products advertised. Second-graders exhibited some confusion, but fourth- and sixth-graders made a clear differentiation between commercials and actual products.

4 *Classes of products recalled* The youngest children spontaneously recalled food product advertisements, while second-graders recalled advertising for products with which they could identify and which they could exhibit some competence in using (car games, dolls). Fourth-graders frequently mentioned household cleaning products, but sixth-graders exhibited no consistent pattern of recall according to product groups. They seem more likely to recall advertisements on the basis of message characteristics.

5 *Complexity of recall* Recall of commercials became more multi-dimensional and complex with age.

6 *Significant others* Older children tended to see parents and celebrities as significant others. Sixth-graders tended to project themselves as significant others ('I'd probably try the product out first').

7 *Perceived validity and credibility of advertisements* Kindergarten students exhibited confusion, but second-graders indicated concrete distrust of commercials, often based on experience with advertised products. Fourth-graders exhibited mistrust for specific commercials and 'tricky' elements of commercials; sixth-graders

exhibited global mistrust — except, if probed, of public service announcements.

8 *Affective response to commercials* The youngest children showed some positive responses to the entertainment value of commercials; second-graders had slightly negative associations, but these were not strongly felt; fourth-graders exhibited distrust, but appeared to enjoy humour (especially slapstick and sadistic humour); sixth-graders enjoyed humour but were generally contemptuous.

The data suggest that kindergarten children's memory of commercials, their reasoning about them, and their responses to them are concerned with concrete products — especially food products which relate to immediate impulsive needs. Second-graders are primarily concerned with competence in sex roles, and their responses to classes of commercials reflect this orientation. Fourth-grade children appear to be concerned with social relationships and the reactions of others to approved roles. Sixth grade children tend to evaluate advertisements on rational, 'conscientious' bases.

Television advertising and intrafamily behaviour

The study by Ward and Wackman is based on mail questionnaires returned from 109 of the 134 mothers recruited for the study of watching behaviour. We were interested in relationships between frequency of children's purchase influence attempts for various products, mother's yielding to these attempts, and mother's perceived influence of commercials in stimulating desires of children for specific products. Data were analysed by the three age groups employed in the watching behaviour study (five to seven, eight to ten, eleven to twelve); however, observation data from that study have not been related to these data from mothers.

The data indicate that mothers feel commercials influence younger children more than older children, and they appear to gauge this influence by the frequency of purchase influence attempts for particular products. Although influence attempts may decrease with age, parental yielding to requests increases with age, probably reflecting the perceived increased competence of older children to make purchase decisions.

Aspects of parent-child conflict are related to influence attempts and yielding. The data suggest that influence attempts may be part of more general parent-child conflict problems; furthermore, mothers who restrict viewing are likely not to yield to purchase influence attempts. Finally, mothers' time spent watching television is positively related to influence attempts, yielding, and perceived influence, while recall of commercials is related to influence attempts and perceived influence. Mothers with positive attitudes toward advertising are more likely than mothers with negative attitudes to yield to influence attempts.

FINDINGS: RESEARCH AMONG ADOLESCENTS

Previous research indicates that patterns of media use change during adolescent years, from childhood years. Time spent with television generally decreases, and use of other media increases. Our general hypothesis was that adolescents would also respond to television advertising differently than would younger children. As we have seen, younger children may respond impulsively to commercials, and cynical attitudes toward commercials may develop by the time a child reaches second grade. Attention to commercials also appears to decrease with age.

While the development of cynical and negative attitudes toward television advertising should probably continue during adolescence, we should also expect commercials to become more relevant to teen-agers, who are becoming increasingly active consumers of goods and services. Therefore, television advertising may be one input to more general processes of consumer learning' — acquiring skills and values relating to consumption behaviour. In the case of pre-teen-age children, television commercials were related to intra-family purchase influence attempts. Such second-order consequences probably also occur during adolescence, but we should also expect different consequences of advertising exposure among teenagers, since adolescents engage in consumption behaviour directly. They have more available money than younger children, and they increasingly assume consumer roles.

The general model for our research with adolescents is described in Figure 14.2.

Adolescent attitudes toward television advertising
One aspect of consumer learning is the development of attitudes toward advertising; the relationship of these attitudes with other aspects of learning and with behaviour is important. In this case 'attitudes' refers both to specific affective attitudes toward

television commercials and to more general attitudes toward the institution of television advertising.

FIGURE 14.2
Major variables in studies of effects of television advertising on adolescents

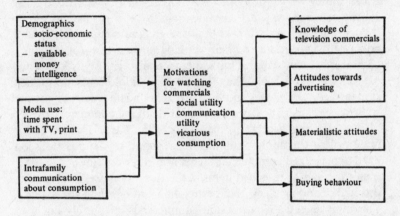

In studies by Ward and Robertson and by Wackman, Reale and Ward, adolescents were asked open-ended questions about the television advertising they felt was representative of the 'best' and the 'worst' on television, and their reasons for these attitudes. While there were slight differences between junior high and senior high school adolescents, the most-liked categories of commercials were those for drug and patent medicines, automobile advertising and soft drink advertising. The most-liked category among black adolescents was advertising for food and gum products; otherwise, their rankings were parallel to those for white adolescents.

The adolescents were most favourable to those commercials seen as 'funny' and/or 'straightforward'. There was some tendency for younger adolescents to cite humour as their primary reason for liking and for older adolescents to cite commercials seen as 'straightforward'. Both black and white adolescents ranked their reasons for liking commercials similarly.

Cigarette advertising was listed as the most disliked category of commercials. Of those adolescents answering the question, over 20 per cent cited this product category as 'worst' advertising. While the data indicate that white adolescents were more critical of cigarette advertising than blacks, this result may reflect the fact that data from black adolescents were gathered during fall 1971, shortly before cigarette advertising was banned from television. The second category of disliked advertising was that for deodorants and cosmetics.

More than one-third of the adolescents criticized commercials because they were 'stupid ... insult intelligence'. The second most salient reason was that commercials were seen as 'false' or 'hypocritical'. Interestingly, junior high and senior high school adolescents are alike in their ranking of reasons for disliking commercials, but senior high adolescents also cite stylistic reasons (eg 'bad acting') more than junior high adolescents do. Black students are somewhat more likely than white students to cite stylistic characteristics as a reason for disliking commercials.

One puzzling aspect of these attitudinal data is that about one-third of the adolescents did not respond to the questions on liked and disliked commercials. This non-response rate was greater than for other open-ended items in the questionnaire, and the rate was higher among black adolescents than among white adolescents. This may suggest that television commercials are simply not very salient for adolescents.

For purposes of analysis, a scale of attitudes toward the institution of television advertising was developed, based on four-point questionnaire items. About three-quarters of the sample agreed with the statement, 'Most commercials are too long', and almost 70 per cent agreed that 'most commercials are in bad taste and are very annoying'. Only about one-third of the adolescents agreed that 'TV commercials tell the truth'.

The higher an adolescent's social class, the more negative were his attitudes toward television advertising. However, social class was not a particularly important predictor of other aspects of consumer learning, nor was it important in analyses comparing black and white adolescents.

Among white adolescents, watching greater amounts of television was associated with positive attitudes toward television advertising, at least among middle and upper social classes.

Adolescents from families in which consumption matters are discussed relatively frequently — in which parents and teenagers seek and give advice about consumption of goods and services — are more likely to have positive attitudes toward advertising than are adolescents from families in which consumption matters are discussed less frequently. However, students who perceive that their parents want them to achieve higher socio-economic status than the family's present status — adolescents who perceive that their parents have high expectations for them — are no more likely to have positive attitudes toward television advertising than adolescents who do not have this perception. Similarly, there are no differences in attitudes between adolescents who hold high occupation expectations for themselves and those who hold less ambitious occupational goals. It might be expected that television advertising, which often portrays success in interpersonal and occupational roles, might be more appealing to adolescents from environments in which striving for success in such roles is important. This does not seem to be the case, however, at least in terms of perceived parental expectations and the adolescent's own expectations.

A mild relationship was found, however, between attitudes toward advertising and 'materialism'. 'Materialism' was defined as an orientation emphasizing material possessions and money for personal happiness and social progress. Adolescents scoring high in materialism had more positive attitudes than less materialistic adolescents.

Consumer learning

During adolescence, most young people begin buying goods and services for themselves. Television advertising often portrays buying behaviour, and attractive life styles are presented as the consequence of buying certain products or services. Thus, we should expect adolescents to use television advertising as one input to learning values and skills as consumers.

Four aspects of such consumer learning were analysed in the present studies: *recall of commercial content* is the measure of knowledge of advertised products: *attitudes toward commercials and 'materialistic' attitudes* are measures of more complex cognitive development; self-reported influence of commercials on specific product purchases is the measure of behaviour.

We expected that various demographic indices would be related to these criterion variables. Our interest was in demographic characteristics of adolescents which, in effect, 'locate' the adolescent in the social environment, such as socio-economic status, intelligence and available money. Within demographically defined groups, however, we expected that adolescent consumer learning would vary depending on the relative presence or absence of intrafamily communication about consumption matters and on the adolescent's media use. Our concern was with two dimensions of media use: amount of print and television use, and motivations or reasons adolescents watch television commercials. The specific 'reasons for watching commercials' in the study by Ward and Wackman were derived from student-written essays on the subject. Content analysis of these essays revealed three major dimensions of reasons adolescents watch commercials. The major dimension was 'social utility' — watching commercials in order to gain information about the 'social significance' of products or brands and association of advertised objects with social roles and life styles.

A second major reason for watching commercials was 'communication utility' — watching in order to provide a basis for later interpersonal communication. Finally, the teenagers indicated that they watch for 'vicarious consumption' reasons — as a means of vicarious participation in desired life styles or as a means of vicarious association with attractive others.

These three clusters of motivations for watching commercials were measured by a series of questionnaire items. While most adolescents indicated that they did not usually watch commercials for these reasons, our interest was in the relative incidence of watching for these reasons among black and white adolescents and in the relative influence of these reasons on the four aspects of consumer learning.

Black adolescents indicated that they watched for social utility, communication utility and vicarious consumption reasons more than white adolescents. Black adolescents also watched television and listened to the radio more than whites; white adolescents spent more time with print media.

No differences were observed between the white and black adolescents in recall of commercials and in attitudes toward advertising. However, blacks were more materialistic than white adolescents, and they indicated that television advertising influenced their purchases more than white adolescents.

Further analyses of consumer learning processes were conducted for white adolescents only, because we had insufficient data from black adolescents. We were interested in differences in consumer learning processes between younger and older adolescents. The data indicated no differences between the two groups on the dependent variables, but some differences between younger and older adolescents on the communication variables. Thus, younger and older adolescents appear to be at the same level of consumer learning, but processes of learning differ for the two groups.

The four aspects of consumer learning appear generally to be independent of each other, and relationships between them do not appear to change over time; intercorrelations among the dependent variables are essentially zero, for both younger and older adolescents.

A step-up regression analysis was used to analyse the relationships between the independent variables and the four measures of consumer learning. The results may be summarised as follows:

1 *Recall* Recall of commercial themes and slogans represents a fundamental aspect of consumer learning. For younger and older adolescents, intelligence was the best predictor of recall. The fact that media exposure is a less certain correlate is not surprising, considering the redundancy of commercial messages. Even minimal exposure to media ensures commercial exposure; but storing and retrieving their content seems mainly a function of intelligence — at least, as measured by tests of 'intelligence'.

2 *Attitudes toward commercials* Markedly different processes seem to be involved in learning general attitudes toward commercials among younger and older adolescents. Social utility reasons for watching commercials and time spent viewing account for much of the variance for younger viewers. By contrast, vicarious consumption reasons and intra-family communication about consumption matters are important variables for older adolescents.

3 *Materialism* Another measure of more complex kinds of consumer learning is 'materialism' — an orientation which views material goods and money as important for personal happiness and social progress. For both younger and older adolescents, social utility and vicarious consumption reasons for watching commercials account for much of the variance. However, for younger adolescents, a third factor was available money; for older adolescents, a third factor was intelligence, which was negatively

related to materialism.

4 *Effects of commercials on buying behaviour* Our measure of
effects of television advertising on buying behaviour is a self-report
item which asks whether the adolescent feels he has been directly
influenced by television advertising in buying a specific product.

The data indicate that three variables are important predictors of
this kind of learning for both younger and older adolescents:
communication in the family about consumption, social utility
reasons for viewing television commercials, and amount of
exposure to magazines.In addition, for younger adolescents, a
fourth variable is important — communicatory utility reasons for
viewing commercials, which is negatively related to effects of
advertisements on buying.

To summarise the research on consumer learning: the data
suggest that television advertising is not a sufficient condition for
buying — especially among older adolescents. Intrafamily communication about consumption intervenes between communication
exposure and purchase. For younger adolescents, reasons for
watching commercials are also important intervening variables
between exposure and behaviour. Specifically, the data suggest
that:

1 Different aspects of consumer learning are not well integrated
among either younger or older adolescents;

2 Different clusters of variables have effects on the different kinds
of consumer learning examined in this study.

3 For any particular kind of consumer learning, essentially the
same cluster of variables affects that kind of learning for both
younger and older adolescents. Therefore, even though younger
adolescents are exposed to more commercial content, talk with
parents more about consumer goods, and watch commercials more
for social utility and communicatory unity reasons, the predictive
power of these variables is essentially the same in both groups of
adolescents.

Three major processes seem to be involved in the different kinds
of consumer learning:
The learning of advertising slogans seems to be mainly a

function of the *intelligence* of the adolescent.

The learning of more cognitive orientations, such as attitudes toward television advertising and a materialistic orientation, seems to be mainly a function of the adolescent's *reasons for viewing* commercials. Thus, these cognitive orientations develop as a function of the adolescent's television behaviour but not simply of exposure time. Rather, the orientations develop as a function of the uses the adolescent makes of commercial content, several of which are basically social uses.

A third process which seems to be involved in the formation of purchasing patterns is clearly an overt social process. In this process, *communication with parents* about advertising, consumer goods and consumption processes seems to be an important variable intervening between exposure to advertising and the purchase of consumer goods.

SUMMARY

Since the overall objective of this programme of research was to bring exploratory data to bear on a broad range of television advertising's effects, no attempt is made to integrate the various findings presented in each of the discrete studies which comprise this research project. We hope that these studies will help make such conceptual integration possible, so that we may have more complete, explicit and integrated knowledge of television advertising's effects on children and adolescents.

Five areas of this research seem particularly important, both in terms of policy implications and in terms of promise for future research possibilities:

1 *Young children's reactions to television advertising reflect stages in cognitive development.* While our data in this area are quite tentative due to several methodological limitations, it appears that responses to television advertising become increasingly differentiated and complex with age. Children progress from confused perceptions of commercials — not discriminating between programme and commercials, nor between advertisements and products — to the beginnings of cynicism about advertising and perceptions of the intent of advertising by second and fourth grade. By sixth grade, we find that children have relatively well-developed attitudes toward commercials; they respond to them in terms of the

message and evaluate advertised objects in terms of their relevance to them.

2 *Selectivity in viewing commercials increases with age, but processes of commerical watching are highly complex.* It does not appear that young children automatically 'tune in' to commercials, as one popular criticism of television advertising suggests. Generally, paying of full attention to commercials decreases with age, although the viewing situation, characteristics of television stimuli, attention to prior programming, and personal characteristics all affect children's attention to commercials.

Just as previous research suggests that adults selectively attend to programming and commercials, the same patterns are observed with pre-teen-age children. Generally, all children seem to pay more attention to programming than adults, but the drop in attention during commercials is not as great as for adults. The drop in attention is greatest for older children, least for younger children.

Perhaps the central importance of the research concerning commercial watching behaviour is that the data may be related to consequences of watching in other aspects of children's lives — ie to learning from commercials, intra-family influence, and attitudinal development.

3 *Mothers perceive that television advertising influences their children, and they estimate commercials' effects by the frequency with which their children attempt to influence purchases.* While most of our research concerns relatively direct effects of television advertising on children's behaviour and cognitive development, the study of intra-family influence is concerned with second-order consequences of television advertising — namely, do television advertisements stimulate desires of children for advertised goods, and do young children then engage in behaviour directed at acquiring these goods? Direct measurement of such effects is impossible, but we asked mothers to estimate the frequency with which commercials influenced their children to want specific advertised products. The mothers had no straightforward, independent measure of commercials' effects, so their estimates of advertising's influence were based on purchase influence attempts. The mothers appeared to reason that, the more their children asked for products which were advertised on television, the more

advertising was influencing their children. (Interestingly, however, even the placing of relatively stringent restrictions on viewing did not seem to inhibit purchase influence attempts, suggesting that television advertising was not the sole cause of such interpersonal influence attempts.)

4 *Adolescents hold negative attitudes toward television adver-tising, and there are only slight differences between black and white adolescents in attitudes.* Generally, adolescents are quite cynical about television advertising, feeling that commercials are not straightforward and are often hypocritical. Cigarette advertising — still on the air at the time of the research — was especially disliked, while advertising for drugs and patent medicines was particularly liked. (Most adolescents who cited drug and patent medicine advertising as most liked advertising seem to like it because it was seen as funny. Thus, the data may reflect the wide-spread popularity of one product in this category which was advertised in quite humourous ways.)

It is interesting to note that most adolescents like advertising for stylistic, entertainment reasons — not because commercials are seen as helpful or informative. On the other hand, the bases of their negative attitudes are along dimensions of trust, truthfulness, straightforwardness.

5 *Adolescents acquire consumer attitudes and skills from television advertising. Such consumer learning occurs as a function of the quality of television advertising use, more than the quantity of media use.* Understanding the broad effects of television adver-tising among adolescents requires an understanding of the context of advertising communication for adolescents. This context reflects the adolescent's growing interest in adult roles and activities and the relevance of television advertising to associated consumer roles and activities. Our interest was in knowledge of advertising, general cognitive orientations (attitudes toward advertising and material-istic attitudes), and buying behaviour as aspects of consumer attitudes and skills.

It appears that the most important predictors of the development of these aspects of consumer behaviour are the motivations of adolescents for watching television commercials. Our data suggest that, beyond verbal attitudes toward television advertising (which are generally negative and cynical), adolescents do learn from television advertising, and this learning is related to developing skills and attitudes relevant to consumer roles.

FUTURE RESEARCH

Future research will require further conceptual development and refinement as well as further empirical work. The conceptual framework shown in Figure 14.1 has guided the present research, but some of the concepts in this framework are too abstract and general for guiding empirical research — 'consumer behaviour'. 'alternatives to commercial watching', etc. Thus, a first step in future research will be the development of lower-level, more specific concepts to describe buying behaviour, reactions to advertisements, etc. Conceptual development in the areas of socialization and personality-cognition development should be especially useful — as indeed they already have been in guiding this research. For example, Brim's conceptualization of role development has been useful in conceptualizing 'consumer role learning', and Piaget's and Erikson's conceptualizations of stages of cognitive development and personality development have been useful in guiding our clinical research on stages of development in children's reactions to television commercials. Besides concept development, further research will need to specify theoretical linkages between concepts, building upon and supplementing the relationships already found in the present research.

At the same time, empirical research to develop adequate measures of these concepts must be carried out. For example, standardized measures of the dimensions of reactions to ads should be developed and administered to larger samples of children, so that baseline estimates of stages of development in reactions to ads can be made. Measures which will tap the several dimensions of buying behaviour should be developed; in fact, a start has been made with two questionnaires which have been administered in Ann Arbor, Michigan, and in the Boston area.

Furthermore, research is needed to fill in gaps in the present research. Some of this research will simply involve analysis of data already collected — for example, analysis of the relation between children's watching behaviour and purchase influence attempts. By collecting more data from the children in the watching behaviour study, we can analyse the relation between attitudes toward advertising, purchase behaviour, and watching behaviour commercial watching behaviour.

Research is also needed to clarify some of the conflicts in the present data. Our research on adolescents indicates that by the seventh grade, adolescent attitudes toward advertising are quite negative, and that these attitudes do not change markedly through junior and senior high schools. The watching behaviour study indicated that negative reactions to commercials occur frequently among eleven- and twelve-year-olds, but not among younger children. On the other hand, the clinical study indicated that most fourth graders (eight- to ten-year-olds) were quite negative toward advertising, and that some second graders (six- to eight-year-olds) were rather negative toward commercials because of their experiences with products advertised. Research is needed to determine when these negative attitudes begin to develop and what variables in the child's media behaviour, interpersonal behaviour, cognitive development, etc., are related to this development.

Finally, subsequent research must fulfill two methodological requirements: (*a*) In order to investigate earlier development in watching behaviour and reactions to advertising, sampling must include children younger than those studied in the present research, those under five years old; (*b*) Cross-sectional research is useful for identifying important variables and for determining age group differences on these variables, but longitudinal research is necessary to investigate developmental phases and trends.

15

The Effects of Television on Children

Dennis Howitt

Contrary to expectation, children are a somewhat forgotten breed as far as studies of the effects of the mass media are concerned. Despite the observation that those most vocal in their criticisms of the media's presentation of violence and sex have frequently used the question of the effects of such content on the immature child as support for the urgency of their claims, researchers have stolidly overlooked children in their studies. This assertion, however, needs some qualification. Obviously it is not true that there is absolutely no research on the effects of the mass media on children, but certainly most effects research, as indeed most mass communications research of any sort, has tended to concentrate on adults. For example, although there is a substantial literature on the contribution of the media to voting and other forms of 'political' behaviour, there has been, as we will see, but a handful of studies assessing the role of the media in the political socialization of children. However, to talk about children as a unity is misleading. We know that the rubric 'child' includes, for our purposes, a toddler just coming up to three as well as a near-adult of sixteen or so. It is not surprising then that with such a wide range of age groups our knowledge is fairly thin. What might be true for a six-year-old may not be true to a sixteen-year-old, but we cannot be sure without exploring the whole age range. Furthermore, the research coverage of children is rather uneven. Relatively, we know a great deal about the effects of television on the child's other leisure activities and his general knowledge,[1] but our knowledge, say, of the effects of television commercials on the young child is scant. Some would offer the opinion, in an extension of this, that although we know little of the effects of the mass media on children, we are hamstrung by a general neglect of the total child as a focus of research in favour of merely considering the child as a consumer of mass communications.

There are some clear reasons why children are ignored in effects research, but ultimately it is an enigmatic state of affairs. Generalizations can be made but every case deserves a distinct explanation. Worries about the impact of sex and pornography, for example, are by and large intertwined with the question of their impact on children. This is readily illustrated by the fact that the American Commission on Obscenity and Pornography, set up by an act of Congress during the Johnson administration, was charged to investigate whether such materials are harmful, particularly to minors.[2] However, this special mention of young people could not be, and was not, interpreted by the Commission as a licence for social scientists to expose children to pornographic and other forms of erotic material (Commission on Obscenity and Pornography, 1970). No Congressman could consider this proper if for reasons of political expediency alone. For ethical reasons there is virtually no research that has wantonly exposed children to the possible influence of pornography. The American Commission which concluded that pornography was not harmful to adults, was hampered in generalizing its findings and recommendations to children simply because there was no available research applicable to this age group. Elthammar's (1967) study of the emotional reactions of eleven- to eighteen-year-olds to films of a violent and sexual nature raises the very ethical questions which have prevented similar studies by others.

There are several studies of the effects of media violence which deal largely with children.[3] These tend to be dominated by correlational field studies where, obviously, the researcher is not exposing children to films or other materials of possible 'harmful' consequences but simply relating their media use to aggressive attitudes or the reports of others about the children's aggressive behaviour (eg *Eron et al*, 1972; *Halloran et al*, 1970; *Pfuhl*, 1970). There could not be the same taboos here as in experimental studies. The experimentalist, because he sets out to show films which he thinks may stand a good chance of influencing the child, is on more dangerous ground. This, to some extent, explains why experimental studies with children have concentrated on 'playful' situations such as 'attacking' an inflated toy clown (*Bandura*, 1963; *Bandura et al.*, 1963a and b), but there are other reasons why experimentalists have tended to neglect children. The most important of these is that he is often concerned primarily with the theoretical[4] rather than the

practical or applied aspects of the mass media-audience relationship. This 'frees' him from the duty to anchor his studies in a wider
social reality and so he is as happy using the constant supply of
university undergraduates available to him as he is using children
who have to be found, transported to the laboratory and
transported back home again.

While it might be expected that the constraints against doing
effects research on children and the violence and pornography
issues do not apply to the effects of advertising, there is a shortage
of relevant studies in this area also. Consumerism may not be such
a taboo effect but still the literature is small. Search, for example,
the psychological and sociological literature for the last few years
and you will be poorly rewarded since few effects studies are to be
found. There is a recent and interesting study by Ward *et al.* (1971)
which documents children's attempts to influence their parents'
purchasing behaviour, but nothing apart from that. This matches
the state of our knowledge of the effects of advertising in general
(*Tunstall,* 1964, p. 17). We can plainly see the large amount of
money spent but are not told of the results of the market research
carried out. Whether this is because relevant work is not done or
whether it is not expedient to publish it is unclear.[5]

This dearth of knowledge of the effects of the mass media on
children perhaps demonstrates that media researchers are not the
slaves of the vocal critics of the media just as they insist they should
not be (*Halloran et al.* 1970).

In several Western or Westernized countries there have been
studies of the impact of television on the young audience. In Great
Britain, Himmelweit *et al.* (1958) produced the prototype and
classic *Television and the Child,* while in the USA (*Schramm et al.*
1961), Japan (*Furu,* 1962) and Australia (*Campbell,* 1962),
amongst others, studies were carried out to evaluate the effects of
the introduction of television on children. Although many of these
discuss the effects of television on moral behaviour, they by and
large concentrate on the effects of television on homework, school
performance, family life, passivity and reading. While it is
interesting to know that children tend to go to bed a few minutes
later due to the influence of television, it is difficult, at face value,
to accept that the matter is of much concern. Once the physical
effects of television on the eyesight of young people was a public
anxiety. Now no one seems to care.[6]

In mass communications research nothing is as simple as it may at first appear. A simple question such as 'What are the effects of the mass media on children?' leads us rapidly to untold complexities. This chapter will elaborate some of the difficulties in mass communications effects research. They are not simply methodological problems or even problems of the lack of research, but fundamental conceptual and theoretical difficulties. Many of the problems of mass communications research have been brought about by the elementary level at which mass communications researchers pitch their interests. The inadequacies of research are only discovered in retrospect. Too often mass communications researchers have progressed laterally. Instead of building from the raw material of established research, the problems have caused them to shift ground to tackle issues which allow them to sidestep the fundamental issues, for the time being at least. The following discussion reaffirms some of the basic issues — methodological, theoretical and conceptual — in the context of our present knowledge of the effects of the mass media on children. The reader will not emerge with a complete perspective on media effects — this just does not exist — but, hopefully, he will gain an insight into the nature and problems of effects research. Rather than concentrating on the issues in abstract, the discussion is centred around research areas. Basic problems are presented in the context, for example, of our knowledge of the effects of the mass media on the child's political development in order that the ideas will have substance.

The theoretical interests of the mass communications researcher and the public concern about the mental health and social well-being of children curiously parallel one another. The layman would be concerned with the effects of television on children because he feels that their personalities are not yet fully developed, that psychologically they are not prepared yet for some aspects of adult life, that they are too impressionable, and that the things that adults can cope with comfortably may be traumatic for the young person. The mass communications theorist would argue something like this: 'I know that the effects of television and the other mass media on adults are pretty minimal — it's difficult to change their opinions, it is difficult to change their voting behaviour and, if anything, the effects of any persuasive communications in the mass media are merely to support the entrenched positions of the audience members, no matter what were the intentions of the message. The reasons for this are largely to do with the fact that the audience comes to the mass media with pre-existing behavioural tendencies, sets of beliefs, and opinions which are not amenable to change. Only when we can expect that the individual has no pre-existing tendencies or when there are circumstances particularly conducive to change can we expect the mass media to have much effect on the audience. Children, since they have had less opportunity to build up such prior tendencies, might be expected to be the most affected sector of the audience.' (cf *Klapper,* 1960)

Cumberbatch and Howitt (1974b) have discussed a similar argument that has been made in connection with adults. It is sometimes argued that adults will be persuaded by communications on topics for which their everyday, non-mass media lives provide no alternative source of opinion or behaviour. Thus, the argument would suggest that we are easily convinced by the mass media of the rights and wrongs of events overseas which are distant from our daily experiences but resistant to arguments which are highly relevant to our everyday life. One would expect that our ideas about crime, because we have little daily contact with it, would be formed by the mass media, and that our conception of mental illness, again since we have so little direct contact with it, should be moulded by the mass media. However, research evidence in both cases suggests quite the opposite. For instance, our images of crime very much reflect the social reality of crime rather than what we read in our newspapers (*Croll,* 1974; *Roshier,* 1969) and our conceptions of mental illness are more realistic (*Nunally,* 1961). This has all the makings of a riddle. Of course, we can always argue that the audience for the mass media discount the content because they know that it is in the nature of the media to sensationalize and to credit the more sensational but, as yet, the adequacy of this assertion is difficult to evaluate. Such a notion has its roots in the work of Dysinger and Ruckmick (1933).

Attempts have been made to extend this 'deficit' argument to research on children. By deficit argument we mean the idea that those amenable to the impact of the same media are those for which countervailing social forces are absent. It might also be termed the 'swings and roundabouts' hypothesis — what one loses on the swings of real life one gains on the roundabouts of the mass media. Howitt (1973) has argued that the mass media relate to violent attitudes only when their content is drastically different from situations which the child will have experienced directly. Howitt and Cumberbatch (1971b) have argued, with empirical support, that since first-born and only children lack older siblings to supply salient models for their behaviour they are likely to adopt the behaviour modelled on television. Hartmann and Husband (1974) suggested that the mass media are a source of racial images for children sharing low contact with immigrants whereas real-life sources are more salient for children in areas where there are a lot of immigrants. But in all of these examples the evidence is relatively slight compared with the total problem and scarcely amounts to a cohesive empirical justification for the idea. A similar conceptualization is integral to the view that mass media portrayals of violence are harmless to all those but the child who lacks the psychological resources of the stable mind. Thus for a proportion of children with certain pre-existing tendencies, the argument is that the mass media *may* 'trigger off' violence (cf *Schramm et al.*, 1961). The only empirical study which has tested this hypothesis using emotionally disturbed children found that they were less likely than normal children to imitate the behaviour of an aggressive model (*Walters* and *Willow*, 1968)! One therefore needs to exercise considerable caution in reaching conclusions about the likely effects of the media on children.

The static and abstract view of the socialization process seemingly held by many media sociologists and psychologists leads them into many assumptions about how the media might influence the child. A very good example comes from the notion that the response of the family to television content can attenuate or reduce the influence of this content on the socialization of the child (eg *Linné*, 1971). The family who comment adversely on TV violence when it appears on the screen are less likely to have an aggressive child grow up in their midst than the family who condone or fail to comment on TV violence, or so the argument goes. But this neglects the critical point that children are socialized in the area of aggression from the age of a few months, well before they can even comprehend television at even the most minimal levels. Not surprisingly, researchers who have tried to study the effects of family communications about television violence on the violent attitudes of the child have found them to have no effects (*McLeod et al.*, 1971). As a general principle, it is a reasonable proposition to suggest that for virtually all areas of social developments, real-life influences will have operated over and above those of the mass media.[7] It strains our credulity rather too much to imagine that parents ignore the socialization of sex and aggression norms until the family group is confronted with bedroom scenes and killings on the television screen. Unfortunately, real life is much too complicated for our models of social life. Restricted models do, of course, have their uses but need to be seen as such.

Not only do we tend to overlook the complexities of social life in the acquisition of socialized forms of behaviour, we also tend to ignore the role of real life in shaping the manifestation of media-learned behaviours. Even if the viewer is taken by Gary Cooper's walk and decides to imitate it, in all seriousness, at school, it is likely that the scorn and derision of schoolmates will rapidly create a jaded perspective on any further excursions into Gary Cooperisms. Socialization of behaviours occurs both in advance of actual manifestations of behaviour and in retrospect. Real life may operate both prior to exposure to the socializing influence of the mass media and in retrospect of any such influence. Should the child test out ideas of social behaviour obtained from the mass media in real life, changes are that real-life experiences will act against those induced by the mass media. Parallel examples come from studies of adults (cf *Simon*, 1967; *Wilcox*, 1968).

Another major difficulty with our conceptions of the effects of the mass media lies in our choice of measures of effects. We may start our investigations with a social-problem orientation, but may finish it by choosing measures which are, in themselves, irrelevant to the social problem. The argument is a familiar one against studies of the effects of media violence; the public's concern is with the seemingly senseless aggression of adolescents and young adults and not with a child's willingness to punch a plastic clown (*Bandura*, 1963; *Bandura et al.*, 1963a and b), or shock someone in 'an experiment on the effects of punishment on learning' (*Berkowitz*, 1967) which form the basis of our measures of aggression. A much more subtle example comes from research on the television programme for pre-school children called *Sesame Street*. The intentions of the research were admirable, but perhaps the socially important questions were neglected. *Sesame Street* was designed to teach pre-school children simple educational skills such as the recognition of numbers and letters (*Cooney*, 1970; *Children's Television Workshop*, 1971). Completely in line with the point of view that the primary function of television is, and must be, entertainment, the producers of this programme used the methods, techniques and pacing of popular entertainment programmes — humour, action, animation and songs — to get over the information they thought important. Research shows that to some extent they were extremely successful at achieving these ends. Ball and Bogatz (1972) studied the effects of the programme on the simple skills the programmes were intended to teach and found that, in line with the producers' intentions, spectacular gains in these educational skills were made by the viewer compared with the non-viewer. Nevertheless, the question remains of whether *Sesame Street* has been an educational success in the sense of solving any real social problems. First of all it was conceived in terms similar to the poverty action research efforts such as Operation Headstart which were intended to bridge the gulf between the educationally advantaged child from the middle-class family and the educationally disadvantaged child from the impoverished environments of the slums. *Headstart* took pre-school children and gave them brief but intensive experience in the classroom with a specially trained teacher. In this period the child was put through an enrichment programme which was designed to try to overcome the disadvantages of the child's educationally poor home environment.

Sesame Street, although not conceived as a substitute for these field efforts, was hoped to be similar in effect. However, far from decreasing the gap between the child from the impoverished environment and the child from the educationally advantaged areas, the gap widened (a possibility noted by Filipson, 1972). More children from the middle-class home watched the programmes and so, on aggregate, the middle-class gained more from the programme than the disadvantaged. Rather than decreasing the disadvantage, the programme may have increased it. The disadvantaged *viewer* may have gained in comparison with the advantaged *non-viewer*, but there were relatively less of them. Another serious problem in regarding such programmes as solutions to the educational problems of the environmentally handicapped young is that they rely exclusively on teaching a few skills which in the end may be irrelevant to the real issues facing educationalists. Although it is not possible to quote chapter and verse on the effects of such programmes, it is clear from the action research such as *Headstart* that while the children with the special training had an advantage in the classroom over other children from a poor environment and compare on simple skills well with the advantaged child, this advantage quickly came to nothing in the educational rough and tumble of the classroom (*Connors* and

Eisenberg, no date; *Connors* and *Walker*, no date; *Walker* and *Connors*, no date). Educational disadvantage is not merely the absence of specific knowledge. It is the absence of good learning skills, good learning environment and satisfactory rewards for progress amongst other things. Educational disadvantage would not be such an intractable problem if it could be overcome by an hour or two's viewing each week. The *Sesame Street* people may well have good reason to be pleased on the basis of the findings of their research team, but it is a moot point whether the real issues have been tackled.

The problem of how to measure effects of *real* mass media on *real* children is another major stumbling block. While the analogies of the laboratory experiment are useful, at least within certain limits, they cannot tell us everything we need or would like to know about the role of the mass media in the development of children. Certain aspects of a child's perceptions of the world, for example, may take years to emerge through processes so gradual that the child may be totally unaware of them. The question is not whether experiments and other short-term methodologies are appropriate or not since they are plainly inapplicable. The more complex the social problems we are dealing with, the more intractable becomes the problem of cause and effect. It is not good enough to compare high and low viewers on a particular sort of measure of the thing we are interested in since this is totally to avoid considering the process by which individuals become viewers of particular sorts of television programme content. One typical procedure which the researcher falls back on is the respondent's subjective reports of the 'sources' of his attitudes and behaviour. The most traditional of all areas of mass communications research — politics — serves well as the illustration.

In the area of political socialization, as we have seen, children tend to be neglected. A person's political beliefs are not the product of a few minutes' exposure to the mass media and their origins and development cannot be tackled using flimsy methodologies. Even with adults the bulk of this literature has tended to concentrate merely on the effects of election campaigns on those relatively few individuals who change voting intentions, and the likelihood that the audience will vote (eg *Berelson et al.*, 1954; *Lazarsfeld et al.*, 1948; *McCombs*, 1972), rather than on the effects of the mass media in the more general field of political socialization.[8] There are few published studies pertinent to the question of the role of the mass media in the political socialization of children, especially if we ignore the demonstration by Himmelweit *et al.* (1958) that the mass media can give to children images of the classes in society other than their own.

The ridiculous thing about mass communications research is that in circumstances where it would seem incontrovertible that the mass media have an effect, such as on political knowledge, it is very difficult to actually prove using the methods of social science. There are correlations between political knowledge and media exposure but how are we to know what is cause and what is effect? However, if we are willing to accept the say-so of children themselves, we have evidence which supports the idea that the mass media are the primary source of political knowledge.

Hollender (1970) even goes so far as to suggest that the new 'parent' is the mass media, particularly television. He was concerned with the sources of knowledge and attitudes about the Vietnam war and war in general for late adolescents. He asked them such questions as what caused the war in Vietnam, what they thought the result of the war in Vietnam might be, and what they thought about war, amongst other things. Having elicited their opinions he then asked them to name the sources of each of these opinions. By and large, the major source claimed by the adolescents was the mass media. Schools came a poor second while parents and peers were the least influential of all. However, Hess and Torney (1967) present evidence that only 5 per cent of children could turn to the mass media as the best place to look for help in making up their minds about voting. But can we believe the kids when they name the mass media as the sources of their opinions? Perhaps the thought that the mass media must be the most important because they contain the most political information had struck the kids as well as the researcher. Obviously there is a need for alternative means of validating what the children said.

A study by Chaffee *et al.* (1970) deserves recounting in that perhaps it pushes our knowledge towards the proof of the obvious which is so often tantalizingly out of our grip. They considered both knowledge and behaviour as distinct aspects of the socializing process. During the 1968 American election campaign measures of political knowledge and campaigning behaviour were taken a few months before the final election day and a few days afterwards, that is, at two distinct times. Political knowledge was measured by such items as the identification of the countries of various political leaders and the naming of local congressmen. Political behaviour was measured by the wearing of campaign badges, the distribution of campaign leaflets, and trying to talk someone into liking a particular candidate. Measures were taken of watching public affairs on television, reading about them in newspapers, watching entertainment programmes on television, and reading the entertainment parts of newspapers. Using stringent statistical criteria they produced evidence which suggested that the consumption of public affairs media increased political knowledge while the consumption of entertainment media seemed to be a negative influence on knowledge. This goes some way towards proving the indisputable. However, in terms of overt political activity the evidence of the effects of the media is so slight that it is best ignored. The children rated the mass media highest in terms of the sources of their information[9] as well as their opinions. Interestingly enough, those who attributed the mass media as being the major source of their knowledge knew more while those who rated parents, friends or teachers as the source tended to know less. A finding which has intriguing implications.

Note that this study was not at all concerned with the particular political orientation of the children (whether they were inclined towards the Republicans or Democrats). We are left with the problem, then, and it is a very old and central one in mass communications research, of whether really the mass media are simply providing a superstructure of ideas and images which are built on the foundations of the individual's pre-existing predilections.

Does the Democratic sympathizer merely take relevant images from the political coverage of the mass media to support these beliefs?

One way of tackling this issue is to look at the dominant content of the media and see if this is reflected in the attitudes of the audience for this particular content. For example, Byrne (1969) administered a questionnaire to eleven-, fifteen- and sixteen-year-old children which included items to measure (a) their affective feeling towards the government and (b) their feelings of the effectiveness of government. Both television and newspapers were considered. Negro children in his sample watched as much televison news as whites and seemed to know as much even though they had less exposure to newspapers. Children from lower social classes watched TV news less, read newspapers less, and had lower levels of political information than those from higher social classes. Those groups of children who were least exposed to newspapers demonstrated more positive attitudes to the government than those groups who were relatively more exposed to the print media. This presents us with serious methodological uncertainties, particularly as we do not know whether these group tendencies apply also within groups, which leaves the problematic issue of cause and effect unresolved. Certainly this seems rather too slight evidence on which to argue that the media engender evaluative attitudes in the audience, but it is all we have on children. If we took recourse to studies using adults and the influences on their voting behaviour, we would be tempted to view the available data as simply representing the absorption of knowledge elements on to an already existing evaluative framework.

While it may appear that we know rather more about the effects or lack of effects of the media on the political attitudes of adults, even this is a contentious proposition. The most outstanding and central piece of knowledge that we have from the voting studies is *not* that we can say that the media contribute little or nothing to final behaviour, but that people change their voting intentions rarely (*Berelson et al.*, 1954; *Lazarsfeld et al.*, 1948). In this context the media could not be a powerful influence, but we still do not know with any precision the role of the media in changing those who vacillate in their voting behaviour. Even less do we know whether the media have any impact in creating the solidly unmoving intentions of the vast majority away from the context of an election campaign. As yet the issues are too big and complex for us.

The studies of children and politics to some extent seem to go rather against the arguments which are commonly accepted concerning the effects of mass communication on voting behaviour. Lazarsfeld *et al.* (1948) provide us with the evidence that taking gross measures of political behaviour the mass media produce little change, whereas taking other measures of effects the media seem more powerful a contribution to political behaviour. Voting change, in terms of a dichotomy in a two-party system, is a very gross measure and perhaps could be likened, as a measure of the political effects of television, to the use of suicide rates as a measure of mental illness. In a sense, both of these measures would merely represent tips of the iceberg of the true effect. For example, in the Lazarsfeld study only 2 per cent of individuals switched parties at all. However, somewhat more than 31 per cent of the individuals changed in some way: they became unsure of their voting intentions, they moved from uncertainty to certainty in their voting intentions, and finally, some of them switched. 53 per cent did not change voting intentions during the course of the election campaign — which still leaves a lot of changers. It is not clear from the study how many of these changers attribute the change to the mass media (although we are told that there were equal numbers claiming the influence of radio and newspapers), but at another point in the book we are told that 61 per cent of the respondents claim that their voting intentions were influenced most by the mass media.[10] Trenaman and McQuail (1961) have analyzed data for changers in vote intention and found that amongst changers the direction of the change has nothing to do with the use of campaign-relevant mass-media content. Blumler (1971) indicates this to be another example of the ineffectiveness of the mass media in producing changes in voting behaviour. However, independent evidence has suggested that voting intention cannot be explained on the basis that maximum exposure should cause maximum effect on voting behaviour (*Lazarsfeld et al.*, 1948). For example, those with the strongest voting intentions even before the election campaign proper are the ones who watch the election coverage most. Those with least firm positions tend to watch the least. Since the least committed are the ones who change most readily and are least exposed, the factors which change their position must have little, if anything, to do with amount of exposure to the media. Yet another example of the 'law' of mass communications research that whoever needs the cultural products of the mass media most, uses them least. The figures that we have for children, then, may not be as drastically different from those for adults as the voting studies might suggest. So long as we use similar sorts of measures (self-reports of influence) we find that the mass media are as effective in affecting adults as children. The big question is whether we should accept such subjective reports.

What evidence is there of the validity of 'source mentions' in influence? Katz and Lazarsfeld (1955) document the adequacy of claims for interpersonal attempts to influence by showing that those who claim to have influenced or have been influenced were supported in this claim by the persons who attempt to influence or who have been influenced. The correspondence is impressive enough. Unfortunately the authors, although they collected information on the mass media as a source of influence, carried out no validity studies. Hartmann and Husband (1974) in a study of the effects of the media treatment of race on the attitudes and images that children had of immigrants into Great Britain pursued the question more thoroughly. For example, they found that children who lived in the area of the country with the least contact with immigrants tended to attribute more of the things that they knew about immigrants to the mass media than did those children in areas with a lot of immigrants in the locality. Furthermore, children who attributed the media as being their source tended to use the mass media more than those who infrequently regarded the media as their source. At least at a minimal level, this is evidence that on the face of it the children's ratings of the sources of the beliefs and knowledge were valid. Interestingly enough, the authors did not ask the sources of evaluative statements on an attitude scale concerned with coloured people, but they did correlate various indices of media exposure with the same measure of attitude and found no relationship. We are left with the same unanswered problems then: if the media have the effects on children that children report that they do, what are the key variables in this socialization process, and how come attitudes are not influenced if, as Hartmann and Husband (1974) report, children claim to have obtained certain kinds of image of immigrants from the mass media? In this case there are several alternatives:

1 Sheer amount of exposure to a medium is not a criterion of the socializing influence of that medium (as the studies of voting behaviour have suggested).

2 The mass media may present a balanced picture of an aspect of social life which may lead the audience in either direction.

3 Self-reports of sources of ideas may be invalid. Any correlations between type of source mentioned and area, and media use and mentions of the mass media as sources are merely rationalizations of the basic inability to name sources.

We do not know which of these alternatives is the most accurate. If we had the answer and knew the validity of source ratings our problems as mass communications researchers would be over.

One day, when the history of mass communications research is finally written, we may be wiser.

It is not to be too pessimistic to suggest that source-reports may not have any long-term credibility as a methodology for estimating audience effects. They may seem intuitively valid (given certain difficulties) on the basis that the media *must* have such and such an effect on the audience, but hard data is something else. In the area of research on the effects of media violence and crime portrayals, reliable source-reports have long been ignored as suitable forms of evidence. While the earliest reports (*Blumer,* 1933; *Blumer* and *Hauser*, 1933) documented claims that criminals and delinquents had made about the sources of their behaviour, more often than not these seemed to be *post hoc* excuses rather than possibilities of 'true' explanations. None of the recent literature has considered such reports valid as sources of data (further research would have not been necessary if they had). But what do they offer as a substitute? Bogart (1972) has reviewed the Surgeon General's Report (1971) on the effects of TV violence and demonstrated the basis on which the committee reached the conclusion that media violence tends to increase the level of violence in society. Undoubtedly the consensus of informed academic opinion is that their conclusion is in general correct (*Paisley*, 1972), but there still remain others who maintain that this is not the case. Consensus does not finally equate with the truth. In recent years, for example, we have had the consensus opinion that environmental deprivation in early life produces 'disadvantaged' adults challenged (eg *Jensen*, 1973) and while we would not wish to get involved in this argument, we may draw a broad parallel between this and the 'media cause violence' argument. Those in favour of this hypothesis tend to work on the basis of the belief that the sum of a series of inadequate experiments and surveys is 'truth' rather than in terms of the relevance and meaningfulness of this hotch-potch of research. Howitt and others (*Howitt*, 1972; *Howitt* and *Cumberbatch*, 1975; *Howitt* and *Dembo*, 1974) argued on the basis of the available evidence that a 'sub-cultural' account of media effects research findings is more adequate than the usual 'effects' explanation. The whole argument is rather too technical to deal with in detail in this paper but consists of the rejection of a number of inadequate studies (by means of detailed statistical analysis) and the emphasis of studies which are, methodologically speaking, more adequate. What emerges after this is the finding that the different media are associated differently with aggression and delinquency. The cinema is the most clearly associated whereas television is not associated at all (bearing in mind the reanalyses). Virtually all the other media are not implicated, with the exception of comic books for which there is some correlational evidence (*Hoult*, 1949). These differential associations cannot be explained easily in terms of the different characteristics of the content of the different media (such as the largeness of the cinema screen *versus* the smallness of the television screen), but are easy to explain in terms of the uses to which the different media are put by children. The cinema has the funtion both of entertainment (the films shown) and of being a place for meeting one's friends, and it is claimed that this forms the basis of an explanation. Delinquency is also a group activity in most instances, rather than being a lone-occupation, and so one can explain the greater frequency of attendance by delinquents at the cinema in terms of their sub-culture rather than in terms of the effects of the films shown.

Those who tend to believe that media violence is dangerous operate in a rather distinct intellectual discipline to that of the mass communications researchers. Social scientists invariably, but to different extents, deal in abstractions from social reality, the laboratory experiment being but an extreme on the continuum on which survey and other field techniques fall. The continuum can also be defined in terms of the distinctions between *could* the media have such and such an effect (eg as represented by laboratory experiments) and *do* the media as they are at present constituted acting in this social and cultural context have such and such an effect. The answers to these questions may neither complement nor supplement each other. We just do not know. Attempts to compromise the two different approaches (laboratory and field) by doing broadly the laboratory experiment in a more naturalistic setting (eg *Milgram* and *Shotland*, 1973) can, of course, only hint at the adequacy of the pure methods. By and large, particularly if one demands that aggression should be distinguished from play,[11] many studies support the null-effects model suggested by the sub-cultural account but, in this field, it is difficult to be more certain than this.

CONCLUSIONS

In many ways mass communications researchers concerned with

the effects question have set themselves a much more stringent task than social scientists do in other fields. In trying to understand the impact of but one element of a social system, albeit a very time-consuming one, which is in a state of gradual but not dramatic change, we have given ourselves an impossible task. Subtle processes, we feel, must affect the child but we have a very limited set of resources — both financial and methodological — for tackling them. We are not alone; the field of socialization in general faces the same problems and yields very similar plati-tudinous assertions.

There was a golden age for effects research but unfortunately very little research was actually done then. It is far easier to study the effects of the introduction of a medium than it is to understand its effects as an ongoing process. When television was introduced into the Western world in the early fifties there was a great opportunity, but little research. We did learn quite a lot from the few studies which were made of the introduction of television into various countries, but we were worried about issues which seem less important today while we ignored those which currently press. Of course we do have at our disposal techniques for answering questions about the effects of individual programmes on limited parameters — the effects of programmes on knowledge, infor-mation, attitude and, perhaps, overt behaviour — but welcome as these studies may be, in the end mass media are more than the sum of the programmes which they present and their effects are not easily measured.

But we must not present too black a picture. Mass com-munications research has helped us to refine our conception of the audience, both adult and child; it has told us that our gravest fears of the monumental impact of the mass media were unfounded — which in itself justified our efforts — but we are unable to say precisely what the effects of the mass media on the audience are. To some extent it is fair to argue that the task of the mass communications researcher is to challenge and check our everyday conceptions of the role of the media in influencing behaviour, but it would be nice to go beyond this.

It is a broad generalization, but not necessarily untrue, to suggest that we have convincing evidence that the media as cultural and leisure activities have influenced the cultural and leisure activities of the audience, but scant evidence that the media, as political and moral systems, have influenced the political and moral behaviour of the audience. We may be groping in the dark when it comes to our knowledge of the effects of the media on adults, but as far as the effects of the media on children are concerned we may well be lost. At the same time, and this will be my final caution, we must avoid rejecting the question of effects in favour of questions of functions. Nothing I have said points to this.[12] We are hampered not by convincing evidence of a complete lack of effects but by the lack of a technology for detecting them with their possibilities of subtle nuances. Although some would like to believe effects research to be dead and buried the issues are very much alive. Even if the mass media were proven to have no effects at all on the socialization of children, it would still be necessary to document why this is the case (eg *Howitt* and *Cumberbatch*, 1971a). However, we do not have sufficient knowledge to be confident that the law of minimal effects (that the effects of the mass media are small and almost negligible) is accurate. Although we can be confident that the law is applicable to the individual film or programme and reasonably descriptive of most campaigns, we have no evidence to prove that it applies to the longer-term effects of the media.

NOTES

The author wishes to thank Guy Cumberbatch and Robin McCron for ideas, time and critical comments in the preparation of this chapter.

1 By and large it is clear that television can influence certain aspects of general knowledge but this needs to be considered against the fact that television can distract from other sources of learning. The displacement effects of television are discussed elsewhere in this book. See, for example, Belson (1967); Coffin (1948); Himmelweit, Oppenheim and Vince (1958); Campbell (1962); Schramm, Lyle and Parker (1961); Furu (1962).

2 Public Law 90-100, Ninetieth Congress, S.188, 3 October 1967.
   Section 1. The congress finds that the traffic in obscenity and pornography is a matter of national concern. The problem, however, is not one which can be solved at any one level of government. The Federal Government has a responsibility to investigate the gravity of the situation and to determine whether such materials are harmful to the public, and *particularly to minors*, and whether more effective methods may be devised to control the transmission of such materials.

3 We distinguish, of course, between studies on young adults (eg university students) and studies employing children. Those of the latter would include Bandura (1963); Bandura *et al.* (1963a); Bandura *et al.* (1963b); Lovibond (1967);

Heinrich (1960); Howitt and Cumberbatch (1972); Cumberbatch and Howitt (1974a); Lovaas (1961); Siegal (1956); Hartmann (1969a); Hartmann (1969b); Feshbach and Singer (1971); McIntyre and Teevan (1971); Eron *et al.* (1972); Halloran *et al.* (1970); Cowden (1969); Pfuhl (1970); Friedrich and Stein (1973).

4 Cf. Berkowitz quoted in Larsen (1968).

5 It is clear from Tunstall (1964) that a lot of research is carried out (£10 million worth each year during the early sixties) but most market research is concerned with the particular product, its packaging and advertising rather than with whether advertising can boost commodity sales in general. For this reason it is probably the former explanation which is the most accurate.

6 Himmelweit *et al.* (1958) document the effects of television on eyesight. There seems to be no effect. However, this is not an explanation of why research is no longer carried out since many of the null effects that Himmelweit *et al.* document have been followed up by later researchers in recent years.

7 This is true only of non-cumulative changes (eg opinion or value change). Knowledge which is cumulative need not necessarily follow this trend.

8 Studies of direct relevance are: Chaffee *et al.* (1970); Byrne (1969); Hollender (1971); Eyre-Brook (1973a); Eyre-Brook (1973b); Halloran and Eyre-Brook (1971).

9 In Eyre-Brook (1973b) it is reported that 64 per cent of ten- to fifteen-year-olds in her sample rated television as their primary source of information for finding out what is going on in the country/world as against 17 per cent, 12 per cent, 6 per cent, 1 per cent and 1 per cent for newspapers, parents, school, friends, and radio respectively.

10 Despite the fact that *Voting* by Berelson *et al.* (1954) is often cited as suggesting the lack of influence of the mass media on voting, the authors did not systematically explore the question and do not even tell us how many of the changers attributed the change to the mass media. The figures are by addition from chart 35 in Lazarsfeld *et al.* (1948).

11 Naturalistic studies often neglect the crucial difference between what is play behaviour and what is truly aggressive behaviour. Those studies which do not delineate between the two (eg *Parke et al.* 1974) tend to show effects due to symbolic violence portrayals whereas others which delineate between the two (eg (Feshbach and Singer, 1971; Hapkiewicz and Roden, 1971) tend to show no effects of filmed violence.

12 Should the reader feel that effects research is a lost cause, I would wish to reiterate the point of this piece which is to argue that we know little about the effects of television on children. Until we can answer the questions of effects satisfactorily, it seems unlikely that we can tackle other issues with any more confidence.

REFERENCES

Ball, S and *Bogatz, L* (1972), 'Summative Research on *Sesame Street*: Implications for the Study of Pre-school Children', in Pick (ed), *Minnesota Symposium on Child Psychology,* VI, University of Minnesota Press, 3-17.

Bandura, A (1963), 'The Role of Imitation in Personality Development', *Journal of Nursery Education,* XVIII, 207-15.

Bandura, A, Ross, D and *Ross, S A* (1963), 'Imitation of Film-mediated Aggressive Models', *Journal of Abnormal and Social Psychology,* LXVI, 3-11.

Bandura, A, Ross, D and *Ross S A* (1963b), 'Vicarious Reinforcement and Imitative Learning', *Journal of Abnormal and Social Psychology,* LXVII, 601-7.

Belson, W (1967), *The Impact of Television,* Crosby Lockwood, London.

Berelson, B P, Lazarsfeld, P and *McPhee, W* (1954), *Voting,* University of Chicago Press, Chicago.

Berkowitz, (1967), 'Experiments on Automatism and Intent in Human Aggression', in Clemente and Lindsley (eds), *Aggression and Defence,* University of California Press, Los Angeles, 242-66.

Blatt, J, Spencer, L and *Ward, S* (1971), 'A Cognitive Developmental Study of Chidren's Reactions to Television Advertising', in Rubinstein, Comstock and Murray (eds), *Television and Social Behavior,* Report to the US Surgeon General's Scientific Committee on Television and Social Behavior, US Government Printing Office, Washington DC, 452-67.

Blumer, H (1933), *Movies and Conduct,* Macmillan, New York.

Blumer, H and *Hauser, P* (1933), *Movies, Delinquency and Crime,* Macmillan, New York.

Blumler, J (1971), 'The Political Effects of Television', in Halloran (ed), *The Effects of Television,* Panther, London.

Bogart, L (1972), 'Warning: The Surgeon General has determined that TV violence is moderately dangerous to your child's mental health', *Public Opinion Quarterly,* (Winter).

Byrne, G C (1969), 'Mass Media and Political Socialization in Children and Pre-adults', *Journalism Quarterly* (Spring), 140-2.

Campbell, W J (1962), *Television and the Australian Adolescent,* Angus and Robertson, Sydney.

Chaffee, S (1972), 'The Interpersonal Context of Mass Communication', in Kline and Tichenor (eds), *Current Perspectives in Mass Communication Research,* Sage, Beverly Hills, 121-68.

Chaffee, S H, Ward, L S and *Tipton* (1970), 'Mass Communication and Political Socialization', *Journalism Quarterly,* (Winter), 647-66.

Children's Television Workshop (1971), *The Electric Company,* Children's Television Workshop, New York.

Coffin, T E (1948), 'Television's Effect on Leisure-time Activities', *Journal of Applied Psychology,* XXXII, 550-8.

Commission on Obscenity and Pornography (1970), *Report,* US Government Printing Office, Washington DC.

Connors, C K and *Eisenberg, L* (undated), 'The Effect of Teacher Behavior on verbal intelligence in *Operation Headstart* Children', unpublished research report, John Hopkins University.

Connors, C K and *Walker, D* (undated), 'Attitudes and Behavior of Teachers of Headstart Children', unpublished research report, John Hopkins University.

Cooney, J G (1970), '*Sesame Street*: The Experiment of One Year', *Television Quarterly*, IX, (Summer), 9-13.

Cowden, J E, Bassett, H T and *Cohen, M F* (1969), 'An Analysis of Some Relationships between Fantasy-aggression and Aggressive Behavior among Institutionalised Delinquents', *Journal of Genetic Psychology*, CXLIX, 179-83.

Croll, P (1974), 'The Deviant Image', unpublished manuscript, University of Leicester.

Cumberbatch, G and *Howitt, D* (1974), 'Identification with Aggressive Television Characters and Children's Moral Judgments' in Hartup and Dewit (eds), *Determinants and Origins of Aggressive Behavior*, Mouton, The Hague.

Cumberbatch, G and *Howitt, D* (1974), *Social Communication and War: The Mass Media*, forthcoming.

Dominick J (1973), 'Crime and Law Enforcement on Prime-Time Television', *Public Opinion Quarterly* (Summer), 296-8.

Dysinger, W S and *Ruckmick, C A* (1933), *The Emotional Responses of Children to the Motion Picture Situation*, Macmillan, New York.

Elthammar, O (1967), *Emotionella reaktioner inför film hos 11-18 aesgrupper*, Almqvist & Wikseil, Stockholm.

Eron, L D, Huesmann, L R, Lefkowitz, M M and *Walder, L O* (1972), 'Does Television Violence Cause Aggression?' *American Psychologist*, XXVII, 253-63.

Eyre-Brook, E (1973a), 'The Relevance of the School and the Mass Media to the Politcal Socialization of English Adolescents', unpublished manuscript, University of Leicester.

Eyre-Brook, E (1973b), 'The Role of the Mass Media in Political Socialization', unpublished manuscript, University of Leicester.

Feshbach, S and *Singer, R D* (1971), *Television and Aggression*, Josey-Bass, San Francisco.

Filipson, L (1972), *Sesame Street in Sweden: a Study of the Pilot Programme Sesame*, Sveriges Radio Audience and Programme Research Department, Stockholm.

Friedrich, L K and *Stein, A H* (1973), 'Aggressive and Prosocial Television Programmes and the Natural Behavior of Pre-school Children', *Monographs of the Society for Research in Child Development*, CLI.

Furu, T (1962), *Television and children's life*, Japanese Broadcasting Corporation, Tokyo.

Halloran, J D, Brown, R and *Chaney, D C* (1970), *Television and Delinquency*, University of Leicester Press.

Halloran, J D and *Eyre-Brook, E* (1971), 'Children's News — Danish Project', unpublished in English, University of Leicester.

Hapkiewicz, W G and *Roden, A* (1971), 'The Effect of Aggressive Cartoons on Children's Interpersonal Play,' *Child Development*, XLII, 1583-5.

Hartmann, D (1969), 'The Influence of Symbolically Modelled Instrumental Aggressive and Pain Cues on the Disinhibition of Aggressive Behavior', unpublished doctoral dissertation, University Microfilms No. 69-12, 789, Ann Arbor, Michigan.

Hartmann, D (1969), 'Influence of Symbolically Modelled Instrumental Aggression and Pain Cues of Aggressive Behavior', *Journal of Personality and Social Psychology* XI, 280-8.

Hartmann, P and Husband, C (1974), *Racism and the Mass Media,* Davis Poynter, London.

Heinrich, K (1961) *Filmerleben, Filmwirkung, Filmerziehung,* Hermann Schroedel, Berlin.

Hess, R and Torney, J (1967), *The Development of Political Attitudes in Children,* Aldine, Chicago.

Himmelweit, H T, Oppenheim, A N and Vince, P (1958), *Television and the Child,* Oxford University Press, London.

Hollender, N (1970), 'Adolescents and the War: the Sources of Socialization', *Journalism Quarterly,* (Autumn), 472-9.

Hoult, T (1949), 'Comic Books and Juvenile Delinquency' *Sociology and Social Research,* XXXIII, 279-84.

Howitt, D (1972), 'Television and Aggression: a Counter-argument', *American Psychologist,* (October), 969-70.

Howitt, D (1973), 'Attitudes towards Violence and Mass Media Exposure', *Gazette,* XVII, 4, 208-34.

Howitt, D and Cumberbatch, G (1971a), 'Children's Moral Judgements of Aggressive Behaviour Set in Different Programme Contents' unpublished manuscript, University of Leicester.

Howitt, D and Cumberbatch, G (1971b), 'The Ethnology of Imitation', unpublished manuscript, University of Leicester.

Howitt, D and Cumberbatch, G (1972), 'Affective Feeling for a Film Character and Evaluation of an Anti-social Act', *British Journal of Social and Clinical Psychology,* XI, 102-8.

Howitt, D and Cumberbatch, G (1975), *Mass Media, Violence and Society,* Paul Elek, London.

Howitt, D and Dembo, R (1974), 'A Subcultural Account of Media Effects', *Human Relations,* XXVII, 25-42.

Jensen, A (1973), *Educability and Group Differences,* Methuen, London.

Katz, E and Lazarsfeld, P (1955), *Personal Influence,* Free Press, New York.

Klapper, J (1960), *The Effects of Mass Communication,* Free Press, New York.

Larsen, O (1968), *Violence and the Mass Media,* Harper and Row, New York.

Lazarsfeld, P, Berelson, B and Gaudet (1948), *The People's Choice,* Columbia University Press, New York.

Lesser, H (1973), *Public Opinion Quarterly,* (Summer), 300-1.

Linné, O (1971), *Reactions of Children to Violence on TV,* Sveriges Radio Audience and Programme Research Department, Stockholm.

Lovaas, I (1961), 'Effect of Exposure to Symbolic Aggression on Aggressive Behavior', *Child Development,* XXXII, 37-44.

Lovibond, S H (1961), 'The Effect of Media Stressing Crime and Violence upon Children's Attitudes', *Social Problems,* XV, 91-100.

McCombs, M E (1972), 'Mass Communication in Political Campaigns: Information Gratification, and Persuasion', in Kline and Tichener (eds), *Current Perspectives In Mass Communications Research,* Sage, Beverly Hills.

McIntyre, J and Teevan, J (1971), 'Television Violence and Deviant Behavior', *Television and Social Behavior,* III, 383-435.

McLeod, J, Atkin, C K and Chaffee, S H (1971), 'Adolescents, Parents and Television Use', ibid, *Television and Social Behavior,* III.

Milgram, S and Shotland, L (1973), *Television and Anti-Social Behavior,* Academic Press, New York.

Mussen, P H and *Rutherford, E* (1961), 'Effects of Aggressive Cartoons on Children's Aggressive Play', *Journal of Abnormal and Social Psychology*, LXII, 461-4.

Nicosia, F (1973), 'Comments on Leo Bogart's *Warning ...*', *Public Opinion Quarterly* (Summer), 295-6.

Nunnally, J C (1961), *Popular Conceptions of Mental Health*, Holt, Rinehart and Winston, New York.

Paisley, M (1972), 'Social Policy Research and the Realities of the System: Violence Done to TV Research', unpublished manuscript, Stanford University, Stanford.

Parke, R, Berkowitz, L, Leyens, J, West, S and *Sebastian, R* (1974), 'The Effects of Repeated Exposure to Movie Violence on Aggressive Behavior in Juvenile Delinquent Boys: A Field Experimental Approach', unpublished manuscript, University of Wisconsin.

Pfuhl, E (1970), 'Mass Media and Reported Delinquent Behavior: A Negative Case', in Wolfgang, Savitz and Johnston (eds), *The Sociology of Crime and Delinquency*, Wiley, New York.

Roshier, R (1969), 'Crime and the press', unpublished doctoral dissertation, University of Newcastle.

Schramm, W, Lyle, J and *Parker, E B* (1961), *Television in the lives of our children*, Stanford University Press, Stanford.

Siegel, A E (1956), 'Film mediated aggression and strength of aggressive drive', *Child Development*, XXVII, 365-78.

Simon, R J (1967), 'Murder, juries and the press', *Transaction* (May-June).

Snow, R F (1971), *Public Opinion Quarterly* (Summer), 298-300.

Television and Growing Up: The Impact of Televised Violence, Report to the US Surgeon General's Scientific Committee on Television and Social Behaviour, US Government Printing Office, Washington DC.

Trenaman, J and *McQuail, D* (1961), *Television and the Political Image*, Methuen, London.

Tunstall, J (1964), *The Advertising Man*, Chapman and Hall, London.

Walker, D and *Connors, C K* (undated), 'A Follow-up Study of Intelligence Changes in Children who Participated in *Project Headstart*', unpublished research report, John Hopkins University.

Walters, R and *Willow, D* (1968), 'Imitative behavior of disturbed and non-disturbed children following exposure to aggressive and non-aggressive models', *Child Development*, XXXIX, 79-89.

Ward, S (1971), 'Effects of television advertising on children and adolescents', *Television and Social Behavior*, IV, US, 432-51.

Ward, S, Beale, G and *Levinson, D* (1971), 'Children's Perceptions, explanations and judgements of television advertising: a further exploration', *Television and Social Behavior*, IV, 468-90.

Ward, S, Levinson, D and *Wackman, D* (1971), 'Children's attention to television advertising', *Television and Social Behavior*, IV.

Ward, S and *Wackman, D* (1971), 'Television advertising and intrafamily influence: children's purchase influence attempts and parental yielding', *Television and Social Behavior*, IV, 516-25.

Wilcox, W (1968), 'The Press, the Jury, and the Behavioral Sciences', *Journalism Monographs*, IX.

16

Alternative Models of Television Influence

Denis McQuail

While the effects of the mass media have remained firmly at the centre of public attention for several decades, the intellectual history of attempts to study their effects has been mixed. The earliest views about film and radio embodied a model of direct and near-inescapable impact. The media were credited with considerable powers to affect beliefs, attitudes and behaviour according to the intentions of the communicator or the basic leaning of the media content. This was believed to be particularly true of the less-educated, less-able and, of course, younger members of audiences. Careful investigation by survey and experiment, especially during the 1940s, led quite rapidly to a much more modest evaluation of the potential of the media for affecting behaviour and attitudes or even for imparting information. The still influential review of research evidence presented by Klapper (1960), along with the development of theories of interpersonal influence (eg *Katz* and *Lazarsfeld*, 1956) firmly established an alternative school of thought about the mass media. In this phase, we became used to stressing the resistance or independence of the audience and the part played by groups' norms and cultural and social-situational factors in determining the direction and degree of any effect from the media. Effects, where they might occur, were thought of as confirming and reinforcing rather than productive of change. Evidence from studies in the fields of politics, education, race relations, delinquency, even advertising, lent support to the view that media effects were usually small and always dependent on other precipitating factors or conditions.

Some were even prepared to conclude that mass media could generally be disregarded as causal factors in matters of public attitude or behaviour. More careful estimates, however, led to a reclassification of the process of mass media effect as an indirect one. Thus Halloran (1970) commented that we must 'ask whether this question about the direct effects of television on attitudes and behaviour is worth asking'. He recommended that we study the 'possibility of television having its influence indirectly, through, or together with the other agencies in the socialization process'. This is in line with what De Fleur (1970) called the 'socio-cultural' model of the influence of mass media. According to this most recent version of the media effects process, the media do not directly affect individuals, but have their important consequences for society by shaping the materials of knowledge, norms and judgements which people acquire and then apply in everyday life. Such views are entirely justified and, as time passes, acquire an increasing degree of empirical confirmation (for instance, *Hartmann* and *Husband*, 1974). However, it is important not to lose sight of the possibility that television, like other mass media, can also have direct effects. In watching television we are, amongst other things, taking part in a communication relationship as receivers and are likely to acquire some information or accept some influence which makes us in some respects different after the event. Such effects are often the ones intended by the 'sender' or sought by us as receivers. The extent of such direct influence may be modest, but it may be cumulative and significant in individual cases.

The discussion in this chapter begins with the observation that direct influence from mass communication has in fact been neglected in the now dominant formulations of the process of media effect. It also rests on the view that this neglect stems more from incompleteness and inadequacy of thinking than from lack of accomplished research. In all the large amount of research which has been carried out during the last two decades, too little attention has been paid to sorting out and identifying the different kinds of effect process which are at work, the mechanisms by which changes related to the viewing experience are produced. The low level of theoretical development in writing about mass communication makes it a good deal easier for simple and general versions of the effect process to gain circulation and credence, versions which make it easy to answer the simple general questions of concerned members of the public. The main purpose of what follows is to draw attention to what we know about processes of influence through communication and to discern in this knowledge the ways in which television can have direct as well as indirect influence on its viewers.

The reasons for the relative neglect of theory merit comment because they take us to the core of the problem. Firstly, research on the effects of television has been mainly stimulated by policy concerns — the wish of broadcasters, educators, parents and others to impose control in what they believe to be the best interests of the audience and society in general, and especially to protect the most 'defenceless' section of the audience who lack real freedom to choose and discriminate, mainly children and young people. The result has been to place a premium on the sort of evidence which is a rational and defensible basis for action and which leaves little room for doubt or challenge. By this standard, theory is not good enough. Secondly, the problem for investigation has acquired a public definition, in the sense that all those interested — legislators, communicators, teachers, parents — regard themselves as in possession of all the components of the problem: they can see the content for themselves, they know about the amount of exposure and they can observe actual or possible consequences. In these rather unusual circumstances (for a scientific investigation) the social scientist is not often credited with special competence except as a technician. His subtleties of thought are less valued than his ability to produce reliable facts and he is under some pressure to work within a theoretical framework of a simple kind which meets the general public understanding of what is going on. A third circumstance reinforcing this tendency is the apparently fixed and unitary character of the *cause* of whatever is going on, that is, television itself. As an object of study, television is indeed relatively easy to identify and come to grips with. If we compare the process of effect from television with other social influence processes, like the effects of family, school, peer groups or locality, it seems strikingly easy to characterize the *source* of influence, and to quantify the amount of influence of a given kind. We can say very little in general about the nature of family, school or locality experience, and attempts by sociologists to do so usually meet public resistance on the grounds that such experience is unique, personal and highly variable. Yet, with television, the reverse is the case and the idea that the experience is variable and personal has instead to be promoted.

There is, of course, some foundation for this prejudice, since, as a result of historical accident, in this country as in many others, television is organized in a semi-monopolistic way so that a very limited amount of content is made simultaneously available to very large numbers throughout a whole society. We can in some sense 'know' about the experience of millions either by personal monitoring or by applying techniques of quantitative content analysis to broadcasting output. We are in a position to say, for instance, for the entire population passing through the ages of five to seven years, what messages they attended to, in aggregate terms, for perhaps 20 per cent of their waking hours. Such a possibility cannot be matched in any other sphere of socialization. We cannot, in the same sense, 'know' what messages parents or friends or teachers are 'transmitting' to this age group. Given what has been said about the constraint of a public definition of the television effect problem, the consequences are serious for those who have the task of investigating these effects. In particular, it makes it difficult for them to adopt theoretical frameworks which adequately reflect the real variability of the television message as the viewer perceives it and of the relationship between audience and source. The public for research findings tends to expect questions to be framed within a rather simple model of cause and effect, in which the stimulus is unproblematic, the process of reception readily accountable and only the reactions of, and consequences for, the individuals 'exposed' remain to be elucidated.

As a result, a good deal of attention has been focused on the concept of *effect*: on what can be observed to happen under given circumstances and degree of 'exposure', rather than on what causes things to happen. In the long run, it is more useful to know *why* effects occur than to know *what* effects actually occurred and one can deduce the former from the latter only to a rather limited extent. The elaboration of thinking about effects is quite striking compared to the vagueness about process. No doubt the practical requirements of conducting research account in part for this — the need to devise indices and measures which are sensitive enough to reflect the consequences of different degrees and types of exposure. Thus, researchers have found it necessary to distinguish between effects which were intended rather than unintended, between those which were short-term rather than long-term and between those which related to cognition, or to behaviour, or to feelings and emotions. Within each category, further sub-divisions were needed for purposes of measurement and for conveying meaningful results. Thus information, attitudes and opinions were separated out amongst cognitive effects, and yet further sub-divisions were called for, as between attitude effects of a 'reinforcing' kind and those reflecting 'conversion'. The catalogue of refinements, all important for the measurement process and all reflecting real aspects of the situation, could be extended. It is noticeable, however, that such thinking remains within the framework of a research methodology which requires no assumptions to be made about why effects should occur. It is enough that the research apparatus should be competent to locate empirical associations between the occurrence of a known message stimulus (the television content viewed) and the various kinds of response, measured as different kinds of effect. The lack of presumption about the exact process leading to such an association might even be regarded as advantageous, since this gap could be filled after the event, with full knowledge of the facts of the case.

Published research on mass communication has typically concerned itself less with the effectiveness, or efficiency of intentional communication (with notable exceptions, like Hovland *et al.* 1949, or Trenaman, 1967) than with the results of communication. Had it been the other way round, it is arguable that we would be better placed than we are now. More thought would have been given to mechanisms for achieving communication results and the besetting conceptual vagueness of many discussions of the effect process might have been avoided. This vagueness is reflected in the terminology used to describe the occurrence of various kinds of effect from television. Thus, in various contexts, television is said to 'stimulate', 'involve', 'trigger off', 'generate', 'induce', 'suggest', 'structure', 'teach', 'persuade', 'gratify', 'arouse', 'reinforce', 'activate'. Receivers on the other hand, may variously 'identify', 'imitate', 'internalize', 'model' their behaviour on it, 'participate', 'adjust' and so on. To list expressions in this way out of context is to make them seem more nonsensical than they actually are, but it may also remind us that such terms are often used in imprecise ways to describe some actual or expected concomitance between message and response and that we would find it difficult to order them in as logical a way as we can the terminology used to describe effects. The world of what happens between sender and receiver is too often regarded by the empirical researcher as *terra incognita*, dealt with mainly in terms of type of effect and conditions of content and viewer characteristics associated with such effects.

There is no real need for this vagueness, a vagueness which in any case conceals some implicit version of the effect process. We do know enough to provide an ordered account of the various effect processes and can do so if we meet certain prerequisites. First, we need to make a conceptual distinction between 'effect' and 'influence'. Secondly, we need to distinguish communication process from other sorts of uses of mass communication. Thirdly, we need to make a choice amongst the available models of influence through communication and it is with the third of these that this article is most concerned. On the distinction between effect and influence, we can treat the former as any sort of behavioural response to any sort of stimulus, while the latter presumes a relationship, between a sender and receiver of messages. Influence can only occur where power is being successfully exercised by one person over another. In the case of television, we are talking about the power of the sender over the receiver, or audience member, once a relationship is established between the two. By contrast, effect refers only to a reaction or response of the receiver. To distinguish the communication process from other related phenomena is to acknowledge that television viewing is not only a message-receiving process; it is also a social activity engaged in for a variety of reasons. For example, it may be simply to fill in empty time; or to meet the expectations of friends and family members; or to help handle some other social situation (like entertaining friends, or to acquire some privacy). On any given occasion of media attention, the whole audience will not be 'in communication' with the source and a formulation of the process in communication terms is only partly appropriate to describe what is going on. It may be in acknowledgement of this fact, that research has tended to make no presumption about the character of the interaction between participants. Nevertheless, we must at times address ourselves to television viewing as communication and the discussion which follows is concerned exclusively where, according to the understanding of those involved on either 'side', genuine communication is intended or taking place.

Although it has already been said that what happens 'in the middle' between message and response need not be uncertain, it is also true that there are alternative formulations of what basically occurs. The problem is to choose the one most appropriate to the case in hand. One way of comparing the different formulations is to think in terms of a simple model of communication as a link between a sender and receiver, along which 'messages' or items of information are transmitted. A first version of what occurs can be labelled as 'information processing', a version which takes this model at its face value and conceives of effects as the outcome of a rational, guided, interaction between a receiver and a sender. A second version is one which focuses on the sender or the message and conceives the effect process as one of response or reaction to the content of the message. We can call this version a 'conditioning' or 'associational' model because of its closeness to theories of learning based on conditioning. Thirdly, there is a version of the process which takes the needs and interests of the receiver as a starting point and conceives the reception of the messages as the result of an adaptive contact with the environment, with consequences of adjustment and need satisfaction. This model we can call a 'functional' one. Fourthly, we can consider the model in 'relational' terms, supposing that communicative contact is subordinate to the social relationship between sender and receiver and to the general character of the orientation of one to the other. Effects, in this view, are governed in kind and degree by the quality of the relationship. To distinguish between the four versions of communication link, we can summarize by saying that the first (information processing) focuses directly on the transfer, or exchange, of information. The second (conditioning) differs from the third (functional) by taking sender rather than receiver as the starting point; and the fourth (relational) is like the first, except for stressing the social definition of the relationship, to which any transfer of information is subordinated. The problem is to decide which of these is the most generally useful for handling the effects of a mass medium like television on children, and to know when variants should be employed. Each needs to be discussed in turn and its relevance to the study of television effects reviewed.

COMMUNICATION AS INFORMATION-PROCESSING

To explain the main features, the basic model of sender-message-receiver needs to be expanded, following the original formulation of Shannon and Weaver (1949), whose work on the mathematical theory of communication underlies most of information theory. Their formulation depicts a basic sequence, beginning with a *source*, from which a *message* is passed to a *transmitter* where it is *encoded* into a *signal* which is subject to *noise* on the way to a *receiver* where it is *decoded* and passed to a *destination*.

In the 'basic model' that we invoked, sender is generally the 'source', while the receiver corresponds to 'destination'. The process described in this way is normally supplemented by a 'feedback' link, using the same or different channels, whereby a response is returned to the source and helps to guide further message sending. Fundamental to information theory, or to any formal theory of communication, is the idea that information has to be defined as the 'reduction of uncertainty', ie its utility for the receiver lies in increasing the capacity to discriminate. Several things should be noted about the bias of this representation of communication. That it has a bias has been argued by Frick (1959), who remarks that 'the information-theoretic approach reflects an attitude, or opinion' and concludes that this theory is essentially normative. He argues that: 'The formalism of the theory is directed at the determination of the efficiency of the communication and the application of information theory to psychological data implies an interest in efficiency rather than the structure of the process under study.' The bias can be summarized as having three main aspects. First it rests on an assumption of purposiveness — it fits situations best where there is a deliberate intention to achieve some specific communicative purpose — in the sense of reducing uncertainty. Consequently the formulation may be misleading in cases where communication is casual, unsystematic or essentially without purpose. Secondly, the framework directs attention to questions of efficiency according to criteria established by the sender. This means, for example, that the problems of communication tend to get defined as ones of inadequacy of 'encoding' by senders, 'noise' in the channels and poor reception, inability or failure to decode 'correctly'. This kind of thinking may be appropriate for teaching machines or very formal learning situations, but it is not so appropriate to circumstances of creative communication or to unstructured viewing situations. Thirdly, as Frick also notes, we are diverted from questions of the structure of relationships towards technical problems and questions of individual difference and varying ability. In sum, the whole framework stresses the *difficulty* of communication and with this, the idea of an optimum solution which should be the goal of communication analysis.

In the light of this brief outline and commentary, how well does the information-processing approach fit the case of television and its effects on the young? For the most part, it would seem to be inappropriate. Much of the television content is not instrumental, in the sense of having informational objectives, and most uses of television by young people are also mainly non-purposive or guided by purposes which are not easily captured by the notion of 'uncertainty reduction'. However, there are certain categories of television programme which can be judged in terms of the efficiency of their results and the results themselves assessed in terms of quantities of information acquired and of the intentions of the senders. We should probably recall, too, that a good deal of research attention has focused on possibly harmful, or unintended effects of television, and that if more notice was taken of positive uses of television then there are circumstances where this way of thinking would come more into its own.

COMMUNICATION AS CONDITIONING

The formulation of effects as responses to given stimuli is familiar enough as a basic element in learning theory for it to need little exposition. Equally, the critique of stimulus-response theory as a guide to the study of mass communication effects has received wide circulation. In essence, the different versions of stimulus-response theory derive from a view of organisms in a shared environment and in a systematic relationship with each other. A change in state in organism or environment stimulates or triggers off changes in other organisms. The association between response and some stimulus is a matter of observation and it is clear that 'learning' effects can be both understood and manipulated with some basic knowledge of the principles of association. The communication process can readily be conceived in such terms. Thus Newcomb (1953) defines communicative acts as 'outcomes of change in the organism-environment relationship actual and/or anticipated'. In this perspective, communication is either response to a prior stimulus (feedback) or a given datum which forms the starting point of a new sequence of S-R associations. Communication process is essentially a *reaction* process and even seemingly 'expressive' acts of communication can be understood as reactions. The critique of this paradigm rests mainly on the observation that complex communication situations in real life involve an important element of unpredictable response by the receiver — response which cannot be understood in terms of the stimulus, but which is accountable in terms of the social situation of the receiver, and guided a good deal by his subjective perception. Thus the receiver can be held to 'act on' the stimulus or message, to 'negotiate' the exchange, to interpret a message according to criteria which are independent of the source. Sometimes the objection is made on the grounds that communication is essentially interactive and inter-subjective and that the 'outcomes' of most communication occasions are constructed in the course of the event, and are not predetermined by the nature of the stimulus in combination with some fixed and knowable attribute of the organism stimulated.

A good deal of thinking about the effects of television rests on suppositions which accord with the conditioning version of communication effects. For example, many of the terms to describe mechanisms of effect evidently derive from or fit this way of thinking: 'triggering', 'imitation', 'suggestion', 'reinforcement', 'stimulation'. The empirical methods of investigation, by experiment or survey, can easily incorporate the observation of association as a basic procedure. Hypotheses about certain effects, especially those which are harmful or unintended, are often framed in terms of the expectation that a representation of action on television will produce a response in line with the stimulus: an aggressive act on the screen 'arouses' aggressive instincts in the viewer; an advertisement for a product stimulates a demand by the viewer, and so on. This version of the effects process has the advantage of requiring knowledge only about the most visible and objectively measurable elements of the television viewing situation: content of programmes; viewing behaviour; audience response. It has taken a long succession of disappointments with the results of associating these ingredients to oblige investigators to take a critical look at the model of effects which is being deployed. Either there are indeed no effects, or measurement is inadequate or impossible, or some more realistic version of what is going on is called for.

FUNCTIONAL THEORY OF COMMUNICATION EFFECTS

The functional approach might well be regarded as a more realistic alternative to studying the process of communication effects, and it has been recommended for this very reason. For instance, according to Katz (1960), we are generally offered two mutually inconsistent and rather vague versions of how people are influenced, both of them failing to account for the available evidence about effects or lack of effects of communication on attitude change. One of these versions he calls an 'irrational model of man' which represents people as prey to any form of powerful suggestion. In essence, this corresponds to the conditioning version of communication influence. The second view is based on a rational model of man using his critical and reasoning faculty to arrive at opinions and beliefs. Again, very approximately, this accords with the 'information-processing' version outlined above. As an alternative, Katz suggests that we look at the motivational basis of attitudes and start from the view that these have varying utility for people. If this is so, then communication effects can be understood in terms of the varying needs of those who attend to messages. He proposes that the main 'functions which attitudes perform for the personality can be grouped according to their motivational base under four headings: the instrumental, adjustive or utilitarian; the ego-defensive; the value-expressive; the knowledge function'. The first of these implies that people respond to communication in order to satisfy some need — the message has utility for them. The second has to do with uses of communication to protect and maintain a bearable self-image and implies a highly selective attention to, and perception of, communication. The 'value-expressive' function of attitudes has similarly to do with maintaining the coherence of the individual personality. The 'knowledge' function refers to people's need to give meaning to what would otherwise be a chaotic and disorganized view of the world. Each of these kinds of function has implications for how people will seek out and respond to communication. By contrast with the previous version of communication, it emphasizes the orientation of the *receiver* as paramount in determining the occurrence of effects.

Akin to a functional theory of communication are the various kinds of balance theory, like that of Festinger (1957), which holds that the psychological discomfort of holding inconsistent views exerts pressure to try and resolve the inconsistency or to avoid situations where it might arise. The implications for communication are that people will seek out information which confirms their existing attitudes and view of the world and avoid information which is disturbing. The theory helps to account for the apparent lack of direct effects from communication and stresses the elements of resistance in the audience, at the level of the individual personality which makes *change* following communication less likely. Despite the support for this way of thinking on logical grounds, there has so far been little or no unambiguous support for the theory from communication research (see *McGuire*, 1974).

In this context, mention should also be made of the 'uses and gratifications' tradition in the sociology of mass communication, which in its dominant form shares some of the basic assumptions of a functional view of communication (see *Blumler* and *Katz*, 1974). This approach assumes that needs arising out of social circumstances and psychological dispositions largely shape both the patterns of media use and of response to mass media content. The process of media effects is held to be mediated through the expectations and needs of the audience members. From at least the time of the seminal study by Riley and Riley (1951), the approach has been deployed on numerous occasions, especially with children, and with some measure of success. For the most part, however, success has been limited to establishing meaningful relationships between social structure and patterns of use and interpretations of media content rather than showing that effects (in the sense of change following communication) can be predicted from knowledge of audience uses or motivations. As a model for conceptualizing the relationship between media and audience and a source of hypotheses, the approach continues to have an appeal.

As a way of formulating the influence of television, the various functional approaches, of which the last mentioned is the most fully elaborated, have some drawbacks. In particular, they only promise to account for a limited range of effects — those which have some connection with an existing need disposition. They are thus less relevant to handling effects which involve new or divergent states of mind or patterns of behaviour. They seem to put a low value on the capacity of the television message to have an independent effect. The messages of television are just aspects of the wider environment, parts of experience which happen to fit what is being looked for at a given point in time. There is the additional risk that a functional approach will lead us to interpret all uses of media as functional, to give meaning to what may have no meaning. If we think in functional terms it is hard to find a place for direct persuasion or cognitive learning or imitation as types of effect, yet we may think that all of these occur sometimes with some people. At best the functional approach can only indicate some of the conditions under which these sorts of process are more, or less, likely to take place.

A RELATIONAL MODEL OF COMMUNICATION INFLUENCE

The starting point is the idea that the use of the term influence implies the use of power to gain the compliance of another, hence indicating that there must be relationship between a sender and a receiver, a co-orientation of one to the other and the participation of both in the outcome. The sender is seeking or expecting to achieve some result with a receiver, to achieve change, to maintain things as they are, or simply to share something and increase the area of commonality between the two. In some definitions, this last is the essence of communication. In mass communication, however, the concept of power has a restricted application, since physical force or the offer of material reward are usually not involved. Rather, we are limited to considering forms of moral or psychological pressure or attraction which can induce the acceptance of influence. Even so, the concept of power is not seriously attenuated, since there remains the essential point that the would-be sender of influence must have some 'assets' relevant to the needs of the receiver, while the latter must actively co-operate if the influence is to succeed. There have been several attempts to analyse the influence process, but most have been concerned with social influence in general (as in *Parsons*, 1963) or with persuasion as a particular form of the exercise of power. Kelman (1961), for instance, suggests that there are three basic processes of influence, with particular reference to communication and opinion change. The first he names 'compliance', by which he means the acceptance of influence in the expectation of receiving some reward or punishment, perhaps of a material kind. The second he calls 'identification', referring to change prompted by the attractiveness of the sender and the wish to please or conform to his views. The third is 'internalization', which is the nearest to a 'pure' communication effect, and means the process whereby change is adopted when it accords with the values of the receiver: 'The individual adopts [the position of the communicator] because he finds it useful for the solution of a problem or because it is congenial to his own orientation, or because it is demanded by his own values.' This is close to the functional view of influence described above. Kelman's proposal goes some way towards stating a relational view of communication influence and in its full statement takes account of many aspects of a communication situation, but it is limited mainly in its rather specific focus on opinion and attitude change.

A more comprehensive approach which offers the main elements needed for a relational model of the communication process is suggested by Cartwright and Zander (1968) and by French and Raven (1968). The former tells us (p 216) that the capacity to influence another depends on two components: certain 'properties' of the agent which they call 'resources of power' and certain needs or values of the person who is the object of the influence attempt, which they call the 'motive bases of power'. They argue that an 'influential act' establishes a relationship between a 'resource' of an agent and a 'motive base' of the person to be influenced. French and Raven, in line with this, provide a classification of the main bases of social power, which, although formulated for the analysis of relationships in small groups, can be applied to communication situations in general and also to mass communication in particular. They suggest five main 'bases of social power' which each refer to attributes of the agent of influence but which, nevertheless, depend conceptually on the co-ordination of a receiver. The first basis of power is called *reward* power which, in communication, implies the ability of the communicator to offer some valued satisfaction to the recipient. The second they call power based on *coercion*. This will be relatively unusual in mass communication, where the communicator does not control the social situation of the receiver, but it can have a marginal reference to mass communication, for instance, when the authoritative source uses television to warn or admonish. Thirdly, there is the more common *referent* power, based on an identification between the receiver and a valued or prestigeful communicator. Fourthly, French and Raven name *legitimate* power, where the sender can expect to be attended to and gain some compliance. Such power depends on a mutual understanding of obligation: 'In all cases the notion of legitimacy involves some sort of code or standard, accepted by the individual by virtue of which the external agent can assert his power.' Again not so usual in mass communication, but there are occasions when the source takes on some of the legitimacy of parent, teacher or authority in society. Fifthly, there is *expert* power, based on the attribution of superior knowledge to the agent of influence. In each case, we can think of a type of co-orientation by the receiver which represents a particular sort of audience attitude. Thus, reward or coercion calls for a calculative orientation; referent power depends on the believed attractiveness of the communicator; legitimate influence is based on the acceptance of certain norms and obligations; expert power on the trust and credence of the receiver. The separate bases of power are ineffective without the appropriate complementary orientation on the part of the recipient.

According to a relational model of communication, constructed in line with this scheme, we would think of communication influence as the outcome of one or more of these basic forms of power relationship. It must be stressed, of course, that in the case of television influence, as in the situations envisaged by French and Raven, the influence process is bound to be more complicated than this typology suggests. Collins and Raven (1969, p 183), in a slightly different account of the same typology, comment that: 'It is seldom that only one source of power is operative at a given time. Usually various combinations of power are involved in the influence situation and ... they operate in a non-additive interactive relationship.' It is nevertheless arguable that actual cases of change or effect from television can be attributed to the working of one or other of the five types of influence process located in this typology.

If a choice has to be made of a single model for handling questions of effect process, there are advantages to this one. It is, first of all, of the four, the only model which is genuinely concerned with influence, in that it takes account of the interaction of sender and receiver and the outcome of that interaction. The first model focuses primarily on the movement of the message between the two, while the second and third focus primarily on source and recipient respectively. Secondly, it is a more comprehensive framework than the other three and captures more of the variety of the range of television situations, a variability of source, message and receiver in various combinations. It could also be argued that none of the other three models add a great deal to this one, even if they can have advantages in dealing with specific sorts of problems. The information processing model is, under one aspect, little more than a generalized version of the much more complex situation indicated by the relational version, while the functional approach, as we saw, fits into the relational typology. Thirdly, the relational model has advantages for a comparative study of communication situations and of different media. It can be a source of precise questions about types of content and appeal and about the kind of relationship typically established between sender and receiver. None of the other models can suggest the content of questions in quite the same way. It might be suggested that a relational model is especially necessary in the case of television, compared for instance with other media used by children like books, comics, films or pop records. This is partly because television does offer more variety of content types and hence more diverse forms of sender-receiver relationship; partly because television is the most authoritative and the most 'external' media source that children and young people are likely to come into much contact with. The other media are sources much more oriented to their own needs and satisfactions, more within their own world and hence easier to account for within a functional frame of reference. Television brings young people into contact with the 'adult' world, the real 'objective' world, as well as providing entertainment and diversion. It is something which they have to respond to and come to terms with, since in the normal course of family viewing they may not be free to ignore it.

A final argument for recommending this approach has already been foreshadowed in comments made about the other approaches. It is useful to have a framework which can apply to the planning or evaluation of 'positive' uses of television — positive in the sense of having some stated policy aim concerned with communication. While the first (information-processing) model has some contribution to make in this respect, its utility may not extend to purposes which relate, for instance to the enlarging of cultural experience, or to creative entertainment, or the stimulation of interests. A framework of relationships between audience and medium, like that described, may suggest a number of ways by which planned influence of this kind may be achieved. The 'conditioning' and 'functional' models seem to embody a rather negative image of mass communication influence. The first stresses the vulnerability of the receiver, the second suggests that the receiver can 'look after himself', since he will only be influenced in a direction which he is already taking. Both reflect an essentially defensive stance and seem designed to pose or answer questions about the undesirable or unintended 'effects' of television.

It is unnecessary to press for the adoption of a single model of the effects process, since there is bound to be room for alternative formulations, given the variety of communication relationships which television establishes between 'senders' and 'receivers'. For the purposes set out above, especially the wish to draw attention to the occurrence of direct effects from television, it should be sufficient to have set out several versions of the ways in which direct influence from television takes place. The discussion should also have helped to indicate what the main components of an influence situation are and, in doing so, have offered guidelines for planning research on influence. Perhaps more importantly, the analysis may be useful in formulating reasonable expectations about what will happen in those more numerous cases when research cannot be carried out. It should be emphasized, in conclusion, that in seeking to revive an appreciation of the potential of television for having direct influence, the intention has been less to revive alarmist views than to promote a more positive approach to television as an instrument of education, in the widest sense. The wide circulation of a belief in the ineffectiveness of television might have discouraged as many as it reassured.

REFERENCES

Blumler, J G and *Katz, E* (eds), (1974), *The Use of Mass Communications: Current Perspectives on Gratifications Research*, Sage, Beverly Hills.
Cartwright, D and *Zander, A* (eds), (1968), *Group Dynamics,* (3rd edn), Tavistock, London.
Collins, B E and *Raven, B H* (1969), 'Groups Structure' in Lindzey and Aronson (eds), *Handbook of Social Psychology* (2nd edn), Addison Wesley.
de Fleur, M L (1970), *Theories of Mass Communication*, David McKay, New York.
Festinger, L A (1957), *A Theory of Cognitive Dissonance,* Row Peterson.
French, J R P and *Raven, B H* (1968), 'The Bases of Social Power', in Cartwright and Zander, (eds), *Group Dynamics*, Tavistock, London.
Frick, F C (1959), 'Information Theory' in Koch (ed), *Psychology: A Study of a Science*, II, McGraw-Hill, New York, 611-36.
Halloran, J D (ed) (1970), *The Effects of Television*, Panther, London.
Hartmann, P and *Husband, C* (1974), *Racism and the Mass Media,* Davis Poynter, London.
Hovland, C I, Lumsdaine, A A and *Sheffield, F D* (1949), *Experiments in Mass Communication,* Princeton University Press.
Katz, D (1960), 'The Functional Approach to the Study of Attitudes', *Public Opinion Quarterly*, XXIV, 163-204.
Katz, E and *Lazarsfeld, P F,* (1956), *Personal Influence,* Free Press, New York.
Kelman, H (1961), 'Processes of Opinion Change', *Public Opinion Quarterly,* XXV, 57-78.
Klapper, J T (1960), *The Effects of Mass Communication,* Free Press, New York.
McGuire, W J (1974), 'Persuasion, Resistance and Attitude Change', in Pool and Schramm, (eds), *Handbook of Communication,* Rand McNally, New York, pp 216-52.

Newcomb, T (1953), 'An Approach to the Study of Communicative Acts', *Psychological Review*, LX, 393-404.

Parsons, T (1963), 'On the Concept of Influence', *Public Opinion Quarterly*, XXVII, 37-62.

Riley, M W and *Riley, J W* (1951), 'A Sociological Approach to Communications Research', *Public Opinion Quarterly*, XV, 445-60.

Shannon, C E and *Weaver, W* (1949), *The Mathematical Theory of Communication*, University of Illinois Press.

Trenaman, J (1967), *Communication and Comprehension*, Longman, London.

Author Index

Subject Index

Brown (ed) (s) Television
K